SIR JOHN OLDCASTLE
of HEREFORDSHIRE

Traitor, Martyr or the real Falstaff?

SIR JOHN OLDCASTLE
of HEREFORDSHIRE

Traitor, Martyr or the real Falstaff?

ANDY JOHNSON

LOGASTON PRESS

LOGASTON PRESS
The Holme, Church Road, Eardisley
Herefordshire HR3 6NJ
www.logastonpress.co.uk

First published by Logaston Press 2020
Copyright text © Andy Johnson
Copyright illustrations © as per credits and acknowledgements

ISBN 978-1-910839-42-3

Typeset by Logaston Press
Printed and bound in Poland by
www.lfbookservices.co.uk

FSC
www.fsc.org
MIX
Paper from
responsible sources
FSC® C105618

CONTENTS

Acknowledgements

My initial enthusiasm for finding out about John Oldcastle was fuelled by conversations with Bob Jenkins, who was once parish clerk for Almeley but at the time I talked with him was running a second-hand bookshop in Kington. He kindly gave me a copy of the notes he had made down the years about Oldcastle, and these gave me leads to many sources of information. When I began my own research it was in the days before the internet, when books and articles either needed to be organised by inter-library loan or listed for a day spent in the British Library, first in its old quarters in the British Museum, and then in its new surroundings near St Pancras Station. This research continued sporadically over the decades and by the time I returned to it with the desire and the time to see it through to conclusion a number of those books were available to read online. It made deciphering and understanding cryptic hand-written notes of years before considerably quicker and easier, and also encouraged wider research than I might otherwise have been able to undertake.

This book would have been far more difficult to research and almost certainly wouldn't have been as detailed if it hadn't been for the work of Charles Kightly, who not only provided the text for several of the entries of the online history of parliament for the period of Oldcastle's life, but also researched Lollardy during this period, together with Oldcastle's rising and subsequent movements.

As for those who have provided help, advice and support, I would particularly like to thank John and Sarah Zaluckyj, who kept an eye out for anything 'Oldcastle' that they came across in their own research and book dealing. Many thanks also to James Pattinson, an old friend and heraldic fiend who helped me make sense of various coats of arms and found out more information than I might have done, notably about the bosses in the cloisters in Canterbury Cathedral; to Jools Holland, who I discovered had Oldcastle interests and gave me some leads regarding Joan Cobham and Cooling Castle in Kent; to Rhys Griffith at Herefordshire Archive and Records Centre, who helped comb the stores for anything that might prove helpful; to Miriam Griffiths of the Longtown & District Historical Society for the loan of a book during lockdown which might otherwise have proven difficult to obtain and for information about Olchon Court; to Richard Ashdowne, former editor of the *Dictionary of Medieval Latin from British Sources*, who translated the letters that Oldcastle wrote to Wenceslas of Bohemia and Woksa of Waldstein; to Michael Brealey, Librarian at Bristol Baptist College, who unearthed the sale details and catalogue entry describing the library's sale of its copy of Wycliffe's translation of The Gospel of St Matthew, Epistles, Acts of the Apostles and the Apocalypse that was thought might have belonged to Oldcastle; to Mark Scott, Bluemantle Pursuivant of Arms, for sourcing the image of Oldcastle's seal; to Sarah Hill of Herefordshire Libraries, who helped me track down and obtain university theses and ancient tomes; to David Styan, who unearthed some details of the early history of the Sir John Oldcastle inn; to staff of many libraries here and in Prague and Bremen who helped unearth and provide illustrations or suggestions regarding something I was trying to uncover, not least Matthew Holford of the Bodleian; to family and friends who either read drafts of the manuscript and gave me their thoughts or who, knowing of my interest, would themselves delve into some corner of Oldcastle's or Falstaff's world that particularly took their interest and unearth something that was often of use, even if only to add or amend a sentence or two. For anyone who feels omitted from the above list, the reason is likely to be down to my appalling hand-writing on countless pieces of paper down the years – please accept my apologies.

I also want to thank Richard and Su Wheeler of Logaston Press, who took on the press, which I had founded in 1985, so allowing me to complete my research and writing, and who agreed to publish the eventual tome. Thanks to them also for their input into drafts of the manuscript. And last, but by no means least, to Karen, my wife – encourager, structure consultant, proofreader, questioner of clarity, literary champion and conjuror of book titles.

Andy Johnson
Logaston, August 2020

Introduction

Falstaff: … And is not my hostess of the tavern a most sweet wench?

Prince Henry: As the honey of Hybla, my old lad of the castle. And is not a buff jerkin a most sweet robe of durance?'

Thus Falstaff and Prince Hal jest in Shakespeare's *Henry IV Part I*, Act I, Scene II before they are joined by Poins, Hal's other close friend, and start to discuss the robbing of pilgrims on Gad's Hill. But why call Falstaff 'my old lad of the castle'? The reason is that Shakespeare originally intended his larger-than-life character – 'sweet Jack Falstaff, kind Jack Falstaff, valiant Jack Falstaff' – to be called John Oldcastle, and here he is playing on the name that he was forced to reject. But who was Oldcastle, and why did Shakespeare initially choose him to be Prince Henry's companion of his 'wilder days'? And what happened to cause the change of name? What resemblance is there between the real Oldcastle and his fictional persona, Falstaff?

It was not long after I came to live on the edge of the parish of Almeley in Herefordshire that I became aware of its connections with the name Oldcastle. The parish has two old castle mounds, locally called twts (pronounced 'toots') after the Anglo-Saxon word for a look-out point. One of them is near the church in typical Norman fashion, but the other is more hidden. To the west of the village centre is the Batch, a deep valley for the size of the stream that flows through it, above which stands a now wooded motte with the remnants of a bailey to the north, close to the more recent Oldcastle Farm. It is this part of the village that was probably John Oldcastle's childhood home.

Over the years, as I gradually discovered more about Oldcastle's life and his links with Falstaff, I came to feel that no-one had really tried to understand the man or fully explore his tangled history. The accounts of his life that we have, six centuries later, tend to be selective, to bolster a particular religious or political belief or stance, or else make a bald statement of certain known facts. The further I looked, the more I realised how my own thoughts had been coloured by the views that chroniclers or other writers sought to propound. I needed to clear my mind of whatever preconceptions had formed from casual enquiry and start afresh. And so this book.

Having now lived near Almeley for almost 40 years, I have gained an awareness of the special characteristics of the Welsh March, which make it like no other place. Free of the central control of the Crown till the Acts of Union with Wales in 1535 and 1542, the semi-independent Marcher lordships had a degree of autonomy where the king's writ did not always run. Stories abound of royal messengers being forced to eat the wax seal of the messages they brought, to show the disdain of local lords for the central government. Many a person avoided the English legal system by seeking refuge somewhere in the Marches, able to slip over into Wales proper when the need arose. Recently, when the referendum was held in 2011 as to whether there should be a Welsh Assembly, I recall discussing – with locals in a pub – how people would vote in what would have been the Mortimer Lordship of Elfael (in what is now eastern Wales). The answer seemed to be that they wanted a different question on the ballot paper, for they preferred a regional government that comprised the English counties of Shropshire and Herefordshire, and the Welsh counties of Breconshire, Radnorshire and Montgomeryshire. The area feels different to the lands on either side.

This book starts with an attempt to give a feeling for Almeley and the surrounding area in the late 1300s, the time when Oldcastle was born. But it's important to get a sense not just of the village and parish, but also the people, for the Oldcastles were part of a tightly knit group of shire gentry often tasked with duties on behalf of central government, Marcher lords or one another. Herefordshire is still a county where you'll soon find you have a mutual connection with someone you meet for the first time, and, after a few minutes' conversation, will discover another. In Oldcastle's day such links appear to have developed into strong bonds of loyalty, and when Oldcastle needed to call upon such links in later life, they were honoured beyond the call of duty.

It was presumably while a young lad in the Marches that Oldcastle first encountered the 'Lollard' teachings of John Wycliffe, along with a host of alternative views on Christianity to those espoused by the established church. There were a number of wandering preachers – some friars, some followers of Wycliffe and some who held a mishmash of views probably more suited to rural gatherings than the halls of Oxford or Cambridge. One of the more charismatic preachers, William Swynderby, a follower of Wycliffe, is known to have preached at Winforton (a parish all but adjoining that of Almeley), and to have made north-west Herefordshire part of his preaching ground. Thus the book moves from considering Almeley and life in Herefordshire to the views of Wycliffe and how these were propagated and supported, as well as adulterated and altered.

Oldcastle's father had been knighted (why and on what occasion is not known) and it appears that his family wished to see the young John follow in his footsteps. The third chapter in the book tells of John's early military career, first in a naval expedition against the French, followed by campaigns in Ireland and Scotland, and then in Wales against Owain Glyndwr, a former comrade-in-arms. Oldcastle was clearly deemed by

Prince Henry (under whom he sometimes served) to be an able military commander; he was given charge of sizeable numbers of troops, and was with the prince at what should have been the final death knell of Glyndwr's war.

And so we come to the connections between Prince Hal and Oldcastle. Chapters Four and Five look at the life of Hal between the defeat of Glyndwr and the death of his own father, and what evidence there may be for any riotous behaviour as ascribed to him by Shakespeare, and then move on to Oldcastle's rise to the peak of his career and his position within government. For Oldcastle married into and became one of the nobility, quite possibly with the prince's support. He was sent as the English champion to a joust at Lille, attended by the duke of Burgundy, perhaps with a subplot to open negotiations between Burgundy and Prince Hal, for just under two years later Oldcastle was one of the commanders of an army sent to France by the prince in support of Burgundy. This was during a time when the prince was in charge of the king's council due to the illness of his father, Henry IV.

There is another side to this chivalric knight that has a chapter of its own. For Oldcastle used the years between 1408 and at least 1411 to support Lollardy, communicating with Jan Hus in Bohemia and probably helping to have Wycliffe's works copied and sent abroad, certainly to Bohemia but perhaps also to Iberia. This brought him into conflict with the Church, in particular with the archbishop of Canterbury. The archbishop needed to tread carefully due to Oldcastle's friendship with Hal, who was now King Henry V, but he laid his ground well and played to the king's orthodoxy and need to hold the kingdom together. Oldcastle was duly tried for heresy and it is in the record of the trial, covered in Chapter Seven, that we can perhaps best gain a picture of the character of Oldcastle. However, we have to be careful. On the one side, we have the records of churchmen who wanted to defame his name and character, and on the other side the works of later writers whose aim it was to enshrine Oldcastle as one of the earliest Protestant martyrs. Much is made of hell and damnation by both sides and one can easily feel the spirit of Christianity is largely missing, except perhaps in some of Oldcastle's stated views.

Henry gave Oldcastle, found guilty of heresy, 40 days grace to reconsider whilst detained in the Tower of London. But the Tower is not the secure place of detention that myth would have it, and Oldcastle escaped to instigate a rebellion which, through a combination of detective work, informants and lessons learnt by the authorities from the Peasants' Revolt of some 30 years earlier, was easily put down. Chapter Eight covers both the rising and Oldcastle's subsequent almost four years on the run, during which he spent most of his time in the company of tradesmen – people with whom he seems to have been as much at ease as when with the prince. Often presumed to have been involved in various plots (and at times definitely involved) at one point Oldcastle returned to Almeley, where he appears to have lived fairly openly, no-one seeking to take up the considerable rewards placed on his head. He was, however, eventually captured close to what is now the border between Shropshire and Wales, quickly taken to London, confirmed by the Lords sitting in parliament as a traitor and hanged. His body was then burnt as that of a heretic.

The penultimate chapter considers what happened to the memory of Oldcastle, the to-ings and fro-ings between being seen as the 'bigot' of Walsingham, the chronicler of the period, and the 'valiant capteine and a hardie gentleman' of the sixteenth-century chronicler and historian Holinshed. The chapter also considers how it was that Shakespeare came to write a character with the name of Oldcastle into his plays – and how and why that name was changed to Falstaff. In untangling this tale, consideration is given to several plays written at the time in which Oldcastle features: to the ordering of certain events, how plays were constantly amended and adapted, and how the scheming politics of the time (which involved several plots against Queen Elizabeth) may possibly have been woven into plays using the Oldcastle story as cover. Almost 200 years after Oldcastle's death, why did it matter whether he was still seen as a traitor? And why the name Falstaff? Could there be a sting in the choice?

And Oldcastle's story doesn't quite end there, as the final part of that chapter and the Afterword will show.

A sketch of Sir John Oldcastle's coat of arms made by
John Duncumb for his *Collections Towards the History and
Antiquities of The County of Hereford* (published in 1804).
(Duncumb's notes are held in Hereford Archive
and Records Centre, CF50/242)

Family Background and Early Life

Sir John Oldcastle was the son of Richard and Isabel Oldcastle of Almeley in north-west Herefordshire. Almeley lies to the west of the line made by Offa's Dyke, the great earthwork erected under King Offa of Mercia in the 780s AD. Part of the dyke still stands tall in Lyonshall parish, just to the north-east of Almeley, from where its course has been traced in the remnants of banks that head south-eastwards to Burton Hill to the south-west of Weobley. Travelling over the western flanks of Burton Hill it then heads south to Garnons Hill and so down to meet the Wye at Bridge Sollers.[1] Almeley therefore lies in an area that includes several place-names owing their origin to Saxon settlements founded beyond the putative Mercian boundary established by the dyke. The settlement's meaning is 'clearing in the elm wood' (an early version of the name has it as Elmlie), and the area is thought to have been heavily wooded until settlers gradually cleared patches of ground. Rather than elms, this part of the country has been better known in post-Saxon times for its oaks, the oak having been called 'the weed of Herefordshire'.

Almeley

Whilst we might imagine Almeley to have been a rural backwater, Hereford, some 15 miles to the south-east, was anything but. With the coming of the Norman Conquest in 1066, William fitzOsbern was created earl of Hereford and began the construction of a major castle in the city, building on the remains of an earlier castle built by Ralph, count of Vexin, who was a nephew of King Edward the Confessor. This castle was destroyed by the Welsh in 1055. After a rebellion by his son, fitzOsbern's castle was to pass into royal hands, where it largely remained for the rest of its existence. Often being near the front line in the wars against the Welsh, the castle was the centre of military activity and supported a number of tradesmen, including money lenders, meaning that Hereford became one of the major cities of England between the twelfth and fourteenth centuries.

Almeley, meanwhile, at the time of the Domesday Survey in 1086, probably had a population of less than a hundred souls, the manor then being held by the 'church', probably in the form of the priory of St Guthlac in Hereford. The manor was sublet to the Norman Roger de Lacy, who also held the manor of Woonton, just to the east of

Almeley and in the same parish, and it wasn't long before he gained full control of the manor of Almeley as well.

By 1242 Roger Picard held the manor of Almeley, when scutage (a tax on those owing feudal duties in lieu of providing military service) to fund Henry III's expedition to Gascony was levied on four hides of land.[2] A hide is generally reckoned to be around 120 acres, making his agricultural landholding some 480 acres. In the same year Picard obtained the right to free warren over the manor, this usually being a right to hunt certain small game – often hares and foxes – over a specified area.

In 1285 Roger granted the rents of a number of properties scattered about Almeley, including at 'Lowgarston' (Logaston) and 'Wotton', to the priory of Wormsley in perpetuity and with right to seek distraint for payment against the tenants, in return for prayers to be said for his soul. The land covered by the grant of rents was some 75 acres, the total annual rental value being 16 shillings, equating to some 2.5d per acre.[3] At this date rents for land on which some feudal duties were owed were usually in the range of 4d – 6d per acre, indicating that the land on which the rents were granted was of less than average quality.[4] Certainly the land around what is now Logaston Common, being subject to flooding, is less agriculturally valuable than that slightly further upslope. The grant does show that hamlets were by then established in the parish outside the village centre. This suggests a landscape of small settlements, often probably comprising just a farm and a few cottages with some cultivated fields in the vicinity, scattered across a landscape containing extensive meres, commons and woods (several patches of common remain to this day).

Many of the houses would have been simple, timber-framed structures, of a mixture of cruck-framed construction (where curving oak trunks and branches were sawn in half to make a matching pair and provide the outline shape of the walls and roof pitch) and square box-framed houses. The frame was rested on a low stone wall to raise it above ground level and help prevent it rotting, and leant against a stone chimney stack. The fireplace would have provided for cooking as well as heat, and possibly had a bread oven built adjacent to it. Many houses would have been single-storey, the occupants living and eating (and possibly even sleeping) in one room, and using the other for storage. Those better off might have had two storeys, but even then the upstairs would generally only have been used for storage, to keep winter food stock dry and away from mice and other rodents. The gaps between the timber frame would have been filled with wattle and daub, the wattle being split ash or hazel wands woven into a sturdy 'mat', the ends of the wands being inserted in holes made in the insides of the framing to anchor the mat in place. A daub of mud and hair from horses or cattle would then have been plastered over each side of this mat. Roofing would almost always have been thatch, of straw in better-off homes, and possibly of bracken or furze in the less well-off. The well-to-do might have used stone slates, pegged on battens. The houses would have been dark and smokey, with the ploughman in *Piers Plowman* (written sometime between 1370 and 1390), for example, complaining that in the home 'smoke and smolder

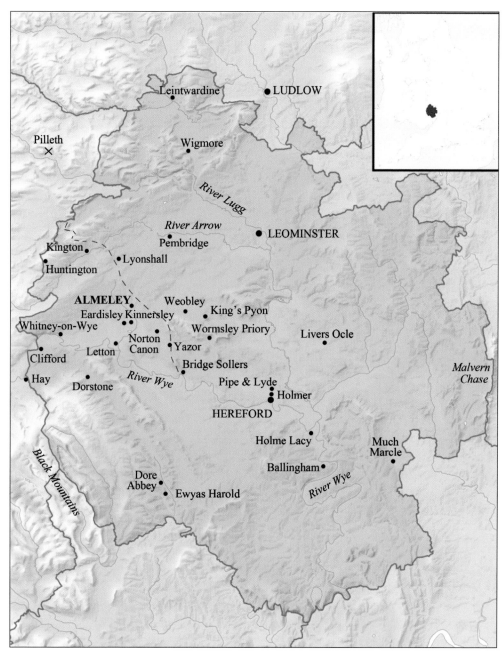

Map of Herefordshire showing many of the places and features mentioned in the text.
The broken red line marks the course of Offa's Dyke between the border with what is now Wales
(it would have been a boundary of a Marcher lordship in the late 1300s) and the River Wye.

smyt in his sihte' (smoke and smoulder smarteth his sight). Few of these houses survive today. Most of the earliest surviving timber-framed buildings in Herefordshire date from the 1400s (commencing from the time that Oldcastle was nearing the end of his life), when box-framed houses of two storeys became more common.

With the coming of the Black Death in 1348 and 1349, somewhere between 30% and 50% of Almeley's population is likely to have died, and this was to have an effect at several levels. Lords needed to hire more people for wages rather than being able to rely on feudal duties owed by a now much smaller pool of tenants. The decline in population also saw a shift towards stock rearing, which was less labour-intensive than growing crops that needed a lot of manual work in sowing, weeding and harvesting. This in turn led to the enclosure of some of the previous open strips within fields that had been farmed in common, as well as of outlying 'wastes' and commons. Many farms and landholdings in Herefordshire, including those around Almeley, would have been turned over to sheep, notably the Ryeland, to make use of extensive untilled land, with the wool being sold for use in the growing cloth trade.

The earliest surviving part of Almeley Church is its tower, which was built around 1200. The rest of the building is in the Decorated style (c.1250–c.1350) so would be much as John Oldcastle knew it (though then it would have been without the Tudor decoration on its ceilure above where a rood screen would have once stood). There are 'deeds preserved conveying land in Almeley for the safety of the donor's soul' and for providing for candles to be burned before the altar,[5] a practice becoming common in the 1300s, perhaps encouraged by the ravages of the Black Death. A chantry chapel on the north side of Almeley church was the abode of a priest who said prayers for the souls of the departed, in return for money left in wills. The church's rood screen was replaced in 1865, but the form of the earlier screen is unknown. Money was spent on new bell ropes for the church in 1390. There was also a chapel at 'wotton', presumably Woonton, served by assistant clergy.

It was during the 1330s that the ownership of the manor of Almeley passed out of the hands of the Picards, but the route by which it came to the Oldcastles is unclear. What is certain is that sometime between 22 June 1378 and 21 June 1379 Sir John Bromwich and Sir John (de) Eynesford, along with the lawyer Philip Holgot (about all three of whom we shall learn more below), applied for a licence from the Crown to grant land in Almeley and the advowson of its church to the prior and convent of Wormsley,[6] which would retain it for around 150 years.

At around the same time that Bromwich, Eynesford and Holgot made their grant to Wormsley Priory, they and others – Henry Arderne, Richard Nash, John II Walwyn, Walter de la Halle and William Barton, some of whom we will meet again later – passed the manor of Almeley to John Oldcastle. This suggests that Bromwich, Eynesford and Holgot, at least, had been trustees of the manor on the death of Richard Oldcastle, John Oldcastle's father, who had therefore presumably died shortly before.

Wormsley Priory, which lay roughly halfway between Almeley and Hereford, had been founded sometime before 1210 and was home to a group of Augustinian canons (the Augustinians being an offshoot of the Benedictines). Amongst its chief benefactors had been John Oldcastle, our John's grandfather.[7] The Wormsley canons used to wear a white scapulary (a short cloak worn over the shoulders) over their black robes, to the end of which was attached a piece of bone to remind them, and those they met, of their mortality. From time to time some of these canons must have trodden or ridden the byways between Almeley and Wormsley in order to conduct any necessary business.[8]

On 12 September 1392, on the death or retirement of the previous vicar, the priory exercised its right for the first time and appointed John Mydale as vicar. Our John Oldcastle obviously took exception to this state of affairs because in 1400 he appeared as the plaintiff in a case in the Court of Common Pleas, trying to regain possession of the advowson of the church in Almeley from the priory. The case was adjourned and no record of the settlement survives, but as the priory retained the advowson until the Dissolution, Oldcastle must have lost the case, or perhaps he withdrew it, as there is no further record of it.[9]

Though the relevant document says the advowson was 'granted' to the priory of Wormsley, it was in fact sold to them, the priory selling lands they held in Cheddar in Somerset in order to buy it.[10] This was a worthwhile transaction for both sellers and purchasers, the sellers receiving a cash payment and the purchasers receiving the right to the major tithes along with the advowson. Although they had to keep the chancel in repair and maintain a priest, the great tithes more than covered these outgoings. The losers were the people of the parish, as money was taken from them that could otherwise have helped either provide for the poor or maintain the church. It was perhaps no wonder that Oldcastle was to contest the transfer of the advowson in the Court of Common Pleas in 1400.

The date for the selling of the advowson and transfer of the manor to John Oldcastle show that John's father must have died sometime before the summer of 1379, which brings us to consideration as to when John was born.

The Birth of John Oldcastle

If Oldcastle's link with Falstaff has any historical accuracy, we could gauge his date of birth from *Henry IV Part I*, Act II, Scene IV. At one point in this scene Falstaff acts the king, Prince Henry's father, and quizzes the prince about 'a virtuous man whom I have often noted in thy company, but I know not his name'. The prince asks for a description and Falstaff goes on to say (describing himself) 'A goodly portly man, i' faith, and a corpulent; of a cheerful look, a pleasing eye, and a most noble carriage, and, as I think, his age some fifty, or, by 'r Lady, inclining to three score …'. As this scene is set in the year of the battle of Shrewsbury, 1403, this would mean that Falstaff/Oldcastle was born between 1343 and 1353, which would make Oldcastle between 64 and 74 years old at the time of his death in December 1417. This is unlikely, though not impossible, as he was still leading a very active life, but for this reason some historians have put his birth date at closer to 1360. This date at first sight appears to be supported by Bale's *Brefe Chronicle*, which recounts Oldcastle's trial for heresy in 1413 after he had become Lord Cobham; however from his introduction it is clear that Bale confused Oldcastle with an earlier Lord Cobham.

A much later birth date, 1378, is given by Elmham, a contemporary of Oldcastle, in his *Liber Metricus*, compiled in 1418.[11] This date may have been chosen for reasons of propaganda, however, for 1378 was the year of the Great Schism in the Church, which began a period in which there were two popes, one based at Rome and one at Avignon. As an ardent papist, Elmham saw this as the start of a period when 'Christ's tunic was rent in two', and as he saw Oldcastle, a leader of the dissenting Lollards, as the Beast of Revelation – a creature with seven heads and 'upon his heads the name of blasphemy' (Revelation 13:1) – he may have thought it useful to equate the date of Oldcastle's birth with that of the start of the Great Schism. Nevertheless, in a more sober piece of writing, his *Chronica Regum*, compiled two years before his *Liber Metricus*, he also gives 1378 as the year of Oldcastle's birth.[12]

Firmer evidence comes from Oldcastle's appearance in the muster roll of Richard Fitzalan, earl of Arundel, for an expedition he was leading in 1387 (for which see Chapter Three). In this roll Oldcastle is listed as an esquire and man-at-arms. This is likely to mean he was in his late teens at this point (as will be shown below), suggesting that a birth date of *c*.1370 will be closer to the truth, and making him eight or nine years old when his father died.

Castles and Property

It is thought that the Oldcastle family took its name from the castle whose mound can still be seen in the deep cutting called The Batch to the north-west of Almeley Church, with various records referring to a mound marking the site of the 'old castle' near which now lies Oldcastle Farm. (Some accounts suggest that the family was of Welsh origin, with John Oldcastle being known as Sion Hendy o Went Iscoed,[13] literally John Oldhouse/castle of Gwent Iscoed, which was the lower part of the old kingdom of Gwent between the rivers Wye and Usk, though there is nothing definite to support this contention. His paternal ancestors appear to have been living in Herefordshire for at least three generations.[14]) This castle site retains a prominent wooded motte some 29 feet in diameter at its top, perched on a spur above the confluence of two streams, one of which runs the length of The Batch. The motte rises some 18 feet above a ditch that separates it from a roughly rectangular bailey marked out by the remnants of a rampart to the north. An eighteenth- or nineteenth-century cottage has been built in what was probably once the entrance on the eastern side.[15] If the Oldcastle home was located here, the buildings were probably largely of timber, though some stone walling may have been used. The mound has never been excavated.

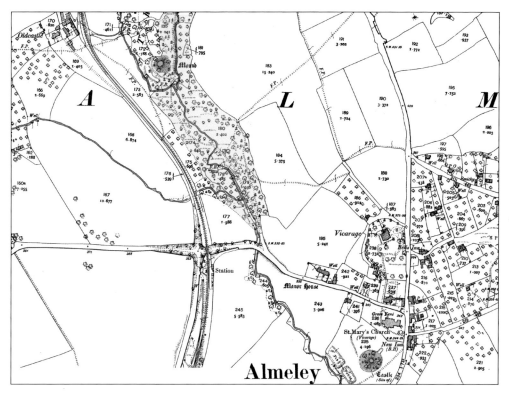

An Ordnance Survey map of Almeley in the late 1800s showing the location of the two castle mottes, (highlighted in red), The Batch (highlighted in light green), the church (highlighted in yellow) and the later Manor House (highlighted in dark green). Newport House, the site of which is another contender for Oldcastle's home, lies about a quarter of a mile to the west of Oldcastle Farm shown in the top left-hand corner.

Oldcastle Motte photographed in the 1930s by Alfred Watkins. (© Herefordshire Libraries)

Aerial photo of Almeley Church and the adjacent motte. (© Paul Davis)

The more prominent castle mound in Almeley is that which lies near the church. This consists of a roughly circular motte some 55 feet in diameter, at the top rising some 20 feet above the surrounding ditch, with associated bailey earthworks to the north, between the motte and the church. There is evidence of a ditch round the bailey, whilst to the south of the motte lie the obvious remnants of fishponds which the castle's occupants would have created to provide some of their food. W.T. Waugh[16] argues that this is the site of Oldcastle's home, suggesting that the family name is derived not on the basis that the castle would have been considered 'old' in the days of Oldcastle's great-grandfather (the first member of the family recorded in the county), but because it was built on the site of an earlier Roman fort or camp.[17] It seems, however, that Waugh confused the Almeley site with the settlement of Oldcastle, situated close to the southernmost eastern flanks of the Black Mountains some 20 miles due south of Almeley, which is said to have begun its life as a Roman station, to be followed by a settlement with a Norman castle and church. This confusion may have been caused by John Howells, a minister for the Baptist community at Olchon (along the flanks of the Black Mountains), who wrote a booklet published in the 1880s which combined elements of local tradition in which he firmly believed, but which we now know to be wide of the mark, with some details of Oldcastle's life which he then often arranged in the wrong order. His booklet therefore includes a somewhat confused and often erroneous account of Oldcastle's life.[18]

It is thought that the castle by the church in Almeley was built during the reign of King John (1199–1216), probably on the site of an earlier structure, but there is no evidence that this was a Roman fort. The Welsh borders are littered with such mottes, possibly built as staging posts by Norman troops in the early days of their conquest of England, as the homes of those who owed military service to their feudal overlords, or during the Anarchy in the wars between Stephen and Matilda (1135–53), when Herefordshire was on the front line and families had to look to their own defence.

Neither castle features markedly in written history, but we do know that the castle by the church was visited by Henry III on 22 September 1231, on his way from Painscastle (some 14 miles south-west of Almeley), which he was in the process of fortifying strongly against the Welsh. He is said to have received homage within the fortifications from Simon de Montfort at a time when Simon was seeking the restoration of lands formerly belonging to the earldom of Leicester.[19] It would seem from this, and the royal appointment of constables, that the castle was in fact held by the king, and therefore could not have been Oldcastle's home. Ruins were still visible on the mound in the seventeenth century.[20]

Although we have barely begun to consider John Oldcastle's life, evidence for the extent of his lands in Almeley and elsewhere in Herefordshire comes from the efforts to regain possession of those lands by his son, Henry, after John Oldcastle's death. An inquisition post mortem[21] was carried out in 1429 and records Oldcastle's lands in the county at the time of their forfeiture, when he was condemned for treason in January 1414, whilst the Calendar of Patent Rolls for 1431 (when Henry gained possession) adds further details.[22]

The Calendar of Patent Rolls for 1431 record that John Oldcastle inherited 'the manor of Almaly, 580 acres of land, 80 acres of meadow, 40 acres of pasture, 25 acres of wood and 100s. rent in Almaly, Upcote, Kynardsley [Kinnersley], Lecton [Letton], Hereford, Holmere, Sheldewyck [Shelwick, north-east of Hereford], Pype and More'.

The inquisition post mortem lists the manor of Almeley's possession as the 'site of the manor' with a grange (barn); three carucates comprising 180 acres of arable land (a carucate was deemed to be the amount of land that could be ploughed in a season by an eight-ox team, so varied in acreage from location to location depending upon the soil); several meadows which are named: Amber or Amury; Locrehamme or Loverham, Oldcastle's, Tweybrokes or Tweybrokes, Oldjack's, Frethemore with an enclosed meadow adjoining, Highmoor or Highmore, Calverhall or Colnerhall, Sokere's Meadow and two-thirds of a meadow called The Plocks. There was also a messuage (a house together with its outbuildings, yards and garden) and a watermill at Oldcastle (presumably on the stream that flows through The Batch, the mill being described as 'ruinous' in 1431), a house and a carucate of land at Upcott and a piece of meadow at 'Wotton' (possibly in the area now known as Almeley Wootton), all within the parish. The later record in the Calendar of Patent Rolls states that the lands identified in the inquisition post mortem as being in 'Oldecastell and Wotton' have always been part of the manor of Almeley.

The map below shows the north-western part of Almeley Parish as depicted on the Tithe Map of 1839. Two of the meadows mentioned in the inquisition, Amber and Sokere's, still retain their name (though the latter as Suckers Meadow), as does Highmore (as High Moors), which was then (and remains) woodland. None of the other names have survived, and nor do they appear on the earlier 1744 estate map (shown opposite) of land owned by the Foley family in that year.

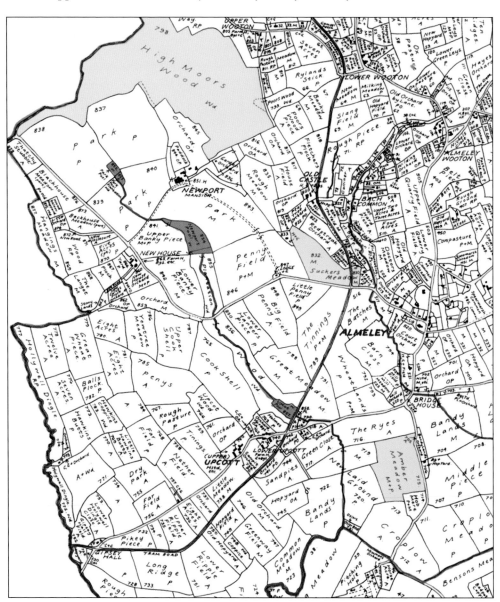

Part of 1839 Tithe Map of Almeley showing lands known to be connected with Oldcastle's landholding shaded in green. The location of Newport House can be seen above the largest blue-shaded pool. (Original map courtesy of Geoff Gwatkin ©)

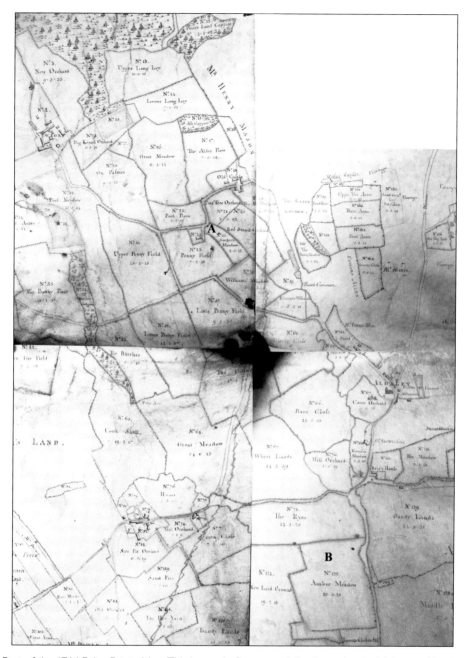

Part of the 1744 Foley Estate Map. This is now in four parts, joined together in this image. Almeley is centre right with 'Old Castle' to its north-west and Newport towards the top left-hand corner. 'Sucker's Meadow' (A) is shown south of 'Old Castle', and 'Amber Meadow' (B) to the west of the road heading south from Almeley. Upcott is the group of buildings to the west of Amber Meadow, just north of Saw Pit Orchard (no.83). Highmore Wood is at the top of the extract and Newport House near the top on the left-hand side. The pencil line that runs the length of the map was added by someone desirous of showing the route of the horse-drawn tramroad built between 1818 and 1820 or its successor railway. (Courtesy of Hereford Archive and Records Centre)

Outside Almeley parish the Oldcastle estate included a messuage in ruins and a carucate of land at Ailey in Kinnersley parish (the parish to the south of Almeley); a messuage in ruins and 30 acres of arable land at Kynley (now Kinley) in Letton parish (to the south of that of Kinnersley); and a messuage in ruins and 120 acres of arable land, 2 of meadow and 2 of pasture at Holmer (north of Hereford). In Hereford itself there were two shops (said, in 1431, to be in the 'butchery'), a messuage containing three shops with a chamber built over with a garden 'hard by at "le Westkarclus"' (as named in 1431, or Westekalerns in 1421), a cellar with a chamber built over it, and another messuage known as 'Fotberesyn' in 1431.[23]

It seems that during his life Oldcastle increased the size of his estate, for other additional lands listed that he held at his death included 14 acres of arable land in Upcott (within Almeley parish), 15 acres of meadow and 10 of pasture in Kinnersley, 68 acres in Letton, and 130 acres of meadow and 13 of pasture in Holmer.

Evidence that John Oldcastle may well have acquired more land, or sold or exchanged land during his lifetime, is borne out by transactions involving either his land or land adjoining it. Thus, in 1407 there was a transfer of land in the parish of Weobley, south-east of Almeley, which mentioned land neighbouring that belonging to Oldcastle,[24] and a separate transaction concerning a quitclaim (a renunciation of a claim to land) to John 'Oldecastelle' and two others of all lands, rents and services, woods, waters and fisheries in Holme Lacy and Ballingham (south-west of Hereford) and 'Hayton' in Shropshire.[25] In the late 1430s and even into the 1440s John Oldcastle's son, Henry, was still trying to assert his claim to lands that his father had owned. Thus, in November 1438, Henry appears to have lost out on regaining some land in Weobley, when 'two places formerly built on, 4 acres of arable land and 3 acres of meadow' were granted to Walter Devereux, lands that were 'in the king's hands by the forfeiture of John Oldecastell'.[26] Henry had greater success in February 1444 when '4 messuages, 4 carucates of land, 40 acres of meadow, 40 acres of wood and 40s. of rent' in parishes to the south of Hereford were granted to him, lands again 'in the king's hands by the forfeiture of John Oldecastell'.[27]

The mention in the inquisition of the 'site of the manor' of Almeley gives little indication as to which building was the lord of the manor's residence. There is no mention of a castle, though as castles became dilapidated the principal domestic residence, which would have been within the castle bailey would come to resemble ever more closely what today would be considered a manor house. In the wars against Glyndwr at the beginning of the fifteenth century, no mention is made of refortifying a castle at Almeley, unlike those at nearby Eardisley, Lyonshall, Dorstone and Huntington,[28] suggesting that both castle sites in the parish were now too decayed to be worth strengthening. It has also been suggested that the site of Oldcastle's Almeley manor might have been where Newport House now stands, half a mile due west of the motte that stands near Oldcastle Farm.[29] Newport is first mentioned in the Close Rolls of King Edward III, so some form of building at least must have been there by

A drawing showing Newport House in 1680.

the time Oldcastle was born.[30] Any mediaeval structure that stood there, however, has long since been erased, the current house dating to *c*.1712–19. It is possible, therefore, that Oldcastle's home stood either in the bailey adjoining Oldcastle motte or on the site where Newport House now stands. The current Almeley Manor, which stands near the church, dates to *c*.1500, the west end having been modified in the seventeenth century.

The village of Almeley would have been clustered near the church and its two castle sites. As for its population, the poll tax return for 1379, which lists names and some occupations, indicate 108 taxpayers in the wider parish.[31] Children under 14 years of age were exempted and as there is known to have been widespread tax evasion where other records for an area can be compared with poll tax returns, the true population may have been closer to between 150 and 180. This represents something of an increase, proportionately, from the likely figure at the time of Domesday, but considerably reduced from the number of inhabitants before the arrival of the Black Death. Isabel Oldcastle, John's mother, by then a widow, is listed in the 1379 tax return as one of the two people paying the largest sum in the parish – 40d (3s 4d). The other listed as paying this sum is John Woutton who is listed as a franklin, and thus a wealthier freeholder, and whose name suggests he might have farmed at Woonton in the east of the parish. Next came the smith John Levyot, yeoman farmers William Hondron and John Neuport, William Drayton the shoemaker and William Wylkoc the carpenter, who each paid 1 shilling. The remainder paid the basic rate of 4d for a married couple or single adult. It is interesting that virtually all the names listed in the poll tax are of English rather than Welsh origin, for records of later times give a higher proportion of Welsh names.

Intriguingly the poll tax return also mentions an 'Isabella' and a 'Willelmo Oldecastile', each paying 4d, meaning they were over 14 years of age.[32] John's uncle, Thomas Oldcastle was to have a daughter called Isabel, but she was not yet aged 12 when Thomas died in 1398 or 1399, so wouldn't have been born by 1379, the year of the poll tax. Isabella and Willelmo make no other appearance in the historical record and are not listed in the poll tax return in close proximity to the name of Isabel, John Oldcastle's mother. Perhaps they took their name from the area of Almeley rather than having any blood connection to the family.

Assessors were appointed in each county to carry out the initial assessment as to who was to pay what amount, collectors being given the duty of gathering in the tax. Those assessed to pay the rate of 3s 4d included a range of occupations: esquires without property who were in service; farmers of manors, parsonages or granges and merchants of animals (depending upon their wealth, they were assessed to pay either half a mark [6s 8d], 3s 4d, 2s or 1s); married pardoners and summoners (assessed at either 3s 4d, 2s or 1s); 'hostelliers' (innkeepers) not of merchant status (again at either 3s 4d, 2s or 1s); and lesser merchants and artisans (assessed at 6s 8d, 3s 4d, 2s, 1s and 6d).[33] As bachelor knights and esquires of knightly estates were assessed at 20s, and as widows were to pay the amount as if the assessment was of her husband, it is surprising that Isabel Oldcastle was not assessed at 20s, given that her husband had been a knight and given the size of their estate, but perhaps she was. Notes passed to me by Robert Jenkins, once Almeley's parish clerk, who had carried out some research into Oldcastle, state that she did indeed pay 20s. Unfortunately, Robert had died by the time I discovered the discrepancy in the two pieces of information and so I don't know on what he based his figure.

The poll tax of 1379 was levied 30 years after the Black Death had swept through the country and fractured the structure of feudal overlordship imposed after the Norman Conquest. With a shift towards a greater emphasis on wages in relation to feudal duties, a lack of available labour then led to wages rising significantly. Anger at legislation aiming to control wage inflation, coupled with unrest at the poll tax, led to the Peasants' Revolt in 1381. Herefordshire, lying as it does well away from London, was relatively untouched by the Revolt, with news of the uprising probably only reaching the county through wandering friars and travellers several weeks later. This is not to say that the villagers would have been unsympathetic to the aims of the uprising. Indeed, the advent of what more closely resembled a wage economy would have changed the nature of the bonds under which society had operated since the Norman Conquest and probably whetted people's appetite for further change. News of the Peasants' Revolt may also have helped prepare the ground for the messages brought by itinerant preachers in the 1390s and 1400s, not least those promoting the views of John Wycliffe, or a version of them.

The inquisition into Oldcastle's lands in Almeley also mentions the holding of a court baron every three weeks, and 3s 4d rent of assize (a fixed rent paid by freeholders or ancient copyholders of an English manor, often in lieu of feudal services once owed) at Upcott (for which, see the map on page 10). The court baron was the manorial court which sorted out disputes in the running of the manorial estate and allocated rights of pasture, and it was normally presided over by the steward appointed by the lord of the manor, rather than the lord himself. The Oldcastles would have appointed someone they knew and trusted as their steward, and he would have done most of the day to day management, the Oldcastles keeping some of the land for farming in hand, using a mixture of labour services still due under feudal law and paid labour. One of the functions of the manorial court was to record changes in landholdings, for many of the Oldcastles' tenants would have held their land under copyhold – defined as a 'holding at the will of the lord according to the custom of the manor' – part of that custom being the provision of labour for certain services. In practice, most manorial courts probably met less frequently than every three weeks, their place of meeting no doubt being in one of the buildings that formed the manor homestead.

The only time that John Oldcastle's mother, Isabel, appears in the records is in regards to her poll tax payment in 1379. Indeed, little is known of any of John's ancestors. His great-grandfather, Peter, is the earliest recorded member of his family. His grandfather, also John Oldcastle, represented Herefordshire in the parliaments of 1368 and 1372. His father, Richard must have come to prominence at some point, for he was the first of the family to be knighted, perhaps as a result of some action in the rekindled wars in France. Edward III's claim to the throne of France through his mother, Isabella, sister of Charles IV of France, led to the battles of Crécy in 1346 and Poitiers in 1356, which saw his efforts reach their peak. But failure to enforce the terms of the resultant treaty, a resuscitation of French arms – notably under Bertrand du Guesclin on land in 1370 and a heavy defeat of an English fleet off La Rochelle in 1372 – contributed to a gradual whittling away of earlier English gains. It is not known when Richard Oldcastle died, but it must have been by 1379, for, as we have seen, his wife was a widow by then, and probably not long after the death of his own father, who died sometime between 1377 and 1379.

The young Oldcastle

John Oldcastle would have been aged about nine at the time of his father, Richard's death, and it would seem likely that his uncle, Thomas Oldcastle, helped to bring up the young John. Thomas, Richard's younger brother, was one of the MPs elected for Herefordshire in 1390 and 1393, and sheriff of the county in 1386–87 and again in 1391–92. He was clearly believed to be an honest and diligent man, for by 1393 he had been made a member of the council of Bishop Trefnant of Hereford, and in 1394 he acted as an arbitrator concerning the bishop's rights on Malvern Chase.[34] He was also known to Edmund III Mortimer, earl of March, for in October 1375 he witnessed the grant of a piece of land at Eaton Tregoz in south Herefordshire, for which the first witness was the earl.[35] Interestingly, two of the other witnesses were John Bromwich and John Eynesford, who were among those involved in the transfer of Almeley manor to John Oldcastle around 1379. It was in 1378 or 1379 that Bromwich was appointed Lord Justice of Ireland,[36] where he commanded a force of 60 men-at-arms and 120 archers, but

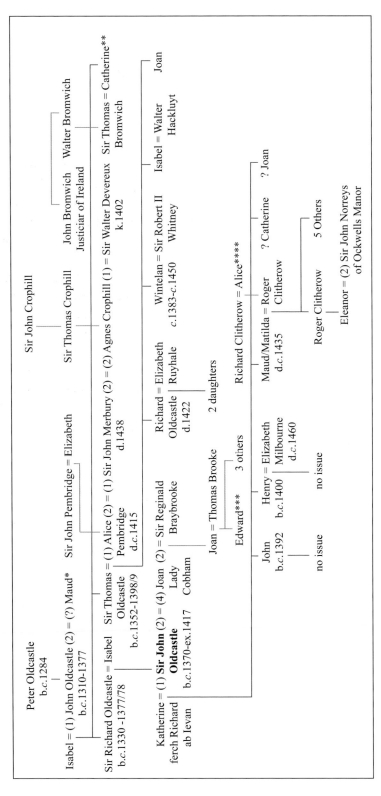

The Oldcastle Family Tree

Red lines link members of the direct Oldcastle family, green either those of ancestors of people whom they married or of stepchildren

* It would seem that Sir John's grandfather remarried on the death of his first wife, with Sir Thomas Oldcastle leaving money in his will to Maud (see page 33).

** For how Catherine Oldcastle is deemed to fit into the family tree at this point, see page 33.

*** Edward regained the title of Lord Cobham, lost with Oldcastle's death. His descendants were Lords Cobham in Shakespeare's time.

**** For details of the Clitherow family, see Chapter 10, note 6 served less than a year, being superseded by Edmund III Mortimer, earl of March, who was placed at the head of the government in Ireland. Sir John Eynesford hailed from Tillington, just north-west of Hereford, and served as a member of parliament ten times between 1365 and 1384.

In July 1397 Thomas Oldcastle and his nephew, John, together with Thomas II Walwyn, were given royal letters of protection (essentially a form of security against issues that arose whilst they were on royal duty) to cover the time that they served in the retinue of Roger VI Mortimer, earl of March, Richard II's lieutenant in Ireland. If John's date of birth was 1370, he would have been aged 27 at this point. The two Thomases, Oldcastle and Walwyn, probably returned to England in January 1398, but John may have stayed on.[37] Thomas Oldcastle is last mentioned in the records during 1398 and must have died in that or the following year, for in January 1400 his widow married John Merbury.

No family papers have survived to tell us of John Oldcastle's youth, but other records tell us that he was a squire and subsequently a knight, so certain inferences can be made. Between the ages of seven and eight a boy whose parents sought knighthood for him would be sent to the home of a relative or wealthy lord to whom they owed allegiance, to become a page. John's father had been knighted, so his mother and uncle may well have thought that he should aim to follow in his father's footsteps. A boy training for knighthood would have learned horsemanship and the use of a lance, archery, sword-play and how to use other weapons such as maces, battle axes and daggers. He would also have become physically fit. A lighter side would see him learn to sing and dance, write in French and Latin, and learn the rules of etiquette and good manners.

Records for Oldcastle's future companion-in-arms, Prince Henry, tell that at the age of ten the prince was playing the harp and learning swordplay, and he might have joined his parents at chess, a game they both enjoyed, and possibly handball with his father, Henry Bolingbroke. He also learned falconry. Henry had a nurse who was probably responsible for his learning English, for in his father's absence on crusade in Lithuania in 1390 and Prussia in 1392 (when Henry was aged between four and six), he was brought up at Peterborough by his mother, Mary Bohun. Mary died when Henry was seven, and though his father had returned home by then, he does not seem to have had much contact with his children. Henry seems instead to have spent much of the rest of his boyhood with his paternal grandfather, John of Gaunt. By the age of eight he was learning Latin; indeed, there is evidence that Bolingbroke's children were being taught to read and write from a young age. Henry's library at his death included books on law, rhetoric, history and logic. Records show payments for the making of copies of books on hunting, and for failing to return two chronicles of the crusades, which he had borrowed from one of his aunts, and the works of Gregory the Great, which he had borrowed from Archbishop Arundel. Unlike his brother Humphrey's more humanist tendencies, Prince Henry's reading would appear traditional, which might explain his support for the established Church in later life (even if given a little reluctantly at times).[38]

We don't know what the young John Oldcastle might have been encouraged to read, but at the age of 14 or 15 a page would become a squire and his skills in warfare would be honed. Wooden weapons were replaced with the real thing and injuries were common. Horsemanship would be perfected. Military strategy would be learnt, not least how to defend and how to besiege a castle, and the chivalric rules of seeking a truce or surrender. The squire could also serve in an actual battle and, should the knight to whom he was apprenticed be injured or killed, he was expected to stand guard over his body. Aged 21 he would be eligible to become a knight, but would need to have the means to purchase and look after the necessary horses and equipment. Not all those who became knights completed this process, however, for another way to be knighted was as a result of prowess on the battlefield, whatever one's previous status.

Kinship and Connections

It is likely that Thomas would have used his connections to secure an appropriate household in which the young John could be trained as a page. In Shakespeare's *Henry IV Part II*, Act II, Scene II, Shallow says: 'Then was Jack Falstaff, now Sir John, a boy, and page to Thomas Mowbray, Duke of Norfolk'. If Shakespeare still had the life of Oldcastle in mind for obtaining some of his information, then Oldcastle's attachment to the household of Thomas Mowbray is supported by John Weever in his 'Mirror of Martyrs', a poetical life of Oldcastle written in 1601. Superficially, it would seem improbable that Oldcastle was a page to Thomas Mowbray, for the duke's lands lay largely in eastern and southern England, making it unlikely that the Oldcastles would have come into contact with the family. Yet there is a possible route.

Lewis Clifford was born sometime soon after 1330 into a cadet branch of the Cliffords of Devonshire. In the 1360s he served under the Black Prince and, following the latter's death, his widow and then her son, King Richard II and Richard's uncle, John of Gaunt. Between 1370 and 1372 Clifford married Eleanor, daughter of John, Lord Mowbray of Axholme, becoming her second husband. Eleanor was of royal descent and aunt of Thomas Mowbray, duke of Norfolk. As a result of the marriage, Clifford obtained the castle and lordship of Ewyas Harold in south-western Herefordshire. This gave Clifford land close to the Cistercian Abbey of Dore, with which John Oldcastle was to have dealings. Clifford was a close colleague of John Clanvowe, who had land at Hergest, near Kington in north-west Herefordshire, close to that of the Oldcastles who were also close colleagues of the Clanvowes (as will be shown below). Clifford served on the king's council in 1392 and that, along with many other appointments and duties, soon raised his income to the equivalent of that derived from a small landed baronial estate.[39] Held in high esteem and with these connections, it is possible that Clifford obtained a position for the young John Oldcastle as a page in Mowbray's household.[40]

On the other hand, it might be that a position as a page was found for him closer to home, for Thomas Oldcastle had extensive connections. Whilst the Oldcastle family would have used the services of the local tailor, shoemaker and most notably the smith (all as recorded in the poll tax records for 1379), their circle of friends would have included those of similar status in nearby parishes, and those with whom they came into contact as a result of business dealings and government appointments. Quite a

The four stages of a man's life, illustrated in the *De proprietatibus rerum* of Bartholomeus Anglicus, translated from Latin into French by Jean Corbechon in the 14th century. (Paris, BnF, fr. 134, f. 92v)

lot is known about these contacts, and it seems that in the late 1300s a closely-knit group of families, with ties of friendship and loyalty, was formed around north-west Herefordshire.

Some of these friendships were made as a result of shared service to the Mortimer earls of March, who were based at Wigmore in north-west Herefordshire and Ludlow in south Shropshire. The Mortimers had risen to prominence during the reign of King Edward I. Roger III Mortimer had given support to Edward when he was prince, including helping in the defeat of Simon de Montfort at the Battle of Evesham in 1265. His grandson, Roger IV Mortimer, allied with Isabella of France to depose her husband, King Edward II, in 1327. He then ruled as king in all but name for three years, before King Edward III, on reaching the age of 18, organised a counter-coup and had Mortimer executed. During those years Mortimer had developed his castles at Wigmore and especially Ludlow into residences fit for a royal court.

The illustrations of the squire and the knight in the Ellesmere manuscript of Geoffrey Chaucer's *Canterbury Tales*. Written between 1387 and Chaucer's death in October 1400, the tales detail a pilgrimage made by 29 assorted members of English society who, on 16 April 1387, left London to head to Canterbury. This was the same year that Oldcastle was to serve in his first military expedition. The Ellesmere manuscript (named after Sir Thomas Egerton [1540–1617], Baron Ellesmere and Viscount Brackley, who acquired it and whose descendants retained it till 1917) was created in the first decade of the fifteenth century, so shortly after the text was first written and not long after Chaucer's death. The illustrations are therefore likely to show a version of the travelling clothing that a squire and a knight of the late 1300s and early 1400s would have worn.
(The illustration of the knight appears on f.10r and of the squire on f.115v)

Ludlow Castle showing the 'state apartments' added by Roger IV Mortimer in the late 1320s.
(© Philip Hume)

A reconstruction drawing showing how Wigmore Castle might have looked in the mid to late 1300s.

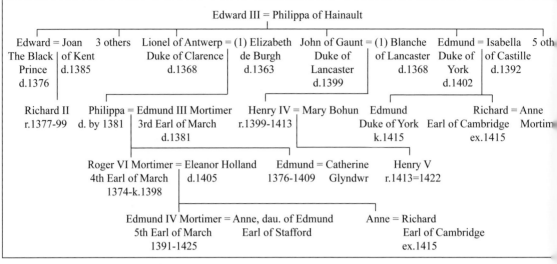

Family Tree showing the linkage of the Mortimer and royal lines

The tree shows:

Edward III = Philippa of Hainault

Children:
- Edward The Black Prince d.1376 = Joan of Kent d.1385
- 3 others
- Lionel of Antwerp Duke of Clarence d.1368 = (1) Elizabeth de Burgh d.1363
- John of Gaunt Duke of Lancaster d.1399 = (1) Blanche of Lancaster d.1368
- Edmund Duke of York d.1402 = Isabella of Castille d.1392
- 5 oth

Next generation:
- Richard II r.1377-99
- Philippa d. by 1381 = Edmund III Mortimer 3rd Earl of March d.1381
- Henry IV r.1399-1413 = Mary Bohun
- Edmund Duke of York k.1415
- Richard Earl of Cambridge ex.1415 = Anne Mortim

Next generation:
- Roger VI Mortimer 4th Earl of March 1374-k.1398 = Eleanor Holland d.1405
- Edmund 1376-1409 = Catherine Glyndwr
- Henry V r.1413=1422

Next generation:
- Edmund IV Mortimer 5th Earl of March 1391-1425 = Anne, dau. of Edmund Earl of Stafford
- Anne = Richard Earl of Cambridge ex.1415

By the time of the death of Roger V Mortimer in 1360, not only had the Mortimers regained the position in the kingdom that they had held before the rebellion of Roger IV, but Roger V had arranged for his son, Edmund III Mortimer, to marry a granddaughter of King Edward III. This put the family very close to the legal succession to the crown. However Edmund was to die in Ireland in 1381, probably as a result of pneumonia arising from a chill caught when on campaign. This resulted in Roger VI Mortimer inheriting his family estates as a minor aged just seven. As was the custom, the young Mortimer became a royal ward and his estates were put into the hands of others to manage until he came of age. In December 1393 the overall responsibility for this was given to a number of earls and lords headed by the earl of Arundel, a responsibility held by the earl until 1394 when Roger VI came of age.

In 1398, Roger VI Mortimer was killed in a skirmish in Ireland, where he was serving as King Richard II's lieutenant, and the Mortimer inheritance passed to another seven-year-old, Edmund IV. With the usurpation of the throne by Gaunt's son Henry Bolingbroke, who became King Henry IV, Edmund IV Mortimer and his younger brother Roger were kept as royal wards, mainly at Windsor. Edmund's uncle, another Edmund, became *de facto* head of the family in the Marches.

Each of these two successive under-age inheritances meant that officials needed to be appointed to oversee the Mortimer estate and manage the individual properties and landholdings. Whilst it is not known if Thomas Oldcastle was one of those called upon, others with whom he formed a close group – Richard Nash, Philip Holgot, Kynard de la Bere and Thomas II Walwyn – did undertake duties on behalf of the Mortimers, and it would seem quite likely that Thomas did too, as he served with Roger VI Mortimer in Ireland.

The effigy of John Gour and his wife in Pembridge Church. Between the late 1350s and his death in the late 1370s John Gour was found in the service of the Mortimer family, often in the office of Steward. In 1355 the patent rolls record a commission to William de Frome, John de Oldecastel (our John's grandfather) and Hugh de Monyton to ensure the enforcement of the Statute of Labourers. That same year William de Frome was mentioned in the company of John Gour in a list head by Roger V Mortimer in a commission of oyer and terminer (literally 'to hear and determine', usually more serious cases such as murder or insurrection). In 1358 John Gour and the older John Oldcastle appear in the same commission recorded in the patent rolls. This indicates that Oldcastle's grandfather and John Gour were colleagues, and that John Oldcastle the elder also served the Mortimers on occasion. When Earl Roger V Mortimer died in 1360, Gour was appointed to look after the family estates in the Marches during the minority of Edmund III Mortimer. His hat or headpiece is unusual and resembles those worn later by apprentices in the law.[41] (© Robert Anderson)

As this group were amongst the first men that John Oldcastle would have come to know, what do we know of them and their connections? Thomas Oldcastle first appears in the records in 1378 when, with Richard Nash, a Hereford lawyer and one of those later appointed to look after the interests of the young Mortimers, he stood surety for Ralph Maylock, who had been given custody of lands of the alien abbey of Lire or Lyre. This abbey had been founded in Normandy by William fitzOsbern, created earl of Hereford by William I following the Norman Conquest. FitzOsbern had continued granting lands to the abbey, including the new foundation of a priory at Livers Ocle near Ocle Pychard east of Hereford. As a dependency of an overseas abbey, Livers Ocle was known as an alien priory, and at times of strife between England and France, and following the loss of Normandy in the early 1200s, the Crown often appointed a custodian who had two duties: to ensure that the monks weren't involved in spying, and to appropriate all the revenues and rents due to the monks, leaving enough for their needs and handing the rest over to the Crown. Livers Ocle's possessions included land and rents in Herefordshire at Livers Ocle, Bridstow, Credenhill, Dinedor, Eardisland, Fownhope, Hereford, Hinton, King's Caple, Linton-by-Ross, Lugwardine, Much Marcle, Sutton, Thornbury and Westhide.[42] By standing surety, Thomas Oldcastle and Richard Nash became legally responsible for ensuring that Ralph Maylock performed the duties placed on him. This meant paying any monies due if he failed to pay any debts – in this case the handing over of the rents due less any agreed cost or proportion retained. The need to stand surety for each other in performing many public and private duties often strengthened ties amongst a group of friends.

The following year Richard Nash and Philip Holgot (another Hereford lawyer), were nominated as attorneys for both the prior of Llanthony and Leonard Hakluyt, who were to travel to Ireland in the service of Edmund III Mortimer. By 1385 the pair were employed by Thomas Oldcastle and his brother, Richard (John's father) as trustees of properties in Herefordshire and Radnorshire. Holgot and Thomas Oldcastle subsequently undertook the same service for Nash. This was becoming a common way of managing estates. Up to 12 trustees, or feoffees, would be appointed, and if the landowner died or was called away on other duties, the feoffees would oversee the income and make necessary payments. This provided certainty for those appointed on official business that their interests would be looked after, and also meant that on their death the land could not pass into the wardship of the feudal overlord, as it was in the hands of trustees. We know that Nash, at least, entered the service of the new earl of March, Roger VI Mortimer, because the records show that by 1387 he was engaged by the earl as an apprentice-at-law or junior advocate, for which service he received an annuity of £2. In 1389 Thomas Oldcastle, Nash and Thomas II Walwyn were joint trustees of an estate at Lower Bullingham in Herefordshire. Thomas Oldcastle, Holgot and Kynard de la Bere then became joint trustees of Nash's property in and around Hereford, and in 1398 Thomas Oldcastle and Holgot were again trustees of land in Shropshire and Herefordshire, this time on behalf of Isabel, widow of Sir John Eynesford.[43]

The links continued. De la Bere was Thomas Oldcastle's fellow MP for Herefordshire in 1390, during which time Thomas provided securities when de la Bere obtained a lease on some royal property in Warwickshire. Two years later, in July 1392, Thomas, along with de la Bere and Walwyn, endowed a chantry chapel at Norton Canon parish church in Herefordshire. The years 1394 and 1395 saw Thomas Oldcastle appointed as an attorney for several knights who were to accompany King Richard II on his campaign in Ireland, including Sir Robert I Whitney of Whitney-on-Wye, Thomas Clanvowe of Hergest and Yazor, and Walter Devereux of Weobley, all of whom lived in north-west Herefordshire. As noted above, in 1397 Thomas was himself called upon to serve in Ireland, together with his nephew John Oldcastle and Thomas II Walwyn.[44]

The lawyer Richard Nash was a busy man. He was elected as an MP for Hereford five times between 1377 and 1390 and then three times for the county, in 1384, 1388 and 1390. Appointed a justice of the peace in 1380, he was much in demand as a lawyer, both privately and on government business. In May 1390 he was appointed a royal justice in South Wales, and the following year he was employed by Thomas, earl of Stafford. Like Thomas Oldcastle, he became a member of Bishop Trefnant's council sometime

Norton Canon Church. Court rolls 1392 show a grant of 'land at Norton, Hynton, Ekkley and Morewys to a chaplain to celebrate divine service daily at the altar of the Blessed Virgin Mary in the church of Saint Nicholas'. Later records show that 'the greater part of Hinton was given for the maintenance of the chantry of the Blessed Virgin Mary in this church, and three acres of land at Ewyas Harold given to supply candles there'.[45] (Author)

before 1393, and with him acted for the bishop in a dispute about episcopal rights in Malvern Chase in 1394. He often acted as an attorney for those overseas on royal business, including the earl of March. Nash had died by February 1395, his lands passing into the hands of trustees who were to found a chantry in Hereford Cathedral where masses were to be sung for the souls of himself and his son, James; his daughter Cecily was not included in this bequest. James was illegitimate, but was trained as a lawyer and supported his father's work, also being a joint trustee of property with Thomas Oldcastle.[46]

The other lawyer in the group, Philip Holgot, had entered the service of the Mortimers in 1375, becoming an executor of the will of Philippa, the wife of Edmund III Mortimer and granddaughter of King Edward III. On Philippa's death, her dower lands would have passed to her son, Roger VI Mortimer, except that he was under age. King Richard II, as was his right, decided to divide the custody of these estates between various Mortimer officials, with Holgot receiving the lion's share. By 1384 these had, however, been passed into the care of a group of noblemen.[47]

Kynard de la Bere was a near neighbour of the Oldcastles, living at Kinnersley Castle,[48] just a couple of miles across the fields to the south of Almeley. Kynard's father, Richard, had been to the wars with the Black Prince and became his chamberlain. Kynard first appears in the records in 1381, when he stood surety for John Croft as lessee for land at Eardisley. He served on a royal commission later that year and the following year was appointed a justice of the peace. He did military service in King Richard II's expedition to Scotland in 1385 (during which campaign he was knighted), and also accompanied the king on his expedition to Ireland in 1394, when he served in the earl of March's retinue. He probably stayed on in Ireland during the earl's lieutenancy of the island, returning to England with the earl in 1398, and then became one of his attorneys on the earl's return to Ireland. Together with Thomas II Walwyn and William Beauchamp Lord Abergavenny, de la Bere was one of the earl's executors when the latter was killed in Ireland. His activities as a justice of the peace recommenced under the new regime of Henry IV, and he was called to attend a great council at Westminster in 1401.[49]

Robert I Whitney, for whom Thomas Oldcastle was appointed an attorney in the mid-1390s, was another close neighbour, his lands lying a few miles south-west of Almeley. He was appointed sheriff of Herefordshire after Richard II's accession. In this role, in an intimation of the wider unrest that would follow the usurpation of the crown by Henry IV, he, along with Walter Devereux and John Eynesford (the then MPs for the county), petitioned parliament for government help in dealing with groups of raiding Welshmen who were plundering Herefordshire. In 1385 he accompanied Richard II on his expedition to Scotland. He soon became closely involved in the affairs of the royal household, becoming responsible for organising the household's lodgings. In 1393 he was in command of the operation that transferred control of Cherbourg back to the kingdom of Navarre, the town having been granted to the English by Charles II of Navarre during his lifetime. (Charles II was the son of Joan of France, queen of Navarre, and Philip, count of Évreux, who gained control of considerable lands in France, including parts of Normandy. His prospects in France were further increased when the English won the battle of Poitiers and took captive the French king, John. However, on John's death Charles II gradually lost his French possessions with the exception of Cherbourg.)[50] Robert I Whitney used nine ships to ferry goods to either Calais or London, selling the remainder to the Navarrese. In 1394 he went to Ireland to make preparations for the arrival of Richard II's expedition. From 1397 he undertook diplomatic missions to Aragon, Foix (in southern France) and Aquitaine, returning in time to head to Ireland once more to make preparations for Richard II's second expedition to the island. With the change of regime to that of Henry IV, and probably now getting on in age, Whitney was happy to relinquish some of his roles for a quieter life.[51] His son, also Robert, was to marry Wintelan, Thomas Oldcastle's daughter, become sheriff of Herefordshire in 1413 and serve in the wars against Owain Glyndwr alongside Richard Oldcastle, who was both Thomas's son and Robert's brother-in-law (see the Oldcastle Family Tree on page 16). But here we start to trespass on territory that belongs to a later chapter.[52]

Thomas II Walwyn was not a neighbour, but one of the most important of this group of Herefordshire gentry in terms of his connections with the magnates of the realm. He came from a junior branch of the Walwyn family based at Hellens near Much Marcle on the eastern side of Herefordshire towards Ledbury, but also had some lands closer to north-west Herefordshire, including at King's Pyon. Like many of the others in this group, he began his career in the service of the Mortimer earls of March, who were also the feudal overlords of Much Marcle. In 1397 he acted as receiver-general of the Mortimer estates, that year going with the earl of March to Ireland, where he moved up the household accounting pecking order to serve as the earl's treasurer. When the earl returned home in early 1398, Walwyn accompanied him, staying in England to act as one of the earl's attorneys when he returned to Ireland. On the earl's death a few months later, he served as one of the executors of his will, alongside Kynard de la Bere and William Beauchamp Lord Abergavenny. A few years later he entered Beauchamp's service, then that of his widow. These connections led him into the circle of Edward, duke of York, a grandson of Edward III and cousin of Richard II.[53]

A geographically closer associate of Thomas Oldcastle was Walter Devereux of Weobley. It was perhaps due to John, Lord Devereux, a friend of the Black Prince and possibly Walter's uncle, that Walter gained an appointment in the royal household, where he was an esquire by 1382. It wasn't long before he was appointed custodian of the castle at Builth Wells during the minority of Roger VI Mortimer. Walter made a very propitious marriage to Agnes, the granddaughter and heir of Sir John Crophill, Sir John dying just two months after the marriage. This inheritance included lands in Nottinghamshire, Leicestershire, Lincolnshire and at Weobley in Herefordshire, the latter becoming his principal residence. Walter served on Richard II's expeditions to

Scotland in 1385 and to Ireland in 1394, when he named Thomas Oldcastle as one of his attorneys. But less is known about him than about many of the others in this group.[54]

The association that starts to take us in a religious direction as far as John Oldcastle is concerned is that with Thomas Clanvowe, though the role of Sir Robert I Whitney (whose daughter, Perrin, married Thomas) may have been as pivotal, as will be shown. The wider Clanvowe family, of Welsh descent, had estates in Radnorshire and Herefordshire, of which Thomas is known to have inherited that of Yazor, about halfway between Almeley and Hereford, and possibly others. Those trying to piece together the family tree of the Clanvowe family of this era have run into many difficulties, but John Clanvowe of Hergest[55] near Kington, who was one of Richard II's intimate court circle, is believed to have been either Thomas Clanvowe's father or his uncle, and it was probably he who gained the young Thomas a position as king's squire in the royal household. As such, he accompanied Richard II on his 1394 expedition to Ireland, where he was presumably knighted, Thomas Oldcastle acting as one of his attorneys in his absence. He was an MP for Herefordshire in both the parliaments of 1397, then became sheriff of the county and a justice of the peace.[56] But it is his father or uncle, John Clanvowe, who may have played a greater role in this unfolding story, as the author of *The Two Ways* – but the unravelling of these clues awaits a later chapter.

And so we have a group of lawyers, esquires and knights bound by a mixture of ties of friendship, neighbourliness, marriage and mutual support and service, who John Oldcastle would have come to know. They also served as members of parliament, sheriffs, and justices of the peace, as John Oldcastle was to do. What did these roles entail and what experience would they give the office holders?

The Oldcastles in Parliament and Government

During these years, and for many thereafter, whenever parliament was summoned by the king, two MPs were elected for Herefordshire (the shire representatives), and two for each of the boroughs of Hereford and Leominster. Statutes of 1330 and 1362 stated that there should be at least one parliament each year, but these were never observed; in Henry IV's reign no parliaments took place between 1407 and 1410, whilst there were two in 1404. It was usual, but not necessary, for MPs to have land or property in the relevant borough or county, and the Oldcastles were elected for the county, these elections taking place at a meeting of the county court in Hereford Castle. Though often termed 'knights of the shire', the county members for Herefordshire were more often squires or lawyers.

The conduct of the elections was the responsibility of the sheriff, who, whilst not allowed to stand himself, could strongly influence if not fix the result – not least as it was he who made the official return, which could be open to falsification. Such misdemeanours by some sheriffs saw statutes issued in 1406, 1410 and 1413, which sought to control their actions more closely, but there is little information about the process of elections before those dates. A statute of 1430 stated that those qualified to vote had to be freeholders of land, or hold land directly from the king, worth at least 40 shillings, that land being in the constituency where they would vote. Before that date, anyone who thought himself eligible might turn up at the county court and seek to cast a vote, although it seems that rarely happened. In essence, only men of the greatest substance in the shire or borough could vote, an electorate that merely numbered about 40 in many locations. What seems to have happened in practice is that those elected had a wider constituency within the population. The Herefordshire electorate also seems to have been quite sophisticated. It would often select, possibly by agreement rather than election, one representative who had previously attended parliament and who therefore had some knowledge of parliamentary procedure, and one novice who might be more vociferous in his views and could gain experience for the future.[57]

There were 135 constituencies represented in the Commons in parliament around this time, though the number fluctuated slightly from year to year depending upon the number of towns sending representatives: 88 in 1384 and 81 in 1399, for example. This made for about 270 representatives in total. Sir John's grandfather and his uncle Thomas Oldcastle were each twice elected for the shire, once as the novice and once as the man of experience. John Oldcastle himself was elected on just one occasion, in 1404. (Sir John's parliamentary record is covered in Chapter Five.)

Having been elected, what could MPs achieve? Parliament was first so named in 1236, when it was an assembly of the most prominent men in the kingdom, summoned on a personal basis and at will by the king to discuss matters of state and of law. Occasionally an assembly of a wider range of representatives was called, the first being in 1211. Initially these were occasions upon which the king could more widely communicate with his subjects and perhaps hear their grievances. With the Crown's income from its lands and feudal dues being relatively constrained, especially when finance was required to fight wars, assemblies began to be required more frequently to authorise the raising of taxes. As those taxes began to impinge on more than just the prominent men who attended the early parliaments, it became customary to seek a wider representation, a cry that was to reverberate in a later century in another country as 'no taxation without representation'. It was Simon de Montfort, when in control of the government in 1265, who first summoned representatives from the towns, a reform that gradually became customary.

Most requests for additional royal finance were to fund wars, and since, under feudal law, the king's subjects had a duty to support the Crown, parliament had little or no option but to consent in principle to the taxation requested. However, the Crown needed to show cause for the taxation and its amount, and this led parliament to becoming a place of barter. The Commons, the Lords, the clergy or the king might propose legislation in the form of statutes; the king would come with requests for taxation; the Lords and/or the Commons might want scrutiny of royal finances and officials; and petitions would be brought for consideration.[58] Electors expected MPs to argue their corner. Over the course of the parliament deals would be struck: taxes assented to (not necessarily at the level requested) so long as certain officials were replaced or records kept, petitions granted and statutes accepted. In participating in all this, the members gained opportunities to make new acquaintances and form new alliances. In Henry IV's reign, 80 of the Acts that were passed originated as petitions presented to parliament, with just seven originating from the Crown; in Henry V's reign only one Act out of 41 was officially inspired.[59] However, the enforcement of these Acts lay in the hands of the king who, if he disliked an Act, could largely ignore it and fail to pursue its enforcement.

As noted above, sheriffs were responsible for managing elections to parliament, and both Sir Thomas Oldcastle and Sir John Oldcastle were sheriffs of Herefordshire, the former in 1386–87 and again in 1391–92, the latter in 1406–07. This was just part of the responsibility of managing the affairs of the county court, which normally met once a month. The sheriffs had had a role in administering justice, a responsibility that had recently passed to the justices of the peace, though they were still responsible for empanelling juries and summoning the shire court, meaning they could affect the outcome of 'justice'. They also retained responsibility for the custody of those awaiting trial and for raising by array forces to defend the county, something that would be put to the test in the wars with Owain Glyndwr. It was their ability to raise or extort money beyond the needs of the array that had, in 1340, resulted in the limitation of their terms of office to a single year on any occasion, a rule not always followed.[60]

A government role in which many more of the gentry were involved over time was that of a justice of the peace. Originally known as keepers of the peace, they had acquired their new name by 1361, when a statute gave them the power to try minor offenders. They were appointed by the Crown from amongst the county gentry, but received no payment for their duties. During Richard II's reign in the late 1300s it became a requirement, as the common law expanded, that at least some of the justices should be trained lawyers. Their role grew with the need, from the government's perspective, to enforce The Statute of Labourers of 1351, which attempted to hold down wages in the aftermath of the Black Death.[61] Amongst their roles the justices had to enforce such statutes locally and take sureties for good behaviour. This involved either the person themselves agreeing a bond that set out the good behaviour to which they were required to adhere and guaranteeing the financial penalty that would be payable if they didn't, or that sum being guaranteed by others. The duty of the justices extended to imprisoning those who could give no sureties. There were around 20 justices of the peace in each county at any one time. With several of those serving also being called upon for military service or other duties alongside others who were currently not serving as justices, this created a fairly wide pool of county gentry who would get to know one another while sharing official duties.

At times members of the gentry would also be appointed as escheators. An escheator had responsibility for ensuring that when a tenant was found guilty of a felony punished by losing their land, or died without an heir, the land was passed back to the landowner. Escheators were often appointed by the king, as he had rights to payments when a new landowner entered into their inheritance. If the land in any event reverted to the king, he could choose whom to favour with the subsequent grant.

The king would also appoint knights of the shire to undertake a range of commissions. These could be: to arrest a named person or persons; to inquire into the ownership of certain lands, or to ensure that lands had been passed on to the rightful owner; to levy forces for protection of the realm; to proclaim commitments or actions by the king; and to ascertain who was trading with Welsh rebels during the fighting with Owain Glyndwr's forces. These appointments usually involved a number of knights, again facilitating a coalescing of local interests and friendships.

John Oldcastle in his teens and twenties

So, we can build up a picture of John Oldcastle as a young man being raised with the help of his uncle in a circle of those responsible for governmental functions and the maintaining of law and order. He may have been a page in the service of Thomas Mowbray, duke of Norfolk, for a while or with one of the families with which Thomas Oldcastle had connections, or even in Thomas's own family, before beginning training as an esquire. The hope must have been that he was developing into a respectable and law-abiding member of the local gentry, and indeed he himself undertook such responsibilities in his time, as we will see. But there is another side to the story, revealed to us through an incident whose details we know through the records of an abbot's petition.

During the late 1390s two monks were contesting the abbacy of Dore, a Cistercian monastery founded in 1147 in the Golden Valley, some 17 miles south of Almeley. For a few years neither monk received the blessing of the bishop and each tried to manage the abbey's properties, for example each appointing his own man as priest of Wigtoft in Lincolnshire, one of the churches of which the abbey had patronage. The dispute between the two appointees got to such a pitch that it led to riot and bloodshed in Wigtoft Church during Mass. In 1398 one of the two monks, Jordan Bykelswade, finally received the support of both the bishop and the pope, and was confirmed as abbot – until he was indicted of a felony in 1403. It was during 1398 that John ap Henry (quite possibly the same man as the John ap Harry who became a close friend of John Oldcastle and whom we will meet later), Griffith ap Henry, Thomas de la Hay, Thomas ap John and John Oldcastle led an armed group of men to the abbey's manor of Morehampton and took away the sheep. Working either individually or in different combinations, between 1396 and 1398 these men also rustled the abbey's cattle, cut down oaks in the abbey's woods for their own use, collected and held onto monetary dues owed the abbey, and carted off stone and felled timber from one of the abbey's granges.

Oldcastle was singled out for bringing a force of armed men at various times between 1396 and 1398 to Treville, not far from Dore, and 'Cantsely', identified as Cantref Selyf, which was centred on Bronllys and Talgarth some 20 miles south-west of Almeley in

Dore Abbey. The transepts, crossing and lady chapel were retained as the parish church after the Reformation. (Author)

what later became Breconshire. Here he cut down 24 great oaks in the abbot's woods for his own use. The alleged crimes are listed in a petition from the abbey seeking redress, which was sent to the king and his council, the abbot stating that he was fearful for his life at the hands of these men or others of their affinity.

On another occasion Oldcastle was involved in the abduction of three monks who were then tied to trees by a combination of ropes and chains, two of them upside down, on and off for three days.[62] Even so, Oldcastle seems to have been among the less culpable of the 'villains', with some of the others going as far as kidnapping monks and ransoming them. Nevertheless the petition hints at a rough and potentially violent character. What happened as a result of the petition is not recorded, and nor is it known whether the actions were part of the power struggle for the abbacy, the result of local feuds, or inspired by Lollard preachings about the sins of the Church.

This incident happened in the years leading up to Thomas Oldcastle's death, when perhaps John was breaking free from his uncle's supervision. By this time he was married, in 1394 having taken as his wife Katherine verch Richard ab Ievan (whose mother was heir to lands in Buckinghamshire). By 1396 they had a son, John.

Thomas Oldcastle died in either 1398 or 1399. In his will he left his armour to his son, Richard, 80 marks to the man who would marry his eldest daughter, Wintelan (later wife of Sir Robert II Whitney), and £40 to the man who would marry his younger daughter Isabel if she should reach the age of 12 (which she did). There was also money left to support Isabel and a third daughter, Joan. Ten marks was to be distributed as alms at his funeral for which there was also provision for 'two candles of wax weighing at least 10lbs', presumably to be lit during the burial service. His will also set out that a sum of 'up to 42 marks' should be used to employ priests to sing masses for his soul, together with the souls of John his father, Isabel his mother, Maud Oldcastle (probably his stepmother, for his mother might have died shortly after giving birth),[63] John Clanvowe, and 'all Christian souls'.[64]

He left his white horse to Thomas Bromwich, one of his executors, who seems to have been the son of Walter Bromwich, the brother of the John Bromwich who briefly became Justiciar of Ireland and who had had dealings with the advowson of Almeley Church and the passing of the manor to John Oldcastle. Various records note that a Thomas Bromwich was married to a Catherine/Katherine Oldcastle. Revd Charles Robinson's *A History of the Castles of Herefordshire and their Lords* gives Catherine as Sir John's sister in Appendix I, a pedigree that is taken from that given by Robert Cooke in a herald's visitation of the county in 1589 (though he must mean 1569). This pedigree also gives Sir Thomas Oldcastle as Sir John's brother, which we subsequently know to be mistaken. Indeed, the 1619 herald's visitation amends the pedigree to state that Catherine was Sir John's aunt, and therefore the sister of Sir Thomas. This makes much more sense of Sir Thomas's will. It was usual for people to leave bequests to their direct family, but not to more distant relatives. Any bequest that Sir Thomas would have left to his sister Catherine would however, under the law prevailing at the time, automatically have become her husband's property, meaning he might just as well leave something of use directly to his son-in-law. It would therefore seem that Thomas Bromwich was that son-in-law, making the bequest understandable in the mores of the times. It is this relationship that is shown in the family tree on page 16.[65]

Towards the end of the 1300s, therefore, John Oldcastle would have been part of a wide group of influential lawyers, gentry and knights centred on, but not restricted to, north-west Herefordshire. The group was bound together by ties of family and intermarriage, friendship and business interests, acting as each other's attorneys and guarantors, and connected through service to the royal household or that of the earls of March. He would have learnt much about the art of warfare, and would have been trained in arms. He could read and write (he was to acquire some books), though we don't know whether he was equally literate in Latin, French and English. As the events concerning the lands of Dore Abbey show, he may not always have been law-abiding. Perhaps behind those episodes lie clues to his views on the Church and Christianity, views that may also have linked him with some of these men.

This brings us close to the issue that is key to understanding John Oldcastle and what was to follow – his views on religion. Those who held views at odds with the thrust of the Church's teachings at this time often hinted at their real views in their wills when referring to their mortal remains and describing how they wished their bodies to be commemorated at their funeral. The fact that Thomas Oldcastle arranged for candles to be burnt and left money for prayers to be said for his soul and the souls of others suggests religious orthodoxy. However, the only non-family member for whose soul a mass was to be sung was John Clanvowe, presumably his colleague, who lived nearby and was the author of the Lollard treatise *The Two Ways* (see pages 151-52). And it is to Lollardy that we turn in the next chapter.

2

Oldcastle and Lollardy

On Monday 1 August 1390, William Swynderby, one of the more charismatic of Lollard preachers, is known to have given a sermon at Whitney-on-Wye, presumably with the blessing of Sir Robert I Whitney, who held the patronage of the church. The sermon gave offence to William Lebyot, the rector of Kinnersley – some six miles to the east, and just to the south of Almeley – who happened to hear it. On 8 September, Swynderby celebrated a mass in what Bishop Trefnant of Hereford subsequently described as a 'profane' (unconsecrated) chapel in the park at Newton near Leintwardine (presumably the Newton that lies some six miles south-west of Leintwardine) and again in a 'profane' cottage in 'Dervaldwood' (Deerfold Forest), also in north Herefordshire. Sometime that year Swynderby is recorded to have been in Monmouth, and his area of preaching seems to have been concentrated in the part of the Marches that runs from Monmouth in the south through Clifford to Wigmore, Leintwardine and Deerfold Forest in the north, and includes Eardisley, Almeley and Kington.[1]

Although what people said in this period is rarely recorded and surviving letters are few, part of what Swynderby said on that occasion is broadly known. He apparently gave a copy of the sermon to Robert I Whitney and although this is long since lost, at his subsequent examination on charges of heresy Swynderby is reported to have said during the sermon that if any prelate 'of the world, of what estate, pre-eminence or degree soever he were, having cure and charge of souls' was full of sin himself, then he could not give absolution of sin to others. Under examination Swynderby tried to find some room for manoeuvre in what he actually said, but even so his meaning is clear – confession to a sinful priest was of no help. In Lollard teaching, this view led to an appreciation that what mattered as regards cleansing oneself of sinfulness was personal contrition. Swynderby may have gone on to say as much in his sermon, for he was subsequently charged with holding such a view.[2]

Oldcastle would have been aged about 20 if he heard this sermon or became aware of its contents, but he was more than likely already well aware of Lollard views. A few years earlier he had served with Walter Brut (as we will see in the following chapter), who was to become a Lollard preacher and who, with land at Pipe and Lyde a few miles north of Hereford, was a neighbour to some land that the Oldcastles had at Holmer.[3] Indeed, as was shown in the previous chapter, a number of those with whom the Oldcastles mingled inclined to Lollard views. But what was Lollardy, and how did its controversial teachings reach Herefordshire?

John Wycliffe

The views Swynderby and others expressed in their own words would have sprung from the thoughts and writings of John Wycliffe. Wycliffe was born in about 1330 in the neighbourhood of Richmond in Yorkshire, an area which between 1342 and 1372 was in the feudal overlordship of John of Gaunt, one of King Edward III's sons. Wycliffe's year of birth is assumed from the fact that his first appearance in the historical record is as a junior fellow at Merton College, Oxford, in 1356, when he would have been one of between 1,200 and 1,500 clerks in residence at the university.[4] Although he became a bachelor of arts that year, he did not become a Doctor of Divinity until 1372, when probably aged over 40. This timescale was not unusual, progress in study being interrupted by administrative and other duties.[5] In Wycliffe's case, having become a master at Balliol College, he left to become vicar of Fillingham in Lincolnshire, a living in the gift of the college. In 1363 and 1368 he was granted permission by the bishop of Lincoln to absent himself from Fillingham in order to continue to study at Oxford, and in 1368 he exchanged Fillingham for Ludgershall in Wiltshire, a parish nearer the university. He was described by William Thorpe, an early Lollard, as 'lean of body, spare and almost deprived of strength, most pure in his life'.[6]

Wycliffe's studies were to lead him to a belief that the Bible was the only ultimate object of faith and that it should be freed from the other teachings and elucidations with which it had been linked down the centuries. This was a not unusual view and one that had been held by many leading churchmen through the ages. Believing that the Bible was timeless and unaffected by a changing world, he held fundamentalist views about Christianity and began to appreciate how the Church's understanding of Christianity had changed down the centuries. He came to feel that the Bible needed to be translated into English so that it was more accessible to understanding by the common man,[7] believing that 'All Christians and lay lords in particular, ought to know holy writ and to defend it' and that 'no man is so rude a scholar but that he may learn the words of the Gospel according to his simplicity'.[8] The Bible had already been translated into French and it would probably have been only a matter of time for someone to make the call for an English translation. However, Wycliffe was to become instrumental, if not directly involved, in the first and very literal translation, subsequently known as the Wycliffe Bible, which made its appearance from about 1382.

Given that Wycliffe believed that the early Church mirrored the teachings of Christ more closely than the theology of later years, it is not surprising that one of the early Church leaders with whom he found himself in agreement was St Augustine of Hippo. In *De Civitate Dei* (*The City of God*), written shortly after the sacking of Rome in 410AD, Augustine distinguished between the heavenly city of the saved and the earthly city of the damned, whilst also believing that in this world all were members

Opening page of the Gospel of St Matthew from a Wycliffe Bible.
(© The British Library Board, BL Arundel MS 104, f.241)

Wycliffe by Henry Adlard, 1800s.

of the Church, only being separated at death into those who were saved and went to heaven and the rest who went to hell.[9] Wycliffe took this view further, believing that only those to be saved could be counted as members of the Church, the damned being eternally excluded. As it was impossible to know in advance who was to be saved by God and who not, it was quite possible, in Wycliffe's view, that the established Church was riddled with the damned. Indeed, if the saved and the damned were already known to God, there was little need for the established Church in its traditional form at all.[10]

Like the Franciscan friars, Wycliffe felt that the Church should follow Christ's life of poverty, humility and chastity, and that the established Church had diverged from this route to become encumbered with property and wealth, and entangled in civil government. In his view the established Church was ripe for reform, and as he looked back to the early Church with its single order of priests and deacons and its lack of property, he came to reject the current Church's hierarchy.[11] Wycliffe's developing thoughts thus gradually led to an attack on the Church as a whole. As any member of the Church could be one of the damned, so any layman could be one of the saved, and had the right of direct access to the Bible without the intercession of a priest. Furthermore, being ordained as a priest gave no assurance of being endowed with God's authority or approval.[12] Priests, Wycliffe felt, should concentrate on preaching rather than the giving of sacraments or the saying of prayers.

It was his attack on the wealth of the Church, which predated his heretical views on the pope as antichrist[13] and his thoughts on transubstantiation, that brought Wycliffe into the secular political sphere. He argued that the wealth of the Church should be redistributed:

Secular lordships, that clerks [clergy] have full falsely against God's law and spend them so wickedly, shulden be given by the King and witty [wise] lords to poor gentlemen, that wolden justly govern the people, and maintain the land against enemies. And then might our land be stronger by many thousand men of arms than it is now, without any new cost of lords, or taliage [tax] of the poor commons, and be discharged of great heavy rent, and wicked customs brought up by covetous clerks, and of many taliages and extorsions, by which they be now cruelly pilled and robbed.[14]

That Wycliffe's views on the structure and organisation of the Church predated his views of certain aspects of the Church's teachings is evidenced by Thomas Walsingham, who had himself studied at Oxford University in the 1360s and possibly into the 1370s. He wrote in his chronicle: 'About the same time [February 1377] there came to prominence in the university of Oxford a man of the north [he was born in West Yorkshire], called Master John Wyclif, a doctor of theology. … he publicly asserted mistaken, heretical doctrines, which were quite absurd and an attack on the position of the universal church. They also contained a particularly poisonous tirade against monks and other property-owning people in religious orders. …'. Walsingham goes on to say that Wycliffe assembled followers and 'dressed them in ankle-length garments of russet, as a sign of their greater perfection. They were to go around barefoot, spreading his heresies amongst the people and preaching them openly and publicly in their sermons.'[15] Henry Knighton in his chronicle of the times also mentions such followers of Wycliffe, who came to be called Lollards, literally meaning 'mumblers', a term derived from the Dutch *lollen*, meaning to mumble or doze, that had been applied to heretics before and covered those with a wide range of views.

As for who Wycliffe's followers were, most is known about them from records of their trials, so it is difficult to be sure of numbers or of any organisation, or indeed whether Wycliffe even encouraged any organisation. There are certainly references to wandering priests in his writings from 1377 onwards – 'with free and constant mingling among the poor' – but no specific instructions appear to have been given to such people.[16]

Wycliffe's views in the early 1370s concerning the organisation of the Church brought him and those who shared them to the attention of those in the lordly and knightly classes, who saw the wealth and power of the Church as something that needed to be curtailed. At their head, if a head they could be said to have, stood John of Gaunt (so-called after an Anglicised form of Ghent, the town in which he was born).

John Wycliffe and John of Gaunt
By the start of the 1370s King Edward III was gradually declining into dotage, with occasional bursts of activity, and it was John of Gaunt who became increasingly responsible for running the government. The heir to the throne was Edward's son, Edward the Black Prince, but his recurrent illnesses from 1369 made it ever more likely that the next

king would in fact be the Black Prince's son, the under-age Richard. If that was to be the case, then it was likely that Gaunt, a younger brother of the Black Prince and Richard's uncle, would continue to run the government during Richard's minority. Contemporary sources paint two contrasting pictures of John of Gaunt, English accounts being less flattering than foreign ones, which concentrated on his chivalrous nature as evidenced by his membership of the Order of the Garter. Enormously wealthy, somewhat proud and arrogant, a soldier and diplomat who was often generous, it is easy to see why some would admire and some mistrust him.

John of Gaunt was concerned about the ability of the pope to intervene in the taxation of the clergy and so interfere in English policy. The clergy numbered some 50–60,000 at this time, rather more than two per cent of England's population, and their combined property yielded about three times more revenue than that of the king.[17] Taxation by the pope had begun as a way to raise funds for the Fourth Crusade in 1199, but had gradually become a standard procedure. Whilst the clergy were unable to object to this taxation, the king could, and did, as it diverted a potential source of income away from his coffers. To ensure the raising of tax without royal interference, it had become accepted that the king would take a share of the papal levy, a percentage that by the end of Edward II's reign had reached 92%; the pope was in effect raising money for the king. This of course made the Crown's finances somewhat easier, but it also gave the pope a means of interfering in English politics. Thus, when the pope disapproved of Edward III's war in France, he desisted from taxing the clergy. Edward therefore had to levy more tax directly on the clergy, which gave rise to arguments in parliament as to what rate should be granted and whether parliament could levy it on its own, or whether the rate needed to be agreed by provincial clerical convocations.

An unspoken alliance was formed between Gaunt and Wycliffe. John of Gaunt found that Wycliffe's views on the organisation of the Church provided helpful arguments in countering the papal interference in the government of the country, whilst association with Gaunt offered Wycliffe and his followers a degree of protection from persecution as they started to question aspects of the Church's teaching. Henry Knighton, referring to this religious unorthodoxy, recorded in the chronicle that bears his name that 'He [Gaunt] believed them [the Lollards] to be holy, because of their appealing speech and appearance, but he was deceived, as were many others'.[18] The chronicle is often deemed to be unreliable, but Knighton was an Augustinian canon at Leicester Abbey, of which Gaunt was the patron, and gained much information from members of the duke's household when they were staying in the abbey. Knighton had once known Swynderby, but came to dislike the Lollards.

With the French gradually whittling away at Edward III's conquests in France, Gaunt was keen to arrange a peace to prevent further losses until such time as Edward's successor became king. In 1374 this would still have been the Black Prince. Thus Gaunt arranged for peace negotiations to be conducted in Bruges between England and France, while at the same time commissioners from England discussed issues of papal rights with delegates from Rome. One of the commissioners was Wycliffe, appointed under a decree dated 26 July 1374, though his role seems to have been more propagandist than negotiator, and he had left by the time the negotiations were reaching their conclusion.[19]

Wycliffe's presence had previously been felt in such matters, in both 1366 and 1371. In 1366 the pope demanded the as yet unpaid part of the tribute that King John had promised when he submitted to Pope Innocent III in 1213, together with 33 years of compound interest owing on the balance, the last payment having been made in 1333. To bolster his position in the parliament that was called to consider this and other matters, Edward III summoned six representatives from the universities of Oxford and Cambridge who, because of the offices they held, would be natural supporters of the Crown against papal authority. It is not clear whether Wycliffe was one of those representatives or simply present during the parliament, but he reported on the deliberations that followed Edward's question 'Was Edward of England the Pope's vassal

A portrait of John of Gaunt commissioned c.1593 and probably modelled on the effigy on Gaunt's tomb in old St Paul's Cathedral in London, which was destroyed in the fire of 1666. His tabard shows the royal arms of Castile and León and those of Plantagenet. (John of Gaunt married Constanza, the daughter of Pedro, the king of Castile, as his second wife in 1371. Her father's half-brother murdered Pedro and seized the crown, but under Spanish law not only was the rightful inheritor Constanza, but her husband was deemed to be the king.)

or no?' Parliament duly deliberated, with the presence of university men seemingly helping to bolster the answer 'No', which of course was what Edward wanted. A vehement attack on the king's cause elicited a treatise from Wycliffe in its defence.[20]

At the parliament of 1371 the king wished to raise £100,000 to fund an army. The Commons agreed to raise half the money if the Church raised the other half. The Church's traditional view had been that they could only agree to any tax if they met separately in convocation and agreed it there – a battle over the supremacy or otherwise of parliament that had been raging in recent years. The Commons argued that the Church's wealth was held for the common good and could be so claimed and used. This was a view supported by some clerics, but not by many in the upper echelons of the Church, whose response was that because the Church wielded its authority from a higher power than did the state, its property should be kept inviolate from all secular uses. As far as is known, Wycliffe himself remained silent in the debate, with the case for a partial confiscation of the Church's temporal wealth at a time of national need through tax agreed in parliament being put by two Austin friars. However, one of these friars, John Bankin, came from a house in Oxford where Wycliffe often lectured, and he expressed similar views.[21]

In 1374 the government, in the person of either the Black Prince or John of Gaunt, asked Wycliffe for a religious answer to the question of the lay power's ability to control the lay aspects of the Church, in terms of taxes and revenues. In the year that Wycliffe arrived at Merton College, the college library appears to have received a copy of *On the Poverty of the Saviour*. In this book by Richard FitzRalph, archbishop of Armagh, FitzRalph argued that not all churchmen automatically delivered good lordship as a result of being churchmen and that the Church needed to weed out those who abused their position. Whilst FitzRalph's book was aimed at the friars, Wycliffe now developed the argument to propound that the laity, in the shape of the king, were responsible for the good governance of the Church.[22] Wycliffe had already argued, in *De Civili Dominio* (written in 1375–76), that when the Church exercised functions which rightly belonged to the state, notably in transactions involving money and land, the state could step in and claim its rights over its affairs. (In *De Officio Regis*, written in 1379, Wycliffe was to argue that the king was set apart from the rest of men as God's vicar and had to be obeyed, even if he was a tyrant.) Wycliffe's view, that the Church was subordinate to the king, was borne out by the fact that it had become a largely secular organisation with extensive property interests and involvement in the administration of the state, meaning that its temporalities were dependent upon the king. Thus it was the king, with the support of the lay lords, who had power over the Church as an organisation and so could bring about change.

The parliament of 1376, which sat between 28 April and 10 July, thus sitting when the Black Prince died in June, was much concerned with the quality of the government of the realm. In what was to become known as the Good Parliament, William Wykeham, bishop of Winchester, was one of those who attacked the corrupt and incompetent

The effigy of the Black Prince in Canterbury Cathedral. (Author)

financial administration of ministers of the Crown, at the head of which group, of course, was John of Gaunt. New councillors were imposed on the king, but later in the year a council called by Gaunt reappointed the old councillors.

As the government needed to raise finance, Gaunt was keen to pursue at least partial disendowment of the Church, so invited Wycliffe to preach his views on the matter in the churches of London. William Courtenay, the recently appointed bishop of London and a defender of Bishop Wykeham, saw this preaching (unauthorised by the Church) as a chance to go on the offensive against Wycliffe, who was summoned to appear before Courtenay in the lady chapel of St Paul's Cathedral on 19 February 1377. John of Gaunt not only hired four doctors of divinity, one from each of the mendicant orders, to defend Wycliffe, but decided to attend in person with the intention of overawing the court. But news had reached London's citizens that Gaunt was proposing to replace the city's mayor and corporation with a royal commissioner with autocratic powers, and they used Gaunt's appearance to vent their displeasure at the rumour. To reach the lady chapel Gaunt's party had to push their way through an expectant throng inside the cathedral. There was a scuffle, and Courtenay had to appear to quieten matters. In the lady chapel insults were traded, Gaunt eventually threatening to drag the bishop out of his cathedral by his hair. The Londoners now drowned out the proceedings in their anger at this treatment of their bishop, whatever their feelings might have been about Wycliffe, and the trial had to be abandoned.

Edward III died four months later, on 21 June 1377, and subsequent mediation by the 11-year-old Richard II eventually restored peace between the parties. Courtenay made no further move against Wycliffe, for the moment. During the rest of the year Richard II's advisers were concerned at how much revenue was still flowing from England to the papal court, partly as taxes and partly as revenues paid to cardinals from their

English benefices. They therefore asked Wycliffe whether England 'might lawfully for its own defence in case of need detain the wealth of the kingdom, so that it be not carried away in foreign parts, even though the pope himself demands it under pain of censure and by virtue of the obedience owing to him'. Wycliffe advised that reason, together with Christ's law as revealed in the gospels and conscience, all favoured the government's ability to do so.

Meanwhile, further moves against Wycliffe were being made. Copies of some of his writings had been gathered at the papal court by English clerics, and in May 1377 Pope Gregory XI issued a number of bulls picking out 18 of Wycliffe's propositions for special condemnation, and sending them to Edward III, the university at Oxford, Archbishop Sudbury of Canterbury and Bishop Courtenay. None of the propositions singled out were considered heretical; all were simply concerned with Church governance. The bulls requested information from Sudbury and Courtenay as to whether Wycliffe really had taught these ideas. If he had, he was to be put in gaol and a confession obtained, and then the prelates were to await further instructions. The bulls only arrived in England at the end of the year, by which time Richard II was king. Wycliffe eventually attended a hearing at Lambeth Palace in March 1378, having been given safe conduct by the king's mother (the Black Prince's widow, Joan of Kent), who insisted that no judgement should be pronounced on his case. The actions of another London mob broke up proceedings early, the bishops being happy to request Wycliffe not to teach the disputed points for the sake of clerical solidarity. It seems he paid little attention to the request.

At this point, the death of Gregory XI in March 1378, and the resulting schism in the Church which led to there being two popes, Urban VI in Rome and Clement VII at Fondi (and later Avignon), meant that concerns about Wycliffe disappeared from the Church's agenda.[23] The schism meanwhile provided good material for Wycliffe's case against the role of the pope, for now there were two popes who were soon each encouraging crusades against the supporters of the other. It was now that Wycliffe came to deny all papal control over the Church. In 1383 Bishop Despenser of Norwich, an ardent suppressor of the Peasants' Revolt of 1381, was calling for a crusade in Flanders against the supporters of Clement VII, and became a chief target of the Lollards. Meanwhile, an attempt by parliament in 1379 to curtail the Church's right to give sanctuary had resulted in such a weak piece of legislation, due to resistance by the Church, that a larger assault on the Church's wealth now seemed improbable.

Wycliffe's heretical teachings

It was in 1379 and 1380 that Wycliffe began to develop his theory on the Eucharist, the taking of wine and bread at Mass or Holy Communion. Church doctrine on transubstantiation stated that the bread and wine became Christ's body and blood after consecration, the two substances only appearing to retain their former physical being.

Wycliffe, however, believed in the continuing reality of the bread and wine, and was therefore faced with trying to explain how Christ's presence was invoked by the consecration, coming to the conclusion that it was a spiritual presence. This in turn led to the questioning of whether officiating priests were a necessary part of taking the sacraments. This was to become the main religious teaching of Wycliffe which the Lollards later espoused, in addition to the more practical and political theories on the teaching of scripture, the organisation and wealth of the Church, and the qualities and experience needed to be a priest.

As Wycliffe wrote in Latin, his initial disciples were those who could read it, namely fellow clerks at Oxford. Whilst Wycliffe's writings are viewed by modern scholars as a hard read and often repetitive, it is believed that he was a charismatic speaker who inspired personal loyalty. At Oxford, his closest adherents were Nicholas Hereford from the city of that name; John Aston from the diocese of Worcester; Laurence Steven from Cornwall; and Philip Repyndon, an Austin canon from Leicester.

Nicholas Hereford was to work with Wycliffe on the translation of the Bible into English. When, in 1382, Hereford appeared before the archbishop of Canterbury, who sought to encourage him to revoke his heresies, he was excommunicated and somewhat bizarrely decided to appeal his innocence to the pope. He fled to Rome, where he was promptly imprisoned. Escaping in 1385, he returned to England and recommenced preaching Lollard views until about 1391, when he sought reconciliation with the Church and became poacher turned gamekeeper, persecuting Lollards. From 1397 to 1417 he was treasurer of Hereford Cathedral, so he may have been known to Oldcastle both as a Lollard and as an anti-Lollard.

We know something of Nicholas Hereford's anti-Lollard phase from a record of 1401. Clearly Lollardy was causing problems within the Hereford diocese that year, for on 22 November the Patent Rolls (Chancery records) note that it was ordered that protection should be given to Nicholas of Hereford,

> clerk, professor of theology, and his men and possessions, as, moved by conscience, in his sermons and preachings, private and open, he is manfully opposing the disciples of Anti-Christ who strive to attract not only laymen but even clergy and literates to their heresies, and many rivals of his, members of Anti-Christ, are suing and purpose to sue false quarrels against him in temporal courts and thereby to imprison and destroy him, to the end that they may continue the destruction of the Christian faith without resistance.[24]

Of Wycliffe's other early adherents, Repyndon quickly recanted his views and was to become bishop of Lincoln, but seems to have retained sympathy with the reformists' views. Aston also recanted, but only briefly, allegedly preaching heresy right up until his death some time before August 1407.

In 1381, Walsingham was once more concerned with Wycliffe's doctrines:

… the old hypocrite himself, the angel of Satan and forerunner of the Antichrist, who should not be called 'John Wyclif' but the heretic 'Weak-belief', was continuing his ravings … He also declared that Christians were wrong to venerate that sacrament, since it was, he claimed, merely bread and inanimate matter, and they rather ought to venerate a toad or any living creature you like rather than that bread, seeing that his argument was that a living thing was more important than something which lacked life. With such ravings …[25]

Walsingham goes on to tell the story of a knight known as Laurence of St Martin who lived near Salisbury. On the eve of Easter he asked for holy communion, and having been given the host, took it, hurried home, divided it into pieces, ate some with oysters, some with onions and some with wine. He defended his actions by saying that any bread in his own house was as worthy as that which he had been given in church, and both could be eaten in a similar vein. Laurence did recant of his 'sin' under pressure from his local bishop, having to build a stone cross in a public place in Salisbury on which would be carved the story of his actions, and at which he had to come bareheaded and barefoot every Friday to make a full confession of what he had done.[26]

But 1381 was going to be remembered best for the Peasants' Revolt, about which Walsingham wrote in great detail. The prime cause of the Revolt lay in the levying in 1380 of a poll tax of 1s per head, regardless of wealth. A poll tax, set at 4d per head on everyone over the age of 14 (excepting 'professional' beggars), had first been raised in 1377 at the end of Edward III's reign, to help pay for his wars in France. It was levied again, but on a graduated basis depending upon status, in 1379. The higher and universal rate set in 1380 was seen as hugely unfair and only added to feelings of discontent already simmering about the expansion of the powers given to justices of the peace at the expense of local and manorial courts, and about statutory wage restraints being imposed at a time when wages would otherwise have risen due to the scarcity of labour following the Black Death. Thus most of the concerns were secular, though in some localities there was also anger at the way that members of the clergy sought to retain or even enhance their powers at the expense of citizens at a time of growing mercantile activity. With evasion of the poll tax widespread, the collectors sent out to gather in the tax became harsher in its enforcement and so fanned the flames of insurrection. There would appear to have been little direct 'Lollard' influence on the Revolt, although the preaching of John Ball, who coined the cry 'When Adam delved and Eve span / Who was then the gentleman?', paid homage to Wycliffe's idea that all property must belong in common to all. To Wycliffe this was an aspiration to be worked for quietly, not sought by violent means. Thus, after the Revolt, Wycliffe decried the peasants' rising. As mentioned earlier, he believed that everyone should obey the orders of the king, however tyrannical, and therefore that the power to change matters was vested with the king and his lords. He confirmed the lords' rights but called for the Church's property to be taken and used to relieve the poor of some of the burdens that had caused

Death of Wat Tyler as depicted in Froissart's Chronicles. (Royal MS 18 E I f.175)

the outbreak. Walsingham, meanwhile, referred to the peasants who took part as the 'lowest of riff-raff and demonical wastrels …'.[27]

What is of particular interest in the Peasants' Revolt relating to the story of John Oldcastle is the effect it was to have on Wycliffe and his followers, and the lessons Oldcastle may have learnt from it when it came to his own uprising. During the course of the Revolt, John of Gaunt's Savoy Palace was burned, whilst the archbishop of Canterbury, Simon Sudbury, and the king's treasurer, Robert Hailes, were the most high-ranking of various officials who were murdered. The man who emerged as the leader of the Revolt, Wat Tyler, was also killed, but the young Richard II managed to charm and disperse the crowds by promising, falsely as it turned out, to deal with their demands.

The Revolt marked a change in attitude on the part of John of Gaunt. Sensing how attacks on the Church's establishment could also lead to attacks on the 'rights' of the nobility, when Wycliffe brought out his book against transubstantiation in the same year, Gaunt endorsed the University of Oxford's decision, prompted by the pope, that the work was heretical. Gaunt was becoming more inclined to support the Church as a stabilising influence in an era when the king was not yet of age.

With the murder of Archbishop Sudbury, Bishop Courtenay of London was elevated to the archbishopric of Canterbury, and now moved decisively against Lollardy and Wycliffe. The Revolt having generated a feeling that the Commons and the Lords were both threatened from below and needed to work more concertedly together, the November parliament of 1381 endorsed Richard II's suppression of the Revolt and requested action against the Lollards. Courtenay focused his attention on Oxford, leaving his bishops to deal with heretics in their dioceses, and called a council at Blackfriars in London the following year to decide on the heresy or otherwise of 24 propositions drawn from Wycliffe's writings; Bishop Trefnant of Hereford was a member of this council. After four days' of discussion, ten of the propositions were deemed heretical, including Wycliffe's teachings on the Eucharist, the papacy, the usefulness of confession and the indefensibility of a property-owning clergy, while the rest were said to be erroneous. As the council ended, an earthquake shook the building and its environs, toppling pinnacles and steeples and dislodging stones from walls. Many saw this as a sign of divine support for their side of the argument.

John of Gaunt went to Oxford to try to convince Wycliffe not to ruin his career over the issue of the Eucharist,[28] but Wycliffe said he could not keep silent about his beliefs. As Gaunt was orthodox in matters of Church doctrine, this brought the two men's relationship to an end, and from this moment on it would seem that Gaunt severed his connections with the Lollards. Wycliffe was now forced to depart for Lutterworth in Leicestershire, a rectory he had received from the Crown in 1374, and where he remained till he died in 1384. After his death, his opponents finally succeeded in having him condemned for heresy, and in 1428 his body was removed from consecrated ground, his bones burned and the ashes thrown into the nearby river.

However, Wycliffe's ideas were to live on. Philip Repyndon, for example, still a Lollard at this time, preached in Leicestershire, where he was supported by William Smith, the first layman to be mentioned as associated with the movement. Smith is described by Knighton in colourful terms, but as Knighton came to detest Lollards his description of Smith as being deformed and ugly may be distorted. Having failed to convince a young woman to marry him, Smith became a vegetarian and teetotaller and taught himself to read and write. Joined by a chaplain, Wayestathe, he established a Lollard school in a deserted chapel.[29] Here he was joined by the man who was to preach on 1 August 1390 in Whitney-on-Wye in Herefordshire, William Swynderby, who may have hailed from the village of Swinderby on the borders of Lincolnshire and Nottinghamshire.

Swynderby had already gone through several transformations. He had begun by denouncing the pride and wantonness of Leicester's women till the town's citizens had forced him to leave, whereupon he decried wealth and merchandising, and so gained further disapprobation. He then decided to become a hermit in the neighbouring woods. At this time he seems to have enjoyed the protection of John of Gaunt. But disliking the hermitic life, it seems, Swynderby returned to Leicester and embarked on a local preaching tour before joining the chapel group.[30] With this background it is perhaps unsurprising that his 'Lollard' views, as later reported, were a bit of a mishmash, lacking the intellectual rigour of Wycliffe's thinking, and much altered to fit the secular world as opposed to the issues within the Church towards which Wycliffe's writings and thoughts were directed. This was common to most of the subsequent Lollard 'preachers': being largely uneducated men, they took a very down-to-earth view of Wycliffe's thoughts, about which they almost certainly learned through intermediaries.

What has become known as the *Twenty-five Points*, a summary of Lollard views, was written down in 1388, some four years after Wycliffe's death, probably by John Purvey. From 1382 Purvey lived with Wycliffe at Lutterworth and revised the translation of the Bible inspired by Wycliffe and probably carried out by Nicholas Hereford.[31] The initial translation had been a verbatim version, following Wycliffe's belief in original scripture, and had not taken into account the differences between Latin and English, making for an end result that was unclear and uncomfortable. On Wycliffe's death, Purvey moved to Bristol and worked in conjunction with others to produce a revised version, probably finished around 1406.[32] The *Twenty-five Points* includes many of Wycliffe's beliefs, but also others. Thus the document refers to the pope as antichrist and as someone who cannot grant indulgences or pass sentences of excommunication; says that contrition alone (without confession) is all that is required to obviate sin; avers that priests have a duty to preach; and condemns the Church hierarchy for the trading of spiritual ministrations for money, the absenteeism of many clergy, the holding of secular offices by the clergy, the non-performance of duties, and clerical self-indulgence. Further, it demands that the Church should be stripped of its endowments, that any property retained should be held in common, and that tithes should not be paid to bad priests. It declares that the bread and wine remain as such after consecration, that sinful priests should not administer the sacraments, and above all proclaims that scripture should be the sole guide for Christians. The document also includes an attack on saints' days, something only touched upon by Wycliffe, and attacks church music and images.[33] Purvey was to become a travelling preacher, some of his discourses being given in Herefordshire and Worcestershire. He was imprisoned for preaching in 1390 but continued writing various sermons and treatises condemning the corruption of the Church.[34] So, in the 1390s a number of preachers were spreading such thoughts and Lollardy was taking root in some areas of the country. But with John of Gaunt no longer giving protection to Lollards, and with their theoretical champion, Wycliffe, dead, what support did they now have amongst the higher social classes?

In north Herefordshire Lollards were clearly obtaining support from John Croft of Croft Castle. A royal esquire and son of Sir John Croft, during the 1380s he was appointed as a justice of the peace and undertook other royal commissions. In 1382 he was excommunicated, however, for withholding the tithes due to Leominster Priory from Newton, the very place where Swynderby was to preach on 8 September 1390. He then appears to have fallen out of royal favour, probably because of his excommunication,

A portrait of King Richard II by an unknown artist in the 1390s.

and on 1 September he was imprisoned without charge in Windsor Castle on suspicion of heresy. He appeared before Richard II just under a year later on 29 August 1395, when he had to swear an oath to foreswear heresy. The text of the oath implies that the authorities saw Croft Castle as a centre of Lollardy, where translations of elements of scripture were either being made or copied out under John Croft's protection. It would seem that his wife, Janet, one of the daughters of Owain Glyndwr (of whom more in the following chapter), and their family may also have been involved. Croft had to repeat his oath before Bishop Trefnant, but it was several months before he complied. Whether Croft adhered to the terms of his oath is unknown, but it's probable that he helped the congregation at Newton and was one of those who gave Swynderby safe conduct on his preaching tours, perhaps providing lodging for him on occasion.[35]

'The Lollard Knights'

Nationally, a group of ten knights is mentioned in the chronicles of Walsingham and Knighton as protecting Lollards during the reign of Richard II, which gives some credence to the belief that Richard showed more favour to Lollards than did his Lancastrian successors, even though his own religious views seem to have been orthodox. Some of the knights are mentioned in only one chronicle, some in both. Those mentioned by both Walsingham and Knighton are Sir Lewis Clifford, Sir Richard Sturry, Sir Thomas Latimer, Sir William Nevill, Sir John Clanvowe, Sir John Montagu and Sir John Cheyne. Those only mentioned by Knighton are Sir John Trussell, Sir John Peachey and Sir Reynold Hilton. Walsingham mentions groups of these knights on two occasions, the first in 1387, when he reports a riot in London caused by the preaching of an Austin friar who had been influenced by Lollard teachings, and the second in 1395, when the Lollards petitioned parliament. Knighton makes just one mention of this group, in 1382.

In *Lancastrian Kings and Lollard Knights*,[36] K.B. McFarlane explores the careers and lives of these knights in some detail, notably the seven mentioned by the more reliable Walsingham. For our purposes it is only necessary to consider the views held by these knights, the effect they had on the spread of Lollardy and the influence they may have had on John Oldcastle, Sir John Clanvowe being the one member of the group to have Herefordshire connections.

It is clear from various documents in which their names appear together that the seven 'Walsingham' knights knew each other, and that there were ties of friendship similar to those existing in the group known to the Oldcastles. Four were knights of Richard's chamber (a group that numbered about 16 at any one time; we have the names of 26 who served Richard during his reign). All seven had served in the wars in France under Edward III, and were retained in times of peace as well as war. They came from different parts of the country, varied in age (their years of birth ranging from the late 1320s to 1351), and came from different levels of society. Nevill was a brother to both John, Lord Nevill of Raby and Alexander, archbishop of York, and became Admiral of the North; Montagu was the eldest son of a peer and became earl of Salisbury in 1390; and Latimer was also of lordly blood, being a grandson of the first Baron Latimer. The others were from the ranks of the lesser gentry but managed to improve their position through marriage and other connections. Three had been retained by Edward III and three had connections with the Black Prince, whilst Montagu became a knight of the royal household due to his existing rank as the son of a peer.

All save Latimer were employed on diplomatic missions which, coupled with their military service, would have made them quite worldly-wise and cultivated men. Clifford was a friend to poets and may have been godfather to Geoffrey Chaucer's son, Lewis. Sturry served on diplomatic missions alongside Geoffrey Chaucer. Chaucer was found guilty of raping Cecily Champaigne in 1380, and when she gave up her rights of action in return for a liberal sum of money, two of those witnessing the trans-action were Clanvowe and Nevill. Cheyne, recognised as a diplomat of rare ability, served on diplomatic missions under Richard II and, after a period in prison at the end of Richard's reign due to his ties with the nobility who thwarted the king, under-took diplomacy for Henry IV as well. Clanvowe (who, as we have seen, was related to Thomas Clanvowe, a colleague of Thomas Oldcastle) was a poet, most noted for *The Cuckoo and the Nightingale* (also known as *The Book of Cupid*), long attributed to Chaucer himself, and Sturry was a friend of the French writer Froissart, so they were a literary group. Latimer was summoned in 1388 to account for the alleged possession of certain books and articles that expressed what were deemed as 'erroneous' views of the Catholic faith, but he escaped any sanctions. (In 1388 parliament had pressured the king's council to ensure that any heretical works were seized.)

Nevill's Lollard sympathies are shown after the arrest of Nicholas Hereford by the civic authorities in Nottingham in 1382 on his return from Rome. The Calendar of Close Rolls for 1385–89 shows that Nevill petitioned for Hereford's transfer to his castle in Nottingham, 'because of the honesty of his person', offering to give bail for Hereford and ensure that he wouldn't allow him to preach or distribute tracts contrary to the Church's faith. His request was granted by the king.[37]

Clanvowe acknowledged the accusations of Lollardy and in a document now known as *The Two Ways* set out his views, which will be covered in a later chapter.[38] But Clanvowe is not the only member of this group of 'Lollard knights' who had connec-tions with the Oldcastles, for Sir Lewis Clifford (who, as we've seen, might have helped Oldcastle in his youth) named John Oldcastle and Richard Colefox at the head of the list of executors in his will, and they are known to have acted in this capacity on his death in 1404. Colefox, a Kentish esquire, was to figure in Oldcastle's rising.

Cheyne was a member of the parliament that met to witness the deposition of Richard II on 30 September 1399, and on 6 October he was elected Speaker of the Commons. However, he resigned this post nine days later, possibly due to pressure from Archbishop Arundel, who declared that Cheyne had long been an enemy of the

Church and held anti-clerical views, though Cheyne gave the reason for his resignation as his physical condition after his long spell of imprisonment. This contretemps didn't harm Cheyne in the eyes of Henry IV, and he was soon a member of the king's council. His will, made on 1 November 1413, is recognisably 'Lollard' in its language, laying emphasis on his unworthiness, expressing contempt for his own human body, and declaring that there should be no pomp associated with his funeral.[39]

Thus, even with the withdrawal of the tacit support of John of Gaunt, there was a group of knights close to the heart of government that was in a position to provide a degree of security to Lollards, at least until the change of regime from Richard II to Henry IV. Clifford, Clanvowe and Cheyne were known to Oldcastle. But what of Swynderby and his activities in Herefordshire?

William Swynderby and Walter Brut

In 1389 (the year before he gave his sermon at Whitney-on-Wye) Swynderby, who had been preaching in the diocese of Lincoln, was examined by the friars. He made a confession setting out the views which were deemed erroneous or heretical, and agreeing not to 'teach, preach, or affirm publicly or privily the same' or to make 'any sermon within the diocese of Lincoln' without license from the bishop. Having done so, he moved west to get away from Lincoln, and so arrived in Herefordshire. He may have chosen this area as it would be easy to move into the comparative safety of the Marches or even Wales, where the king's writ didn't fully run. This would have limited the bishops' ability to use the power of the Crown to arrest him as a heretic.

Swynderby's words may have fallen on receptive ears, for there seems to have been a pervasive feeling of anti-clericalism in the central Marches in the late fourteenth century. Apart from the goings-on at Dore Abbey mentioned previously, the behaviour exhibited by the local clergy, as evidenced in the bishop of Hereford's visitation returns for 1397, shows that it fell far below what would have been expected, even by fourteenth-century standards. Twenty-one parish priests, including the chaplain at Kinnersley, were accused of openly keeping a concubine, with seven more keeping two, three or even four. The chaplain at Kilpeck was said to have two mistresses, whilst the vicar had turned to pagan practices. At Eardisley the priest was seemingly having sexual relations with both his maidservants, failed to give the sacrament to dying parishioners, refused the Communion to his enemies and acted as a moneylender. Elsewhere priests gave confessions whilst drunk, and kept pigs in the cemetery and calves in the church tower.[40] It is not surprising that people refused to pay tithes to the Church, and even resorted to violence against priests.

Swynderby was the area's main proselytiser of Lollard and other heretical views, and he soon came to the notice of the friars and John Trefnant, bishop of Hereford, who had been a member of the archbishop's council that passed judgement on Wycliffe's writings in 1382. Much of Trefnant's register (essentially a record of the bishop's administration of his diocese) is taken up with what followed as regards Swynderby and another Lollard preacher, Walter Brut, setting out the written answers that each gave to questions about their belief. Whilst the registers are in Latin, Swynderby's and Brut's responses are given in the English in which they were delivered. On 14 June 1391 Trefnant called Swynderby to appear before him at Kington Church, to answer questions of heresy. At this meeting, Trefnant, being convinced of the heretical nature of Swynderby's views, gave him a list of the articles of the Catholic faith, to which he was required to respond in person some two weeks later, at 6 o'clock on 30 June at Bodenham Church.

Swynderby duly appeared and read out his prepared answers. 'Which thing being done, the same William (without any more with him) did depart from our presence, because we, at the instance of certain noble personages, had promised the same William free access; that is, to wit, on that day for the exhibiting of those answers, and also free departing …'. The guarantee of Swynderby's safety is evidence of knightly support. His answers fell into three sections: some refuted the specific claim made against him, some argued that he had been misquoted, and some suggested that there could be better practice within the Church. According to William Capes, in his introduction to Trefnant's register, 'They show intimate familiarity with the text of Scripture, unfailing hostility to papal claims … but they are free of the scurrilous bitterness of much of Wycliffe's language, and their tone though uncompromising is respectful.'[41]

Over the course of the proceedings, Swynderby's views were clarified and it was established that they included the usual Lollard view on transubstantiation, coupled with a mixed bag of Lollard beliefs: that tithes could be withheld from evil-living parish priests, that any priest could preach without licence from the bishop, that no priest should take money for presiding over any religious service, and that no child was truly baptised if the priest or godparents were in mortal sin.[42]

Having considered the answers, Swynderby, 'pretending to be priest', was cited by the bishop to appear before him at 'North Lodebury' (Lydbury North) on 20 July to discuss further some of the points raised which had 'been judged to be false, heretical, erroneous and schismatical'. The citation provides a clue as to where Swynderby was then most likely to be found, for people to whom the citation was to be specifically sent included 'the dean of Leamster [Leominster], the parsons of Croft, Almaly [Almeley], and Whitney, and also the vicars of Kington, Eardisley, Wiggemore [Wigmore], Monmouth, Clifford and of St John's altar in our cathedral church of Hereford [the altar for the parish in which the cathedral then sat].'

William Swynderby did not appear at Lydbury North, and nor did he keep subsequent appointments set by the bishop for 9 July at Pontesbury, 8 August at Cleobury Mortimer and 16 August, 2 September and 7 October at Whitbourne. In due course Trefnant therefore did duly 'pronounce, decree, and declare the said William to have been, and to be, a heretic, schismatic, and a false informer of the people, and such as is to be avoided of faithful Christians'. Swynderby appealed to the king and his

Parts of the original record of Swynderby's trial.
Swynderby's testimony is given in English, the part here showing his replies regarding his preaching at a chapel in Deerfold and another at Newton near Leintwardine, for which the transcription of the text of the 12th and 13th articles reads:

The xii article is this, that oure byschoppe putes to me that I mony tymes and ofte have comen, he sais, to a desert wode cleped Derwaldeswode of his diocese, and there in a chapell noght halwed but a curset schepherdeshutte be myne owne foly, he says, have presumet to syng but rather to curse in contempte off the keyes. Hereto I say that this falsely put upon me of hem that tolde yow this – for hit is a chapel where a prest synges certain dayes in the yere with great solempnitiee, and certes I song never thereynne sethen I was borne ynto this world.
The xiii article is this, that I should also presume to syng in an unhallwet chapel that stondes in the park of Newton besides the toun of Leintwardy of his same diocese. Trwely I wot not where that place stondes.

The form of citation to Swynderby issued through the Clergy where it mentions the area of his preaching. This is given in Latin, for which the transcription is:

Johannes, dilectis filiis, decano nostro de Leomestre, et rectoribus de Crofte at Almaly et Whyteney, necnon vicariis de Kyngtone, Yardesley, et Monemonth, Clyfford, ac altaris sancti Johannis in ecclesia nostra cathedrali Herefordensis, ceterisque decanis rectoribus, vicariis, etc., salutem, etc. Vobis committimus, etc., quatinus Willelmum Swynderby presbiterum se pretendentem citetis seu citari faciatis peremptorie et sub excommunicacionis pena quod compareat coram nobis etc. vicesimo die instantis mensis Julii apud Ledebury North cum continuacione dierum sequentium eciam …

(© Herefordshire Archive Service, AL19/7)

council against the sentence, as well as sending a long letter addressed to the nobles and burgesses of parliament.

In 1392 Richard II had issued a commission which legalised the church authorities' imprisonment of Lollards in their own prisons 'or any other at their own pleasure' until either they repented or the king and council decided their future. On 9 March, therefore, a royal mandate was issued, ordering the authorities in the diocese of Hereford and the 'dominion of Wales' to arrest Swynderby and another Herefordshire preacher, Stephen Bell. Included in the list of officials to whom the commission was addressed is Thomas Oldcastle, uncle of John Oldcastle. It is not known what finally happened to Swynderby, as there is no account of his arrest or of his preaching again. Perhaps he headed into Wales and continued his work out of reach of the Crown until he died.[43]

Swynderby was not alone in preaching Lollard views along the borders; presumably Stephen Bell also preached them, and so did Walter Brut (who, in January 1392 confessed that he had drunk, eaten and communicated with Swynderby, by then a convicted heretic, earlier that month).[44] Brut was a small landowner near Lyde, north of Hereford, where he had a share in three messuages, 120 acres of agricultural land and 5 acres of meadow.[45] His land lay close to some of that owned by the Oldcastles, and he had served with John Oldcastle in the naval expedition of 1387. He has tentatively been connected with a Walter Brut of this date who was educated at Oxford and was the author of *Theorica planetarum*, a book that developed the mechanics of the motions of the planets, notably Venus. It would appear that Brut had an older brother and that he therefore trained for the Church (often the role of a younger son), not coming into the lands at Lyde until his brother's death. This would explain his time at Oxford whilst also becoming a landowner.[46]

Brut was denounced to Trefnant in 1390 and tried by him over the course of 1392 and 1393, Trefnant being supported by the ex-Lollard, Nicholas Hereford. Brut was a Welsh speaker and his home was near Hereford, so his preaching was probably centred on the Marches and seems to have expressed views that were more extreme and anti-sacramental than those of Swynderby, in whose company he spent some time. The bishop followed the same procedure for Brut as for Swynderby – Brut was called to various churches at set times, at which he attended either in person or via messengers, presenting a series of long scrolls (one of them over 20,000 words long) written in his own hand with copious references to verses in the Bible, including the Apocalypse, to answer the questions levelled at him. Whether he was the author of *Theorica planetarum* or not, his answers included the proposition that the conjunction of Saturn and Jupiter would presage the Second Coming.[47] Most, but not all of his views took a fairly standard Lollard viewpoint (except for the role that the Welsh were supposed to have played in the Creation)[48] albeit with a few extra twists, such as that women had the power to preach, make the sacrament, and perform other priestly duties – reinforcing the variety of Lollard views propounded by the various preachers. (Unusually for the times in terms of how women were seen, Brut settled his estates in his lifetime on his mother and his wife, presumably to safeguard them should he come to harm, perhaps as a result of his heretical preachings.)[49] He also believed that all wars were illegal, quoting Christ's sayings that one should love one's neighbour as one's self and that one should turn the other cheek, and declaring that Christ, 'the king of peace, the Saviour of mankind, … came to save, and not to destroy …'.[50]

Towards the end of Brut's trial, which took place in Hereford, there were rumours of a violent form of protest in his support, and in September 1393 Richard II issued an order to 14 Marcher knights and esquires, along with the mayor of Hereford and the sheriff, to imprison all those who joined together in whatever form to resist Brut's judges. No information is given as to who these people were or their rank in society but clearly they were potentially a force to be reckoned with, which again suggests that tacit support was given to Lollard preachers in the Marches during these years.[51]

On 3 October 1393 Brut's trial reached its climax and he agreed to recant, reading his submission to the Church in English by the cross in the cathedral close to a large number of people on the 6th. There is no indication that he reverted to Lollardy; indeed, he appears to have given up his pacifist views in favour of his Welsh pride and joined the rising of Owain Glyndwr. He was killed sometime between September 1401 and September 1402, being put to death for treason as adjudged by a military court under the office of the constable and marshal of England.[52] The dates suggest that he was captured by the English in the months following the Battle of Pilleth, perhaps adjudged to be one of those who turned on their English compatriots during the battle (for details of which see page 71). Nevertheless, during his time as a Lollard preacher his standing as a landowner would potentially have made his views carry more weight with the men of his class than those of Swynderby and the other wandering preachers.

Oldcastle's views

What do we make of all this as far as Oldcastle is concerned? It would seem that during Richard II's reign the group now referred to as the 'Lollard Knights' was able to go about its business unmolested for any taint of heresy, and that Richard's uncle, John of Gaunt, supported John Wycliffe, at least for several years. That was probably because there was widespread discontent amongst the magnates of the realm and many of the gentry at the scale of the Church's wealth, the ability of Rome to milk some of that wealth, the overbearing nature of some clerics, and the schism in the Church, with the existence of more than one pope seeming to make a mockery of the Church's authority. In addition, many of that class may already have possessed a Bible that had been translated into French, a language they could read, and thus may have been forming their own views on reading scripture without any intercession from priests. But as soon as Wycliffe's views appeared to threaten the power and wealth of secular lords, the support of John of Gaunt, the most important magnate to have protected Lollard preachers, was withdrawn. Nevertheless, the coterie of 'Lollard Knights' close to the Crown seems to have restrained the clergy from energetically pursuing heretics, allowing their views to take hold. There was, in a sense, a national revolt by the laity at all levels of society against the visible Church, combined with individual and disparate ideas on the errors in various elements of Church teaching.

When Oldcastle was around 20 years old, he could well have heard Swynderby preach at Whitney. Swynderby was rated as one of the more charismatic of Lollard preachers, but there were others too, such as Stephen Bell and Walter Brut, and perhaps more – we only know of those who were persecuted for their beliefs. Whilst some, such as Nicholas Hereford, recanted, we do not know how many others were active but are unknown to history, having slipped below the radar of the authorities. They may or may not have been wandering preachers, as encouraged by Wycliffe; they may simply have been people who discussed their views with friends and family. It would seem that the Marches of Wales were particularly rife with Lollard views, perhaps because preachers could easily put themselves beyond the reach of English law.

From the likely training he received when young, from the correspondence in which Oldcastle was involved in later life and because it is known that he owned books, it can be presumed that Oldcastle could read. In about 1394 on the other side of Herefordshire, near the Malvern Hills, or just over the county boundary on the other side of the hills in Worcestershire, *Piers Plowman* was written by William Langland. In part because he could read the Bible in English, the ploughman of the title sees through the words of the friars, who, starting from poor beginnings, had become rich and renowned for attacking each other's Order – 'the fat friar with his double chin shaking about as big as a goose's egg, and the ploughman with his hood full of holes, his mittens made of patches, and his poor wife going barefoot on the ice so that her blood followed'.[53] The poor would have turned from the friars to these poor Lollard preachers, and perhaps Oldcastle was influenced by both text and spoken word.

A suggestion has been made that it was Oldcastle who wrote the *Twelve Conclusions of the Lollards* put to parliament in 1395. The *Conclusions*, which set out to refute the heresies with which the Lollards were charged, were presented to parliament (which took no notice of them) and also posted on the doors of St Paul's Cathedral and possibly Westminster Abbey, then a common method of publicising views and thoughts. They are preserved in their original Middle English (other summaries in Latin survive) in the Dominican friar Roger Dymock's *Determinationes contra XII haereses Lollardorum* (*Against the Twelve Heresies of the Lollards*) written for Richard II in 1396-97, from which the following brief summary of the heresies is made.[54]

1) The English Church had become too involved in issues relating to temporal, as opposed to spiritual, power, in doing so following 'her stepmother', the Church in Rome.
2) There was no biblical basis for the ceremonies that had grown up around the ordination of bishops.
3) The practice of clerical celibacy had served to encourage sodomy.

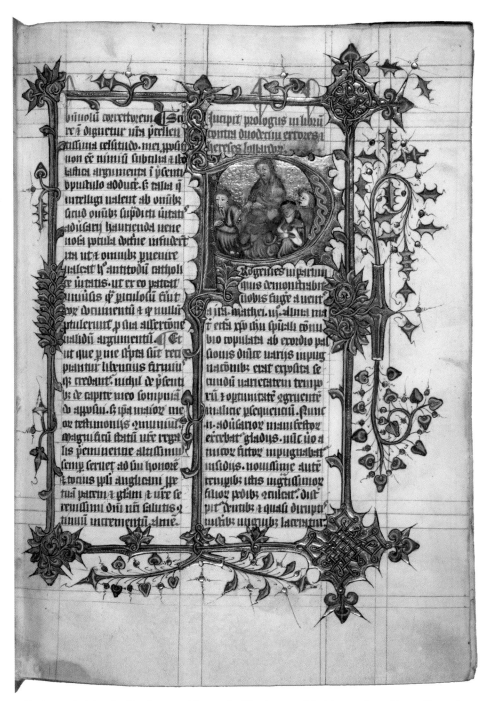

Prologue, St John the Baptist preaching to the Pharisees and Sadducees, from Roger Dymock, *Determinationes contra XII haereses Lollardorum*. This luxurious copy of the book refuting *The Twelve Conclusions* was almost certainly the one that was given to the king.
(© Image reproduced by kind permission of the Master and Fellows of Trinity Hall, Cambridge, Trinity Hall MS 17, f. 5r)

4) Belief in transubstantiation had led to the idolatrous worship of everyday objects such as the bread used for communion.

5) Exorcisms were a form of 'necromancy' and not Christian.

6) Clerics should not hold temporal offices in addition to those in the Church ('Us thinketh that hermaphrodite or ambidexter were a good name to such men of double estate').

7) Saying prayers for named individuals who had died excluded everyone else who had died, and granting sums of money for the saying of prayers for named deceased individuals was a form of simony or bribery that corrupted the Church (the creation of chantry chapels and paying for chantry priests to say masses for the souls of the named dead was an increasing phenomenon).

8) Pilgrimages were ineffectual and saying prayers in front of statues of saints was a form of idolatry.

9) Hearing confessions by priests was blasphemous as only God had the power to forgive sins, and it also led to rich people being able to purchase forgiveness from priests (a process that led to the issuing of indulgences that were sold, a system mentioned in the full form of the next Conclusion as a way of raising money to fund Crusades).

10) Man should refrain from war as the New Testament forbade manslaughter so that even going on Crusade was against God's teaching.

11) Some women who had made vows of chastity were in fact having sex and then abortions to conceal the fact that they had broken their vows, a practice to be condemned ('we would [that such women] were wedded').

12) People were devoting too much time to the manufacture of beautiful objects in churches and elsewhere and instead should simplify their lives and devote more time to godliness, mentioning the crafts of goldsmiths and armourers as examples of those that should be abolished.

Oldcastle's authorship of the *Twelve Conclusions* was first suggested by John Bale in his chronicle written in the mid-1500s. This attribution was picked up by Bishop Tanner of St Asaph, who included it in his entry for Oldcastle in *Bibliotheca Britannico-Hibernica*, published in 1748. It was repeated by Horace Walpole in his *A catalogue of the royal and noble authors of England, Scotland, and Ireland*, which was first published in 1758,[55] since when there appears to have been silence as to Oldcastle's possible authorship. This is not surprising. Oldcastle, who is likely to have been aged around 25 in 1395, was yet to make any name for himself. Nothing indicates that he was yet so steeped in Lollard thought, and he was never a pacifist, so would not have written the tenth Conclusion. Even so, he was probably well aware of a variety of Lollard views by the time he began his military career, to which we turn next.

3

The Military Life

Service at sea

It was shown in Chapter One that by the mid 1380s Oldcastle was probably in training as a squire, a watchful eye being kept on him by his uncle. That this is likely to have been the case is suggested by his appearance in both the retinue roll and muster roll as an esquire and a man-at-arms in the naval expedition mounted by Richard Fitzalan, earl of Arundel in 1387, when Oldcastle is likely to have been aged about 17. Intriguingly, two others who also appear on both rolls are Owain Glyndwr (born c.1354, so some 16 years older than Oldcastle), then a loyal adherent of the English Crown, and Walter Brut. Brut's date of birth is not known but, as set out in the previous chapter, we know he inherited his father's lands at Lyde, north of Hereford, in late 1386 or early 1387 when he was an adult.[1] Glyndwr served directly under Arundel, whilst Oldcastle served under Sir Edward Dallingridge and Brut under Sir Thomas Mortimer (part of Brut's lands at Lyde were held from the Mortimers).[2] Dallingridge was a veteran of wars with France. His base was at Bodiam in Sussex, where he was granted a licence to crenellate his manor house so as to help protect the countryside around from French raids. This led to the construction of Bodiam Castle. He had served the earls of Arundel in many capacities, including as a trustee of Arundel's lordships of Chirk and Chirksland in the Welsh Marches. On the current expedition he helped organise the fleet, and served on Arundel's flagship.[3] Sir Thomas Mortimer was an illegitimate half-brother of Edmund III Mortimer, 3rd earl of March.

In the decades at the end of fourteenth century and the first of the fifteenth, England was at constant risk of raids from France – and worse, invasion. In 1385 Philip the Bold, duke of Burgundy, was intent on strengthening his duchy as the power behind the throne of France. With kings Charles VI of France and Richard II of England both young and inexperienced, Philip thought the time was ripe to mount an invasion of

Part of the muster and retinue roll for the Earl of Arundel's expedition in 1387.
John Oldcastle's name (here written as John Oldecastell) is indicated by the arrow.
(TNA E101/40/33)

England at the head of a Burgundian-Franco alliance. The intention was to remove the English threat and cement his position as pre-eminent in an enlarged and strengthened France. Furthering his plans through alliances with Brittany and Scotland, he sent a force of some 2,400 men to Scotland to support Scottish attacks on northern England, whilst assembling a large force at Sluys in Flanders preparing to invade. However Ghent rose in rebellion and, in alliance with England, attacked and seized a town near Sluys, cutting off Philip's lines to Bruges and forcing him to divert his attention. Peace was not made between Burgundy and Ghent until December, delaying thought of invasion until the following year.

From March 1386 Philip began assembling his forces once more, but poor weather kept delaying his plans to cross the Channel, and the longer his army stayed at Sluys the more difficult it became to feed them, leading them to plunder the local countryside. When one of his allies was attacked, Philip was again forced to abandon his invasion plans and turn his attention elsewhere.[4]

In October 1386 the English parliament approved the raising of finance for an expedition to be mounted the following year in support of allies such as Ghent, to take the war to the duke of Burgundy and forestall any further thoughts of invasion by attacking the duke's assembled ships. Richard Fitzalan, earl of Arundel, was appointed admiral and given a commission to raise a force of 2,500 men who would serve for three months, beginning on 1 March 1387. According to Walsingham, rather than taking any men and paying them cheaply, Arundel 'spared no expense but chose valiant men whom he knew'. This would refer to the captains he selected, and Arundel knew Dallingridge from previous campaigns, but how Oldcastle came to serve under Dallingridge is unclear. There is no obvious campaign or event in Dallingridge's military career[5] which might suggest how the two men came to know of each other, so perhaps the connection was made via the family with which Oldcastle had commenced his military training. As mentioned, two of those serving in the force with Oldcastle were Walter Brut and Owain Glyndwr, but it is not possible to learn anything of their individual exploits or how well they might have come to know each other during the course of the expedition.

On 16 March, Arundel was at Sandwich with a fleet of 60 ships with which to oppose the duke of Burgundy's 1,200 ships. The duke, meanwhile, had fallen ill and dispersed most of his army, and many of the ships had been put to use as trading vessels.

Arundel put to sea and on 23 March sighted somewhere between 250 and 360 ships of the duke's fleet which were in the process of bringing wine from La Rochelle to Sluys. Walsingham says these ships were not well armed because 'English traitors' had informed the duke that Arundel's fleet would not be ready till May. Arundel attacked, whereupon some of the German and Flemish vessels that formed part of the French fleet changed sides. The action that followed became known as both the Battle of Margate and the Battle of Cadzand, the fighting stretching over several nautical miles as the French fleet tried to make for safety.

A fleet of Richard II, depicted in British Library Harley 1319 f. 18. (© The British Library Board)

The remains of a cog, the commonest type of vessel built in England in the late 1300s, raised from the sea bed and preserved in Bremen. (© Deutsches Schifffahrtsmuseum, Bremen)

Many English ships in those days were cogs, high-sided ships suited for weathering storms in the Channel and providing stowage for transporting both goods and men, whilst many French ships were flat-bottomed galleys equipped with both oars and sails, thus able to work in shallow water and manoeuvre in light or contrary winds. Out at sea, if the English ships could position themselves so as to use the wind to gradually close in on their enemy, the high-sided vessels would provide a platform from which to rain arrows on the crew and soldiers of the French ships. This put the English at a distinct advantage by the time it came to boarding, for naval warfare was then a series of miniature land battles, each fought on the deck of a ship; cannon were yet to make their appearance to any extent in sea warfare. Knights were not keen on naval warfare, armour being a distinct disadvantage if you fell or were pushed overboard, often causing drowning (a common occurrence in the records of naval battles of the time), and there was little prospect of retreat, making naval battles all the more brutal.[6] (Reporting on the English naval victory at the Battle of Sluys in 1340, the court jester told the French king 'Our knights are much braver than the English'. 'How so?' replied the king. 'The English do not dare to jump into the sea in full armour', replied the jester.)

It would seem, according to Walsingham, that Arundel manoeuvred his ships to windward of the French fleet, then bore down on them, leading to small scale battles as described above, in which John Oldcastle, Owain Glyndwr and Walter Brut would have been involved. Arundel pursued the fleet into Sluys, capturing ships as he went, before blockading the harbour. Over the next couple of weeks, before returning to England, he sent raiding parties ashore to plunder the nearby coast, whilst seizing more ships that tried to enter the harbour. English losses are reported to have been light, while 12 French ships were sunk or burned and some 68, possibly more, were captured, these vessels containing some 8,000 or more tuns of wine. The wine was taken to England and sold at a fraction of the normal price, earning Arundel and his men much gratitude from the populace.

Having restocked his own ships, Arundel sailed to Brest to resupply the English garrison that held the town, then under siege, capturing two castles built to prosecute the siege in the process, subsequently adding one to the defences of the town and burning the other. Dallingridge was made Captain of Brest for a while, so Oldcastle might have been based there for at least part of the winter.[7]

Service in Ireland

Oldcastle's next military exploit was to take him to Ireland. In the Calendar Rolls for 11 July 1397, along with his uncle Thomas Oldcastle and Thomas II Walwyn, he was given a letter of protection for a period of one year to serve Roger VI Mortimer, 4th earl of March, who had been appointed Richard II's lieutenant in the country.[8]

Richard had recently led an expedition to Ireland with the aim of bolstering English power on the island, landing at Waterford on 2 October 1394 at the head of a force of some 5,000 men-at-arms and up to 2,000 archers. Combined with a local force of some 2,000 men, this made for a sizeable army for a campaign in Ireland, and it soon won some skirmishing victories over the Irish, leading to the submission to the English Crown of many of the leading Irish fiefdoms (excepting some in the far west and north-west). Richard re-embarked for England on 1 May 1395, leaving Roger VI Mortimer as his lieutenant. It wasn't long before some Irish kings and clan heads reassessed their loyalties, some regarding their fealty as lying direct to the English king and not to Mortimer, who, as earl of Ulster, was in some cases an intervening lord between the Irish and the king. Mortimer soon found himself at war in north Leinster, south of his main base at Dublin, where he suffered a defeat, and south Ulster, north of Dublin, where he was successful.

At this period the Irish had adapted their style of warfare to operating with a mixture of mounted and armoured knights on horseback (whose armour was light and supple enough to allow the rider to throw spears), combined with archers (who had smaller bows than the English longbow), and lightly armoured and armed infantry. At times such a force would be bolstered by heavily armoured Gaelic mercenaries from Scotland. It was a style of army that fitted their desired way of fighting, using forests as their natural cover and launching raids against English troops and towns. Richard II countered this by landing in the autumn when the forests had lost their leaf cover, lessening the Irish capacity for surprise and giving the English archers a clearer field of fire. Roads were cut through the forests to make it easier to attack the Irish. This would have been quite a different form of warfare to that experienced by Oldcastle to date.

By the time Oldcastle arrived in Ireland, sometime in the summer of 1397, Mortimer was still at war in Leinster and Ulster. In the former the Irish had a capable leader and in the latter they were led by the energetic new king of Ulster, whose elderly father had died earlier in the year. No records survive as to which actions Oldcastle took part in, but during the year Mortimer won a victory in Leinster, and in the following year the English, who had settled in the area known as the Pale of Dublin, consolidated that success. But then, on 20 July 1398, Mortimer was killed at the Battle of Kellistown on the western side of Leinster near the town of Carlow, apparently whilst dressed in Irish attire riding out ahead of his troops, in what was a defeat for the English.[9] It was this death that caused Richard II to lead another expedition to Ireland in 1399, which in turn gave Henry Bolingbroke the chance to return to England from his banishment on the Continent, so leading to the chain of events that culminated in Bolingbroke's usurpation of the Crown.

Service in Scotland
It is not clear when Oldcastle returned to England, but as his next summons to a royal force (in 1400) was as a knight, he presumably gained his knighthood during his time in Ireland and before the death of Roger VI Mortimer. Perhaps it was during the successful campaign in Leinster in 1397.

Upon Henry Bolingbroke's accession as Henry IV in 1399 and Richard II's subsequent death while held at Pontefract Castle, the kingdom became unstable. Armed bands were breaking into properties in Devon and making off with horses; quantities of arms and arrows were stolen from St Briavels Castle in Gloucestershire; mobs assembled in Bristol, Oxford, Gloucester, York and Hereford; and highway robbery was frequent.[10]

France was also keen to cause trouble for England. Isabella, the eldest daughter of the French king, Charles VI, had been Richard II's second wife, so French sympathies lay with her and her dead husband, and they also hoped to use the unrest for their own benefit. They wooed Scotland in the hope of creating war for England on two fronts, but Scotland had its own internal divisions. George Dunbar, earl of the March of Scotland, had taken offence because the heir to the Scottish throne, the duke of Rothsay, had rejected his daughter, to whom he had been formally betrothed, and had instead married the daughter of his rival, Archibald, earl of Douglas. Dunbar's and King Henry's grandmothers had been sisters, and Dunbar now sought Henry's help.[11]

The existing truce with Scotland had expired on Michaelmas Day 1399 and negotiations were being tardily pursued for its renewal. On 24 May 1400 Henry informed the Scots that he considered that the treaty agreed in 1396 was still in force, and demanded reparation for all the infringements that the Scots had subsequently made. At the same time, he called for an army to be assembled at York on 24 June. Here, Henry received a message that the Scots considered that the relevant treaty was the one made in 1328 between Edward III and Robert the Bruce, under which Scotland was recognised as independent and Edward resigned for himself and his successors all claim to the Scottish throne. This was a treaty made when Edward was under age and, according to the Lanercost chronicler, acting 'on the pestilent advice' of his mother, Isabella of France, and her lover Roger IV Mortimer. (The two had agreed to recognise the independence of Scotland, which, after the battle of Bannockburn in 1314, was a reality at least on the ground, if not sealed by treaty, in return for the Scots not attacking England whilst Roger and Isabella effected their coup against Edward II.[12]) Henry had his army but not yet its provisions, and while the weeks passed as the necessary ships and supplies were assembled, negotiations with the Scots continued.[13] At the end of July the army was ready. And in its ranks was John Oldcastle, recorded as a knight and man-at-arms.[14]

Oldcastle, then around 30 years old, initially served in the retinue of Richard, Lord Grey of Codnor, a military leader who had gained some renown under Edward III. The Greys had previously been allies of the Mortimers, Richard's grandfather supporting Roger IV Mortimer during the reign of Edward II, for example, and it might have been this connection that secured a place for Oldcastle in Richard's retinue. Another possible connection is given by a seventeenth-century pedigree which suggests ties of kinship between Oldcastle's mother and the Greys.[15] The army advanced into Scotland, reinforcing garrisons en route, but the year's campaigning season, which was subject

Roxburgh Castle from an old print

to the vagaries of the climate, had been shortened by the delay at York. The summer was a poor one with much rain, and the Scots' use of a scorched earth policy in front of the advancing army put pressure on provisions. As a result, the advance ground to a halt at the castle of Dalhousie, some eight miles south of Edinburgh, where the army settled down for what proved to be an unsuccessful siege. At the end of August, the Scots promised to look into Henry's complaints and his renewed claim of overlordship, and the bulk of the army then retired south, but Oldcastle remained for three months in the retinue of Lord Grey, defending Roxburgh and the eastern Scottish March. It was a useful precaution, for the Scots followed up the retreating army, the garrisons harassing the Scots in return, with that stationed at Harbottle under Sir Richard Umfraville routing a large Scottish force and taking many prisoners.[16] In September and October Oldcastle appears to have been in Newcastle, seemingly now in the king's own retinue.[17] If he hadn't already met Prince Henry during the campaign, he would now surely have done so, for the prince, the future Henry V, was also serving in the king's retinue, in command of a troop of 17 men-at-arms and 99 archers. The prince would turn 14 years old that September.

Service on the Marches and in Wales
Oldcastle's next military experience came as a result of the revolt by Owain Glyndwr in Wales. The event that sparked this rising is often said to have been a dispute over territory between Glyndwr and Lord Grey of Ruthin (a distant cousin of Richard, Lord Grey of Codnor), but matters ran deeper.

Glyndwr was descended from Llewelyn ap Iorwerth, prince of Gwynedd. He was educated in London, where he studied law at the Inns of Court, and entered the service of the earl of Arundel. He may have left the earl's service before Arundel fell foul of Richard II, for the chronicler Walsingham mentions him as being an esquire in the service of Henry Bolingbroke before he became king.[18] Glyndwr's lands lay close to those of Lord Grey of Ruthin, and when the latter laid claim to a piece of land that Glyndwr believed he owned, Glyndwr petitioned parliament to seek redress. His petition was rudely dismissed – 'they answered and said they set nought by him'.[19] Anti-Welsh sentiment was flourishing at the time, with many Englishmen feeling that the Scots were their equals but that Welshmen and Irishmen were not. To compound the offence, Grey then withheld the summons sent to Glyndwr from Henry Bolingbroke, now Henry IV, to join the king's expedition against the Scots in 1400 until it was too late for him to join the muster at York. Glyndwr excused himself by the lateness of the notice, but knew that Grey was a close associate of the king who had been involved in preparing the document of abdication signed by Richard II. Glyndwr feared that Henry would naturally side with Grey and that he could never obtain justice, indeed that Grey might even suggest that Glyndwr had missed the muster on purpose.[20]

What is not clear is whether, shortly after these events, the Welsh rose against Henry and elected Glyndwr as their leader, or whether Glyndwr himself raised the

Left: A painting reputedly depicting Owain Glyndwr. The painting is held at Kentchurch Court in south-west Herefordshire, the Court being depicted in the left-hand background. Sir John Scudamore, owner of the Court, married Alice, one of the daughters of Owain Glyndwr. Claims are also made for it being a portrait of John Kent, a local priest, remembered as Jack of Kent, a local sage and sorcerer. (Courtesy of Jan Lucas Scudamore ©)

Right: King Henry IV by an unknown artist, oil on panel, 1597–1618. (NPG 4980(9) © National Portrait Gallery, London)

standard of revolt. Whichever was the case, the revolt quickly became national in character as a protest against English rule and lack of respect for the Welsh. Glyndwr was proclaimed Prince of Wales on 16 September 1400, and two days later the Welsh set fire to Ruthin, attacked Denbigh and marched towards Oswestry and Welshpool. On 24 September their advance was checked by a locally-raised force under Hugh Burnell.[21]

In January 1401 it was widely reported that Welsh students at Oxford were leaving for the principality in order to join Glyndwr. Labourers, carrying arms, were doing likewise. On 1 April the Welsh took Conwy Castle whilst most of the garrison were in church. In October 1399, Henry IV had created the son of the earl of Northumberland, Harry Hotspur – already warden of the east Marches of Scotland and governor of Berwick – chief justice of north Wales and Chester as well as constable of Chester, Flint, Conwy and Caernarvon castles. In effect this made him chief counsellor and military adviser to Henry's son, now the English prince of Wales, and the two men set about retaking Conwy Castle. Lack of pay for soldiers and supplies meant that the siege dragged on, and a negotiated surrender was only obtained in the June of 1401. Nevertheless, on 3 May Hotspur had been able to write to the king's council that: '... the commons of the said country of North Wales, ... have humbly offered their thanks to my lord the Prince for the great exertions of his kindness and goodwill in procuring their pardon at the hands of our sovereign lord the King'. The pardon itself was dated 10 March 1401, but excluded Glyndwr from its provisions. Not only that, the parliament that ended that day had, according to Adam of Usk, debated many potential anti-Welsh laws, including that they should not intermarry with the English, or even dwell in England. Whilst these laws were not actually passed, parliament did approve, with Prince Henry's support, that the English of the Marches could legally take reprisals against Welshmen who were their debtors or had injured them.

Perhaps news of these debates and actions fanned the flames, for in a letter to the king on 17 May 1401, Hotspur stressed the still perilous state of the Welsh Marches and said that he could do little more without additional finance. A lengthy siege of Conwy was then still in prospect, and the mercurial Glyndwr was reported to be actively encouraging risings in several parts of Wales. On the previous day, according to the Patent Rolls, a commission had been granted to John Chandos, Walter Devereux, Kynard de la Bere, John Pauncefoot, John Greyndour, John ap Harry, John Skydemore (Scudamore) and John Oldcastle to investigate information 'that divers evildoers have assembled in the part of South Wales in the lordship of Bergevenny and there committed divers homicides and other evils and propose to go from thence to the county of Hereford and the March of Wales to do the same or worse, to resist and take all such with the posse of the County and March if necessary, and after obtaining sufficient information to punish them'.[22]

The king responded to Hotspur's plea by announcing that he would head towards Worcester with the intention of crushing the rebellion in person, but in the intervening time the situation worsened. Abergavenny Castle was besieged, and in the town itself three men who had been condemned to hang for theft were released when townspeople slew Sir William Lucy, the knight appointed to carry out the execution.[23] Carmarthen was also under attack, Shropshire was invaded and the suburbs of Welshpool were burned. Glyndwr did suffer a defeat at the hands of John Charlton, Lord Powis, probably towards the end of May, but he won another encounter in the vicinity of Plynlimon in the summer. In the autumn of 1401 Henry IV, accompanied by Prince Henry, finally ventured into Wales in what was termed a *chevauchée* – an armed raid which kept on the move and aimed to take prisoners and booty whilst disrupting the governance of the area through which it passed by burning crops, stores, houses and mills – reaching Bangor on 8 October and thence, via Caernarvon, Strata Florida Abbey. The fighting was hard and retribution merciless. Adam of Usk records that the English used the abbey as stables, pillaging its contents, and that more than a thousand children, boys and girls, were carried off into England to be servants. English losses were also high.[24]

This *chevauchée* was over by mid-October 1401, after which Henry appointed the earl of Rutland as governor of north Wales, and the earl of Worcester as lieutenant of south Wales. Worcester was a member of the Percy family who had supported Henry's usurpation of the throne and was now placed in charge of the castles of Lampeter and Cardigan, receiving three months' wages for 50 men-at-arms and 120 archers. Corn was to be supplied from Ireland. Prince Henry was given charge of Anglesey and overall command. At this point, according to the ordinances of the privy council, 'Monsieur Johan Oldecastle' was ordered up the Wye on Prince Henry's authority and under his

An aerial view of Builth Castle looking slightly south of due west.
The photograph shows evidence of a barbican on the edge of the bailey and at the entrance to the motte, together with evidence of structures on the motte. (© Paul Davis)

command to take charge of the castle at Builth with 20 men-at-arms and 40 archers,[25] part of a ring of garrisons aiming to pin Glyndwr back into Snowdonia. At this stage in the war men for such garrisons are likely to have been raised by a commission of array for a short term of service, and paid wages by the king (the commissioners were appointed for each county by the Crown to raise men from muster rolls compiled for each township or hundred).

An informal truce seems to have lasted over the winter of 1401–02, but 1402 was to be a year that saw great success for the Welsh. At the end of January Glyndwr led a raid against Ruthin, burning the town. He returned a few days later and led Lord Grey of Ruthin, smarting from the attack, into an ambush and took him prisoner. Greater calamity was soon to befall the English. On 22 June at Pilleth, a few miles south-west of Knighton, an English army under the 26-year-old Sir Edmund Mortimer (the acting head of the Mortimer family during the minority of Edmund IV Mortimer) was heavily defeated, Sir Edmund himself being taken prisoner. The English forces would have been drawn from the Marcher lands of the Mortimers (which straddled the modern English-Welsh border as well as encompassing part of the current county of Herefordshire), and included members of families that had served the Mortimers over the years. The troops, therefore, would have been a mixture of English and Welsh. It appears that Mortimer was encouraged to attack uphill, Glyndwr's forces withdrawing out of range of the archers. Then, in an act of brutal treachery, a number of Welsh archers in the English ranks turned upon their previous comrades. Attacked unexpectedly and on all sides, some 800 English soldiers were probably killed, a casualty rate that would have approached 50 per cent. Several members of the Oldcastle circle were killed, including Sir Kynard de la Bere of Kinnersley, and Sir Robert I Whitney and his brother, whilst Sir Walter Devereux of Weobley was mortally wounded and died five days later. Sir Thomas Clanvowe was taken prisoner but released by November, presumably after paying a ransom. Walsingham reports that many of the bodies on the battlefield were afterwards obscenely mutilated by Welshwomen, almost certainly camp followers.[26]

News of this battle, without the name being given, is famously reported in Shakespeare's *Henry IV Part I*, Act I, Scene I, in which Westmoreland breaks the news to the king:

> … the noble Mortimer,
> Leading the men of Herefordshire to fight
> Against the irregular and wild Glendower,
> Was by the rude hands of that Welshman taken,
> A thousand of his people butcherèd,
> Upon whose dead corpse there was such misuse,
> Such beastly shameless transformation
> By those Welshwomen done, as may not be
> Without much shame retold or spoken of.

Overlooking the site of the Battle of Pilleth. The army led by Sir Edmund Mortimer was advancing up the valley in which the church sits. The group of Wellingtonia trees to the left of the church is believed to mark the burial pace of many of those killed. (Author)

The tomb of Sir Walter Devereux, mortally wounded at the Battle of Pilleth, in Weobley Church. (Author)

From analysis of damage caused during the Glyndwr revolt, it would seem that north-west Herefordshire suffered considerably in the period immediately following the Battle of Pilleth. In July licence was granted to the inhabitants of Leominster, some 19 miles south-east of Pilleth and 13 miles north of Hereford, to strengthen their defences with walls, pales and ditches.[27] Alarm may even have spread to Hereford, the base for supplying the garrisons of Hay, Brecon and other castles in the central Marches. Food supplies included wheat, oats, fish, ale and wine, possibly enlivened by honey and salt,[29] whilst weaponry would have included equipment for the archers, such as the 50 bows and 54 sheaves of arrows sent to the garrison at Harlech in 1403.[28]

Henry IV paid 10,000 marks for the release of Lord Grey of Ruthin, taken in the ambush by Glyndwr, but refused to pay any ransom for Mortimer, captured at Pilleth, on the excuse that his coffers were virtually empty, which indeed they were. It is just possible that Henry might have been happy to see Sir Edmund safely in a Welsh prison, for he was the acting head of a family that had a claim to the throne that Henry had usurped – Edmund's nephew, Edmund IV Mortimer, was the son of Roger VI, whom some believed had been declared heir to the throne by King Richard II. Richard II had not been so specific, however. In 1376 his grandfather, King Edward III, had made a decree limiting the succession to male heirs and their male offspring, so cutting out the line of succession through female heirs and thus any Mortimer offspring. At a parliament held in 1386, Richard II revoked this decree, restoring the previous position whereby succession could be to a female heir and thence to her female or male offspring.[30] There is a suggestion that Richard made this change in part to counter the influence of his uncle, John of Gaunt, who had aspirations that his son, Henry Bolingbroke, would inherit the Crown if Richard died childless. Whether that is true or not, the Mortimers, descended through the female offspring of Edward III's second son, still had a strong claim to the throne, Henry IV being descended from Edward's third son. (Richard II was the son of Edward the Black Prince, Edward's first son, who had died in 1376.) In the meantime, the heir to the Mortimer claim, Edmund IV Mortimer (then a boy aged 11), was being brought up in the close confines of the royal household.

The king's attitude towards ransoming Sir Edmund Mortimer brought remonstrances from his other commanders, notably Hotspur (who was married to Edmund's sister) and the rest of the Percies, the family of the earls of Northumberland. They feared the attitude that Henry might take if they too were captured in battles with the Welsh or the Scots. Could they expect to be ransomed? Henry's decision certainly contributed to the disaffection of the Percies, as reported by Holinshed and faithfully reproduced by Shakespeare. Holinshed writes:

> The king, when he had studied on the matter, made answer, that the earle of March was not taken prisoner for his cause, nor in his seruice, but willinglie suffered himselfe to be taken, bicause he would not withstand the attempts of Owen Glendouer, and his complices; & therefore he would neither ransome him, nor releeue him.

The Persies with this answer and fraudulent excuse were not a little fumed, insomuch that Henrie Hotspur said openlie: 'Behold, the heire of the relme is robbed of his right, and yet the robber with his owne will not redeeme him.'[31]

Meanwhile, in the late summer of 1402, three armies were gathered eventually to comprise an improbably large force stated to be of 100,000 men for an assault on Glyndwr. One force assembled at Hereford under the joint command of the earls of Arundel, Stafford and Warwick, a second at Shrewsbury under the king, and a third in Chester under Prince Henry. (In the earlier part of the year the prince spent at least some of the time away from his command in south Wales; he is known to have been in London on 8 May and a week later at Berkhamsted.) The advance commenced at the beginning of September, but the size of the combined force outstripped the ability to supply it – especially in view of the awful weather, for September 1402 was a month of uninterrupted rain and hail. The armies never acted in concert and many men perished from exposure. The king himself was only saved from being badly hurt when his tent collapsed on top of him in a storm because he had lain down to sleep in his armour. The armies retreated and Oldcastle's former colleague-in-arms Richard, Lord Grey of Codnor, was appointed the king's lieutenant in Brecon, Aberystwyth, Cardigan, Carmarthen, Builth and Hay from 30 September until Christmas, with a force of 150 men-at-arms and 600 archers. There was some good news for the English Crown that September, however, when the king received news of a crushing victory over the Scots by the Percies at Homildon Hill on the 14th of the month.[32]

Sir Edmund Mortimer, realising that he was not going to be released, made a compact with Glyndwr, cementing it by marrying his daughter Catherine. In the lull between campaigning seasons, on 13 December, Sir Edmund called for the people of Radnor and Presteigne to support Glyndwr in restoring the rightful king, Richard II, if he was still alive; or if not, his nephew, Edmund IV Mortimer, the earl of March.

On 7 March 1403 Prince Henry was appointed as his father's lieutenant in the Marches of Wales, with effect from 1 April, with orders to prosecute the war with vigour. The prince made his headquarters at Shrewsbury and was soon in the field, leading a *chevauchée* along the valley of the Dee and back to Shrewsbury by way of relieving Harlech and thence Montgomery.[33] En route he had sought Glyndwr at his home of Sycharth, but finding no one there, had burned it to the ground, and then continued to another of his manors, Glyndyfrdwy, with similar results.

The prince seems to have quickly realised that mounting occasional *chevauchées* was not a strategy that would defeat Glyndwr, but he lacked the resources to put a more methodical plan into action. This would have seen garrisons placed in castles not simply to resist the Welsh but to be proactive in harrying them, preferably in a coordinated manner. He was expected to fund the war, in part at least, from the income from his own lands, for suppressing internal rebellion was seen as something for which the lords of the lands concerned should shoulder responsibility in terms of finance.[34] In 1404, the prince's lands were estimated to produce an annual income of over £10,500, but that was in a peaceful year. Almost half that income came from lands in south and north Wales which were for the moment largely outside his control, whilst the revenues from Devon and Cornwall – almost a quarter of the total, mostly derived from tin mining – were also reduced in scale due to the widespread instability in the country. (Prince Henry's annual income compares to that of just under £3,000 per annum listed for the earls of Stafford and Warwick in 1401.)[35] As a stop-gap he raised funds by pawning his jewels and plate, while he wrote to his father to report the danger to both Harlech and Aberystwyth castles (then besieged by Glyndwr), and urgently requested more finance so that he could keep troops in the field to counter a general threat to the Marches. As it was, during the summer the Welsh harried central and southern Wales almost at will, plundering and destroying the neighbourhood of Builth and surrounding Brecon. They were beaten back from the latter by John Bodenham, the sheriff of Herefordshire, on 1 July, but returned once he had withdrawn. Castles in south-west Wales fell one after another until a section of Glyndwr's army was routed by Lord Carew. The knights and gentry of Herefordshire again called for the king's help and intervention, and this time it was speedily forthcoming, but not directed at south Wales, but rather towards Shrewsbury.

In July the Percies, seemingly frustrated at not having received adequate recompense from the king for their wardenship of the Scottish March and for their work in Wales, coupled with whatever resentment they had over Henry's refusal to ransom Sir Edmund Mortimer, rose in revolt. The earl of Worcester joined them with more troops and the force marched south, hoping to join with Glyndwr and adherents of the former king, Richard II, from Cheshire. Henry led his forces speedily to Shrewsbury, to put himself between Hotspur and Glyndwr, and on 21 July he defeated Hotspur, who was killed; the earl of Worcester was captured and executed. Prince Henry was wounded in the face by an arrow, a wound which kept him from playing an active role in the Welsh war for the next few months, whilst the king headed north in pursuit of the earl of Northumberland, Hotspur's father.

Meanwhile, matters in south Wales and the southern Marches continued to deteriorate, with banditry rife. King Henry, now that Northumberland had re-sworn allegiance (for the moment), once more prepared to advance into Wales. He reached Worcester on 3 September 1403, but did not leave the city till 10 September, once again tarrying to raise finance to pay for troops. However, by the 14th he was in Hereford and then advanced into Wales to regain Carmarthen.[36] Oldcastle seems to have been in the expedition, assisting the constable of Kidwelly Castle with a force comprising 40 men-at-arms and 120 archers.[37] Such a force appears to have been quite a constant command in these wars, even for the earl of Worcester at the commencement of the war, though hardly compares with Henry IV's personal command of 144 men-at-arms and 720 archers in 1405.[38]

By this stage in the war, troops were being raised to serve for longer than a brief period, with those commissioned as arrayers given a specified number of men to recruit

This watercolour of Kidwelly Castle by J.M.W. Turner well indicates the strength of this castle, which withstood the forces of Owain Glyndwr.

with the promise of immediate payment of wages by treasurers of war appointed by parliament. In November 1404 commissioners of array were appointed in five counties, each given orders to recruit 20 men-at-arms and 200 archers. Little is certain about the methods of recruitment, but after revisions made to commissions of array in 1404 most service was by indenture. Under this system, a lord or knight contracted with the king or the prince to bring a retinue raised from amongst their own tenants and followers rather than raised from amongst the inhabitants of a hundred or some other area of a county.[39] The abominable troops that Falstaff raises in *Henry IV Parts I* and *II* would have been recruited through the earlier form of commission of array, albeit that he took bribes from those who could afford it to avoid recruitment. (The scene in *Part II* where Falstaff examines his troops was painted by William Hogarth in 1730, the first Shakespearean scene to be depicted by an English artist.) The size of Oldcastle's force indicates that it was intended to go on the offensive – in October 1404 just 28 men managed to hold Caernarvon Castle against a combined force of French and Welsh,[40] and garrisons of even lesser size managed to hold the smaller castles.

But what would have been the nature and equipment of the force that Oldcastle commanded at Kidwelly? The Assize of Arms promulgated by Henry II in 1181 decreed: 'Let every holder of a knight's fee have a hauberk, a helmet, a shield and a lance.'[41] It was common at this time for knights to have a minimum of three horses, though custom and practice changed down the years with different categories of knights having different requirements. By the time of Henry III's reign (1216–72) knights banneret formed the highest class, below whom came simple 'knights' along with knights bachelor and shield-knights. Each was required to have a squire and sometimes 'boys', who might also be lightly armed with a dagger and a sword.[42] By the mid 1200s many of those who could have become knights in England, were choosing not to do so because of the cost of maintaining horses and squires, coupled with the onerous duties that a knight could be called upon to undertake on behalf of the Crown. As a result, Henry III began to issue 'distraints of knighthood' on all those who owned land valued at or above £20 per annum in order to boost the numbers of those he could summon to serve him in war, regardless of whether or not they were in possession of an old feudal knight's fee. This was one of several causes that led to the disintegration of the original feudal system.[43] Those with land valued at an annual income of £10 (sometimes £15) were recruited to serve as 'sergeants', a form of lighter cavalry, a term that gradually morphed into hobelars and men-at-arms.[44] Archers often chose to be lightly armed to retain agility, and as time wore on they were increasingly mounted when on the move. Their equipment would have included a breastplate (often of leather), an iron helmet (usually shaped like those used by the British in the First World War), mail gloves, a bow, arrows, sword and dagger.

In October 1339, Edward III mustered an army in northern France that included some 1,600 men-at-arms (cavalry), 1,500 mounted archers (who dismounted to fight) and 1,650 foot-archers and pikemen. By 1475, when Edward IV sent an expedition to France he had over 1,600 men-at-arms but over ten times that number of mounted archers[45] (albeit this army was intended to overawe the French and lead to a peace treaty). As mounted archers grew in quantity in English armies, so the number of infantry declined. In a summer campaign against the Scots in 1335, just over half Edward III's army of 15,000 men was made up of infantry. As the Hundred Years War progressed, English armies on the Continent came to include no pikemen, with nearly all the archers mounted for speed of movement around the countryside, and this seems to have been the model largely adopted by Prince Henry in his wars against Glyndwr, except when besieging castles.[46]

Thus it was that Oldcastle's force would have comprised 40 cavalry (the men-at-arms) and 120 archers, most of whom are likely to have been mounted. In a large force there might even be a medical corps: a physician is recorded in what became the Agincourt campaign, and was given three archers for protection;[47] however, such provision might only have been made in the wars in Wales for a campaign such as the prolonged siege of Aberystwyth.

When Oldcastle was in command of such a force, much of his time must have been occupied ensuring that his men and horses were fed, in keeping discipline and stopping men from deserting (the latter was certainly to be an issue at the siege of Aberystwyth Castle during 1407). As for pay, in 1300, albeit just over a hundred years earlier, the daily rate paid to a knight was around 2 shillings a day. This was enough to buy the equivalent of between 8 and 12lbs of bread, and on such as sum he had to feed himself, his squire, any boys and his horses. The daily rate for a foot soldier was about the same as that for a labourer, barely a subsistence level, equating to a third of a loaf of bread a day.[48] It's unlikely that the rate of pay in the early 1400s would have purchased much more, and the temptation to take food and other goods by force would have been high; added to that, there would have been a number of felons within the troops, for pardons were often granted to men who agreed to serve. (There are records of 850 pardons being granted to men who served in France in 1339–40.)[49]

On 21 September 1403, whilst at Defynog in the Usk valley, John Oldcastle and John ap Harry were given power 'to receive into the king's grace any Welsh rebels of Brekenok [Brecknock], Buyllt [Builth], Cantresselly [Cantref Selyf], Hay, Glynbough [Glyn Bwch] and Dynas [Dinas]so that they surrender their bows, arrows, swords and other armour offensive and defensive and take oaths of loyalty, saving to the king the forfeiture of their lands and goods.'[50]

John ap Harry seems to have been a particularly close companion of Oldcastle's, each of them acting as feoffee or trustee for the other's landholdings. Ap Harry was a staunch supporter of the house of Lancaster, having been in the service of Henry Bolingbroke before Bolingbroke became king. The ap Harry family estates lay in Herefordshire's Golden Valley, and in 1397 John ap Harry received, by royal grant, an estate in Dorstone previously owned by a felon, giving him lands even closer to those of the Oldcastles. It was during this time that Oldcastle and, in all probability, ap Harry became involved in the depredations against Dore Abbey mentioned in Chapter One. With Henry IV's accession to the throne in 1399, ap Harry's father-in-law Hugh Waterton became chamberlain of the duchy of Lancaster and steward of Lancaster's lands in south Wales. Ap Harry himself was made constable of Aberystwyth Castle, a post he held till 1402, though such a post was really a way of providing patronage, as constables rarely dwelt in their castles. He also became sheriff of Herefordshire, and during the minority of Edmund IV Mortimer he was made steward of the lordships of Builth and Dinas (Brecknock). His brothers are said to have joined Owain Glyndwr's rising, but John ap Harry remained loyal to Henry, garrisoning Clifford Castle the day after the Battle of Pilleth, and spending the remainder of the year repairing it and the nearby Mortimer castles of Glasbury, Dinas and Blaenllyfni. In September that year he was commissioned, along with John Merbury (whom we shall meet again in Chapter Eight), to muster the forces being assembled under the command of Richard, Lord Grey of Codnor, the king's lieutenant in south Wales. In 1407 ap Harry and Sir John Oldcastle, along with John Bodenham, were granted the Mortimer lordship of Dinas, to be held jointly. The two men also had many mutual property dealings. In 1405 ap Harry was a trustee for Oldcastle when he received the reversion of Sir John Chandos's manor of Wellington in central Herefordshire; Oldcastle repaid the favour a year later when ap Harry had custody of Ewyas Lacy in western Herefordshire. Ap Harry was also a feoffee (trustee) of Oldcastle's principal manor at Almeley, from which, in 1408, he granted an annuity to one of the tenants, Thomas Corbet, for the services he had rendered Sir John. In his turn, Sir John was a trustee of ap Harry's manors of Poston and Turnstone in the Golden Valley.[51] Despite his close alliance with the house of Lancaster and thus with Henry IV and V, ap Harry's friendship with Oldcastle was to prove the stronger in later years.

During 1403 an event of a different kind concerned the Oldcastle and ap Harry families. The Patent Rolls for 3 November that year record that John Smyth, one of Oldcastle's yeomen from Lyonshall (a neighbouring parish to Almeley), was ambushed at night and murdered by four men. They were granted a pardon at the intercession of Lady Waterton, John ap Harry's mother-in-law, but no other details survive.[52]

From 14 January 1404 Oldcastle sat as a knight of the shire for Herefordshire in a parliament that met in January, the meeting of which is covered in Chapter Five. Shortly after parliament finished Oldcastle was named as one of the eight justices of the peace for Herefordshire (and was so-named again the following February).[53]

In the meantime Glyndwr's forces continued to ravage the Marches. Now styling himself Prince of Wales, he sent envoys to the French court with the aim of concluding an alliance, and in the summer he launched his own *chevauchée* through south Wales and Herefordshire. Prince Henry initially moved his headquarters to Worcester to meet the threat – and then, from 29 June, to Hereford, only 15 miles from Oldcastle's home at Almeley, whilst also maintaining a household at Leominster between 20 July and 21 November.[54] The king's council, which met towards the end of August, affirmed that Hay was to be guarded strongly until the end of September, and Oldcastle and John ap Harry were put in charge of the castle, along with that at Brecon.[55] Government expenses show payment for 20 archers at Brecon between July and September. (As an

The Norman keep and adjacent gateway of Hay Castle. The castle is currently being restored. (Author)

idea of costs, John Greyndour calculated the wages for the garrison at Radnor Castle between 1402 and 1405 at £877 4s 6d.[56])

As seen in Chapter One, at times of tension with France, what were known as alien priories and monasteries (those with a mother-house in France to which they remitted receipts) were often placed in the care of a royal custodian. He gathered in the monies due to the monks, ensured that they had enough to live on and paid the rest over to the Crown. It appears that Oldcastle was appointed at around this time as custodian of Craswall Priory, for which Hay Castle would have been a good base, Craswall being in the hills above the town.[57]

A lack of funds still restricted Prince Henry's operations. In June he had a force of only 129 men-at-arms and 256 archers, though by 1 October this is believed to have grown to 500 men-at-arms and 2,000 archers. On 13 November he set out to relieve Coity Castle near Bridgend, but failed to do so.[58] It would appear that Oldcastle remained at Hay during this expedition, for, in November, a John Treloscan was appointed to serve Oldcastle and ap Harry in its defence.[59]

During this period Oldcastle's personal estates seem to have been growing, for he received a life beneficiary in a manor owned by Sir John Chandos at Wellington in Herefordshire, with John ap Harry acting as a trustee.

It was in October that Oldcastle was placed on a commission (which also included his colleague Thomas II Walwyn) entrusted with the impossible task of stopping the

The ruins of Craswall Priory in the Herefordshire hills to the east of the Black Mountains. This photograph is taken looking down the nave of the priory church to the altar. (Author)

conveyance of provisions and arms into the rebel districts of Wales.[60] Proclamations had been issued in 1402 making it illegal for Englishmen to trade with the Welsh on pain of confiscation of their goods, but people all along the border were less concerned about loyalty to the king than their own survival, and certainly preferred to sell their goods to whomsoever would buy them rather than have them stolen. This originally low-level trade had extended to smuggling oats, beer, malt, grain and fish into Wales, whilst goods stolen by the Welsh from English farms were bought back. On 15 October Oldcastle reported to parliament that cattle were still being bought from the Welsh, whereupon an order was issued that all such cattle should be confiscated.

Over the winter of 1404–05 pressure on the English in Wales remained high. Harlech Castle was garrisoned for a while by just five Englishmen and 16 loyal Welshmen, whilst Caernarvon had only 28 fighting men, 11 of the garrison from an earlier siege having died from wounds or disease. Over these months Cardiff, Harlech and Aberystwyth were all to fall to Glyndwr.

At the end of January 1405, Prince Henry was still based in Hereford when he learnt that the Welsh were gathering at Builth in preparation for an attack on the city. They believed that with most of the court in London, and the county already weakened by previous raids, they stood a good chance of success. What they did not yet appreciate was that the prince's plans for the conduct of the war were at last bearing fruit. He now had the assistance of two treasurers of war, appointed during the parliament held in early 1404, at which Oldcastle had been an MP, providing for more regular payment of soldiers and thereby increasing morale. Also, the policy of providing detachments of troops based in castles scattered about the principality, such as those under the command of John Oldcastle, was bringing more information about the movements of Welsh soldiery and an ability to concentrate forces quickly where and when required. (In 1405 the treasurers of war record a payment of £252 for 80 men-at-arms and 200 archers stationed at Monmouth, Hay and Radnor, in addition to a further 120 men-at-arms and 500 archers.)[61] The majority of the archers in the garrison at Carmarthen in 1404, for example, were mounted, allowing for rapid sorties.[62]

That spring saw concrete results from the new strategy, for on 11 March Prince Henry was able to write to his father, '... on Wednesday, the eleventh day of this present month of March, your rebels of the parts of Glamorgan, Morgannoc, Usk, Netherwent, and Overwent, were assembled to the number of eight thousand men according to their own account; and they went on the said Wednesday in the morning, and burnt part of your town of Grosmont.' The letter went on to explain how the prince decided to bolster the local contingent under William Neuport and John Greyndour with forces from his own household under Lord Talbot which, when combined, attacked the Welsh, killing some 800 to 1,000.[63]

A further victory was scored at Pwll Melyn in May, when 1,500 Welshmen were killed, including Glyndwr's younger brother Tudor, whilst one of his sons, Gruffydd, was taken prisoner.[64] With south Wales once more coming under English control,

Prince Henry moved to north Wales, but he was not there for long. Both he and his father moved to quell another northern rebellion, led by Hotspur's father, the earl of Northumberland, who had once again risen in revolt, this time in conjunction with Lord Bardolph of Wormegay and Richard Scrope, archbishop of York. The revolt was put down easily, largely because the rebel 'army' consisted of untrained levies who melted away. Scrope was executed, an action which appears to have haunted Henry IV for the rest of his life. Northumberland and Bardolph sought refuge in Scotland.

Early in August 1405 the French landed a force in support of Glyndwr at Milford Haven. Consisting of some 800 heavy cavalry, 600 crossbowmen and 1,200 men-at-arms, the force was not as formidable as it sounds, for most of the cavalry's horses died of thirst during the crossing. Joining with the Welsh, the army captured Carmarthen and possibly Cardigan castles, but was driven back from Haverfordwest and Tenby. Continuing to advance eastwards, they reached the outskirts of Worcester, where they were confronted by a force mustered by Henry IV, who, having put down the northern rebellion, had hurried south on hearing the news. For eight days the two armies faced each other before the Franco-Welsh force retreated westwards, followed by Henry's army.[65]

During August and September, the prince was back in south Wales and seems to have completed the task of bringing most of south-east Wales once more under full English control. He also finally relieved Coity Castle, though much of the countryside of south-west Wales remained in Franco-Welsh hands over the winter, during which time some of the French departed for home, the rest leaving the following Lent.

In August, Oldcastle, together with 'Thomas Barre knight of Herefordshire, John Somenour of Worcestershire and Thomas Chirbury of Herefordshire', stood surety under a potential penalty of £100 for Thomas II Walwyn, who seems to have got into a dispute with the wealthy widow Elizabeth le Despenser and had injured one of her servants.[66]

On 30 November 1405 a commission of oyer and terminer (a commission authorising those named to hear and determine cases of treason, felony, or misdemeanor) was granted to 'Richard, lord of Grey [of Codnor], John Oldcastell, John Greyndore [the victor at Grosmont], Stephen White and Thomas Holcote in the counties of Gloucester and Hereford on information that divers persons of the realm have for no small time brought victuals, armour and other harness to Wales for the relief and recreation of the rebels there'.[67] Once more Oldcastle was charged with hunting down and bringing to trial those trading with Welsh rebels. Over the winter the prince seems to have been in London once more.

The year 1406 was to see a series of setbacks for Owain Glyndwr. All of south-west Wales came back under English control, and Walsingham records that on St George's Day, 23 April, a Welsh force was defeated and one of Owain's sons slain, though where this happened and who was the commander of the victorious force is not stated. In June, the earl of Northumberland and Bardolph, who had managed to reach Wales from Scotland, were defeated by Edward Charlton and fled to France. With Glyndwr's support collapsing, Prince Henry, whilst still in overall charge, spent more time in London dealing with the work of the king's council, as Henry IV was ill. In November, Anglesey, the breadbasket of north Wales, returned to English rule.[68]

By 1407 only parts of north and west Wales still remained in Glyndwr's hands. On 20 January Oldcastle was at Carmarthen, presumably on business connected with the Glyndwr revolt,[69] and in May he accompanied Prince Henry on an expedition to retake Aberystwyth Castle. The force was rich with commanders and included the duke of York, the earl of Warwick, Lord Carew, Sir Roger Leche and John Talbot, with Sir John Greyndor and Sir John Oldcastle as sheriffs of Gloucestershire and Herefordshire respectively. Oldcastle had been appointed sheriff of Herefordshire for the year 1406–07. One of his duties, on receipt of the relevant royal writ, was to muster the required knights, squires, archers and others at an appointed time and place, ready to depart on the king's service. Overall command of the operations against Aberystwyth Castle was given to the Admiral, Thomas, Lord Berkeley. Cannons were assembled, including the king's own 4.5-ton gun, which arrived from Nottingham via Hereford, together with 538lbs of powder, 971lbs of saltpetre and 303lbs of sulphur. These were the early days of artillery, and cannon were usually only used during sieges, being hugely unreliable. Indeed, one known as the Messenger burst when fired during the siege of Aberystwyth, despite the English gaining a reputation for their skilful manufacture. Used against decaying castle walls they could be quite effective, but they

A reconstruction of Aberystwyth Castle as it would have been in the late 1300s, based on information supplied by Tim Strickland, Archaeological Director and consultant at Gifford and Partners, Chester. (Drawn by Graham Sumner, who has copyright)

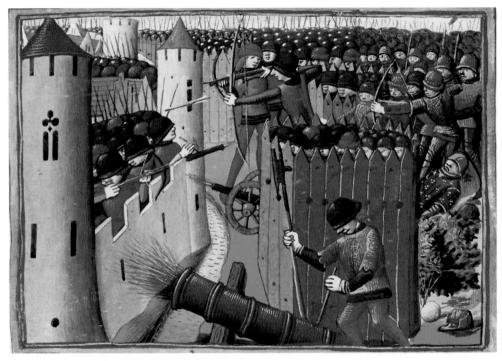

A medieval siege, that of Orléans in 1429, as depicted in the Martial d'Auvergne (1493)

don't appear to have been of much help on this occasion, and the English settled in for a long blockade.[70] Around the end of May and the beginning of June Oldcastle must have spent some time back in Herefordshire, for there is a charter dated 1 June regarding Lyonshall and Dorstone castles for which he is one of the witnesses, along with Thomas II Walwyn, John ap Harry and three others.[71]

The Welsh, commanded by Rhys ap Griffith ap Llewelyn ap Jenkin, were soon reduced to near starvation, and on 12 September they invited 17 of the English commanders into the castle to negotiate terms. An indenture was signed that the castle would be surrendered if Glyndwr had not driven off the besiegers by the week ending 1 November, until which time an armistice was agreed, Oldcastle signing as one of the witnesses.[72] Those in the garrison who refused to abide by the terms of the agreement were to be turned out to fare as they could, whilst the rest would be pardoned on the castle's surrender. The abbot of Strata Florida and three squires were handed over as hostages. Agreement having been reached, Prince Henry returned to Hereford, leaving 120 men-at-arms and 360 archers to maintain the siege. This was so that he could participate in the parliament being held at Gloucester that autumn, his father being unwell. On 16 September Prince Henry turned 21 and came of age. His father proposed being present at the surrender of Abersytwyth, perhaps to celebrate both the final defeat of Glyndwr and his son's coming of age, but there was to be no surrender. Before 1 November, Glyndwr managed to enter the castle, rescind the terms of the agreement and brand those who had agreed the terms as traitors. It is not clear how he gained access. Certainly many of the English troops appear to have deserted once the agreement had been reached, but it is possible that the duke of York, a known schemer, allowed him to enter the castle. Despite his reputation, the duke was always well spoken of by Prince Henry, and indeed was to die fighting at Agincourt.[73]

We know a little about Oldcastle's duties as sheriff during this year. The Patent Rolls for 28 November 1407 tell of a petition brought before parliament concerning liability for the escape of a prisoner in the sheriff's custody:

> Whereas one David Hardeman of Kyngeslane [Kingsland], groom, indicted before justices of the peace in the county of Hereford on sunday after Circumcision last [the celebration of the circumcision of Christ, then celebrated on 1 January, so referring to the Sunday after 1 January 1407], gone to Shorlieheath [Shirlheath] by Kyngeslane county Hereford and there lain with one Margaret ap Llewelyn and violated her against her will and struck her on the head with a stick and killed her. When charged with felony remained dumb, adjudged and committed to the law and committed to Geoffrey Porter, deputy of John Oldcastell, then Sheriff of Hereford, in the office of gaoler – but escaped and fled to the cathedral. The king at supplication of the commons of the realm and in parliament and in consideration of John Oldcastell at the time of the judgement having been on the king's service in the safe-keeping of Kaermerdyn [Carmarthen], pardons to him the escape.[74]

This also shows Oldcastle to have been in command of Carmarthen Castle in November after the lifting of the siege at Aberystwyth.

During the winter of 1407–08 Prince Henry's household seems to have maintained a presence at Hereford and at Llanthony Priory near Gloucester where parliament was sitting,[75] and the following summer Henry attempted the capture of Aberystwyth for the second time. Stores of arrows, sulphur and saltpetre were assembled at Hereford, from where Henry set off on 29 June, this time with fewer commanders at his side. The castle was captured during the winter, whilst Harlech fell to Gilbert Talbot and his brother, Lord Furnival in February 1409. Sir Edmund Mortimer, who had joined with Glyndwr having not been ransomed by Henry IV after his capture at Pilleth, died during the siege of Harlech, and his wife, their children and Glyndwr's wife were all captured.

With the later capture of two of Glyndwr's most trusted leaders, Rhys Dhu and Philip Skidmere (Scudamore), the Welsh war was essentially over. The occasional raid still took place and Owain was never captured, but people were weary of some eight years of hardship and looked forward to peace to restore their fortunes. There are records of negotiations for the release of Owain's prisoner Dafydd Gam (of later Agincourt fame) during 1412. Thereafter, Glyndwr effectively disappeared. When Prince Henry, now king, tried to reach a final settlement with him in 1415 he could not be found. His burial place is still not known.

In 1406 Oldcastle had been awarded a pension of £40 a year, along with other honours for his service in the wars.[76] At the end of 1407 he was also granted, together with John ap Harry and John Bodenham, wardship of the lordship of Dinas in Brecknock during the continuing minority of Edmund IV Mortimer, the heir of Roger VI Mortimer earl of March, who had been killed in Ireland in 1398.[77]

With the fall of Harlech in 1409, Prince Henry's focus moved from the Marches to London and the centre of government. And Oldcastle's geographical focus was also on the move – to Cooling in Kent. The move was more than geographical, however. Oldcastle was leaving Herefordshire to enter a new world – that of the aristocracy.

A view over the remains of Castell Dinas – built on the site of an Iron Age fort – the castle at the centre of the lordship of Dinas of which Oldcastle, John ap Harry and John Bodenham were granted wardship (Mynydd Troed is in the background). They were to hold the wardship from 7 December 1407 during the minority of Edmund IV Mortimer 'and so from heir to heir until an heir child reach his majority, paying yearly to the Exchequer the extent made or to be made thereof or as much as can be agreed on between them and the treasurer by the advice of the king's council'.[78] The holding of wardships was a valuable source of income for the Crown, or a way of granting patronage. In this instance the Crown should have been better able to receive the monies due to it, but because of the disturbed circumstances prevailing it was realised that not all might be forthcoming that should have been, no doubt a situation that unscrupulous men in charge of a wardship could use to their advantage. There is no evidence to judge the three men one way or the other in this instance. (Author)

4

Wilder Days?

During 1407, when his father was ill, Prince Henry started to devote much of his time to the work of the king's council. Henry IV had already suffered a sudden illness not long after he had executed Archbishop Scrope of York in 1405 for his support of rebellion in the north. Whilst some saw his ailment as divine retribution, others said it was an outbreak of leprosy as it included a skin disease on the face. Alternatively, the problem may have been syphilis or blood clots in the brain, for he suffered a seizure, though he soon recovered. In 1406 the king's legs swelled up to the extent that he could not travel by horse.[1] In June 1408 he suffered a second seizure and was unconscious for several hours, after which his strength and faculties never fully recovered. In the winter of 1408–09 he was ill again for several weeks, and successive seizures followed, each making him weaker and less able to conduct the business of government, whilst a prolapse of the rectum again prevented him from sitting upon a horse. These changes in his physical state must have been hard to bear given his active past, complicated by the belief, prevalent at the time, that such misfortune must be punishment for one's sins.[2] With the ending of active warfare against Owain Glyndwr after the fall of Aberystwyth and Harlech castles in 1409 and his father's continuing illness, London, the centre of government, now became the prince's focus.

The king had been responsible for appointing staff to Prince Henry's household till about 1405 when the prince began to appoint them himself. The king's household often numbered around 200 men,[3] the prince's probably somewhat fewer. Over time, several of those who had been in the service of Henry IV switched to the prince's service, including John Merbury (whom we met on page 78 and will meet again in Chapter Eight) and Thomas Erpingham. His household soon included 11 men from Herefordshire – Oldcastle's home county – five of them appointed on the same day, 15 November 1408. They included Walter Devereux, son of the Walter killed at Pilleth in 1402, who had been associated with the Oldcastles; John Bodenham, who had been sheriff of Herefordshire in 1402–04 and was to hold the office again in 1415–16; Thomas de la Hay, a neighbour of John ap Harry, who had lands at Peterchurch and had served in south Wales in 1405; John Scudamore; and Sir John Greyndour.[4] Scudamore and Greyndour had been appointed to the same commission at the start of the Glyndwr revolt (see page 69), and Greyndour had been involved in the victory against the Welsh at Grosmont in March 1495 (see page 81). Many of these connections would have been made during the war against Glyndwr and many in the prince's household were presumably selected as a result of an appreciation of their character gained in that conflict. Also of the prince's party was the young earl of Arundel, nephew of the archbishop of Canterbury. With the prince now in London with his own body of young Turks, tensions were bound to arise between the son and the father whom he knew so little, and between their advisors.

It is the next few years that would have seen the riotous youth of Prince Henry, as described by Shakespeare; however, this would be following the battle of Shrewsbury, fought in 1403, and subsequent northern rebellion, and not during those times as portrayed in the plays. But is there any basis for these stories, and what role might Oldcastle have played?

The two men had had several opportunities to become well acquainted: Oldcastle's appointment by Henry to be the captain of Builth Castle in 1401; their probable co-operation in the parliament of 1404 (covered in the next chapter); their close proximity from June 1404 into the early months of 1405, with Henry based at Hereford and Leominster, and Oldcastle at Almeley, Hay and Brecon, serving under him; and then in close company during the abortive siege of Aberystwyth Castle in 1407.

It is not clear whether Oldcastle took part in the second campaign against Aberystwyth in 1408, but by then he was a widower. With his first wife, Katherine (daughter of Richard ap Ievan, whom he had married before 1394), he had three daughters, Maud or Matilda, Catherine and Joan, and two sons, John and Henry. A second marriage, to an unknown woman, is mentioned by John Philipot, who was Somerset Herald from 1624 until his death in 1645, but he has an unreliable reputation as a genealogist.[5] Some sources, notably G.E. Cockayne in *Complete Peerage*, suggest that Oldcastle's first wife, Katherine, died soon after they married and that Oldcastle had most of his children with his second wife, but there seems to be little evidence for this.[6] In any case, sometime between 15 February and 18 July 1408 Oldcastle married Joan, Lady Cobham. (We know these parameters because, on the former date, Joan is mentioned in a settlement of some property without the mention of a husband, and on the latter Oldcastle is mentioned in conjunction with Joan in another such settlement.[7]) Lady Cobham had lost her third husband, Sir Nicholas Hawberk, in October 1407.[8] Hawberk had also served in Wales, though in the north, receiving payments for services rendered in 1403.

Joan was born c.1378, so she and Oldcastle were both in their thirties when they married. She was the granddaughter of John, third Lord Cobham of Kent, a prominent figure during the reign of Richard II, who died at an extreme old age (some say in his 90s) on 10 January 1408.[9] The third Lord Cobham left no male heirs, so his granddaughter now inherited all his possessions. Through the marriage Oldcastle thus came into a life interest in Cobham Manor and Cowling, or Cooling, Castle, just north of Rochester in Kent. But it wasn't just Cooling that came into Oldcastle's possession.

The list of the Cobham estates differs in the various sources, but all seem to agree that they included six manors and the revenues of the hundred of Shamley in Kent, a manor in Norfolk and two each in Northamptonshire and Wiltshire. There may have been other estates in Shropshire and Essex, and Joan also held properties in dower from her three earlier marriages.[10] All of this would have supplied Oldcastle with a considerably increased income. It is probable that he met Joan through Richard, Lord Grey of Codnor, under whom he had served in Scotland and possibly at times in the wars in the Marches, and with whom his mother is thought to have had some shared kinship. Richard's mother was another Joan de Cobham, daughter of Reginald, the first Lord Cobham, through whom he had succeeded to half of the manor of Hoo, which bordered Cooling. Richard had subsequently bought the balance of the manor and also held that of neighbouring Halstow.[11] Richard was under-chamberlain to Henry IV between 1404 and 1413, a position which carried much influence in terms of who had access to the king and how any personal petitions or requests were dealt with. He may also have helped obtain the licence necessary for a widow to remarry, as royal approval was necessary.[12] There is also some suggestion that Prince Henry encouraged the marriage.[13]

The estates of which Oldcastle now had the benefit through his marriage included Cobham's Inn in the parish of St Dunstan-in-the-East in London. John Stow in his *Survey of London*, written in 1598, noted 'Also I read, that in the 6th of Henry V [1419] there was in the Tower ward a messuage, or great house, called Cobham's Inn',[14] which suggests that the building lay close to the Tower of London. This probably would have functioned as an inn, whilst affording the Cobhams a London residence when required.

The wording of Stow's entry indicates that Cobham's Inn near the Tower was no longer standing by 1598. It would seem that at some point a replacement Cobham's Inn was erected on a corner of what was then Coppice Row but is now an enlarged Farringdon Road, near where the Royal Mail's Mount Pleasant Sorting Office now stands. In 1300 there was a settlement at Clerkenwell, then a village to the north-west of London, which by 1593, when John Norden drew his map of London, had become part of the growing city, encompassing the area where the later Cobham's Inn was erected. Though this building is likely to post-date the times of John Oldcastle, his name is remembered in the current Sir John Oldcastle pub at 29-35 Farringdon Road.

For Shakespeare's purposes, the later Cobham's Inn lay a little to the north-west of Eastcheap, where Shakespeare sets the inn in which many of the notorious scenes featuring Prince Hal and Falstaff take place. But what is the evidence for a 'riotous' Hal during these years? In *Henry IV Part I*, Act I, Scene I, the king says of his son, when comparing him with Hotspur:

> Whilst I, by looking on the praise of him,
> See riot and dishonour stain the brow
> Of my young Harry.

The Sir John Oldcastle pub at 29–35 Farringdon Road. For a while, an inn known as the Cobham's Head stood near the replacement Cobham's Inn, on the site of what became Clerkenwell Fire Station. It had become a lodging house by the time that the Metropolitan railway line was built in the 1860s, during the construction of which it became unsafe. Nevertheless it survived a few more years till destroyed by a fire in 1866. In the meantime an inn called the Sir John Oldcastle was operating on the west side of Coppice Row, but further north, and supposedly built in the grounds of Sir John's house, though, from Stow's comments (see previous page) it is likely that the Cobham's Inn used by Sir John was an earlier building located near the Tower of London. Rather than the inn being built in the grounds of Sir John's house, as tradition holds, it seems to have been built adjacent to Sir John Oldcastle's Field, a block of pasture that was sold, together with the adjacent pasture called Gardiner's Field, in the 1690s. The pasture may have formed part of the estate of Cobham's Inn, which is perhaps how the Oldcastle connections with this part of London commenced. The Sir John Oldcastle inn began life as a small wayside hostelry, then, as London expanded, became popular for its large rear garden which was used for concerts and firework displays. By 1762 it had been pulled down. The current Sir John Oldcastle pub is further to the south along Farringdon Road, at the junction with Greville Street, but carries on the tradition of the name.[15] (Author)

Thomas Walsingham, who was recording the times in which he lived (he died about a year after Henry), wrote that '… as soon as he [Henry] was invested with the emblems of royalty, he suddenly became a different man. His care now was for self-restraint and goodness and gravity, and there was no kind of virtue which he put on one side and did not desire to practise himself.'[16] Later chroniclers gradually increased the distance in character between the new king and the earlier prince. Writing more than 25 years after the event, the chronicler who wrote what is now known as the Pseudo-Elmham – the *Vita et Gesta Henrici Quinti, Anglorum Regis* – stated that, during the banquet that celebrated his coronation, Henry neither ate nor drank. Instead he focused his mind on the responsibilities that lay ahead, and for the next three days fasted, prayed and implored God to help in the good governance of his people. This could be seen as a recognition of former dissolute days, but equally as a measure of the moral and religious outlook by which he already tried to live.[17]

One of the chronicles of English history known as the *Brut* recounts a fabled history of early England, the chronicle's name being derived from Brutus of Troy, great-great-grandson of Aeneas, the legendary founder of Britain. Over 50 copies exist in Anglo-Norman and a further 184 in English, many of these taking the history on from the date of the death of King Henry II in 1272, where the early versions ended. One of these, written anonymously in 1478-79 and known as Lambeth MS 84, takes the story as far as 1475, during the reign of Edward IV, and therefore has a Yorkist slant – Hal being a Lancastrian prince. This is the one version of the *Brut* that includes (in its account of 1403) tales of Prince Hal's riotous youth, as well as describing a change that came over him when he became king.[18] It says of Henry:

> And before he was Kyng, what tyme he regnyd Prince of Walyes, he fylle & yntendyd gretly to ryot, and drew to wylde company … [except three] men of his howsolde … [who advised] hym to doon wele, & forsake ryot. and þerfor he hatyd them iij. [three] most of al men in his house, vnto þe tyme þat his fadyr was dede. And thanne he beganne to regne for Kyng, & he remembryd þe gret charge & wourship þat he shulde take vpon hym; And anon he comaundyd al his peple þat were attendaunt to his mysgouernaunce … to come before hym. And … þe Prynce … sayde to them: 'Syrys ye are þe peple þat I haue cherysyd & mayntynyd in Ryot & wylde gouernaunce; and here I … charge yow þat from this day forward þat ye forsake al mysgouernaunce' … And thus he voydyd al his housolde, savyng tho iij. personys þat he hatyd most, … & them he lovyd aftyrward best … & made them aftyrward gret lordys …[19]

The *Brut* was first printed by William Caxton in 1480, and was mined by the historians Edward Hall and Raphael Holinshed, and so provided Shakespeare with ideas.

Equivalent tales and a change of Henry's heart on becoming king are recounted by the person known simply as the Translator of Titus Livio's life of Henry V, *Vita Henrici Quinti*, who undertook his translation between the spring of 1513 and the following autumn. Livio, an Italian who had travelled to England and gained employment in the household of Henry's youngest brother, Humphrey, duke of Gloucester, appears to have gleaned much of his information from James Butler, earl of Ormonde. Ormonde accompanied Thomas, duke of Clarence (another of Henry's brothers) on the expedition to France in 1412 (see pages 122-23), fought at Agincourt and then served in both France and Ireland, and appears to have been a man with a particular liking for history and heraldry; also, he had the opportunity to learn a lot about Henry. To his translation the Translator added information from a now lost book of reminiscences or another biography of Henry V that also owes much to information from Ormonde. The Translator recounts that the young Henry would, with a band of friends, rob his own receivers (those gathering in rents and payments due to him), later reimbursing them for any losses they had personally suffered and rewarding the man who had resisted best. The Translator then tells of Henry's conversion to a sober king and his dismissal of his youthful companions.[20]

What are the known facts? On 18 March 1410, aged 23, Prince Henry was made Captain of Calais and was also given Coldharbour, his father's house in Eastcheap, as a present for life: 'Know ye, that, of our especial grace, we have granted to our dearest son, Henry Prince of Wales, a certain hostel or place called Coldharbour, in our city of London, with its appurtenances, to hold for the terms of his life, without payment to us for the same.'[21] In the late 1350s Coldharbour was described as having a quay (on the River Thames) that lay along Haywharf Lane, Stow calling it a 'right fair and stately house'.[22] As for Eastcheap itself, it was then (and had been for a while) the centre for London's butchers and pieshops. Lydgate, writing during Henry's subsequent reign, had his *London Lyckpenny* say:

> Then I hyed me into Estchepe;
> One cryes 'rybbes of befe and many a pye';
> Pewter pots they clattered on a heap;
> There was a harp, pype and minstrelsy.

So Eastcheap was not just a district where butchers plied their trade, but a centre for musicians. It was thus ideal as the location in a play for an inn in a setting that Londoners would have recognised, as they would Hal's reference to Falstaff being like a roasted 'Manningtree ox with the pudding in his belly'.[23] (Manningtree in Essex used to have a Whitsun Fair for the sale of oxen,[24] some of which would have made their way to London butchers.) But, as Chapter Nine will show, there were no inns in Eastcheap at the time, though there was one fracas which involved Henry IV's offspring.

Most magnates owned or rented hostelries in London, which they used as their base when their presence was required in the city (as with the Cobhams' own inn), and which were also used by their retainers and entourage. It is quite likely that Prince Henry was resident at Coldharbour for a while himself, as a meeting of the king's

Inside of an inn from Cocharelli's *Cuttings from a Latin prose treatise on the Seven Vices* produced in Italy c.1330–40. (© The British Library Board, BL Add 27695, f.14)

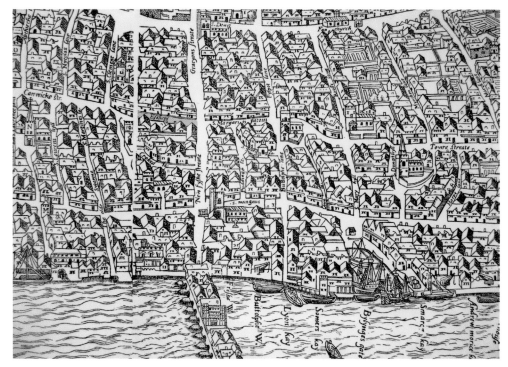

Map of London showing Eastcheap (in pink) and area. This is known as the 'Agas' map (or more properly 'map view') after Ralph Agas, who, it has since been determined, was not its originator. It was printed c.1561 using a series of woodblocks to produce an original that was roughly two metres wide. As seen in this illustration, the map does not form a precise join where the woodblocks align. Heading north from London Bridge, Eastcheap is marked as the third road off to the left; the modern Eastcheap heads east at this point, Cannon Street taking the line of Eastcheap shown on the map.

council was held there on 8 February 1410, at which he presided. He may then have gone to Calais, but by the middle of June he was back in London and involved with governmental affairs, attending two meetings of the council on the 16th, one of them held at Coldharbour. Further meetings followed on the 18th and 19th, and another, at which Hal acted as president, took place on 11 July. Between those dates an event occurred which the *Chronicle of London* recorded as 'an affray in East-Cheap between the townsmen and the Princes Thomas and John', two of Henry's younger brothers. Stow enlarged on, and embroidered, this in his later account:

> In the year 1410 … upon the eve of St John the Baptist, [23 June] the King's sons, Thomas and John, being in Eastcheape at supper (or rather at breakfast, for it was after the watch was broken up, betwixt two and three of the clock after midnight), a great debate happened between their men and other of the court, which lasted one hour, till the mayor and sheriffs with other citizens, appeased the same; for the which afterwards the said mayor, aldermen, and sheriffs were called to answer before the King, his sons, and divers lords, being highly moved against the city. At which time, William Gascoyne, chief justice, required the

mayor and aldermen, for the citizens, to put them in the king's grace; whereunto they answered, that they had not offended, but (according to the law) had done their best in stinting debate and maintaining of the peace; upon which answer the king remitted all his ire, and dismissed them.[25]

A year later the *Chronicle of London*[26] again records Thomas's men being involved in a fracas in the city. These stories have since been extrapolated to build up a portrayal of wantonness in Prince Henry, even though he is not mentioned, and many believe it is the story on which Shakespeare built his picture of the young Prince Hal. Stow also says he heard that Henry once enjoyed a supper with his brothers and numbers of London Merchants at the house of Lewes John in the Vintry. (Deriving its name from the Worshipful Company of Vintners, who, from the mid-1360s, had a monopoly of the wine trade with Gascony, the Vintry is one of the wards of the City of London, encompassing that part at the northern end of Southwark Bridge.) But Stow, far from describing them as getting up to any riotous behaviour, suggests that this is where they were sent a ballad by Henry Scogan which encouraged the princes not to waste time in 'lust and vice', but rather to spend it in 'virtue and Godliness'.[27] The episodes are referred to much more succinctly in *Gregory's Chronicle*: 'And the same tyme was the hurlynge in Estechepe by the lorde Thomas and the lorde John, the kyngys sone, &c.'[28] Again, there is no mention of Prince Henry.

Effigy of Henry's brother, Thomas, duke of Clarence in Canterbury Cathedral. Clarence was possibly Henry IV's favourite son, but blotted his copybook in Prince Henry's eyes by not attending to his duties in Ireland where he was Henry IV's lieutenant in 1410. Clarence had a more dashing attitude to warfare than Prince Henry, though Henry managed his brother's flair as part of his campaign strategy in the years in France from 1417. However, it was whilst Henry was in England in 1421 that Clarence acted rashly and without the support of most of his archers and led his troops to defeat at Baugé. (Author)

Henry's brother, John, duke of Bedford, from the 'Bedford Hours' c.1410–1430. Bedford had Henry's complete trust and was both a good administrator and an able soldier. As such, during Henry's absences in France in the years from 1415, Bedford was often made Regent in England. On Henry's death he became Regent of France. (© The British Library Board, BL Add Ms 18850, f256v)

Wherever Henry was on the occasion of the Eastcheap fracas on 23 June 1410, he was once again presiding as president of the council at meetings held on 22, 29 and 30 July. Where he spent that winter is not recorded but he was in London for a meeting of the council in March 1411, by which time he had helped set the royal finances in order, benefiting from lessons learnt during his campaigns against Owain Glyndwr.

This would all suggest that Prince Henry was a rather sober character, although there is some cause to think otherwise. The privy purse accounts of his cousin, Edmund IV Mortimer, earl of March (who spent part of the first two years of Henry's subsequent reign at Court) record losses at cards, backgammon, raffles and chess, some of them large and many of them frequent, totalling over £150 between mid-September 1413 and the end of April 1414.[29] There are also references to other entertainments, with Henry playing the harp and having a fondness for music and mummers. The prince was also a patron of poets and actors.

Drawing of the effigy of Judge Sir William Gascoigne from the effigy on his tomb at All Saints Church, Harewood, West Yorkshire.

And then there is the story concerning the prince and the judge. Several sources tell of Prince Hal being arrested by the mayor of Coventry and subsequently hitting the chief justice.[30] It was Thomas Elyot, a friend of Cardinal Wolsey, Thomas More and Thomas Cromwell, who first recorded the story in his *Boke Named The Governour* in 1531, over a century after it might have happened but presumably recording some legend circulating at Court. The book's purpose was to help educate young men who might become 'governors', and the tale relates that one of the prince's servants had committed a felony and was due to appear at the court of the King's Bench. Hearing of this, Henry arrived at the court and demanded that his servant be set free. The judge was not to be overawed and asked the prince to ensure that either the law took its course or a royal pardon be granted by his father. The prince grew angry and attempted to take his servant away, whereupon the judge ordered the prince to leave him be. Onlookers felt that the prince then came close to injuring or even killing the judge, who nevertheless continued to sit still and ordered the arrest of the prince for contempt of court. The prince calmed down, set down his weapons and took himself off to the prison of the King's Bench.[31] In a life of Henry V, probably written about 1575, Robert Redmayne embellished the story, suggesting that Henry hit the judge, and connecting the episode with his removal from the king's council. These embellishments remained in Edward Hall's and Holinshed's accounts and provided the background to the story that passed onto the stage.[32]

If the scene described above ever took place, the chief justice concerned, due to the likely date when it occurred, would have been Sir William Gascoigne. According to Wylie, two searches of the prison records for the period have not shown the prince's name, so either the imprisonment was very short-lived or it never happened, whatever the truth behind the rest of the story.[33] Certainly the incident is not impossible, given standards of behaviour in the fifteenth century. Richard II, for example, is said to have knocked down a judge and kicked him while he lay on the ground, whilst in 1411 one of the newly appointed justices of the King's Bench, Robert Tirwhit, accompanied by 500 armed men, tried to ambush Lord Ross, with whom he had a dispute about grazing rights, rather than resorting to the courts of which he was part.[34]

Gascoigne, incidentally, was a Yorkshireman, the eldest of eight children, and had studied law at Gray's Inn. He rose to prominence during the reign of Richard II and by 1391 had attained the degree of sergeant-at-law, the necessary stepping-stone to becoming a judge. He would attend the courts from 8 in the morning till 11, then head for St Paul's, where all the sergeants-at-law had an allotted pillar beside which they would meet their clients and transact business (this was a time when most if not all large churches provided space for lawyers, scribes, hawkers, beggars, and even players of palm tennis).[35]

In Shakespeare's *Henry IV Part II*, Act V, Scene II, the chief justice with whom the prince has had a brush – he is never named – is confirmed in his position as one of the first acts of Henry when he becomes king. In fact, when Henry V assumed the crown, Gascoigne's appointment as chief justice was not renewed, an action often taken to signify Henry's latent enmity for him. But Gascoigne was then close on 70 years old, a good retirement age even now, and he was well treated by Henry until his death in December 1419.

Whether the story has any element of truth or not, there is a possibility that a similar episode, but involving different people, had an impact on the name change from Oldcastle to Falstaff in Shakespeare's plays. However, that awaits telling in a later chapter.

French chroniclers, who would not be expected to write favourably of someone who caused so much bloodshed in France, recorded that Henry was a just prince 'both in relation to himself, for the sake of example, and in relation to others' and 'a great administrator of justice'. They noted that he was honest, upright in his dealings, temperate of speech and action, brave and loyal.[36]

So, the impression is that the young prince was not a riotous character, though he may well have enjoyed gambling and playing pranks on officials. If he was considered such a just and upright man in later years, these youthful indiscretions might have grown in importance in the eyes of some, allowing them to perceive a change in

King Henry V by an unknown artist, oil on panel, late sixteenth or early seventeenth century.
(NPG 545 © National Portrait Gallery, London)

attitude on his becoming king. And there was a change from the man who was at odds with his father in the last years of Henry IV's reign and possibly causing considerable tension within the state. But there seems no justification for seeing in the prince the youth portrayed by Shakespeare in the company of Falstaff. And as for Oldcastle, there is no evidence for his living a life of debauchery at this time. In his *Brefe Chronicle* of the later trial of Oldcastle for heresy, Bale has Oldcastle confessing early on in the second part of his trial that 'in my frail youth I offended thee, Lord, most grievously in pride, wrath and gluttony, in covetousness and in lechery. Many men have I hurt in mine anger, and done many other horrible sins', adding in his preface that Oldcastle's 'youth was full of wanton wildness before he knew the scriptures'. His activities against the monks of Dore noted in Chapter One could be cited as evidence for such wildness, but there is nothing of further note recorded at a time when Oldcastle would have been better known and more in the public eye – no affrays or misdemeanours of the type with which many others were charged.

Whatever precisely happened in these years, it is more than likely that the prince and Oldcastle maintained contact of some sort; Cooling was not far from London which could be reached by boat up the Thames, and Cobham's Inn was not far from Coldharbour. In 1411 the prince was to choose Oldcastle as one of the commanders of an expedition he sent to France during a period when Oldcastle appears to have been a member of Henry's household. Indeed, as the next chapter shows, Oldcastle, being a member of the Lords, was now at the heart of government.

Oldcastle Near the Centre of Government

Parliament, Politics and Jousting

Oldcastle married Joan, Lady Cobham, sometime between 15 February and 18 July 1408, after which he was based at Cooling Castle in Kent. On 26 October 1409 the chancellor, Archbishop Arundel, issued writs for a parliament to meet in Bristol on 27 January 1410. One writ was addressed to Oldcastle, who was summoned to attend the upper house of parliament as Lord Cobham, a baron of the realm. The title had technically died with the death of Joan's grandfather, as there had been no son to inherit it, and Joan's second husband was only referred to as Dominus de Cowling, whereas Oldcastle was allowed the title of Johannes Oldcastell, chevalier and Dominus de Cobham.[1] G.E. Cockayne's *Complete Peerage* notes that Oldcastle signed a declaration of his beliefs in 1413 as 'John Oldcastle, Knt, and Lord Cobham', and in the proceedings of parliament in 1417 he was referred to as 'Dominum Joh'an Oldcastell, Militem, Dominum de Cobham'.[2] It has to be presumed that he was therefore created Lord Cobham in his own right.

This would not be his first experience of parliament, for (as noted earlier) he was elected as a representative for Herefordshire in 1404, in what became the fifth parliament held during the reign of Henry IV. His companion for the shire was Thomas II Walwyn, who had previously served in the parliaments of 1397 and 1399. Expenses were paid, records showing that the two men received £15 each for 75 days attendance.[3]

As we have seen, parliament was usually called because the king required to raise more finance. The parliamentary process involved a system of bartering a finally agreed level of taxation in return for attempting to oversee the administration of the Crown's finances, coupled with consideration of statutes presented by – and petitions presented to – parliament. In addition, the king might propose some statutes of his own. During Henry IV's reign the majority of those elected as knights of the shire were supporters of the Lancastrian regime, either because they were connected with the Duchy of Lancaster in some way, or because they had gained from Henry's patronage since he became king. Henry appreciated that, as a king who had usurped the Crown, he needed to spread his patronage widely – the issuing of royal appointments and benefits of wardship, along with favourable responses to individual petitioners – in order to widen the base of his support. Edward II and Richard II, meanwhile, had showered patronage on a small group of favourites, leading to widespread resentment and calamitous ends to their reigns. Henry IV's actions meant that his parliaments were essentially loyal in flavour, although concerned about the constant demands for tax and how the money raised was spent and accounted for.[4]

At the commencement of any parliament the first act was often its adjournment, as many of its members had yet to arrive. When it was reconvened a few days later an address was given, normally by the chancellor, setting out the state of the kingdom and why the parliament had been summoned – usually with a preamble setting out the taxation that the king required together with the business that the parliament was 'charged' to consider concerning governance and finance. The receivers of private petitions were named, along with their 'triers'– all drawn from the Lords, not the Commons. Their job was to try to see that the petitioners' needs were satisfied without so clogging up parliament that it didn't have time to conduct the business for which it had been summoned. Often there would be one group of triers for those petitions from within the British Isles, and one for those from outside (those parts of France in English hands), and a few days were given for the petitions to be received. On the second day, the Lords and Commons would start their separate sessions to consider the business with which they were charged. In addition, the Commons would present public petitions setting out the general grievances of the Commons to the Lords (usually some 20 to 30 petitions each parliament), and consider private petitions referred to the Commons by the triers in the Lords. The Lords, meanwhile, would consider the business they were charged with, and would also sit as a court hearing appeals from the King's Bench and cases referred directly to parliament, notably cases of treason. This process necessitated much 'intercommuning' between Lords and Commons; small groups from the two would meet throughout the course of parliament.[5]

The clergy were represented in parliament in this period by a potential 21 bishops, 27 abbots and 60 archdeacons, together with cathedral deans or priors, one representative of each cathedral chapter and two representatives of the clergy from each diocese, making for a possible grand total of 192. However, not all always took their seats, absences being due to age, pluralism (the holding of more than one post), or to save on cost (as the clergy received no payment for attending) through one person serving as a representative for several of those due to attend. They were also able to appoint proxies to attend in their place, some of these almost becoming professional parliamentarians over a number of years, and again often acting for a number of different people or bodies. Although forming part of the parliament, the clergy also sat in convocation while parliament met, for whilst they could be asked to pay a certain level of tax, parliament could not enforce payment. The clergy met separately and agreed what they would grant, often in the knowledge of what parliament expected of them. These convocations also considered matters of Church discipline and faith.[6] Sittings began at 8am each morning and the business of parliament would gradually be done.

Oldcastle's first parliament of 1404 lasted for an unusually long time, almost three months. It was noted, among many chroniclers of the age, for much talk and little result. Unfortunately, no records of the debates were kept, parliamentary records simply recording outcomes and decisions, and only a little information about each parliament can be gleaned from other sources. No record exists, therefore, of any individual part that Oldcastle played in the parliament of January 1404 at Westminster, which is especially unfortunate as he was the junior member for Herefordshire and perhaps expected to be the more vociferous (see page 29).

The chancellor, Henry Beaufort, bishop of Lincoln,[7] opened proceedings with a résumé of why the parliament had been called: the need for money to counter the rebellion in Wales; the expected attacks on the south coast by the French; the danger to Calais and Guienne, also from the French; the wars in Scotland and Ireland, and the recent insurrection of the Percies. There were also new problems concerning Flanders, to which much English wool was exported and where the towns valued their independence from the overall authority of the duke of Burgundy. Poverty, distress and misery were reported as the norm along the Marches and in Calais. Payments to garrisons were in arrears, whilst revenue from the wool trade was declining due to brigandage on land and sea. With less revenue coming in from Wales and the north because of the disturbed state of the country, other methods of raising money had to be considered, and the king and council came up with a proposal for an early form of income tax. As this would fall most heavily on the classes represented in parliament, this led to a degree of agreement between the Lords and the Commons as to how to respond to the request, not least because parliament was becoming slightly exasperated by the king's continual requests for money.

Sir Arnold Savage, who had been elected Speaker (a post first introduced in 1376), noted that even if the Crown's revenues had fallen, the king also had all the revenues of the immense duchy of Lancaster, together with the wardships of all the lands belonging to the nobility then under age – a system devised in earlier years to cover the cost of warfare. Savage complained that castles, manors and lands held under wardship were being granted on poor terms by the king as a way of gaining support through patronage, with the effect of reducing what would otherwise have been revenue due to the king in respect of rents and other payments. Concern was also expressed about waste within the king's own household: Henry had establishments at Westminster, Windsor, the Tower (of London), Berkhamsted, Wallingford, Rockingham, Nottingham, Odiham in Hampshire and Leeds in Kent, together with manors at Kenton (near Kingston), Eltham, Claryngton, Shene, Sutton, Byfleet, Chiltern Langley, Woodstock, Easthampstead, Havering-atte-Bower, Henley on the Heath, Cosham, Bickley, Clipstone, Isleworth, and two lodges in the New Forest.

The Crown also argued for what had become a common tax of tenths and fifteenths. This was based on each person's loosely defined 'movables', and was levied at a tenth in cities and towns and a fifteenth in rural areas; it was subject to much evasion. The Crown suggested that one third of the revenue so raised should be used to cover the king's and queen's expenses, and the other two-thirds to meet the loan repayments due to merchants together with the costs of necessary measures in Calais, Scotland, Wales and Ireland.

In the end a compromise was reached. The king agreed to make some changes to his household staff to try to ensure greater financial control. Some foreigners at Court were to be dispensed with to reduce costs, and others (mainly Dutch and Germans) would be sent to serve in the border fortresses. In return, the Commons assented to two new taxes: a shilling in the pound (a 5% tax) on the annual rental of all lands and tenements, and the same percentage on the value of all movable goods. However, it was stipulated that these taxes were not be taken as a precedent, with all records to be burned once the tax had been accounted for. Four men – a clergyman from Rutland and three citizens of London – were appointed by the Commons to receive and account for the money and control its expenditure. They became known as the treasurers of war, and they would remit money to Prince Henry and so provide for the war against Glyndwr. As we have seen, this was part of the prince's strategy to enable him to have a reliable form of finance so that he could wage the war more determinedly. It seems probable that Oldcastle would have been one of those supporting the prince in advocating the appointment of treasurers of war, as he was one of those appointed to collect the tax.[8]

This measure set in train Henry's ability to fund his campaigns in France when king, so the 'much talk and little result' suggested by the chroniclers may be inaccurate when viewed with the benefit of hindsight. Indeed, one matter of constitutional importance happened at the end of the parliament: the king published the list of those appointed to act as his permanent council. The names included those of six bishops, the duke of York, the earls of Somerset and Westmorland, six lords, four knights (one of whom was Sir John Cheyne, a Lollard, and another was the Speaker, Sir Arnold Savage), and three commoners. Though the king could still choose whom he wished, the fact that he had done so in parliament gave the council a veneer of parliamentary approval. Knowing who was on the council also gave MPs and their circle of electors in the counties and boroughs a better chance to scrutinise their actions between parliaments, and decide where to focus any future grievances. Henry sought another parliament soon afterwards, apparently to reverse the seeming parliamentary veneer of approval. It was an issue which would oscillate between king and parliament during Henry IV's reign.[9]

Though the next parliament, which met at Coventry that October, did not include Oldcastle, one imagines that he would have been interested in being part of one of its key debates. The parliament was known as the 'Illiterate' or 'Unlearned' parliament because Henry IV had asked for no lawyers to be returned as MPs, feeling that their contributions wasted time and their absence would make life easier for him. (Summons to parliament had started 'at the pleasure of the king' but had gradually been taken by the Commons to mean election 'by custom and practice', so there was room for disagreement between king and Commons as to the election process.) In response to a request for yet more taxes, the Commons raised questions about the hardship that the general population was undergoing, contrasting this with how the clergy appeared to be idling in luxury. But rather than simply propose that the burden of taxation should fall on the clergy, the Commons suggested that their possessions should be seized for one year and the revenue be used by the government.

A key proponent of this move was Sir John Cheyne, one of those appointed to the king's council at the previous parliament and one of the 'Lollard knights' encountered in Chapter Two, who had briefly been Speaker of the parliament that assembled to witness the deposition of Richard II and to commence business under Henry IV. Some have seen this as proof that the Lollard 'party' had obtained a majority in the Commons, but it is probably no more than a sign of weariness at the king's continual financial demands, widespread indignation at the way the Church conducted itself, and a proposal for an alternative way of raising finance that went some way to dealing with the frustrations surrounding both issues. There is no mention of permanently stripping the Church of its endowments, a common Lollard proposal.

In reaction to the suggested seizure of Church property for one year, Archbishop Arundel rounded on the knights and the Speaker, reminding them that they had already urged the king to confiscate the wealth of foreign priories and abbeys, 'promising untold riches, yet his necessities are as great as before. Now you urge him to seize the wealth of the Church at home, that you may be the gainers. My head shall rather bow unto the sword than Holy Church should lose any part of her rights.' Arundel went on to warn the Lords that if the knights' request was granted, their own property might be next. But he need not have worried. The clergy represented an important source of loans to the king, revenue which could be obtained without the necessity for the bargaining that went on in parliament, and Henry did not want to run the risk of alienating a group who were, in effect, the majority of his private bankers. The Church held the day.[10]

It is worth considering the relationships between Henry IV, his son Prince Henry and Archbishop Arundel, especially between prince and archbishop, as it perhaps led Oldcastle to make certain assumptions about the course of action the prince would follow once he became king. A few months after the Battle of Shrewsbury in 1403, the prince had called a meeting of his council whilst he was at Worcester trying to co-ordinate support for the defence of the Marches against Glyndwr. He asked for an advance of money or loans from those present, but Arundel pleaded poverty. The lay members of the council were somewhat irked by this, considering the comparative luxury of the archbishop's retinue. 'Was it fair', they asked, 'that they should be spending their lives toiling on the battlefield, that these churchmen might lead a life of luxury?'[11] They suggested that they strip the churchmen of their ornaments and horses, and send them home on foot. Arundel replied angrily that whoever first raised his hand to spoil the Church 'he schal for his spoyling have as good knokkis [fight] as ever had Englischman'.[12] The prince managed to calm matters, but as his uncles the Beauforts

– Henry, bishop of Lincoln and then Winchester, and Thomas, earl of Dorset – disliked Arundel, he found himself in the middle of a fiery mix.

At the parliament of 1406, held at Westminster, Prince Henry presented a petition for the revision of the statute *De Haeretico Comburendo* in reaction to concern about the excessive power it was thought that the statute, passed in 1401, had given to the Church courts. This statute imposed a penalty of death by burning on heretics who relapsed or who refused to abjure their opinions, and had been supported by Henry IV as a way more of cementing his dynasty in the eyes of the Church, given the threats to his reign from various rebellions, than of supporting an attack on heresy. The revision was to seek a change so that the arrest of preachers and teachers of doctrine contrary to that of the Church should be handled by the secular arm of government, not the ecclesiastical, and that those arrested should be tried by king and lords in parliament, not by ecclesiastical courts, as they posed a threat to society. The petition was presented in parliament by the Speaker, Sir John Tiptoft, itself a novel procedure.[13]

The king accepted the petition, but no statute was enacted and nothing seems to have been done. It may be that the procedures proposed were unworkable,[14] or perhaps nothing was done because of a crisis in government. Henry IV and others involved in the execution of Archbishop Scrope of York had been excommunicated by Pope Innocent VII, and Henry had started showing signs of illness shortly after the execution. (Henry was to be formally absolved in April 1408 by Innocent's successor, Gregory XII.) Archbishop Arundel had failed to stop Henry's actions, but was now seen as the possible stabilising influence in government, yet was himself ill and most concerned with defending the Church whilst balancing his feelings about Scrope's execution and dealing with a king who was currently excommunicated.[15] That nothing was done regarding the petition to amend *De Haeretico Comburendo*, was therefore largely due to the need to resolve matters of weightier import and Arundel's desire not to see the powers of the Church diminished. However, it shows that the prince was already thinking that Lollardy, because of its attack on the structure of the Church, was as treasonable as it was heretical for the views it held on Christian beliefs. It seems an early indication as to how he would handle the Lollard rising that was to come in 1414.

The parliament of 1406, which considered this petition, lasted for much of the year. It had been summoned initially to meet at Coventry, then Gloucester, so as to be convenient for campaigning in Wales, and finally at Westminster, where it opened on 2 March, to be adjourned to 3 April, resuming again on 23 April. Adjourned once more on 19 June, it recommenced on 15 October and continued till just before Christmas. Its length was largely because parliament was increasingly frustrated by the king's constant demands for money and was becoming obdurate, whilst also seeking different ways both to raise funds and to oversee how they were spent. Somewhat ironically, Walsingham was to say that the length of this parliament meant that much of the tax it finally consented to raise went to cover its own expenses.[16]

In January 1407 Henry IV appointed Arundel as his chancellor, and to act as his deputy during periods of illness. Still excommunicated at the time, Henry appreciated that he needed Arundel to shore up his government and ensure a degree of stability. Around the prince (who was still engaged in managing the campaign against Glyndwr) gathered an opposition party which included the Beauforts, Richard Beauchamp, earl of Warwick, and Henry Lord Scrope of Masham (subsequently involved in the Southampton Plot; see pages 172-73). Thus, Henry IV's reign entered a period in which he was sometimes so ill that his ability to govern was affected. Power was wrestled between three men: a king worn down by years of conflict since taking the Crown; an energetic prince who was surrounded by old councillors offering guidance and young bloods who had tasted warfare, and who appeared orthodox in his religious views but was wary of the Church's power; and an archbishop of Canterbury who was the country's chancellor and intent on protecting the power and wealth of the Church – and rooting out heresy.

Whilst parliament was meeting at Gloucester in the autumn of 1407, Archbishop Arundel called a convocation of the province of Canterbury in Oxford, which issued a series of 13 'constitutions' that were to be binding on all clerks within the province.[17]

The gateway to Cooling Castle, Oldcastle's Kent home, in 2010. Note the enamelled sign above the arrow slit in the right-hand tower, for details of which see overleaf. (Author)

Cooling Castle, as depicted in 1784.
On the right-hand tower flanking the entrance to the outer ward is an enamelled sign
erected by Joan's grandfather that says (though now hard to read):
Knouwyth that beth [are] and shul be
That i am mad[e] in help of the cuntre [country]
In knowying of whyche thyng
Thys is chartre and wytnessyng
and a pendant seal of the arms of Cobham, *gules* on a chevron *or* three lions rampant *sable*.[18]
A photograph and drawing of the sign is shown opposite.

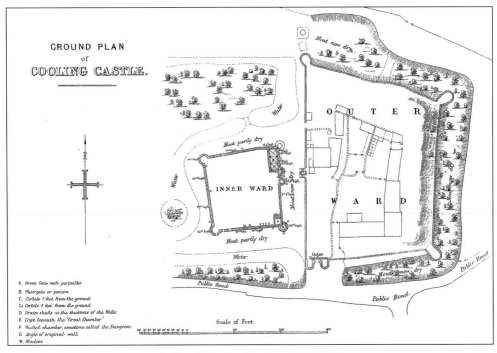

A plan of Cooling Castle made in 1877.

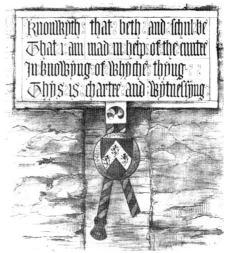

These stipulated that no-one was to preach in a church or churchyard without the special authority of the bishop of the diocese; no-one could preach against the mass, marriage, confession or any sacrament or article of faith; teachers were not to be allowed to discuss theology or scripture 'except as they had been expounded of old'; no writings of Wycliffe or his contemporaries, or produced since his time, were to circulate in schools, halls, hostels or elsewhere unless sanctioned by 12 doctors and masters to be appointed by the universities of Oxford and Cambridge; and no one should translate any part of the Bible into English, or read such translation, until an authorised version was approved. Arundel was trying to clamp down on unorthodoxy in Christian teachings and practice, especially that of the Lollards. It may have been a warning to Oldcastle, but he seems to have been unperturbed.

Oldcastle, meanwhile, was settling into life at Cooling in Kent with Lady Cobham. In February 1381 Sir John Cobham, Joan's grandfather, had received licence to crenellate his castle, the reconstruction of which had started in response to a raid up the Thames by a force of French and Spanish in 1379. The work was still in progress in 1385. The plan opposite shows the form of the castle, which had an inner and an outer ward that actually stood adjacent to each other. What was referred to as the Great Chamber stood in the north-east corner of the inner ward, and was reached by a drawbridge across what would have been a water-filled moat in the early 1400s. This Great Chamber, which would have been the principal abode in Oldcastle's time, consisted of a basement with two storeys above. An inspection of the castle carried out in the 1870s showed that the building commenced life as the Cobhams' manor house, the defensive walls around it being added when it was decided to fortify the site. It appears to have been well constructed, with fireplaces and an eye to privacy. There is even a suggestion that it had a separate room in which to take a bath, and the bedrooms had garderobes or toilets that drained into the moat. The outer ward was probably on the scale shown so as to include higher ground to the east of the inner ward, which would otherwise have over-looked the castle and been of use to those attacking it. A lease of nearby properties in 1429 included the condition that the then tenant had to strew fresh rushes on the floors of the hall and chambers whenever the lord of the castle was coming to stay; presumably, a similar clause would have existed some 20 years earlier in Oldcastle's time.

Oldcastle was soon involved in official duties reflecting his new status and place of abode. On 1 July 1409 he was granted commissions of de wallis et fossatis (walls and ditches) along the shore of the Thames between Greenhithe and Deptford, meaning he had to investigate the state of drainage of low-lying lands and any flood prevention works. (Just over two years later, on 18 September 1411, he was to be on a commission to inquire into damage to bridges and walls along the Thames between Northfleet and Greenwich.[19])

It was in December 1409 that another side of Oldcastle comes to the fore, that of the chivalric knight, for that month Oldcastle was one of three Englishmen who met three Frenchmen in a jousting tournament at Lille. Jousts were often used to serve two purposes: to foster a sense of chivalric brotherliness amongst the ruling elite of a nation, and as a forum for diplomatic, exploratory talks between the two sides involved. During much of Henry IV's reign challenges had been thrown down to the English Crown by various French nobles as more of a taunt, often referring to Henry as simply 'of Lancaster' rather than as king, and hoping to provoke a response that might lead to the outbreak of hostilities, or at least royal sanction from Charles VI of France for hostilities that were already taking place. Henry IV was keen to try to keep peace with France, at least until the latter years of his reign, as he already had war in Wales and in the north to deal with and had limited revenue, so he found ways of deflecting the challenges. The Flanders cloth towns were also keen to keep the peace, to ensure the continued flow of English wool on which much of their prosperity depended (a cause now supported by the current duke of Burgundy in contrast to his father's plans to invade England as noted in Chapter Three). In July 1408 a tournament, comprising eight combatants on each side, had taken place in Smithfield, London between Hainault (an area to the south of Flanders) and England, the hosts winning by seven to one.[20]

From around 1300, towns in north-eastern France and the Low Countries, such as Ghent, Lille, Douai and Bruges, had started to sponsor jousting tournaments in which important citizens would take part – even, at times, competing against knights and noble squires. Lille hosted an annual *fête de L'Épinette* which involved at least two days of jousting, with separate jousts for noblemen and burghers. This festival was held at the start of Lent, however, so Oldcastle's joust in December would have been part of another occasion. On Sunday 1 December Oldcastle (called Jehan d'Opchastel in the record of the event) jousted with Antoine de Craon from Anjou. How the competition went is not told, but neither of the combatants can have been severely hurt, for that evening they dined with the count of Nevers, the master of ceremonies, together

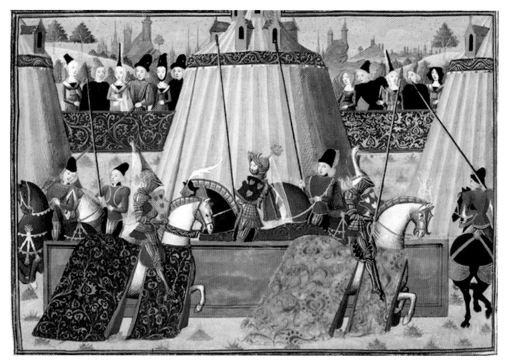

How Oldcastle's joust at Lille might have appeared. This picture is of a jousting tournament at St Inglevert, France in 1390 from volume IV of Froissart's Chronicles, produced in Bruges in the period 1470–1475. In this royal tournament three French knights defended the lists for 30 days against all comers from around Europe. (Harley MS 4379, f.23v.)

with several knights and esquires (de Craon was to die at Agincourt). The duke of Burgundy also seems to have been present, and in light of Prince Henry's desire for an alliance with Burgundy in the years to come and the role that Oldcastle would play in it, one wonders how much of the prince's influence lay behind his selection for this tournament. Oldcastle's two companions were two esquires, de Aufreville (Gilbert Umfraville, then aged 19) and Roger Rambur (probably Roger Brembre), who fought their opponents on the following two days.[21]

It was just over a month before the tournament that Archbishop Arundel had issued a writ to Oldcastle, in the name of Lord Cobham as a member of the Lords, to attend a parliament that was due to meet in Bristol on 27 January 1410. Temporal lords – dukes, earls and those of baronial rank – were usually summoned to parliament, though not always – some might be ill, on duty overseas or out of favour. The number of peers had declined in the past few decades, despite Richard II's elevation to the peerage of various of his favourites, for with the arrival of Henry IV, some of these lost their titles or had them reduced; the rank of marquess disappeared and the rank of duke was restricted to members of the royal family. When peers rebelled against Henry and were condemned as traitors, though their families were well treated their titles were forfeited. Oldcastle was to become one of the few new peers of the reign of Henry IV.

There were only 49 peers in total when they assembled at the first parliament of Henry IV's reign in October 1399, so Oldcastle's elevation to the peerage indicates the esteem in which he was held and his seniority in the realm.[22]

Between the date when parliament was summoned and its meeting, what has been described as 'an obscure crisis' took place.[23] Early in December it seems that the king met with opposition from the council over financial matters and on the 11th Sir John Tiptoft, then treasurer, was relieved of his office. Ten days later Arundel resigned as chancellor, the chief power in the government now clearly lying with the prince's party. On 6 January 1410, Henry Lord Scrope was appointed treasurer, whilst Sir Thomas Beaufort was proposed as chancellor. The king retired initially to Lambeth Palace, then to Windsor, and was not seen in London again till 1411. From January 1410 to November 1411 a council consisting of the prince and his allies essentially governed the country.[24]

It was six years since Oldcastle had last sat in parliament, years in which his views on the Church had hardened, and in which he had grown in stature and influence, and his presence was clearly felt.

The parliament eventually assembled in Westminster, the venue having been changed from Bristol, partly because the stores gathered for feeding those present were plundered in the Forest of Dean. On 31 January Admiral Sir Thomas Beaufort was confirmed as chancellor, the only layman to take this role during the reign, and the Commons chose Thomas Chaucer, a representative of Oxford and son of the poet Geoffrey Chaucer as well as Prince Henry's cousin, as Speaker. The proceedings continued until 9 May, with a three-week recess at Easter.

The first session appears to have been turbulent, with no agreement reached as regards taxation. This may have been because the Commons was presented with a petition with clear Lollard leanings, that set out in some detail a plan for the confiscation of the lands of the bishops and greater abbots. It is not recorded who sponsored the petition, but several historians have surmised that Oldcastle, now in the Lords, must have played a leading role.[25] It is not known if Prince Henry, now head of the king's council, was aware of this petition in advance, nor do we know what his reaction to it was. Given the conservatism towards faith he had shown over the years, one suspects that he would not have been in favour, but was perhaps tempted to give lukewarm support as a counter to Arundel, still a power in the land even if not chancellor, and to put pressure on the Church for finance in general. The petition is recorded in Latin in Walsingham's chronicle, the version given below being an English translation of Walsingham's record that is included in the *Chronicle of London*, which amended a couple of Walsingham's figures:

> To the most excellent and redoutable lord and king, and to all the noble lords of this present parliament, all the true commons show meekly as follows. They say truly that our liege lord the king could receive [the maintenance of] 15 earls, 1,500 knights, 6,200 squires, and 100 almshouses, more than he has at the present time,

well maintained and sustained by lands and tenements – all this from the temporalities occupied and proudly wasted by bishops, abbots and priors. And when all this has been taken, our lord the king may still receive £20,000 in his Treasury for the defence of his realm, free of encumbrance, as may be truly proved. …

And also to ordain that every town throughout the realm should keep all poor men and beggars who are not able to work for their livelihood …

And in order to understand how all this may be done, may you understand that the temporalities of the bishops, abbots and priors extend to the sum of 322,000 marks [£214,666 13s 4d] a year. …

And thus in all the realm men may have 15 earls, and 1,500 knights and more squires than now, sufficiently maintained in rents. Added to this, there could be five universities and 15,000 priests and clerks sufficiently funded by temporal alms, if the king and the lords prefer to spend them for this purpose. And the king may deliver into his Treasury £20,000 a year. And over and above that 100 almshouses; and in every house a hundred marks with lands to feed the indigent poor withall, at no cost to the town. …[26]

Other estimates of the time indicate that the Church possessed a third of the land in England, and that the larger dioceses yielded an income of 22,000 marks each per annum.[27] The petition was not acted upon, but was used by Shakespeare in the opening scene of *Henry V*, in which the archbishop of Canterbury says to the bishop of Ely:

> My lord, I'll tell you; that self bill is urged,
> Which in the eleventh year of the last king's reign [i.e. 1410]
> Was like, and had indeed against us pass'd,
> But that the scambling and unquiet time
> Did push it out of farther question.

To which Ely replies 'But how, my lord, shall we resist it now?'
  The archbishop continues:

> It must be thought on. If it pass against us,
> We lose the better half of our possession:
> For all the temporal lands which men devout
> By testament have given to the church
> Would they strip from us; being valued thus:
> As much as would maintain, to the king's honour,
> Full fifteen earls and fifteen hundred knights,
> Six thousand and two hundred good esquires;
> And, to relief of lazars [lepers] and weak age,
> Of indigent faint souls past corporal toil.
> A hundred almshouses right well supplied;
> And to the coffers of the king beside,
> A thousand pounds by the year: thus runs the bill.

Parliament's mind was more focused after the recess. The complaints were largely as they had been in previous years: the need for impartial justice; the king to tighten his expenditure; a firmer hand required in the Marches and on the sea to counter brigandage; a reduction in the short truces made with neighbouring states, which were only loosely observed, and instead the creation of permanent peace; reform in the rule of Calais, Guienne and Ireland; wages to be promptly paid and no-one to obtain any office that would put him above the law and to be answerable only to the king; complaints of bribery amongst officials; and concerns about the number of foreigners based in England. As usual, action on the list of complaints was to be traded against the amount of revenue which parliament would consent to raise. Another Lollard-inspired petition was also presented, seeking protection from violent and arbitrary arrest under the Statute *De Haeretico Comburendo*, but this was rejected by Henry IV.[28] The parliament eventually agreed to only half the level of taxation initially requested, which was expected to raise £48,000. It also refused to agree a grant of a tenth and fifteenth for the remainder of the king's life, which he had proposed, it was said, so as to save the expense of holding parliaments.

During the Easter recess the king's half-brother, John Beaufort, earl of Somerset, died, releasing many valuable offices that the king could use to bestow patronage. Prince Henry, also in London for the parliament, was made Captain of Calais in Beaufort's place. This signified a new energy in overseeing the defence of Calais, and perhaps the start of the prince's greater interest in matters French.

As we have seen, on making London his base after the fall of Harlech in 1409, the prince regularly attended meetings of the king's council, often acting as its president. These meetings took place at Coldharbour, the residence he was given by his father in 1410, or in the London home of the bishop of Hereford, and sometimes elsewhere. Henry's initial concern was to sort out the management of England's finances after his success in getting treasurers of war appointed at the parliament of 1404. But now he had to turn from domestic matters to events taking place across the Channel. Having been made Captain of Calais in March 1410, he possibly spent part of that winter there, and this would have made him acutely aware of the intrigues swirling around the French court, intrigues in which he and Oldcastle were to become involved.

Oldcastle in France

King Charles VI of France was prone to bouts of madness during which he had to be confined and the country ruled by a council headed by the queen, Isabeau, with whom, it was rumoured, Charles's brother Louis, duke of Orléans, was having an intimate affair. The key magnate on the council, however, was Philip the Bold, duke of Burgundy, who used his authority to maintain a semi-independent existence for the newly created duchy centred on Dijon with lands that lay between France, the English enclave of Calais and Flanders. The supporters of the two dukes divided into parties known to later historians as the Orléanists and the Burgundians. Philip the Bold died

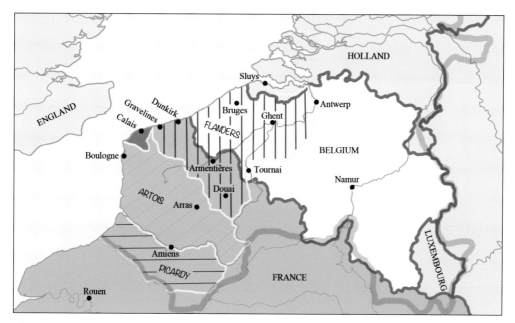

A map showing the rough extent of territories at this period in what is now northern France, Belgium and part of Holland. The wide, semi-translucent line in purple shows the approximate maximum extent of Burgundian control (with the exception of the Calais enclave) reached in 1429. Between 1411 and 1429 there was a pattern of increasing Burgundian control across this area.

in April 1404, to be succeeded by his son, John the Fearless, and Louis used the opportunity to try to oust the Burgundians from the council. In November 1407 John the Fearless arranged for Louis to be murdered in Paris, claiming that the act was a release from tyranny. Charles VI, back in sound mind but with the Burgundians popular in the capital and strongly armed, had little choice but to pardon Duke John. The king sought to pacify relations between the dukedoms and an uneasy peace was restored until 1410. On 15 August that year Louis's son Charles, aged 11, married Bonne, the daughter of Bernard VII, count of Armagnac and Constable of France. During the wedding celebrations at Gien on the Loire, the Orléanists and Armagnacs together with the dukes of Brittany and Berry formed a league to fight against the duke of Burgundy. John the Fearless, duke of Burgundy, then in control of the government, declared this an act of rebellion and, after the league had refused to disband their forces, Charles VI announced that he would lead an army against them. At his approach the league resolved to sue for peace, which was restored, but only on the surface. By the following year France was once more on the brink of civil war.[29]

Both sides now looked for English support. The wars with Wales, the continual need to be ready to defend Calais, and fighting to keep the French at bay around Aquitaine (the strategic castle of Bourg had withstood a long siege in 1407 carried out by the Orléanists) meant that there were plenty of English captains well trained in the art of war and ready to be hired.

John the Fearless (1371–1419),
duke of Burgundy,
by an unknown artist.

A manuscript illustration of the young Charles
VI of France. (Bibliothèque Nationale de France,
Département des Manuscrits, Division occidentale,
Français 2705, Folio C recto)

The effigy of Henry IV on his tomb
in Canterbury Cathedral. (Author)

In 1407 it had been suggested that Prince Henry should marry one of Charles VI's daughters, but the suggestion had not developed into a firm proposal. Now, in July 1411, the duke of Burgundy, seeking an alliance with England, suggested that his daughter Anne marry Prince Henry, and offered to hand over four of his Flemish towns – Gravelines, Dunkirk, Dixmuiden and Sluys – to the English, and also help them reconquer Normandy.[30] Henry IV sought further clarification as to the details of the potential alliance and sent a group of four emissaries to discuss matters with the duke of Burgundy, not least to ascertain whether he would definitely rise against his sovereign to help an English attack on Normandy. In the meantime, Henry IV started to assemble the forces that might be needed if the outcome of the negotiations was successful, intending to lead the troops in person. Preparations began in August and continued apace in September, but the king fell ill whilst events in France moved on.

The countryside to the north of the Seine and the Oise was in the hands of the Armagnacs, whose German and Gascon mercenaries were terrorising the countryside and whose activities were starting to spread southwards. The council in Paris urged the duke of Burgundy to defend the capital, and in early September he brought a sizeable army, supposedly of 60,000 men, westwards. It comprised French and Fleming troops together with 300 men from Calais under the command of Sir William Bardolph. No longer was Burgundy planning to rise against his sovereign; he was now defending him and denying that he had been in negotiations with the English Crown, even though this appears to have been widely known.

After capturing Ham on the River Somme south-east of Amiens, the force rested at Montdidier between 22 and 26 September. By this time the Flemings' commitment of 40 days' service was nearing its end, and with winter approaching the army began to disintegrate. Rather than pursuing them, the Armagnacs pushed on towards Paris, capturing St Denys on 11 October and the following night the bridge at St Cloud, so cutting off all supplies that might have entered the city from the north and west whilst extending their ravages to the south of Paris. Burgundy had drawn back to Arras, where he consolidated a smaller army of some 15,000 men and was joined by a larger force which had arrived from England, sent on its way by Prince Henry, who was then in charge of the king's council. The force comprised 200 men-at-arms and 800 archers under the leadership of the earl of Arundel, Sir Francis Court, Sir Robert Umfraville and his nephew Gilbert Umfraville (popularly called the earl of Kyme from the time of this expedition, though it was never an official title and he was never an earl), Sir John Gray and Sir John Oldcastle, Lord Cobham. (The *Chronicle of London*, in mentioning the only commanders as the earl of Arundel and Lord Cobham, suggests that Oldcastle was second-in-command, whilst Walsingham suggests that Richard Beauchamp, earl of Warwick, was also present, though this seems unlikely and is unsupported by any other record. The *Brut* says the force was led by 'the Erle of Arundell, Ser Gylbarde Umfravylle, Erle of Kyme and the Lorde of Cobham, Ser Iohn Oldecastell, and many other gode knyhts'.[31] Gilbert Umfraville had been one of the esquires accompanying

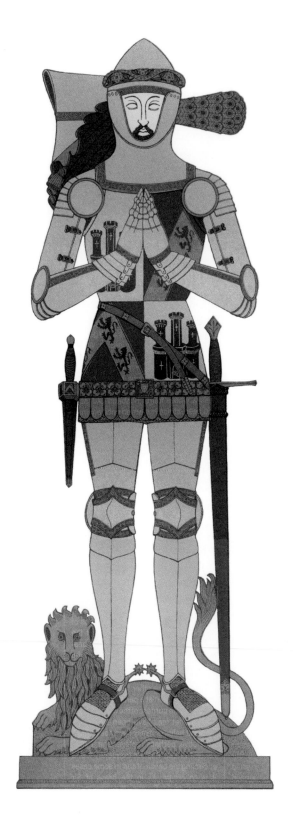

Oldcastle to the tournament in Lille.) Sir William Bardolph's contingent probably now became part of Arundel's command. The English commanders, accompanied by three of the four emissaries sent earlier by Henry IV, were greeted by the duke in the abbey of St Vaast, a meeting followed by much feasting and discussion of the marriage proposals.

Advancing towards Paris, by 16 October the combined expedition reached Pontoise to the north-west of the city. On the 22nd they crossed the Seine at Meulan, where they were met by 3,000 Parisians and escorted into the city. There was some reluctance to house the English and apparently the streets echoed all night with the tramp of horsemen seeking quarters. On the 25th they attacked the Orléanists at La Chapelle, just outside the city beyond Montmartre, and drove them into St Denys. Hearing

---

Opposite: Oldcastle as he might have appeared

This image of how Sir John Oldcastle might have appeared as an effigy on a tomb or in stained glass was created in the 1960s by the artist John Mollo and John Brooke-Little, then Bluemantle Pursuivant at the College of Arms in London.

Oldcastle's coat of arms – as it appeared on his seal to an indenture document in the Cobham archives that may no longer exist (see illustration on page 133) – was recorded by Robert Glover (1544–88) when Somerset Herald as follows: Quarterly, 1 and 4, castle; 2 and 3, on a chevron three lions, Cobham; Supporters, two lions sejant, affrontée; Crest, on a helmet and wreath, a Saracen's head, wearing a cap.

The drawing with the greatest detail of Oldcastle's Arms is contained in the notes made by John Duncumb for his *Collections Towards the History and Antiquities of The County of Hereford* (published in 1804) (see illustration on page *xii*).[32]

The illustration shows the quarters as stated by Glover, though there is debate as to whether the castle should be black on silver, as shown, or silver on black. The seal would not disclose this. The Rouen Roll, so called because it supposedly lists 'The names and arms of those that were with King Henry V at the siege of Rouen … 1418', reverses the quarters, putting the Cobham arms of three lions on a chevron in quarters 1 and 4, and the Oldcastle castle in quarters 2 and 3. The Roll is clearly not a list of the names and arms of those who were at the siege of Rouen, as Oldcastle was dead by then, and it has since been deemed to list those who were prominent at around that time. Oldcastle's own seal is presumably more accurate in the order of the quarters, and this order is given in John Foster's *Some Feudal Coat of Arms*, published in 1902. There were few set heraldic rules at this point, and thus some people thought that Oldcastle's arms should take preference in the 1st quarter, others that as Lord Cobham, the Cobham arms should take first preference. In addition, Burke's *General Armory* of 1844, whilst not always accurate, gives Oldcastle's arms (prior to his marriage to Joan, Lady Cobham) as 'Ar[gent] a tower triple-towered sa[ble] chained transverse, the port or', more accurately describing the 'castle' and indicating it was black (sable) on a silver (argent) background, with a chain in gold across its gate, which is just visible in the illustration (partially hidden by a gauntlet and a belt in each of the quarters).

In Glover's description of Oldcastle's seal, the crest is the same as that used by some branches of the Cobham family, to which Oldcastle was now linked. In the illustration by John Mollo and John Brook-Little, the suggested wreath round the bascinet (the small headpiece) could either have been to support the great helm on which Oldcastle's head rests, or have been purely decorative, perhaps representing a tournament favour gained at Lille, for example (see pages 110–11). It is not known if Oldcastle possessed a great helm, but in including it Mollo and Brook-Little have given it a 'panache' – in its original meaning as a plume of feathers on a headdress or helmet.[33]

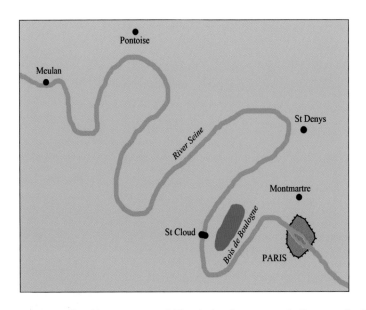

Map showing the location of places in the vicinity of Paris mentioned in the text.

of the officially sanctioned English alliance with Burgundy, English mercenaries who were fighting with the Orléanists were given leave to cancel their contracts, and withdrew from the fray.

It was next decided to drive the Armagnacs from St Cloud, which was held by some 1,500 troops comprising knights and esquires from Brittany, Gascony and the Auvergne rather than more common soldiery. The town was undefended by walls, so the troops had dug trenches, made walls of barrels filled with stones and blocked the roads and lanes with barricades of carts. The bridge across the River Seine was made of timber, with a tower at one end controlling a drawbridge, and various mills constructed against the piers. A surprise attack was planned, and three detachments numbering some 9,000 men in total and including English, Burgundians, Parisians and men from Picardy, left Paris by the city's southern gates on the night of 8 November, whilst fire ships were prepared to be floated down upon the bridge and its associated mills. All were in position at about sunrise and the defences were rushed. The Armagnacs were forced into the centre of the town, where the English archers crawled onto the roofs of houses and fired into the mêlée. The defenders tried to force a route out towards the bridge, but found that their comrades in the tower had raised the drawbridge, only laying some planks across the opening to be used for mounting sorties. In the resulting chaos, horses and men were forced into the river to drown. Chroniclers say that between 600 and 1,400 knights and squires died, including the massacre of some who had fled into the church or into the cellars of houses: this against the loss of 20 of the attackers. Many more were wounded, some badly, and they were treated with salves and ointments at the duke of Burgundy's expense. Other sources put the English losses higher but also say that they distinguished themselves in the fighting. They also tell of arguments between the allies over the treatment of prisoners. The English had taken some of the Armagnac captains hostage in the hope of ransom (as was normal in war), whilst their allies saw all the enemy as traitors, and so deserving of death. The English response apparently provoked a riot in which some Parisians were killed and the prisoners taken by the English were seized, many then being murdered.[34] After their defeat, the Armagnacs immediately evacuated St Denys, which was turned over to the Picards and the English to plunder.

The English joined in the siege of Étampes, some 25 miles south of Paris, which fell on 15 December, and then that of Dourdan, a few miles to the north-west of Étampes. Here, there was more trouble over prisoners, whom the French wished to massacre. The English, largely at the instigation of the Umfravilles, at first prevented their slaughter, but once they had received their ransom money from the royal treasury, they waived further objections and left the French to torture and behead the rebels 'according to the customs of the country'.[35] (In *The Life and Times of the Good Lord Cobham*[36] Gaspey says it was Oldcastle who first stood up for the prisoners, but this book reads as rather an essay in hero worship and contains many an unsupported statement.) With a harsh winter setting in, the English troops returned to Paris, where, on the 23rd December, the duke of Burgundy entertained them at his Hostel d'Artois and gave gold goblets, hanaps (goblets with a lid), ewers and other presents to their leaders. After Christmas, a small force of some 400 men under the Umfravilles stayed with the duke of Burgundy, whilst the rest returned home.

A change of policy towards France

The service provided by this small English army did not go unrecognised by either side. The duke of Burgundy renewed negotiations concerning his daughter's marriage whilst the dukes of Berry, Bourbon and Orléans, together with the count of Armagnac, made a counter offer. They proposed an alternative alliance under which the ancient duchy of Aquitaine would be restored to the king of England as his by hereditary right, and offering any of their daughters in marriage to any of Henry IV's sons. The opportunity for English involvement in the internal affairs of France had been opened wide.

But then matters stalled. In France the duke of Burgundy came by the papers that the envoy to England from the Armagnacs was carrying, which showed that the Armagnacs were even prepared to recognise the English king as their feudal overlord. The news of the depth of the Armagnacs' potential treachery caused Burgundy to fore-stall his plans of alliance with England whilst vowing, with the Dauphin, to crush any rebellion before help from England might arrive.

England, meanwhile, had its own political crisis, the roots of which are difficult to fathom, but it meant that control of the king's council was about to be seized back from Prince Henry by the king. Chroniclers tell of tensions between the king and his eldest son, but not the cause. The parliament in 1406 had approved an Act of Succession whereby the Crown would descend through male heirs, essentially ruling out any daughter of Prince Henry should he not have male heirs. The parliamentary petition which led to this Act referred to errors made by Prince Henry, whilst showering praise on him, in language that hints at strains in the father-son relationship. This Act was rescinded in the following December,[37] but it nevertheless indicates that Henry's next oldest brother, Thomas, was their father's favourite. It may also be that in periods of good health the king realised that Prince Henry was taking ever greater control of the government, and that he saw the Burgundian offer of an alliance as now much less appealing than one with the Armagnacs. Rather than Burgundian support for the retaking of Normandy, the more attractive offer appeared to be actual recognition of the king of England's suzerainty over Aquitaine and the regaining of lands lost over recent years in Guienne, Poitou and Angoulème.

Archbishop Arundel, who had resigned from the chancellorship in December 1410 when Prince Henry took control of the government, seems to have made the first move to regain control of events for Henry IV. In late summer 1411, Arundel conducted a visitation of Oxford University (essentially an investigation into its governance), which was under the prince's protection, as part of his continuing actions against Lollardy. In the autumn, six of the prince's household knights were arrested, including Roger Leche, Richard Stanhope and Thomas Chaworth. At about the same time, writs were issued for a parliament to be held at Westminster on 3 November, with Oldcastle being one of those summoned. The charges against the six knights are nowhere recorded: they were examined on 6 November and soon afterwards released.[38] One can only suspect that the arrests were designed to weaken the prince's party on the eve of the parliament.

Once the parliamentary session had opened, the Beauforts proposed that the king should abdicate in favour of his son, Henry. The motion was debated, with the king warning the Speaker that he would accept no changes to normal custom in this parliament – a clear warning of his stance. Parliament duly supported the king, who had recovered some of his zest and energy, and the prince and his supporters were removed from the council.[39] Another victory for the archbishop concerned the Oxford visitation. The legality of this had been challenged by the university's chancellor, Richard Courtenay, and the dispute now reached parliament, which confirmed the archbishop's view, paving the way for a return to greater orthodoxy within the university.

With Henry IV back in control, English policy towards France was now to support the Armagnacs, and on 18 May 1412 an agreement was drawn up in London between the two sides. Henry was to send 1,000 men-at-arms and 3,000 archers, to be assembled at Blois as soon as possible. Meanwhile, Burgundy, now the opponent of England, prepared to attack Guienne on the borders of Aquitaine, where the English had been losing ground in recent years. The English in turn sought support from the duke's Flemings, threatening them with the loss of all that had been gained in a recently agreed commercial treaty. While Henry IV made preparations for leading an army to France (he was determined to be at its head), events were running strongly against the Armagnacs. Small parties of English did make raids from Calais and caused some of Charles VI's forces to be directed against them, but as midsummer passed there was still no sign of the promised English force at Blois. Henry IV was now ill again and with relations with Prince Henry still sour, command of the army was passed to the prince's brother, Thomas, duke of Clarence. Neither Oldcastle, nor any of those who had been associated with the Prince's French policy, was named as one of the leaders. It also seems that Clarence's force contained few of those lords and knights who were part of Henry IV's close affinity. This can be read as indicating the personal nature of military service (owed due to previous family bonds or landowning ties) whereby military commanders recruited and took on campaign those whom they knew and trusted. However, the fact that the army was to have been led by the king, yet that most of his affinity were not included, could indicate that Henry IV wished to retain a loyal military entourage in England in case of complications with Prince Henry.[40] (On Prince Henry's accession to the throne, the two brothers managed to patch up any differences they had, and Clarence worked solidly and loyally for Henry.)

The army finally landed at St Vaast in the bay of La Hogue, and proceeded to ravage the Cotentin, before heading south to Maine, where they joined troops of the count of Alençon and duke of Brittany, part of the Armagnac alliance. Meantime, a fearful siege had been raging at Bourges, where Burgundians and the Dauphin, the son of King Charles VI, besieged the Armagnacs. This seems to have brought the leading men to their senses and to an understanding of the death and destruction that they were causing. During August 1412, as the English army headed into Maine, a treaty of reconciliation was hammered out between the dukes of Orléans and Burgundy. The count of Alençon did not recognise this and, in his name, the English now advanced along the Loire, capturing towns and plundering parts of the duchy of Orléans. The French resorted to buying off the English and, during November, works of art in the shape of gold crosses, and even younger sons as prisoners, were given as pledges that the amounts agreed would be found. (One son would remain a prisoner for 30 years till the account for which he was surety was fully paid.) The ease of the campaign along the Loire, and the sums of money that the French were prepared to hand over to pay off the English, would have registered with Clarence and his brother Prince Henry.

Meanwhile, the summer saw rumour and counter-rumour in England as to the proposed actions of the king's party on the one hand and the prince's on the other, with civil war even seen as a possibility – the possibility of Henry abdicating in favour of his son had been raised just the previous autumn, after all. The prince certainly seems to have been gathering a sizeable force in Coventry, and some put it about that he was aiming to seize the throne. The prince wrote a letter to his father (given verbatim by Walsingham), in which he maintained that the force he had been allocated to accompany Clarence's army to France was too 'feeble'. He pointed out that his father had agreed to allow him more time to collect together a larger force, whereupon he had gone to Coventry to assemble those troops.[41] Henry came to London in person to deliver the letter and seek reconciliation with his father, arriving on 30 June 'with moche peple of lordes and gentyles', and in September 'with an huge peple'.[42] It was also a time when rumours circulated that the prince had misspent the money allocated to him as Captain of Calais, though this was later disproved when the accounts were audited.[43]

During this period Oldcastle appears to have been officially attached to Prince Henry's household, so he was presumably in the prince's company when he arrived in London. So here we see Oldcastle at his zenith: now Lord Cobham, with all the estates and wealth that this entailed; and a respected military commander, close to the heir to the throne. As later events were to show, he was clearly a much-loved member of the prince's company. But he was also involved in promoting the spread of Lollardy, getting ever more deeply involved with the Lollard views to which he had been sympathetic since his youth.

Calais as depicted in Froissart's Chronicles when produced in 1410,
though showing the French siege of the city in 1350.
(Bibliothèque Nationale de France, MS Fr. 2643, Folio 399, Public Domain,
https://commons.wikimedia.org/w/index.php?curid=14869512)

6

Oldcastle's Increasing Commitment to Lollardy

Lollardy was clearly a threat to the established Church, not just because it sought to take away its possessions but also because it attacked some of the core elements of its teachings. The Church had already sought to control the activities of unlicensed priests through a series of regulations set out in 1408 and confirmed by a convocation of clergy that began at Canterbury on 14 January 1409,[1] and in 1410 the penalties were extended to include anyone who supported them. Thus, on 3 April that year, during the recess of the first parliament to which Oldcastle had been summoned as Lord Cobham, Arundel wrote to the dean of Rochester noting that a 'pretended chaplain', one John, who was living with Oldcastle at Cooling Castle, was preaching heresies at Cooling, Hoo and Halstow. The bishop was asked to proclaim an interdict in those places, to prevent their use, and to provide a citation for the chaplain. The churches were duly placed under this interdict, but it was lifted two days later to allow for the marriage by a licensed priest of Oldcastle's stepdaughter, Joan, daughter of Lady Cobham, and never reimposed.[2] If the interdict was meant to be seen as a threat against Oldcastle, he seems to have paid it little heed, for he continued to support Lollard preachers, maintaining one of their number, Robert Chapell, in his household for six months.[3]

Oldcastle's Lollard connections were indeed strengthened through this new family alliance. It had been agreed on 20 February 1410 that Oldcastle's stepdaughter would marry Sir Thomas Brooke of Holditch in Dorset, with Brooke's father, also Sir Thomas Brooke, agreeing to pay Oldcastle 1,300 marks on the day of the wedding. In return the Brookes were given an assurance that Joan would inherit her mother's extensive and valuable possessions; as a widow, in medieval law Joan had control over estates held in her name, unlike the position of a woman who married for the first time, whose estates became the property of her husband to do with as he liked. Sir Thomas Brooke the elder had inherited a number of properties but also debts, resolving matters to his gain by marrying the widow of a rich merchant, Robert Cheddar. He nurtured the Cheddars' numerous estates and properties spread around the south-west to the extent that when Robert Cheddar's son Richard came of age in 1400, he confirmed his step-father's life tenure of his inheritance. This left Sir Thomas as the largest landowner in Somerset, and he also owned properties in Devon, Bristol, Dorset, Gloucestershire and Wiltshire. Unlike Oldcastle's wife, Lady Cobham, the Brookes appear to have shared

Oldcastle's Lollard opinions. His new son-in-law was to join Oldcastle's rising and spent part of 1414 in fetters in the Tower.[4]

Contacts with Jan Hus, King Wenceslas and reform in Prague

Oldcastle was certainly stepping up his involvement in Lollard affairs, for in September 1410 he wrote to the religious reformer Jan Hus in Prague and to others of the reformist party in Bohemia. When Charles IV, King of Bohemia and Holy Roman Emperor, decided that Prague should rival Rome or Constantinople, one of his acts was to found a university in 1348, donating a library. In a golden age for universities, the number of students had reached 7,000 by the time of Charles's death in 1378, and rose further thereafter. The vast majority of students came from outside Bohemia, notably Germany and including England.

Charles encouraged both popular piety and a sense of provincial loyalty in his kingdom, and support for these policies continued under his more erratic successor, Wenceslas. As a result, from about 1360 a number of evangelical preachers were soon at work, notably in Prague. They urged private devotion and purity, and attacked the sloth and corruption of the clergy. A number of prominent laymen aided reform, and in 1391 Wenceslas Krizand and John of Mühlheim founded the Bethlehem Chapel in Prague, where preaching in Czech was to take place every Sunday and every feast day. In 1402 Jan Hus was appointed the chapel's priest.[5]

Jan Hus, as depicted in a copperplate engraving.

A copy of an illustration made in 1572 as displayed in the Bethlehem Chapel in Prague showing
Top: Wycliffe 'striking the spark' with a pair of flints.
Middle: Hus 'showing the way' with a lighted candle.
Bottom: Luther 'blazing the way' with a torch.
(Author)

Hus, born in 1369, had learned his theology at Charles's university in Prague. One of the earliest statutes governing the university had encouraged its lecturers to discourse on the writings emanating from Paris or Oxford,[6] and in the religious fervour of the new university the writings of Wycliffe soon found their way into the library. In 1388 a canon of Prague Cathedral, who had studied at Oxford, left money to establish a number of bursaries at Oxford, and connections between the two universities continued to grow. Students from Bohemia would often copy Wycliffe's writings to take home with them. Relations between Bohemia and England were augmented when Anne, the Emperor's daughter, married Richard II as his first wife. The close ties between Bohemia and Oxford resulted in some Czech students becoming keen supporters of Wycliffe's views on reform and enthusing Czech teachers of philosophy in Prague with his ideas, leading to differences in belief and approach between the Czech and German elements in the university.[7]

The attack on the papacy received much support in Prague in light of the Great Schism (see pages 44 and 57), not least from Hus, who also supported Wycliffe's view on the authority of the Bible over that of the Church, and so supported the teaching of the Bible in the native tongue as opposed to Latin. He nevertheless still held orthodox views on the Eucharist, unlike other Czech reformers. Events in Prague soon mirrored the split in the Church, with Wenceslas's largely ineffectual rule leading to the German parts of the Holy Roman Empire electing their own emperor in 1400, whilst Wenceslas remained king of Bohemia and still claimed the title of Holy Roman Emperor. Wenceslas busied himself with trying to reunite the church

Satan selling indulgences from the Jensky kodex, c.1490–1510, an image which is displayed in the museum at the Bethlehem Chapel in Prague, which had been founded in 1391 by those dedicated to Church reform and where Hus preached – in Czech as opposed to Latin.

under one pope, and in 1409 cardinals obedient to each pope came to a council at Pisa which elected a third pope, Alexander V, who was acceptable to both sides, in an attempt to bring the Church together. This move was supported by those Czechs who supported reform, but opposed by many, notably those German masters who taught at Prague University. As the structure of the university allowed the German masters to outvote the Czechs, Wenceslas changed the university constitution to achieve the direct opposite. The German masters resigned en masse and Hus was appointed rector of the now Czech dominated university.

Thus at the time when Oldcastle was in communication with Hus, the latter was at the height of his influence. This period was to last until 1412, when Alexander V's successor, John XXIII, began to sell indulgences to finance a campaign against Gregory XII, the pope based in Rome, an action which Hus denounced. As Wenceslas would have taken a share of the monies raised from the sale, he withdrew his support from Hus. With more determined moves to reunite the Church being made in many countries, both by prelates and influential laymen, in 1414 Hus was invited, under a pass of safe conduct which was not honoured, to attend a council at Constance, where he was tried for heresy and eventually condemned to death.

In the meantime, Alexander V had authorised the archbishop of Prague to seize those books of Wycliffe's that contained any article from a list of 45 which were deemed heretical, and to restrict preaching to parish churches. Hus and his supporters complied to an extent, in that some 200 copies of Wycliffe's books were handed in with their request that the heretical passages should be marked and then disclaimed. The archbishop instead burned the books, and Hus and his comrades were excommunicated.

However, Prague's populace was largely on Hus's side and he continued to preach to large crowds. The pope urged the archbishop to invoke the power of the secular arm of government, but the secular arm supported Hus, protesting at the burning of the books and the attempt to silence the preachers. Copying of books continued apace as replacements for those burned. Hus then challenged the Church to discuss some of the condemned books to ascertain if they contained heretical thoughts, whilst four of his friends took up the challenge over the contents of other books. One of these four was Zdislaw of Wartenberg, a baron of the realm and a university friend of Hus, who had defended Wycliffe's *De Universalibus*.[8]

News of events in Prague must have reached Oldcastle, for on 8 September 1410 he wrote a letter from Cooling Castle addressed to both Zdislaw (probably the intermediary in this correspondence as he had been in England, knew Oxford well, and may have met with Oldcastle) and Woksa of Waldstein, one of the leading burgesses of Prague. (Woksa was later to be found parading a cart around Prague collecting papal indulgences which were then burned. He was also a friend of Zdislaw.) Oldcastle's letter was written in Latin, the translation of which follows:

To the noble Woksa, but in his absence to the lord Zdyslaus of Zwerzitcz, dearest brothers in Christ to me, knowledge of the Lord's ways, a great love of them, and health.

I give thanks to my God, who has, as I have heard through certain lovers of truth, animated your heart to be zealous and strive for the justice of the law of God: if only it may in accordance with the judgement of the wise man be until death. For as the Saviour says: whoever perseveres in truth until the end shall be saved. Yea, dearest brother, I rejoice greatly concerning you, and more than I am able to write, my soul is delighted in you in as much as the vainglory of the opponents of Christ give you no terror but because with boldness you promote the word of God and those who are true in making it known, so far as you are able. For already, as we can clearly see, the law of the Lord had been spotless, for too long a time suffocated by priests who are the enemies of Christ and excessively feebly thought of little value by those to whom Christ had entrusted the sword for the purpose of the defence of his law. To this fact kings and temporal lords are paying too little attention, and for that, as Isidore says, they will render account to the Lord, from whom they have received the church to defend by their power. O how much we wretched can fear, who expend our own strength and efforts so often on carnal sins and the affairs of the world but in the cause of the Lord wickedly draw back from putting ourselves out on any matter. Let us for this reason recall Malachi, Phineas, Judas Maccabeus, and the others who had zeal for God, who merited being commended by God in the holy scriptures as their zeal and deeds are left for posterity to be examples. Let us be imitators of them destined in the end to receive a reward with them. What, therefore, would move us, given the vain character of this age, which passes like a shadow or the lucre of temporal transient things, to put ourselves forward so boldly but in the cause of Christ after accepting so many benefits to fear too stupidly because of a false terrifying statue? Certainly only that fear that opposes Christ, pride and the abundance of temporal things has excessively blinded us. Let us, you and I and others like us, therefore, reckon that it is not sufficient for justice to believe in the heart unless we also confess the lord Jesus Christ with the mouth. For he himself in the gospel bears for us merit and punishment: merit when he says, whoever has confessed me before men, I too will confess him before my father; and on the other hand, punishment when he says, whoever has denied me or blushed before men, I will deny him and blush in the sight of my father and the holy angels.

Let us for this reason love the lord Jesus Christ by humbly confessing him with our heart and work, and in no way defend any who block the free action of his law, since whoever stands in the way of the word of God bringing benefit literally to his church is without doubt like the Antichrist, when Christ as the source of salvation underwent the most cruel punishments and death for the sake of the revelation of his law; and let false excommunications from men not scare us from good works, since the Lord says through the prophet Isaiah: Who are you, that you are afraid of mortal man and the son of man who dries out like hay and have forgotten the lord your God? And as Chrysostom testifies with

Oldcastle's letter to Woksa of Waldstein no longer exists, but the text survives in a transcript made of a collection of letters dating to the 1400s that also includes letters by Pope Innocent III, Jan Hus and Richard Wyche. The illustration shows the opening part which starts with his greeting, and the ending, which includes the text *Ideo sigillum armorum nostrorum, quod nunquam apponimus ad litteram que deberet in posterum cessari, decrevi hanc litteram eodem sigillare* ('For this reason, I have decided to seal this letter with the seal of our arms, which I never affix to a letter that should be set aside in future.')
(The transcript is held by Charles University, Prague, with the reference E cod. bibl. univ. Prag. XIII. F. 21 Fol. 146v r)[10]

certainty: The betrayer of the truth is not only he who by transgressing speaks lies in public in place of the truth, but also he who does not proclaim truth as freely as he ought to proclaim it or does not defend it as freely as he should defend it. For like the priest is the debtor, that he should preach the truth freely that he has heard from God and in no way, neither out of fear nor out of love, should fail to defend boldly, since it is a very serious thing, the truth which he has heard from priests to be shown in the scriptures. And if he does not do this, he betrays the truth. Behold dearest ones: these and similar things move me; may they move you too and your like, that we may all boldly stand together with the truth; and if in the end we stand firm, the lord of truth will not defraud us of our rightful renunciation; and if the lord deigns not to help us, as we hope, let us not intend to hold back from this truth, even until death. For this reason, I have decided to seal this letter with the seal of our arms, which I never affix to a letter that should be set aside in future.

Given at our castle of Culing [Cooling] on the Nativity of St Mary in the year of the Lord 1410 by John Oldcastle, lord of Cobham.[9]

Richard Ashdowne, the former editor of the *Dictionary of Medieval Latin from British Sources*, who translated this letter (and the other from Oldcastle that follows) describes the language used as 'rather flowery Latin which he is not fully in control of', going on to say 'The vocabulary is clearly in line with that of Wycliffe, as one would expect. The style is perhaps one that suggests dictation but I'd be very hesitant about thinking that with any confidence.' Even if dictated by Oldcastle rather than written by him, it shows that Oldcastle had learned to write in Latin, and had the education to quote from St Augustine, Isidore (archbishop of Seville in the 630s) and John Chrysostum (archbishop of Constantinople from 397 to 404). At the very least the sentiments expressed show that Oldcastle fully accepted the leading principles of Lollardy, laying emphasis on the duty of priests to preach the truth and, indeed, insisting that anyone striving to prevent such preaching was to be deemed the Antichrist. He signs himself John Oldcastle, lord of Cobham, and affixed his seal with the comment 'I have decided to seal this letter with the seal of our arms, which I never affix to a letter that should be set aside in future', indicating that he was prepared to stand by his views. It would not be surprising if those in Prague thereby saw him as the leader of the English Lollards. How he signed his letter and his comment regarding when he used his seal have an interesting parallel in *Henry IV Part II*, Act II, Scene II, when Poins reads Falstaff's letter addressed to Prince Henry in which Falstaff says, of how he signs his letters: 'JACK FALSTAFF with my familiars, JOHN with my brothers and sisters, and SIR JOHN with all Europe'.

On the same date that Oldcastle wrote his letter, Richard Wyche, who had already suffered for his Lollardy and in 1440 would be burned for heresy on Tower Hill, wrote a letter to Hus addressed from London (he was then a priest in Deptford) urging him

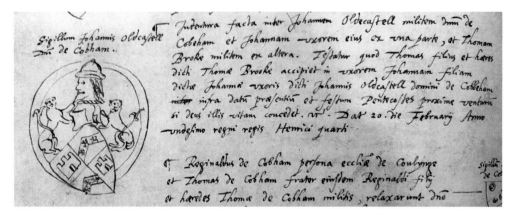

A drawing of Oldcastle's seal reproduced from notes made by Robert Glover, Somerset Herald between 1544 and 1588, on the basis of charters and other documents he inspected belonging to the Lords Cobham. The crest of a Saracen's head wearing a cap is the same as that used by some branches of the Cobham family, so probably reflects Oldcastle's connection with that family. As for the supporters – two lions sejant, affrontée – these might purely be fillers between the sides of the shield and the edge of the seal, a fairly common design feature of the time. Even the figures chosen as supporters on the royal coat of arms varied at this time.

The Latin text alongside reads (with its various spellings of names): *Indenture made between John Oldecastell knight, lord of Cobeham and Joan his wife of the one part and Thomas Broke knight of the other part. It is witnessed that Thomas son and heir of the said Thomas Brooke shall take to wife Joan daughter of the said Joan wife of the said John Oldcastell lord of Cobbeham, between the date of this deed and the next feast of Pentecost, if God grant them life. Given on the 20th day of February in the 11th year of the reign of King Henry the Fourth [1410].* Above the seal is written 'The seal of John Oldcastell Lord of Cobham'. (Courtesy of The Kings, Heralds and Pursuivants of Arms)

and his colleagues to persevere. Presumably Wyche and Oldcastle knew each other at least well enough to use the same messenger, perhaps a student travelling between England and Bohemia, to take the letters. It may also be that the two men were more than simply acquaintances, for in October 1417 Wyche was questioned about monies that had belonged to Oldcastle and had been forfeited to the king.[11]

Richard Wyche's letter to Hus and Hus's reply have both survived, Hus writing:

> … Turning over in my mind its [Wyche's letter's] marrow and strength, I said in a large assembly of people, numbering, I suppose, nearly ten thousand, as I was preaching in public, 'See, my beloved brothers, what a care for your salvation is shown by the faithful preachers of Christ in other countries; they yearn to point out their whole soul, if only they can keep us in the gospel of Christ, even the Lord.' And I added, 'Why, our dear brother Richard, partner of Master John Wyclif in the toils of the gospel, hath written you a letter of so much cheer, that if I possessed no other writing, I should feel bound by it to offer myself for the gospel of Christ, even unto death. Yea, and this I will do, with the help of our Lord Jesus Christ.' Christ's faithful ones were fired with such ardour by the letter that they begged me to translate it into our mother tongue.[12]

Another letter from Oldcastle is dated 7 September, this one from London and to King Wenzel (Wenceslas). The year is not given but it is likely to be 1411. It can't be any earlier as Wenceslas only became Margrave of Moravia (one of the terms of address used by Oldcastle, the Margrave being the title of the administrator of Moravia, one of the dependencies of the Bohemian Crown) on 17 January that year. It is also not likely to have been sent later than 1411 as it is written before Oldcastle might have known that Wenceslas had turned upon Hus, and Oldcastle himself is clearly still operating as a free man.[13]

The original letter has been lost, but a transcription was made. Translated from the Latin it reads:

> To the most serene and illustrious prince and lord, lord Wenceslas, king of the Romans and Bohemia, Margrave of Moravia and prince of Luczburg, health from him who is, and who is able to rouse the sons of Abraham from the stones. May he, I say, grant health, strength, comfort and protection in everything good throughout all endless ages. Since pleasing news delights the mind and encourages the heart to great joy, it is from this, most serene prince, that the news of your earnest soldiering in the gospel of Christ brought to me in letters by master Hus, in my judgement a priest of Christ, and to others, has very much fed my mind with happiness and my heart jumping for joy has enriched my bones and indeed my limbs and prepared me, though unworthy, to write to your serenity since love does not stay idle. O what a fine thing it is that Wenceslas, king of the Romans and Bohemia, an example and mirror and first-fruits of other kings, wisely and carefully separated from the wheat the darnel of false priests gathered into the barn, and strengthened the wheat, the true priests of Christ, in their state of evangelical poverty. O what a delightful thing so excellent a prince, so excellent a solider of Christ has been made! O how remarkable and inexpressible but unsurprisingly laudable it is that a king carry out the duty of his position in modern times! And I do not doubt that the view of Augustine in his letter to Boniface, giving instruction in the duty of a king, has readied you as king to have first to serve God, by regulating one's laws to the law of God, by destroying those who oppose the law of Christ and by forcing the people into observance of the commands of the lord, since you are the representative of divinity. And if without doubt your kingdom, magnificent king, shall thus stand undivided, since it is divided only by transgressing the commands of the lord and unified only by observing the same, and if you shall so be protected by mercy and virtue, your throne will be strengthened by clemency and in consequence you shall be made a destroyer of all evil in destroying false brothers and prelates, they are terrified even by your gaze as if by the roar of a lion. O if only God were granting perseverance in grace. Most illustrious prince, to your majesty and to the whole of your gospel community, to barons and knights, by the teaching of Christ and zeal for love, I offer myself in service, without prejudice to my lawful lord, together with all my friends and those who join to me in the way of gospel truth and I stand ready since you have called many quite earnestly to the word of

God by your example. O if only the lord were granting such a heart to all kings or at least were arousing a Daniel in all the regions of the world, who would put himself forward so attentively for the law of God and establish you more and more in the practice of the law of the lord and afterwards grant eternal life, and may he whose kingdom shall never be destroyed deign to bring this about.

Written at London on the seventh day of September
by your humble servant
John Oldcastle, knight,
lord of Cobham.

Oldcastle's letter says that he has 'news of your earnest soldiering in the gospel of Christ brought to me in letters by master Hus, in my judgement a priest of Christ', showing that he had previously been communicating with Hus, but only the two letters by Oldcastle included above have come down to us. There is, however, a reference to the wider role that Oldcastle might have played in the dissemination of Wycliffe's works in Thomas Netter's *Doctrinale*, produced just a few years later in the 1420s.[14] Netter was a Carmelite friar and a confessor to Henry V, for whom he also served on diplomatic missions. He was also one of those who sat in judgement at Oldcastle's trial and his *Doctrinale* sets out arguments against those who supported Wycliffe and Hus. In it he says that Hus specifically requested copies of Wycliffe's works from Oldcastle, a request that Oldcastle fulfilled.[15]

Of particular interest in the letter to Wenceslas are the views that Oldcastle sees as being those that should be espoused by a prince or king: to be rid of 'false priests' and to strengthen 'the wheat, the true priests of Christ, in their state of evangelical poverty'. This echoes the views of Wycliffe as to the role of the king in relation to the Church, and perhaps in these lines we see the disappointment Oldcastle is to face when his prince, Henry, fails to take on the Church.

The two letters mentioned are the only known surviving writings by Oldcastle. In 1905 W.T. Waugh, in his essays on Oldcastle, described him as a man of few intellectual abilities, referring to Archbishop Arundel's reference to the need to have some of the doctrinal questions posed at his subsequent trial translated into English to make up for his lack of learning ('*pro leviori intellectu eiusdem*') (but see page 132 above and also page 58).[16] Yet the letter to Woksa suggests he was widely read and informed in matters relating to Christianity and he is known to have possessed various books, one of which played a crucial role in Arundel's moves against him (as will be seen in the following chapter). The records of his subsequent trial show that he had an easy literary style at least in English (the chosen language of Church reform) and an ability to write clearly without implicating himself in heresy. He also appears to have conducted his own defence with clarity.

Oldcastle's other possible writings

Other writings have been credited to Oldcastle. In his *Brefe Chronicle*, which covers the trial of Oldcastle for heresy, John Bale mentions that Oldcastle wrote six Latin 'verses', by which he means lines, that summarised the *Twelve Conclusions* of the Lollards, which had been written in 1395 and which Bale also ascribed to Oldcastle (see pages 58-60). Bale says that these 'verses' were 'copyed out by divers men and set upon theyre windows, gates and doors, which were then known for obstinate hypocrites and fleshly livers, which made the prelates madde'. This sounds more like the antics of a religious Falstaff; even Bale calls them 'grosse and vnperfect, according to the time than, wherin all fresh literature was cleverly extinguished, yet is the sentence of them lyvely, and of a fresh faithfull spyrite, …'.

Bale wrote his *Brefe Chronicle* in 1544. The lines also appear in John Weever's 'Mirror of Martyrs, or The life and death of that thrice valiant Capitaine, and most godly martyr Sir John Oldcastle knight, Lord Cobham', published in 1601, and in Thomas Wright's *Political Poems and Songs*,[17] published in the mid-1800s, each in a marginally different form. The version given below is taken from Weever's poem, along with the two verses that precede it:

> That I had caused Wickleues bookes be sent,
> Faire writ, to Boheme, France, and Germanie,
> Whereof two hundred openly were brent
> By Prag[u]es Archbishops great authoritie,
> That I preferd vp Bills in Parliament,
> Where to the King and Lords gaue all consent.
>
> Of all the Cleargies villainous abusion,
> Which I put vp in open Parlement,
> Writ in a briefe containing sharpe conclusion,
> These verses were the summarie content,
> Whose soules with sin empoisning hate did anguish,
> That they ne're left me till they saw me languish.
>
> *Plangunt Anglorum Gentes crimen Sodomorum.*
> *Paulus fert horum sunt idola causa malorum.*
> *Surgunt ingrati Giezite Symone nati,*
> *Nomine prelati, hoc defensare parati,*
> *Qui reges estis, populis quicunque praestis,*
> *Qualiter hijs estis gladios prohibere potestis.*

This last verse Bale translates as:

> Bewayle maye Inglande the syn of Sodomites:
> For Idolles and they are ground of all theyr wo.

Of Symon Magus a secte of hypocrites,
Surnamed Prelates, are vp wyth them to go:
And, to vpholde them in all that they may do.
You that be rulers, peculiarly selected,
How can ye suffre such mischeues to go vncorrected?[18]

This has been paraphrased by others to:

The horrors of the Cities of the plain,
Idolatry, and hypocrites, for gain
Prepared with Satan any lengths to go
Called prelates, are the source of England's woe.
Oh! ye who have for rulers been selected,
Why let such wickedness pass uncorrected?[19]

But were these lines actually Oldcastle's? I doubt if we will ever know.

Weever repeated an assertion made by Bale that Oldcastle was also responsible for sending copies of Wycliffe's works to France and Spain, but no hard evidence for this has ever been found, just a shred. One of those who is known to have transmitted letters between Prague and England was the student Mikuláš Faulfiš. In 1414 Hus was to say that Faulfiš had died 'somewhere, I believe between Spain and England'. Could he have been a courier for the wider dissemination of Wycliffe's works, perhaps helped in so doing by Oldcastle?[20]

Tantalisingly, in his account published in 1884 of the most distinguished alumni of Bristol Baptist College, S.A. Swaine noted:

Among the manuscript curiosities of the Museum is a copy of Wycliffe's Translation of the Gospels. It was most likely made in Wycliffe's own time by one of the numerous copyists employed for the purpose of multiplying the translations he made. An inscription at the beginning informs us that it was presented to John Oldcastle, more generally known as Lord Cobham … The donor was a certain FitzHenry, *alias* Harrison. By Lord Cobham the book was 'bequeathed by wille' to Sir H. Brooke ….[21]

Revd R. Hyett-Warner, vicar of Almeley in the early 1900s, tried to find out more. Contacting the librarian of the Bristol Baptist College, he discovered that the book was only a copy of Wycliffe's translation of the Gospel of St Matthew and the Acts of the Apostles, not the complete Gospels. Not only had Swaine got the contents of the book wrong, but also the dedication, for the librarian also told Hyett-Warner that this read 'Fitz Henry ats Harrison, 1364 ? Gyven by him to the Lord Wilton Cobham: by whom it was willed to his son Sir George Brooke.'[22] This does not make sense, for there is no Lord Wilton Cobham known to history, but Hyett-Warner did not pursue it further. On checking the details in 2020 it would seem that the librarian in the early

1900s had also got it wrong. The book itself, measuring 4.25 inches by 3 inches, actually included The Gospel of St Matthew, Epistles, Acts of the Apostles and the Apocalypse. It was sold by the college at a Sotheby's auction in December 1977, along with other old manuscripts, the buyer believed to have been a Japanese collector. The catalogue description included the following summary of the dedication from 1564 (not 1364): 'fitzhenry alias harrison, 1564; given by him to the Lord William Cobham: by whom it was willed to his son Mr. George Brooke and by him given to William Lambarde'.[23] Lord William Cobham and son George Brooke make sense: Lord William Cobham, the tenth Lord Cobham, was Lord Chamberlain in Shakespeare's time (as will be recounted in Chapter Nine), and he died in 1597. George Brooke was one of his sons, and William Lambarde was one of Lord William's executors, a lawyer who held strongly Protestant views.[24] Thus, unfortunately, the book in question is not known to have belonged to Sir John Oldcastle, but did belong to his great-great-great-great stepson, the tenth Lord Cobham.

In 1748 Bishop Tanner's work of some 40 years, *Bibliotheca Britannico-Hibernica*, was published 13 years after his death. In it he credits Oldcastle with writing the *Twelve Conclusions* of Lollard beliefs (as recounted in Chapter Two), but also mentions something called *Agricolae querimonias* (Farmers' complaints): '*Agricolae querimonias*, lib. i "Christus Jesus, qui erat "de." Quia ab Oldcastello dispersus erat hic liber, illi attribuit Baleus, sed Wiclefo debetuir.' (This translates as '*Farmers' complaints*', book i, "Christ Jesus, who was "down". Because this book was dispersed from/by Oldcastle, [John] Bale wrongly attributed this book to him but it should be to Wycliffe.') *Agricolae querimonias* and its connection with Oldcastle was mentioned some 160 years previously, in *Bibliotheca, Instituta Et Collecta Primum A Conrado Gesnero*, published in 1583; and again in *Index librorum prohibitorum et expurgandorum novissimi, Hispanicus et Romanus*, published in 1667. Gesnero, normally known as Conrad Gesner or Gessner, was a Swiss physician and naturalist best known to history for his compilations of lists, mainly concerning plants and animals. In 1545 he completed his first bibliography, which listed 1,800 authors and their works with associated comments. If Oldcastle was credited in Switzerland in the 1500s with

Ioannes Oldencastel, Anglus, armatæ militiæ eques auratus, regulus de Cobham, scripsit contra monachorum & sacerdotum Sodomiam lib.i. Agricolæ querimonias lib.i. Symbolū suæ fidei. Londini ob fidei confessionem ferreis catenis suspensus, vitam m igne finiuit, anno 1418.

Excerpt from *Bibliotheca, Instituta Et Collecta Primum A Conrado Gesnero* crediting Oldcastle with the authorship of *Agricolae querimonias*.

writing *Agricolae querimonias*, that suggests that Oldcastle had contacts further afield than just Bohemia, or at least that his reputation had spread. But did he write it, and what was it about? It was presumably heretical in content, given that the title of the second bibliographic volume, published in 1667, says it is an index of prohibited books.

The title suggests that the work might be something akin to *The Praier and complaynte of the ploweman unto Christe*, one of a number of works in which a ploughman was the central character.[25] William Langland's more famous *Piers Plowman* was written sometime between 1370 and 1390. Another such work, *Pierce the Ploughman's Crede*, was an alliterative poem of 855 lines which made fun of the orders of friars, and was written sometime between 1393 and 1400. *The Plowman's Tale*, written around 1400, was thought for a while to be have been penned by Geoffrey Chaucer as one of *The Canterbury Tales*. As for *The Praier and complaynte of the ploweman unto Christe*, it was printed first in Antwerp in 1531 and then in England the following year, but the original would appear to pre-date even *Piers Plowman*. The editor of the Antwerp edition, thought most likely to be William Tyndale, included in the frontispiece that it was 'written nat longe after the yere of our Lords. M and three hundred' (i.e. sometime shortly after 1300).[26] Foxe believed it had been originally composed around 1360, and incorporated the full text in the second volume (that printed in 1570) of his *Actes and monuments*.[27]

A polemical text, *The Praier and complaynte of the ploweman unto Christe* focuses on the quality of priests and what they should be doing with their time (living as true Christian men, teaching and preaching as opposed to practicing simony – the selling of indulgences and shriving of sins, or robbing people of tithes, or 'feeding' people with songs in Latin that they don't understand). It also attacks the papacy, and calls for a better sharing of wealth between the rich and the poor. Several of these subjects would have been ones on which Oldcastle is likely to have shared the author's views, as will be seen in the evidence of his trial in the next chapter. From what we have seen of Oldcastle's character, however, they don't sound like subjects which he would have chosen to write about, and all the dates suggested for its composition would rule out Oldcastle as its author in any event. Most likely Gesnero, and presumably others, were aware of some tract which had a farmer or plowman as its main 'speaker' who iterated some of Wycliffe's views and which Oldcastle helped to have copied and disseminated, and of which Bale and Tanner subsequently became aware. Searching lists of Wycliffe's extensive writings and their contents has not revealed a likely source, but the large volume of his work is somewhat fragmented.[28] As will be explored more in Chapter Nine, Foxe would have seen a work such as *The Praier and complaynte of the ploweman unto Christe* and any similar works of agrarian discontent as a tradition of the true call for Church reform that ran via Wycliffe and through Oldcastle.[29] Thus linking such a text with Oldcastle's name would be welcome in furthering a 'Protestant history'.

There is one other writing that might have been by Oldcastle. A jury trying people in Leicestershire charged with supporting Oldcastle's rising in 1414 suggested that some of the bills promoting his cause had been written by Oldcastle himself. These bills included attacks on the Church's view of sacraments, on confession and on pilgrimages,[30] but whether actually written by Oldcastle is not known, and the bills have not survived.

Even given these unknowns, it seems that much of Oldcastle's time in the last part of 1410 and during 1411 was taken up with supporting the spread of Wycliffe's views and wider Lollardy at home and abroad. Indeed the antiquary John Leland singled out Oldcastle as preserving Wycliffe's writings at his own considerable expense, 'to the honour of [his] contrey'.[31] He was also engaged, on behalf of the prince, with military duties in France (as recounted in the previous chapter). But with Henry's accession to the throne the relationships between the new king, Archbishop Arundel and Oldcastle were set to change.

7

The Trial

In October 1412 Henry IV and Prince Henry managed to patch up their differences. The king was seriously ill once again and perhaps the prince felt it wouldn't be long before he would inherit the kingship. In December Henry IV was unconscious for periods of time. He rallied at Christmas, but died on 20 March 1413. A parliament that had been summoned for 3 February was still in session, but was dissolved as a result of the king's death, and no records remain of its actions.

With Prince Henry's accession to the throne as Henry V he found himself in a more formal relationship with the Church. As prince, Henry seems to have had a prickly relationship with Archbishop Arundel, as evidenced in the power struggle between his fraternity and that of his father, in which the archbishop was a key player. How would that relationship now play out, given Arundel's desire to suppress heresy, and what would that mean for Oldcastle?

Henry's accession to the throne was unlike that of most English kings: he had had his own independent military command since his mid-teens, albeit with senior, well-versed commanders such as the earl of Arundel and Lord Grey of Codnor in close supporting roles. It meant that he had learnt to command men, had built up a degree of knowledge as to the strengths and weaknesses of a number of lords and knights, already formed bonds of loyalty and shared experiences with a host of men and was entering the kingship with these men as a phalanx behind him. Most Princes of Wales would have reached this point with a household of knights appointed by their father, and would have taken up a throne surrounded by their father's appointees. The Black Prince, Edward III's son, would have been in a similar position to Henry, but he died before he could become king. Also, Henry's group of household knights and favourites (if favourites they could be called) was spread over a large number of men, meaning that a small clique never emerged. So, perhaps by design or perhaps by the chance events of his formative years, he was never surrounded by a close-knit faction that sought lands and wealth for themselves, so putting at risk the Crown under which they profited, as had been the case most spectacularly with Edward II and to a lesser extent with Richard II.

But Henry's position as king was not necessarily very strong. His father had usurped the throne and his reign had been dogged by rebellions which partially sprang from this. The defeat of the rebellion of the Percies had left a power vacuum in the north that was now being filled by the twice-married Ralph Neville, earl of Westmorland and his 22 children. This situation was to build up resentment in those of the Percy affinity who saw their status being eroded, and this probably played a part in the Southampton Plot (see pages 172-73).

Henry would have been aware of such continuing threats, an awareness that may well have lain behind his decision to dabble in the affairs of France. He may have seen this both as a way of 'bringing the country together' (as war is still deemed to do today), by restoring the country's prestige after its comparative humiliations on the Continent towards the end of Edward III's reign and during the reign of Richard II, and as employing productively those who had learned the art of war in Wales. But to do this, and be absent from England himself, he needed to ensure he had peace at home.

We have seen that the prince was minded to regard those who were deemed heretics as also being a threat to the state given some of their views, meaning that consideration should be given to trying them as traitors and not just as heretics (see page 106). The prince's attitude to those individuals convicted of heresy by the Church can be seen in an episode that happened during the parliament of 1410, when Archbishop Arundel moved against John Badby, an Evesham tailor, who held what were seen as heretical views, possibly as a counter to the Lollard views being expressed in that parliament (see pages 112-13). Badby could not accept the Church's teaching on transubstantiation, and he expressed his views in a way that was an attack on the whole Church: 'John Rakyer of Bristol had the same power and the same authority to make the body of Christ as any priest', he is reported as saying. Badby had been condemned by the bishop of Worcester as a heretic in January of the previous year, and since then he had been in prison in Worcester. He was now brought to London to face judgement before a panel of ecclesiastics and laymen, including Archbishop Arundel, the duke of York and the new chancellor, Thomas Beaufort, which met on 1 March.

Duly condemned, on 15 March (the first day of the parliamentary recess), Badby was taken to Smithfield, bound with iron chains, and placed in an empty barrel. The barrel was fastened to a stake and wood piled around it. Many of the bishops who had judged Badby were present and so was Prince Henry, though the reason for his being there is unclear. As this was only the second sentence of death for heresy carried out in England, there was little precedent to follow. (William Sawtre's death by burning at the stake on 2 March 1401 had been authorised by a writ issued by Henry IV on 26 February, as the statute *De Haeretico Comburendo* had not yet passed into law.) It may be that, as the then head of the king's council and with the secular arm of government being responsible for the execution, Prince Henry felt his presence was warranted. Perhaps he hoped to convince Badby to recant and save himself, and so either relieve the potential pressure on Oldcastle or encourage him also to recant should the need arise. Perhaps he wished to show Arundel that he would work with the Church whilst also wanting to show the authority of the secular arm, especially since he had replaced

Badby's execution as depicted in Foxe's *Actes and monuments* or *Book of Martyrs*, showing Prince Henry's intervention. The dress depicted is of a rather later date than that of 1410.

Arundel at the head of the king's council just three months earlier. Perhaps he thought if he succeeded in getting Badby to recant where the Church had failed, it would enhance the position of the secular arm in relation to Church affairs. Perhaps he went with mixed hopes and emotions.

The fire had not been long lit under Badby when Henry ordered it to be put out so that he could talk with him. The prince encouraged Badby to renounce his views, pointing out what would soon happen to him if he didn't. But when Badby was asked whether the sacrament was bread or the body of Christ, the tailor answered that it was bread, and the wood was again set alight. As soon as he felt the heat of the fire, Badby cried out 'Mercy', and Henry ordered the fire to be quenched again, thinking that the cry might mean that the prisoner was reconsidering. He then asked Badby whether he would forsake heresy, and even offered him a daily allowance of 3 pence if he did so, but Badby declined – or, as the *Chronicle of London* records, '... the cursed shrew would not, but continued forth in his heresy: wherefore he was burnt'. With Badby's death by burning, what Henry's presence did show was that he was willing to see heretics burned. Lollards had received a warning and Arundel seized the moment. A few days later a William Taillour of London, who had made an outspoken attack on clerical possessions in 1406, was cited for heresy and soon afterwards several London Lollards were arrested.[1] Arundel was exerting counter-pressure on Oldcastle and the Lollard influences on parliament.

On Henry V's accession to the throne, both the Lollards and the Catholic Church made moves to improve their position. The Lollards trusted that the friendship between the king and Oldcastle would aid their cause, perhaps even with changes to the statute of *De Haeretico Comburendo*. They are said by Walsingham to have fixed papers to the doors of all the churches in London proclaiming their doctrines and threatening violence to those who opposed them.[2] Meanwhile, the Church was preparing for its reunification under one pope at the council of Constance held in 1414, at which Hus was tried for heresy. In addition, a council held at Rome in early 1413 condemned many of Wycliffe's writings as unfit to be read or possessed by sound Christians and as deserving to be burned. In England, Henry V was considering his claim to France and, like his father before him, needed money and the means of ensuring stability in England. He saw that he could solve both these problems by raising taxes from the Church in return for dealing with their grievances, whilst also using the Church's power to help maintain control in England whilst he was in France.

It seems that Henry, as king, had already made moves to distance himself from Oldcastle, presumably because of his heretical views. According to the Pseudo-Elmham, Henry had already 'dismissed [Oldcastle] from his household because of his insane ideas' (*causa opinionis insanae a suo famulato domestic repellebat*).[3] This is borne out by an analysis of a list of Henry's household knights and esquires in 1413–14, in which Oldcastle's name does not feature; nor does Oldcastle's name feature in the list of those to whom Henry gave lengths of scarlet cloth from which to fashion cloaks to wear at his coronation.[4]

Henry called a parliament soon after Easter 1413 to pursue his plans, and Archbishop Arundel likewise convened an assembly of prelates and clergy at St Paul's Cathedral. The latter quickly agreed that the breaches in the Church could not be repaired if heresy was rampant, and that certain notable leaders of Lollardy needed either to be removed or to be brought back to allegiance to the Church. Oldcastle was specifically named; indeed, the *Chronicle of London* states that 'the archbishop and bishops, at St Paul's Cross, accursed Sir John Oldcastle on the Sunday'. But Arundel was keen to proceed cautiously, for Oldcastle was one of Henry's 'most-loved courtiers', '*unum de praecarissimus ex magnis domesticis suis*', as he was described by the anonymous author of the *Gesta HENRICI QUINTI, REGIS Angliae*. Described as a particularly authoritative account of the next few years of England's history, the *Gesta* was written by someone who was an eyewitness to events, although the writer couched it in propagandist terms to justify Henry's policy, particularly towards France.[5] Arundel himself, in his letter to the bishop of London after the trial, which details many of the events leading up to the trial and the course of the trial itself, says: 'Notwithstandinge for the reuerence of oure Lord the king in whose fauor the said sir Ihon at that present was, ...'.[6]

Arundel had, in fact, already made his first move against Oldcastle. While the parliament that ended with the death of Henry IV was in session, he called a convocation of clergy, that commenced its session on 6 March. That same day a chaplain by the name of John Lay, who was suspected of heresy and who had celebrated mass in Oldcastle's presence earlier in the day, was brought before Arundel, cross-examined and asked to produce his certificate of ordination and his licence to celebrate Mass. Lay said he had brought neither with him, and was asked to return with these documents the following Saturday. But nothing more is heard of Lay and no further action was taken.[7]

According to Archbishop Arundel's own memoirs, he now helped to create an occasion which would help bring Oldcastle's beliefs and actions into the open. At a convocation of clergy held the previous summer, some 300 texts were deemed heretical and burned. Other heretical writings were now brought to the attention of a provincial synod in July 1413, among them a number of unbound short tracts that had been discovered at the address of an illuminator in Paternoster Row, who confessed that they belonged to Lord Cobham.[8] Arundel retained this evidence against Oldcastle for use at an appropriate moment, which he adjudged to be an assembly at which both Henry and Oldcastle would be present. According to the archbishop the tracts were read

> before the King, and almost all the prelates and nobles of England, in the closet of the King at Kennington [a palace built by the Black Prince in the 1340s and demolished in 1531 by Henry VIII, who used materials from it to construct his palace at Whitehall]. ... Then our King himself expressed his abhorrence of those conclusions, as the worst against the faith and the church he had ever heard. And the said Lord John Oldcastle, being asked by the King whether he thought the said tract was justly and deservedly condemned, said that it was so. On being asked how he could use or possess a tract of this sort, he said that he had never read more than two leaves.[9]

Arundel certainly believed that Oldcastle had supported clergy with Lollard tendencies and thoughts in the dioceses of Hereford, London and Rochester, and possibly elsewhere. Walsingham records that Oldcastle 'had been present in person during their wicked sermons, and put down any hecklers he found by terrifying threats of what the power of the secular sword would do to them', whilst stating that the archbishop of Canterbury did not possess, and never had possessed, the power to license preachers.[10]

Arundel now mentioned to Henry in private that he was concerned to question Oldcastle regarding his potentially heretical beliefs and even to press charges of heresy. In reply Henry said he would approach Oldcastle personally and try to bring him round to the Church's way of thinking. If that proved impossible, he would allow the Church to pursue its own actions with the support of the secular arm of government. It is quite likely that Henry already knew most of Oldcastle's views, for the king's personal chaplain (no friend of Oldcastle) declared that the knight 'attempted to infect the king's highness himself with his deadly poison by his crafty wiles of argument'.[11]

It certainly seems very unlikely that the closeness between the prince and Oldcastle had any effect on Henry's views on Christian beliefs and practices, even if they shared, up to a certain point, a desire for reform in the organisation of the Church. The prince's religious convictions always seem to have been orthodox and it appears that he was desirous that those of others should be so too. The prince is known to have made a pilgrimage to Canterbury in 1403 before the Battle of Shrewsbury, and before taking up the command at Aberystwyth in 1407 he visited Bridlington. Here, fulfilling a vow made earlier, he offered 5 marks at the shrine of his patron saint, John Twenge, the last Englishman to be canonised before the Reformation. (His father had placed Prince Henry under the special protection of John Twenge when he was baptised, at the height of miracles ascribed to Twenge.) This acceptance of the efficacy of pilgrimage, a belief in patron saints and Henry's use of priests in chantry chapels to say Masses for the souls of the dead (not least that of Richard II),[12] is quite at odds with Wycliffe's teachings on how to gain pardon for sins, which was through public confession or confession to a suitable person where this would help ensure repentance, coupled with contrition. On the other hand, Henry was clearly interested in the reform of the Church. In 1421, for example, during a visit to England from his campaigns in France, he addressed a meeting of some 60 abbots and over 300 doctors and monks of the Benedictine Order covering, amongst other matters, the negligence and carelessness of the current masters of the Order.[13] Henry also sought to limit the papacy's claim to fill certain high ecclesiastical offices in England when they fell vacant.[14]

Henry and Oldcastle were still on good terms in July 1413, and Henry must have been hopeful of convincing his friend of the errors of his ways, as he saw it. Thus, the Patent Rolls show that on the 20th Henry issued a warrant to settle, at Michaelmas 1414, the outstanding balance of 400 marks still owed to Oldcastle, Richard Colefox, Thomas Berboure, Walter Gayton and John Andrewe for the clasp (*firmaculum*) that had belonged to Sir Lewis Clifford, Oldcastle and Colefox having been among the executors of Clifford's will.[15] But his attempts to bring Oldcastle back to orthodox thinking failed. At a meeting of the two men in early August at Windsor, Oldcastle expressed unequivocal support and loyalty to the king, but said he could not accept the pope's authority on tenets of Christian teaching where he felt that the Bible either contradicted the Church or at least was ambivalent. This meeting seems to have caused a deep breach in their personal relationship, for it appears that Henry launched a verbal attack on Oldcastle. Fearing for his safety, Oldcastle left without taking his leave of the king, and retreated to Cooling Castle. He was rightly apprehensive, for the king kept to his agreement with the archbishop and, meeting him in Windsor Park on 21 August, ordered him to proceed against Oldcastle.[16]

As recounted earlier, Cooling Castle was a manor house that had been fortified as recently as 1381 by Sir John de Cobham, so its fortifications were fairly new and in good

The west front of Rochester Cathedral, showing the doors on which Oldcastle's citations to appear at Leeds Castle would have been posted. (Author)

repair. Given Oldcastle's known military prowess, church officials were reluctant to approach it, and John Butler, one of Henry's officials, accompanied the messenger sent by the archbishop to summon Oldcastle to a hearing. Both were admitted to Cooling Castle, but Oldcastle refused to attend the hearing. Arundel therefore posted citations on the doors of Rochester Cathedral summoning Oldcastle to appear at Leeds Castle on 11 September,[17] but these were torn down, as were replacements. In his absence, Oldcastle was denounced, condemned and excommunicated, before further attempts at citation were considered for 28 September. It was meanwhile reported to the archbishop that Oldcastle was preparing to defend Cooling.

Deciding to seek Henry's help, Oldcastle wrote out a confession of his faith and went to see the king. At first Henry refused to receive the confession and said it should be sent to the Church as his judge, but Oldcastle persevered and eventually Henry summoned him to his privy chamber. Henry told Oldcastle he had to resolve his beliefs with the Church and not the king, and, following the earlier breach in their friendship and his agreement with Arundel, Henry had him arrested and taken to the Tower. His examination by the clergy, in the persons of Archbishop Arundel, Henry Beaufort, bishop of Winchester and currently chancellor of England,[18] and Richard Clifford,

A brefe Chronycle concernynge the Examinacyon and death of the blessed martyr of Christ syr Johan Oldecastell the lorde Cobham/collected togyther by Johan Bale.

Syr.Iohan.Oldecastel.the.worthy

lorde.Cobham.and.moste.valyaunt.

warryoure.of.Iesus.Christ.

suffred.death.at.London.Anno.1418.

In the latter tyme shall manye be chosen/proued/and puryfyed by fyre/ yet shall the ungodly lyue wyckedly styll and haue no understandynge. Dan.12.

The frontispiece to Bale's *Brefe Chronicle* with its depiction of Sir John Oldcastle.

bishop of London, was fixed to take place on 23 September in the chapter house of St Paul's. Oldcastle prepared himself by copying out his confession, retaining one copy for himself and sending one to the archbishop.

This confession and the record of the subsequent questioning gives us the chance to look in depth at Oldcastle's views on religion and its relationship with the state. As we have seen, those who called themselves Lollards, and even those who didn't, expressed a wide range of ideas and beliefs. Although the belief that the bread taken at Communion remained materially bread, rather than being literally transformed into the body of Christ, was common amongst Lollards, views on such matters as pilgrimages, the worshipping of images, the power of the pope, the need for intercession by clergy, the wealth of the Church and the relationship between the Church and the state varied between individuals, and some held their views more strongly than others. Of concern in understanding Oldcastle's thoughts is how well we can trust the accuracy of the record of his trial. Fortunately, we have the archbishop's official account of the proceedings, which gives us at least a clear impression of the hearings and the statements that Oldcastle read out, so we can be fairly sure of their authenticity. Where accounts of the trial start going into actual dialogue rather than summaries of what was said, we enter the realm of faction – extrapolation from the known facts. Some 130 years later, Arundel's dry account in Latin of the trial was reworked, together with that of the trial in 1407 of John Thorpe, another heretic, into a stirring story of Protestant martyrdom: *A Boke of Thorpe or of John Oldcastelle*. (According to Sir Thomas More, its author was George Constantine, who had helped William Tyndale translate the Bible into English in the 1520s whilst in exile in Antwerp, and who also compiled books that attacked the Catholic church.) Much of it was written as if it was a verbatim record of accusation, with defence and counter-accusation, and it was one of the sources of John Bale's *Brefe Chronicle* record of the trial. Thence, with some further refinement, it made its way into John Foxe's *Actes and monuments*, which was first published in English in 1563.[19]

Both John Bale and John Foxe were champions of Sir John Oldcastle. Of humble origins, Bale was sent to a Carmelite convent to be educated and became a zealous Catholic, only to convert to Protestantism and begin writing plays attacking Catholicism, as a result coming to the attention of Thomas Cromwell, who provided support. With Cromwell's fall, Bale fled to Germany, where he continued writing plays, but also, in 1544, *A Brefe Chronicle concerning the Examination and Death of Sir John Oldcastle, collected by John Bale out of the books and writings of those Popish Prelates which were present*. With the accession of Edward VI in 1547, Bale returned to England and continued writing, his works of this period being described as examples of 'polemical power, showing his learning, his rude vigour of expression, and his want of good taste and moderation'.[20] *A Brefe Chronicle* is not far short of that mark, the preface commenting on those who judged Oldcastle, 'What beastly blockheads these bloody belly-gods were in their unsavoury interrogations.'

John Foxe was a Puritan preacher and author who fled overseas on the accession of Queen Mary in 1553. He had already begun work on a book of Protestant martyrs, and now carried on writing, publishing in 1554 in Latin a first edition of what became *Actes and monuments of these latter and perillous dayes, touching matters of the Church, wherein ar comprehended and described the great persecutions horrible troubles, that have bene wrought and practised by the Romishe prelates, speciallye in this Realme of England and Scotlande, from the yeare of our Lorde, a thousande, unto the tyme nowe present. Gathered and collected according to the true copies*, usually shortened to *Actes and monuments* and popularly known by the rather shorter title as *The Book of Martyrs*. With the aid of manuscripts sent to him from England, Foxe carried on his work, publishing in 1559 a second edition which included those martyred up to 1556. With the accession of Elizabeth I, Foxe returned to England and continued updating his work, including new details from sources he could now access, publishing a first edition in English in 1563, and a further improved second edition in 1570. Minor changes were made to the third and fourth editions, published in 1576 and 1583. Foxe's work has been criticised as one-sided and at times credulous, but his research was detailed and he availed himself of sources which have since been lost. Bale's work is much more propagandist in style. It should also be borne in mind that Foxe is thought to have had a moderating influence on Calvinism when he was living on the Continent, and also opposed the martyrdom of Anabaptists and Jesuits, writing strongly worded letters to Queen Elizabeth on the subject.[21] As the probably 'truer' versions of events, Archbishop Arundel's record and Foxe's account form the core of what follows regarding Oldcastle's trial, with the occasional reference to Bale's chronicle.

In his initial confession to the king, Oldcastle propounded the view that those on earth are divided into

> three divers estates, that is to say, into priesthood, knighthood, and the commons; among whom the will of God is, that the one should aid the other, but not destroy the other. The priests, first of all, secluded from all worldliness, should conform their lives utterly to the examples of Christ and his apostles. Evermore should they be occupied in preaching and teaching the Scriptures purely, and in giving wholesome examples of good living to the other two degrees of men. More modest also, more loving, gentle, and lowly in spirit, should they be, than any other sort of people.

The duties of the knighthood included 'to preserve God's people from oppressors, tyrants and thieves, and to see the clergy supported so long as they teach purely, pray rightly, and minister the sacraments freely'. Of the commons, he wrote that they should bear 'true obedience to the aforesaid ministers of God, their kings, civil governors, and priests. The right office of these is justly to occupy every man his faculty, be it merchandise, handicraft, or the tilth of the ground.'

... Finally, this is my faith also, That God will ask no more of a Christian believer in this life, but only to obey the precepts of that most blessed law. If any prelate of the church require more, or else any other kind of obedience, than this to be used, he contemneth Christ, exalting himself above God, and so becomes an open antichrist.[22]

As was usual in such statements of faith, including Swynderby's to Bishop Trefnant in the 1390s (see pages 54-56), few would openly condemn themselves in what they wrote. What really mattered was what they didn't write. Even earlier than Swynderby's statement was Sir John Clanvowe's in *The Two Ways*. Sir John Clanvowe, (as mentioned in Chapter One) was either the uncle or the father of Sir Thomas Clanvowe, a colleague of Thomas Oldcastle, John's uncle, and was one of the 'Lollard knights' close to Richard II. *The Two Ways*,[23] a treatise of some 10,000 words, sets out his views on Christianity, which largely follow what is written in the Bible: to be meek, to fear God, to shun the seven deadly sins ('coveting to have too muchel of the world is a vice'), 'to travail truly for that that men needeth, and, if men get more over that, for to help therewith their needy brethren and neighbours'. Clanvowe denounces the 'foul stinking muck of this false failing world', and goes on to decry the failings of his own class:

> For the world hold them worshipful that been great warriors and fighters and that destroyen and winned many lands and wasten and given much good [wealth] to them that have enough and that dispenden outrageously in meat, in drink, in clothing, in building, and in living in ease, sloth and many other sins ... And of such folk men make books and songs and readen and singen of them for to hold the mind of their deeds the longer here upon earth.

He goes on to reject swearing, drinking, gaming and killing, *The Two Ways* thereby becoming an early pacifist writing, but all based on Biblical text and no other theological writings as far as can be discovered.[24] Clanvowe followed Wycliffe and others in going back to what the Bible says without the need for a clerical intermediary, but there is nothing heretical in what he writes: nothing against worshipping images, going on pilgrimage, the effectiveness of a priest in administering the sacraments, or even the payment of tithes to clergy who are not carrying out their duties in a proper manner. The Church as an institution is not mentioned. Assuming the role of a lay preacher, and an unlicensed one at that, Clanvowe was suggesting that the layman had no need of an intermediary between himself and God. He was well aware that the Church would resent such a suggestion. After he had denounced those who lived 'outrageously' luxurious lives and commended those who live meekly 'and suffer patiently wrongs that other folks doen and sayen to them', he went on to say 'such folk the world scorneth and holdeth them lollers and losels [good-for-nothing] fools and shameful wretches. But surely God holdeth them most wise and most worshipful ...'. Towards the end of his life Clanvowe praised the Lollards and aspired to become one. Are we to see a similar journey reflected in the life of Sir John Oldcastle?

At the start of the hearing Arundel offered Oldcastle absolution if he were to meekly ask for it. In reply Oldcastle replied that he needed no absolution and read out a further statement that he had prepared. From this we can be fairly certain of his views (the spelling is adjusted to that in current use):

> … I believe that most worshipful sacrament of the altar is Christ's body in form of bread, the same body that was born of the blessed virgin, Our Lady Saint Mary, hung on the cross, died, and buried, the third day rose from the death to life, the which body is now glorified in heaven.
>
> Also as for the sacrament of penance I believe that it is necessary to every man that shall be saved to forsake sin and do due penance for his sin previously done with true confession and contrition and due satisfaction as God's law defines and teaches and otherwise may he not be saved. Which penance I desire all men to do.
>
> And as of images I understand that they are not of belief but that they were ordained since the belief was given of Christ by sufferance of the Church to be calendars [guides] to simple men to represent and bring to mind the Passion of Our Jesus Christ, and martyrdom and good living of other saints, and that whosoever does worship to dead images that is due to God or puts faith hope or trust in help of them as he should do to God or has affection in one more than in another he does in that the great sin of idolatry.
>
> Also I believe this full that every man on this earth is a pilgrim towards bliss or towards pain and that he knows not nor will know nor keep the holy commandments of God in his living here, although he go on pilgrimage to the whole world, shall be damned when he dies, and he who knows the holy commandments of God and keeps them to his end, he shall be saved, even though he never in his life went on pilgrimage as men use now to Canterbury or to Rome or to any other place.[25]

Having heard Oldcastle's statement and noticed the omissions regarding areas where the Church and Lollard preachings diverged, it is not surprising that Arundel replied: 'Come hither, sir John: in this your writing are many good things contained, and right catholic also, we deny it not; but ye must consider those articles whereof, as yet, no mention is made in this your bill: and, therefore, ye must yet declare us your mind more plainly. As thus, whether ye hold, affirm, and believe, that in the sacrament of the altar, after the consecration rightly done by a priest, remaineth material bread, or not?' This question, and that of the supremacy of the pope, became the two main issues debated over the next few days.

With no answer forthcoming from Oldcastle, other than his referring to what he had already written, the archbishop deferred the proceedings to the following Monday, 25 September, when Oldcastle would have to respond to a list of four questions which

Portrait of Archbishop Arundel.
(Lambeth Palace)

the archbishop would provide him with on the Saturday. Those questions covered transubstantiation, the power and authority of the pope, whether any priest – once ordained – had the power to hear confessions and give absolution, and pilgrimage: 'Holy Church hath determined, that it is meritorious to a christian man, to go on pilgrimage to holy places, and there specially to worship holy relics and images of saints, apostles, and martyrs, confessors, and all other saints besides, approved by the church of Rome. – How feel ye this article?'

The hearing resumed on the Monday, this time at the home of the Dominican Friars at Ludgate, in the presence of Arundel and the bishops of London, Winchester and Bangor, together with 11 doctors of divinity and friars, plus 'a great sort more of priests, monks, canons, friars, parish-clerks, bell-ringers, pardoners, [who] disdained [Oldcastle] with innumerable mocks and scorns, reckoning him to be a horrible heretic, and a man accursed of God', as described by the partial Bale. We now move into the world of faction developed from the bones of Arundel's account of the proceedings.[26]

Oldcastle was asked by Archbishop Arundel whether he was prepared to ask for absolution. In a letter Arundel sent to the bishops, who were to be encouraged to see it used by preachers combatting Lollard heresies, he simply says that Oldcastle 'would seek no absolution on these matters from us, but from God alone'.[27] Foxe, following Bale, goes somewhat further and says that Oldcastle fell to his knees and asked God for forgiveness. Rising again, he said, 'Lo, good people! lo!; for the breaking of God's law and his great commandments, they never yet cursed me, but, for their own laws and traditions, most cruelly do they handle both me and other men; and therefore, both they and their laws, by the promise of God, shall be utterly destroyed.' Foxe and Bale recount that 'At this the archbishop and his company were not a little blemished', to which, if the exchange is accurately reported, one might add the assumption that they were angered by Oldcastle's words and determined to deal harshly with him.

Arundel now pressed Oldcastle to state his beliefs. In his letter to the bishops, Arundel says he asked him his views on the sacrament, summing up Oldcastle's reply as follows:

> Just as Christ, passing here on earth, had in himself divinity and humanity, but with his divinity veiled and invisible under his humanity, which was evident and visible in him, so in the sacrament of the altar is the true body and the true bread; it is bread indeed which we see, and the body of Christ, which we do not see, is veiled beneath it. And he explicitly denied the faith concerning matters to do with the sacrament in the aforementioned paper, the decision of the Church, translated for him by us, determined by the Holy Roman Church and blessed men of learning, for the future and the present. But he said that if it is the decision of the Church, and after the Church became endowed, and poison was spread in the Church, and not before, it is done against the sacred Scripture.

Foxe recounts the exchange as follows: 'I believe fully and faithfully in the universal laws of God; I believe that all is true which is contained in the holy sacred scriptures of the Bible; finally I believe all that my Lord God would I should believe', quoting what the Bible said concerning the sacrament. Arundel pressed on, trying to establish whether Oldcastle believed that the bread and wine were still bread and wine after the consecration, or were the body and blood of Christ. Oldcastle responded with his own interpretation of the Bible, repeating what he had said in his statement to Henry: 'I believe that in the sacrament of the altar is Christ's very body in form of bread, the same that was born of the Virgin Mary, done on the cross, dead, and buried, and that on the third day arose from death to life, which is now glorified in heaven.' Oldcastle having again avoided answering the direct question, many of the assembled clergy now pressed the point, reiterating the question as to whether or not the host was material bread after the consecration. Oldcastle repeated that he believed it was Christ's body in the form of bread and gained agreement for this view from Arundel.

But still the doctrinal question remained, and Oldcastle elaborated his view further: 'It is both Christ's body and bread; I shall prove it thus: for like as Christ's dwelling here upon the earth had in him both Godhead and manhood, and had the invisible Godhead covered under that manhood, which was only visible and seen in him; so, in the sacrament of the altar, is Christ's very body and bread also, as I believe. The bread is the thing that we see with our eyes; the body of Christ, which is his flesh and his blood, is thereunder hid, and not seen but in faith' – a view that the process was a spiritual one and not a material transformation. The clergy 'smiled'

Portraits of Oldcastle all stem from an initial image, probably that shown top left, which some image libraries claim was made c.1410. From the dates of later versions all that can be said with some degree of certainty is that the original was drawn by the end of the 1600s. That bottom right was being used in 2020 on the cover of the menu at the Sir John Oldcastle pub in Farringdon Road, London.

and stated that that was a 'foul heresy'. Oldcastle retorted that nowhere did the Bible use the word 'material', and that therefore 'my faith hath nothing to do therewith ... St Paul the apostle was, I am sure, as wise as you be now, and more godly learned, and he called it bread, writing to the Corinthians: The bread that we break, saith he, is it not the partaking of the body of Christ? Lo! he called it bread! and not Christ's body, but a means whereby we receive Christ's body.' The clergy responded that 'Paul must be otherwise understood'. Oldcastle, asking how the clergy justified their view that the bread became the body of Christ, was answered that the Church had so determined.

According to Walsingham, who is mellow in his choice of words recording the trial (unlike when sometimes writing about Oldcastle, which suggests he was working from a copy of Arundel's record of events), Oldcastle then gave his views on

> the sacrament of repentance and confession, [saying and asserting] that if someone found himself trapped in a serious sin from which he could not see how to escape by his own efforts, it was expedient and good for such a person to go to a holy and wise priest for counsel from him. But it was not necessary for salvation that the man should make confession of this sin of his to his own curate or some other priest, even if one was available, seeing that through contrition alone a sin of this kind could be wiped out and the sinner cleansed.[28]

Arundel continued his questioning: 'Sir John, we sent you a writing concerning the faith of this blessed sacrament, clearly determined by the Church of Rome our mother, and by the holy doctors.'

Oldcastle retorted, 'I know none holier than is Christ and his apostles. And as for that determination, I wot it is none of theirs; for it standeth not with the Scriptures, but manifestly against them. If it be the Church's as ye say it is, it hath been hers only since she received the great poison of worldly possessions, and not before.'

This caused some mutterings within the ranks of the clergy and brought the hearing to the subject of the position of the Church and pope. This, it soon becomes clear, was the issue that most concerned Oldcastle. The teaching of the Church concerning the material of the bread was just a part of what he felt had gone wrong as the Church moved away from its roots and core beliefs. It was not long before he was telling the assembly that 'the laws that ye have made are nothing to His glory, but only for your vain glory and abominable covetousness'. This was quickly denounced as heresy. Oldcastle was unsurprised at this reaction, saying that

> they that rebuke your vicious living must needs be heretics, and that must your doctors prove, when you have no Scripture to do it. ... To judge you as you be, we need go no further than to your own proper acts. Where do you find in all God's law, that ye should thus sit in judgement on any Christian man, or yet give sentence upon any other man unto death, as ye do here daily?

The clergy tried to justify their actions by comparing them with Christ judging Judas, but Oldcastle argued that Christ judged himself and not his apostle, returning to his theme that the bishops of Rome were initially martyrs and true followers of Christ.

> But indeed since that same time, one [pope] hath put down another, one hath poisoned another, one hath cursed another, and one hath slain another, and done much more mischief besides, as all the chronicles tell. And let all men consider well this, that Christ was meek and merciful; the pope is proud and a tyrant: Christ was poor and forgave; the pope is rich and a malicious manslayer, as his daily acts do prove him: Rome is the very nest of Antichrist; and out of that nest come all the disciples of him; of whom prelates, priests and monks, are the body, these pilled [shaven] friars are the tail behind.

The hearing continued, with members of the panel often becoming frustrated by the strength of Oldcastle's arguments, a description of the trial that first Bale and then Foxe would be only too happy to recount. The questioning moved on to the ability of all priests to hear confession. Oldcastle's reply was again direct and to the point. 'But if he be an idiot, or a man of vicious living that is my curate, I ought rather to flee from him than to seek unto him; for sooner might I catch evil of him that is naught, than any goodness towards my soul-health.'

On the fourth article, concerning pilgrimages, he stated: 'But I say this unto you, and I would all the world should mark it, that with your shrines and idols, your feigned absolutions and pardons, ye draw unto you the substance, wealth, and chief pleasures of all christian realms.'

'Why Sir,' said one of the clerks, 'will ye not worship good images?' to which Oldcastle replied 'What worship should I give unto them?'

One of the friars present then suggested 'Sir, will ye worship the cross of Christ, that he died upon?' to which Oldcastle replied 'Yet once again I ask you, What worship I should do unto it?' One of the clerks responded this time, saying 'Such worship as Paul speaketh of, and that is this; God forbid that I should joy, but only in the cross of Jesus Christ.' Oldcastle then spread his arms out wide, saying 'This is a very cross, yea, and so much better than your cross of wood, in that it was created of God; yet will not I seek to have it worshipped.' The bishop of London then chipped in: 'Sir, ye wot well that he died on a material cross', to which Oldcastle retorted 'Yea, and I wot also, that our salvation came not in by that material cross, but alone by him who died thereupon.'

Questioned towards the end of the proceedings by Thomas Netter, a Carmelite friar and afterwards Henry V's confessor, as to what he felt of the pope, Oldcastle's frustrations seemed to come ever more to the fore: '... he and you together make up the great Antichrist, of whom he is the great head, you bishops, priests, prelates, and monks are the body; and the begging friars are the tail, for they cover the filthiness of you both, with their subtle sophistry ...'.[29]

This dialogue makes for good reading, but how does it relate to Arundel's account of the proceedings, from which these exchanges are developed? Arundel himself says that Oldcastle

> denied that the faith, as touching the said sacrament, determined by the Romish church and holy doctors … was the determination of the holy church. But if it be the determination of the church, he said that it was done contrary to the scriptures; after the church was endowed, and after that poison was poured into the church, and not before.

Then he records that Oldcastle said it was not necessary to seek a priest as an intermediary to confess one's sins in order to gain salvation,

> forasmuch as only by contrition such sin can be wiped away, and the sinner himself purged. As concerning worshipping the cross, he said and affirmed, That only the body of Christ which did hang upon the cross, is to be worshipped … And being demanded what honour he would do unto the image of the cross, he answered by express words: That he would only do it that honour, that he would make it clean and lay it up safe. As touching the power and authority of … the archbishops, bishops and other prelates, he said, that the pope is very Antichrist, that is, the head; that the archbishops, bishops and other prelates be his members, and that the friars be his tail.

Arundel's words are gentler, but the meaning and the spirit of Oldcastle are the same.

The day wore on, and wanting to draw the hearing to a close, Arundel asked whether Oldcastle would submit to the Church or leave himself in great danger.

Oldcastle was defiant and spirited to the end. 'I know not to what purpose I should otherwise submit me. Much more have you offended me, than ever I offended you, in thus troubling me before this multitude. … Do with me what you will.' Without more ado, Arundel stood up and read out a bill condemning Oldcastle as a heretic, and delivered him to the secular jurisdiction to be put to death.

8

Rising, Flight and Capture

Oldcastle was condemned to death as a heretic on 25 September 1413 and returned to the Tower of London, but Henry persuaded Arundel to grant a stay of execution for 40 days in the hope that Oldcastle would use this time to recant.[1] The Tower was not, however, noted for holding its prisoners securely. People escaped through bribing or drugging the guards, or by wearing their wife's clothes.[2] When Roger IV Mortimer was imprisoned in the Tower in 1323, he was able to have letters smuggled out to a surprising number of people, and escaped when one of the guards drugged most of the garrison who were celebrating the feast of St Peter ad Vincula. The guard then crowbarred Mortimer's cell door open, completing the escape in company with Roger, the cook turning a blind eye as the pair scrambled up a chimney onto the rooftops, and fled over the walls with the help of rope ladders.[3] In July 1414 John Whitlooke or Whitlock, who had been a groom to Richard II and who encouraged belief that the king was still alive, was also to escape with the help of those working at the Tower, although a porter who was accused of aiding the escape was executed.[4]

Oldcastle was able to use the laxness in security to make contact with London's community of Lollards, arranging for them to post bills in various parts of London that urged their readers not to believe the 'slanders and lies' that his 'enemies' had been putting about. The bills asserted that he had been wrongfully convicted and imprisoned, and proclaimed that he believed that 'in the blessed sacrament of the altar is verily and truly Christ's Body, in form of bread'. This of course left much unsaid on this core, potentially heretical belief. An abjuration by Oldcastle of his beliefs, which exists from this time, seems to have been drawn up by the clergy in the hope that Oldcastle would recant and sign it, though possibly it was designed as 'fake news', counter-propaganda to the bills being posted around London.[5] Perhaps Oldcastle encouraged the notion amongst his gaolers that he might abjure Lollardy to ease his conditions in the Tower, for those prisoners deemed most troublesome to the state were shackled. For whatever reason, the conditions of his imprisonment seem to have been relaxed and he was soon released from his fetters.[6]

On 19 October, Oldcastle escaped. Stow records that he got over the walls at night,[7] but most chroniclers simply state the fact of the escape, not how it was done. In the sixteenth century Robert Redmayne, possibly having access to records since lost, surmised that he bribed some of the guards.[8] But there is yet another possibility. On his escape Oldcastle was immediately given refuge by William Fisher (also known as William Parceminer/Parchmyner/Parchmener), a parchment maker in Smithfield,[9] who was eventually captured in October 1416.[10] At his trial, which quickly followed his arrest, Fisher was charged with having, along with others unnamed, broken into the Tower to effect Oldcastle's release. According to one version of this tale, Oldcastle was imprisoned in the Beauchamp Tower in the inner ward, when a group of London's citizens broke into it (possibly with the connivance of the guards), and set him free.[11]

The Rising

Oldcastle appears to have remained at Fisher's house until the outbreak of the Lollard revolt on 6 January the following year, or so at least Fisher testified at his trial. Having turned down several opportunities to recant his beliefs, and now at liberty, Oldcastle seems to have set himself on the course of rebellion, sending out messages to Lollard groups around the country. Clearly, he held his religious views deeply, but it is unclear what his personal feelings now were towards his old companion, Henry V. It would seem that Oldcastle, and perhaps those Lollards whom he knew, had decided that, with attempts to take some worldly wealth from the Church via parliament having failed, and with any hope dashed that Henry as king would push for major reform of the Church and show a leniency towards heterodox views, to go for broke with rebellion was the only remaining alternative. The shape of the plan emerged from the confessions made at the trials after the rising, some of which were to result in execution and some in pardon, often depending on the individual's degree of involvement in the plot. The first part of the plan was to seize the king and his brothers at Eltham Palace, to the east of London. The plotters were to be disguised as a group of mummers, the scheme perhaps being modelled on an attempt on Henry IV's life in the early years of his reign. A gathering of Lollards in London would then lend their support to the new government.[12] According to the *Chronicle of London* for 1413–18 the plan was to kill 'the king and his lords', and the official indictment after the event certainly charged the plotters with the intention of killing the king, his brothers, the prelates and other magnates, as well as despoiling churches, forcing members of religious orders to earn their living, and dividing the kingdom into fiefdoms. Oldcastle was to be declared regent.[13] But those charges could have been exaggerated to stir up resentment against the plotters and Lollards in general.

Oldcastle may have hoped that there would be support for the rising from those who believed that Richard II was still alive (a pretender then lived in Scotland), from Scotland and perhaps from Wales. But England had grown tired of the warfare in its own lands brought about by the Welsh rising on the border counties of England and recent raids by the French on the southern coast from Dartmouth in the west to Winchelsea in the east.

The Peasants' Revolt was now over 30 years in the past, but one wonders what memories of it lingered on in different sections of society, for in some ways Oldcastle's

An illustration that shows the betrayal of Oldcastle's rising from the *Pageant of the Birth, Life and Death of Richard Beauchamp, Earl of Warwick, K.G., 1389–1439*, written between 1485 and 1490.
The caption that accompanies the illustration says:
Here sheweth, howe after the cummyng home of Erle Richard from the holy lands Henry Vth then beyng king of Englond was secretly enfourmed of a prevey and sodeyn Insurrection of traiterous heretikes, which sodenly by nyght purposed to have taken & kept the kyng undre their rule & subieccion and after by his autoritie to have destroied the Church of Englond and to slee the p[re]lates, and distribute their possessions ayenst the honor of God after their indiscrete advises and pleasirs.

rebellion resembled it. The leaders of that Revolt had met on occasion in London, where they could be in contact with groups of its citizens who were entrusted with seizing the city's gates, whilst supporters gathered from the counties closest to London. Messengers were sent to centres of potential support to lay the plan for a wider uprising. This seems to have been Oldcastle's pattern too.

The lessons of the Peasants' Revolt also informed Henry's response, with early action replacing the inaction of the authorities in 1381. After ten days in which the government appeared to be making no moves, though they may have organised searches of the homes of known Lollard sympathisers in the hope of finding Oldcastle, on 28 October they finally broadcast news of his escape and issued a proclamation forbidding anyone from harbouring him.[14] Meanwhile, Archbishop Arundel had been sending out his reports on the trial to all the bishops in the province of Canterbury, along with a set of condemnations of Oldcastle's opinions to be read out in all churches. On 10 December he publicly excommunicated Oldcastle. It's possible, of course, that these measures helped to inform those who held Lollard sympathies of events in London, and so swelled support for the forthcoming rising.[15]

On 28 October Henry dismissed the keeper of the Tower, Robert Morley, for his negligence,[16] and spies were employed to try to uncover Oldcastle's plans. It was through one of these spies that the plot began to unravel. (After the rising was over, Thomas Burton, recorded as the king's spy, was paid 100 shillings for his services.)[17] It would seem that Oldcastle had sent letters to groups of Lollards in the Midlands, the West Country and the south-east, urging them to rendezvous at St Giles's Fields (or the part then known as Fickett's Field), which lay between London and Westminster in the vicinity of what is now Lincoln's Inn Fields, over the night of 9 January to the early morning of the 10th, to coincide with a rising of the city's apprentices. The better-off were asked to take up arms, and the less well-off were offered money to do so.

On 5 January 1414 two London Lollards, John de Burgh, a carpenter, and Thomas Kempford lost their nerve and gave details of the plot to the government; they were each to be rewarded with an annuity of 10 marks a year. Now fully cognisant of the plans, Henry had a group of Oldcastle's supporters seized at 10 o'clock on the evening of Twelfth Night at the Sign of the Axe, the premises of a Lollard carpenter by the name of John Burgate, just outside Bishopsgate.[18] It appears that this group were the counterfeit mummers, who soon confessed and were imprisoned.[19] Stow and *Gregory's Chronicle* suggest that the seizure of the king and his brothers was to be attempted on Epiphany (6 January), a date on which it would have been appropriate for mummers to perform, but three days before the proposed assembly on St Giles's Fields, which would have left a three-day vacuum. Certainly, if the mummers were arrested at 10pm, they weren't leaving much time to get to Eltham to perform that evening.

Two drawings in the marginalia of a Flemish manuscript illustrated by Jehan de Grise in 1344 showing mummers of that period. (MS. Bodl. 264, fols. 21v & 181v, © Bodleian Libraries)

Above: Illustration of Eltham Palace from the south-west, c.1320, drawn by Peter Urmston. In 1295 the bishop of Durham, Antony Bek, acquired the manor of Eltham. He proceeded to develop the site into one of his palaces, constructing a defensive stone wall and a great hall with an elaborate tiled floor, known from excavations. On his death, Bek left the palace to Prince Edward, the future Edward II, who extended the area within the fortified walls. Edward III carried out extensive renovations in the mid-1300s, and Henry IV built a new set of timber-framed apartments including a bath-house. He was to spend 10 of his 13 Christmases as king at Eltham, and created a fine palace for his son Henry V.[20] (© Historic England)
Below: The stone bridge built across the moat of Eltham Palace in 1396. (Author)

Henry then set about preparing to deal with the planned rising. He warned the mayor of London about the plot, and, probably now aware of at least the vicinity in which Oldcastle was hiding, set spies to watch any move he made in Smithfield. It seems that on 6 January Oldcastle left Fisher's house, possibly moving to an inn in Smithfield known as 'The Wrasteleyre on the Hope'. Certainly the inn acted as an interim gathering place for incoming groups of Lollards, and was where a leader of Essex Lollards distributed wages to his men.[21] By now, Oldcastle must have known of the failure of the first part of his plan, and to also have surmised that details of the rising were therefore known to the king; hence the need to move his lodgings. However, it would have been impossible, at that late date, to prevent those already on the move to London from continuing their journey and making their fateful rendezvous.

On 7 January, Henry notified sheriffs throughout England of the plot which sought 'the destruction of the catholic faith, of the king's person and the estate of the lords and great men of the realm spiritual and temporal', and ordered them to announce proclamations against making, procuring or attending unlawful assemblies of any kind.[22] On the 8th he moved his family from Eltham to Westminster so he was better placed to take action against those assembling on St Giles's Fields.

On the evening of the 9th, Henry had the gates of the city held by his own men to prevent London Lollards and apprentices leaving for the rendezvous. Walsingham states that rumours suggested 'that about fifty thousand servants and apprentices together with some of the citizens who were their masters would have left the city that night to oppose the king'.[23] This seems an unlikely number, but even so, Oldcastle must have expected Londoners to provide the majority of his army. Not long after midnight, accompanied by his brothers, Archbishop Arundel, the earl of Warwick and other lords, the king led an armed force to St Giles's Fields.[24] Some of his counsellors thought this an unwise move, fearing that some 25,000 armed men might be assembled, and they advised that waiting for daylight might be the better plan.[25] Possibly already aware of rumours of the discovery of their plot, and now faced with this force, the Lollards tried to disperse as fast as they assembled. Chroniclers of the times talk of up to 20,000 trying to reach St Giles's Fields, but clearer analysis of those captured and brought to trial afterwards – just some 80 souls – would suggest that far fewer were involved. It may well be that the chroniclers, usually members of religious foundations, were keen to exaggerate the numbers to indicate the threat to the established order that Lollardy posed, and show how thoroughly the rising was crushed. Adding together the names of those known to have been arrested, wanted, tried, executed or pardoned, produces a total of only two to three hundred known supporters of the rising.[26] A further unspecified number may have been killed in the fracas in the dark, though most of the chronicles do not mention that anyone was slain; whilst those arriving later would have become aware of what was happening, and had a chance to turn tail and warn others still en route to the rendezvous. Oldcastle himself escaped – perhaps he never even went to St Giles's Fields, fearful of what he might find there.

The Rising's supporters

Of those known to have taken part in the rising, one of the most prominent, after Oldcastle, was Sir Roger Acton, a fellow campaigner on the Welsh Marches against Glyndwr. Acton was a weaver's son from Shrewsbury, who had done well enough in the wars to establish himself as a landowner at Sutton, near Tenbury in Worcestershire. In 1403 he was a squire in the king's household and served with Sir John Greyndour. He later became sheriff of Shropshire, in which role he relieved Montgomery Castle from a siege by Glyndwr's forces in 1405, despite having to borrow money to pay his soldiers.[27] He had also served as constable of Criccieth and Ludlow castles.[28] Since 1407 Acton had been encouraging preachers to speak out against images and pilgrimages.[29]

Another veteran of those wars who was involved in the rising was Sir Thomas Talbot of Davington, near Faversham in Kent, though he was a relative newcomer to the county, hailing from the Yorkshire/Lancashire border; he had been close to Richard II. His brother, Henry, was involved in pro-Ricardian plots against both Henry IV and Henry V, plots that were eventually to bring about his own death. Sir Thomas was constable of Montgomery Castle in 1403 and 1405, and as such might have known Sir Roger Acton, if not Oldcastle himself. Thomas managed to become reconciled with Henry IV.

Along with the handful of knights, there were 15 esquires and gentlemen, including Richard Colefox[30] (who, together with Oldcastle, had been an executor of the will of Sir Lewis Clifford, one of the 'Lollard knights', probably appointed to that role by Thomas Clanvowe);[31] Robert Harley of London, who was possibly an esquire of Oldcastle's; likewise John (or Nicholas) Hooper, who remained at large at least until 1428, although his servant Howel ap David was amongst those taken prisoner and executed;[32] and Thomas Noverary of Leicestershire. The rest mainly comprised an assortment of chaplains, weavers, shoemakers, glovers, tailors, goldsmiths, brewers, carpenters, ploughmen, smiths, thatchers and labourers. Amongst them was William Morley, a rich brewer from Dunstable, Hertfordshire, who is alleged to have been offered overlordship of the county if the rising was a success. He brought with him two horses with gold trappings and a pair of gilt spurs ready for his promotion. Having escaped from St Giles's Fields, he was apprehended, along with Robert Harley and John Purvey, an influential Lollard writer and a former secretary to Wycliffe, at the Cock Inn in Turnmill Street, where they sought lodgings with sympathisers to the Lollard cause.[33]

The involvement of Oldcastle's relatives, the Brookes, has been mentioned, and through them we meet again Richard Cheddar. During the first session of parliament in 1404 (at which Oldcastle represented Herefordshire), Cheddar accompanied Sir Thomas Brooke, one of Somerset's MPs and the father-in-law of Oldcastle's step-daughter. Cheddar was assaulted for reasons unknown by John Savage, one of the king's esquires, during which his head was badly injured and his nose almost severed. The assault resulted in a petition to parliament, which eventually led to the passing of the Assaulting Servants of Knights of Parliament Act, a statute that is important in the history of Commons privilege. Cheddar was a particularly violent man who subsequently sought to ambush Savage. He had to undertake not to harm the bishop of Salisbury or his ministers or servants, and was charged with haranguing and threatening jurors who were about to decide against him in a case concerning tenants on one of his estates. He was also accused by a woman of imprisoning and murdering her husband, then planning to rape her, it being the manorial custom that any widow committing fornication would lose her tenurial rights. Cheddar does not seem like a typical Lollard, but after Oldcastle's rising – though there is no indication he was present – he had to give surety for not supporting or aiding Oldcastle. This was probably due to his close ties with the Brookes rather than because of any religious leanings.[34]

During 10 January a commission of oyer and terminer was established, consisting of the lord mayor, two lords and three judges, to try the 80 Lollards who had been captured in the preceding 24 hours.[35] On the following day the government had to issue proclamations that no-one was to seize the goods of anyone accused of Lollardy, or take any action against those accused except by order of the king, for some citizens appear to have been taking advantage of the situation, sometimes accusing their neighbours of Lollardy simply with the aim of pilfering their goods in their absence upon arrest.[36] That same day the commission started its work, probably finding 11 guilty and sentencing them to death forthwith, for on 12 January the balance of those captured, 69 in number, were condemned to death, an ecclesiastical court working alongside the secular one finding seven of them heretics. On the 13th, somewhere between 36 and 39 people were hanged as traitors at St Giles's Fields in batches on four pairs of gallows, the bodies of the seven who had been found guilty of heresy then being burned.[37] Those executed included Robert Harley, William Reyneham, son and heir of Sir Edward Reyneham, a tenant of some of Oldcastle's lands in Suffolk[38] (each described as a gentleman), and the brewer William Morley, who was one of those condemned as a heretic. A week later four more were hanged: a priest by the name of John Beverley, an unnamed 'textwriter' of Clerkenwell, a glover of London Bridge and possibly the Eltham plotter John Burgate.[39] At the same time commissions had been sent to the sheriffs in the counties on 11 January to arrest leading plotters, resulting in the arrest, convictions and deaths of Oldcastle's squire, John Brown, seized in Oxford;[40] the chaplain Walter Blake, leader of a contingent of Lollards from Bristol;[41] and Sir Roger Acton, who was convicted of treason. Acton's body was left hanging from the gallows for a month before being cut down and buried beneath them.[42]

The low number of those arrested who were found guilty of heresy might indicate either that most of them recanted (though there was little point, as they had already been condemned to death and would only be burned after their death), or that they had other grievances against Lancastrian rule, joining the rising in the hope of personal gain and thus convicted 'solely' of treason. Perhaps some of them were simply adventurers, attracted by offers of money and high rewards for high stakes. One of the problems the prosecutors faced was determining whether the beliefs held by those accused arose from ignorance due to a lack of education or were truly heretical views, which may provide a better explanation as to why so few were burned as heretics. From what we know of this period, it seems that individuals held a wide range of views with little consistency amongst those described as Lollards. Yet one point would seem to be clear: the inquiries made after the rising showed that most of those involved had come from the areas that had always been most affected by Lollardy.

From Derbyshire came a contingent headed by a chaplain named William Ederyk, who had been preaching Lollard views for a while, thanks to the protection of his patron Thomas Tykhill. It seems that Tykhill equipped the London-bound party, for the weavers, smiths and thatchers of which it comprised were well supplied. Three of the Derbyshire men were taken and hanged, while Ederyk escaped, and although he was later captured, he was treated very leniently. He seems to have had influential backers. Tykhill himself was arrested, although he had not taken part in the rising, and was eventually released. Bail was provided by Sir Richard Stanhope and Sir Roger Leche, the latter being one of the knights thrown into the Tower in the autumn of 1411 during the crisis in which it was suggested that Henry IV should abdicate in favour of Prince Henry.[43] Another of those knights was Sir Thomas Chaworth, who was somehow implicated in the rising despite his loyalty to Henry V, orders for his arrest being issued on 8 January. Once taken, he was put in the Tower, but released from his chains in early February after bonds worth 1,000 marks were given by his friends, and pardoned and freed from the Tower altogether in May.[44]

As for those from neighbouring Leicestershire, on 5 January a group that included those subsequently described as a farmer, a ploughman, a chaplain, a 'webster' or weaver, and an ironmonger assembled in Leicester, equipped with swords and bows. They seem to have been genuine Lollards, three of their number preaching that confession to priests was unnecessary and that pilgrimages were valueless, but then Leicester had been an important centre of Lollard heresy, hosting preachers such as John Aston, Philip Repyndon and William Swynderby (the latter apparently inspiring considerable support amongst the townspeople). Also present at St Giles's Fields and imprisoned in London after the rising was Roger Goldsmith, a Leicester burgess who had represented the town in the parliament of 1406. From south Leicestershire came another group, where a 'scrivener' or clerk by the name of Thomas Scott was known to have distributed Lollard bills. Some of these bills were said by a subsequent jury to have been composed by Oldcastle himself, and included attacks on the Church's view of sacraments, confession and pilgrimages. The south Leicestershire group included Thomas Noveray, described as a gentleman, and another who was probably his son. A further, larger group gathered at Kibworth Harcourt under the leadership of Walter Gilbert. Some of these men may have been 'bought', two of them receiving the large sum of 20s for their aid, with the money possibly being provided by Noveray, who is known to have sold his goods before departing for London. Walter Gilbert and his brother were amongst those hanged after being captured on St Giles's Fields, whilst Scott was pardoned in December 1414. Noveray gained a pardon in January 1415 and then recanted his heretical views.[45]

Others, including a hosier and a fuller, came from Northampton, and there was a group from Daventry led by a 'hostiler' (presumably an inn-keeper) and a parchment-maker, that included a woman called Eleanora Warde, one of the few female Lollards known by name.[46]

One of the larger groups came from Bristol, as we know from information gathered by commissions sent out by the government on 11 January to investigate those who might have supported the rising. On 8 February local juries sat in Bristol and handed out their indictments, which were sent to the court of the King's Bench. The leader was a chaplain by the name of Walter Blake, and a large proportion of the 40 or so followers he took were weavers, but there were also servants, spinners, skinners and hosiers. They were well-armed, Blake himself being equipped with body-armour worth £5 and a sword worth 20 shillings. Some of them were amongst the 80 captured at St Giles's Fields and hanged, Blake himself escaping but being arrested in Oxford and taken to London, where he was tried and then executed on 27 January. Blake's employer, Christina More (a member of Bristol's government class), was to find herself in hot water for a number of years due to her support of Lollardy.[47]

Sir Roger Acton is believed to have brought 16 armed men, gathering them as he came through Worcestershire.[48] Other groups came from the Kidlington area of Oxfordshire, Coventry and parts of Warwickshire. The Oxfordshire group was led by a glover and included a mason, a miller, a labourer, a tailor, a fuller, a cooper, a weaver and a carpenter. Other Oxfordshire support came in the form of three clerks from Oxford University, including John Mybbe, the principal of Cuthbert Hall.[49] In Coventry Lollardy was supported by Ralph Gorton, a wealthy mercer. Whether he went to St Giles's Fields is not known, but he was arrested on 30 January on suspicion of Lollardy. Those who gave surety for him, totalling 1,000 marks, included previous MPs, sheriffs and lord mayors of London, which shows how friendships made through shared activities often overrode political difficulties and differences. The Coventry contingent included a hosier, a glover and a servant, but none seems to have been executed, all receiving pardons.[50]

The overall numbers joining the rising seem pitifully small, and it clearly did not have the backing of enough influential and moneyed people to successfully take over the government. The band of fake mummers seems to have been far too small to have captured the king and his brothers. Oldcastle must have hoped that many more would assemble at St Giles's Fields than managed to do so, the numbers perhaps most notably lessened because Londoners were prevented from leaving the city by Henry's manning of the gates with men of known loyalty. The lack of any major figure with a large retinue meant that the groups travelling to London at best numbered in their tens, not the hundreds necessary for success. Even though Oldcastle was a member of the nobility, his 'noble' roots in Kent were recent, and the few years he had been based there had not been sufficient to build up ties of friendship and loyalty such as he had in the Marches; from Kent, only Sir Thomas Talbot, a recent newcomer to the county, is known to have taken part in the rising. As for the Marches, Oldcastle had been absent from there for a few years, and in any event they lay at a distance from London that would have made it difficult for supporters wishing to join the rising to get there. The lack of names from Norfolk is at odds with its soon flourishing Lollard congregations, but this again may simply reflect its physical distance from the capital. Essex, an area not previously noted for Lollardy, provided many names, along with Buckinghamshire, where Lollards had benefited from the patronage of the Cheynes of Drayton Beauchamp, and continued to do so in subsequent decades. A handful of individuals made the journey from as far away as Westmoreland. The vast majority of those involved were craftsmen and tradesmen of relatively low standing.

Oldcastle on the run

With the failure of the rising, Oldcastle needed to go into hiding. On 11 January Henry ordered the sheriff of Kent to offer large rewards for his apprehension: 500 marks for anyone giving information which led to his arrest, 1,000 marks to the person actually arresting him, and freedom from all taxes to the city, borough or township where he was seized. In addition the king would look favourably on anyone who otherwise distinguished themselves in Oldcastle's capture.[51] Similar orders were sent out to the sheriffs of other counties, with that for Herefordshire being issued on 23 January.[52] However, with the limited extent of the rising becoming apparent, and with the few known ringleaders soon being caught and executed, the exception being Oldcastle himself, it wasn't long before Henry decided it was time to show leniency towards most of those involved. On 23 January, William Dene, a fuller from London, was pardoned even though he had been condemned and sentenced on 11 January.[53] At the same time, however, arrests continued to be made. Roger Cheyne, probably a cousin of the 'Lollard knight' Sir John Cheyne, and his son John were handed over for imprisonment in the Tower on 18 January. Sir William Beauchamp of Somerset was imprisoned on the 23rd, as also was Thomas Brooke, the husband of Oldcastle's stepdaughter, at about the same time.[54] These must have been precautionary measures, as John Cheyne, Sir William Beauchamp and Thomas Brooke were subsequently released, or perhaps they had only been arrested in the hope that they might provide information as to Oldcastle's whereabouts. On 28 March a proclamation pardoned many others, providing the pardon was applied for by 24 June. There were exceptions, including William Fisher, who had sheltered Oldcastle in London, and Roger Cheyne of Drayton Beauchamp and his vicar, Thomas Drayton. (Roger Cheyne was to die as a prisoner in the Tower on 14 May 1414.) On 20 May another proclamation granted pardon to a further few named individuals. Those excepted from the pardon were, besides Oldcastle, a single knight (Sir Thomas Talbot) and several 'clerks', but most were merchants. On 9 December

1414 and 18 February 1415 Henry offered a pardon to Oldcastle himself if he came out of hiding and surrendered, and sent letters to Oldcastle's friends and associates setting out the details, but no submission came.[55]

Another explanation why so few of those caught were found guilty of heresy might be that Henry was leaning on the courts to concentrate on finding people guilty of treason, so making the holding of Lollard views treasonable against the state and not simply an issue of heresy that concerned the Church. The parliament held at Leicester in 1414 passed a statute whose preamble declared that Lollard beliefs were not only subversive to the Church but also to the state. These thoughts were in tune with a poem of the time:

> ... under colour of suiche lollynge,
> To shape sodeyn surreccioun
> Against oure liege lord Kinge.[56]

Oldcastle's rising certainly did the cause of Lollardy little good if it was to be perceived in future as both treasonous and heretical.

Oldcastle was to spend much of his time on the run either in the Midlands, which was a particular centre of Lollardy, or in the Welsh Marches, notably close to his home village of Almeley, where ties of friendship both supported him and left him in peace. It is to the Marches or even Wales that Oldcastle is believed to have first hurried, though he may have remained in hiding in London for up to a month, waiting for the initial hue and cry to subside. Certainly, the authorities continued looking for him in London for a while after the rising, finding two horses and two red robes lined with gold that belonged to him in the premises of Matthew Toly, a barber, and John Joynour, an ironmonger, in St John's Street. They subsequently claimed that an unknown squire had left them for safekeeping on the morning of the rising.[57]

The government feared that Oldcastle might seek to rekindle Welsh revolt, so reinforced the garrison at Cardigan 'lest John Oldcastle and other heretics … should take the said castle by night after they had fled from England into Wales, as the King is informed and rumour hath it'.[58] These orders even affected Oldcastle's own cousin Richard, son of Sir Thomas Oldcastle, for he was then constable of Aberystwyth Castle and was ordered to reinforce it with eight additional archers.[59]

On 14 June 1414 Oldcastle was formally outlawed.[60] His properties had already been seized by the king, but during the summer Henry granted Roger Clitherow, a Kentish esquire and Oldcastle's son-in-law by marriage to Maud, his daughter by his first wife,[61] together with Thomas Brooke, his son-in-law by marriage to his stepdaughter, the custody of all the possessions held by Sir John in his own right or conjointly with his wife. These would have included Oldcastle's original lands in Herefordshire, but Clitherow and Brooke did not seem to consider them part of the grant, nor were they seized by John Darell, the escheator responsible for handing on the management of the lands in Kent and Middlesex. Darrell compiled a list of possessions found at Cooling Castle, which shows that no valuable ones were to be found, presumably having been removed so as to preserve them from the escheator's hands. Though no Lollards are known to have come to St Giles's Fields from Kent or Middlesex (with the possible exception of John Wykeham, an esquire from near Banbury in Oxfordshire, who held some lands in Middlesex), Darell was later paid expenses of £6 13s 4d to cover the cost of an escort of 20 to 30 horsemen for fear of those adhering to Oldcastle.[62] As will be seen below, these efforts to cut off the flow of income to Oldcastle were not completely successful, with rents from lands in Herefordshire, including from tenements in Hereford, still reaching him.[63]

In June Oldcastle was possibly in Daventry at the houses of Simon Horn and Philip Turnour. The latter had been pardoned both for treason and for Lollardy after the rising of 1414 but was to be arrested again in 1417, this time dying of disease whilst in prison. Around the end of July or early August, Oldcastle appears to have been at Chesterton in Warwickshire, some seven miles south of Coventry, where he stayed with the vicar. By 11 August, when Henry V left for France on the campaign that led to Agincourt, or soon after, Oldcastle had moved to the Malvern area.[64]

An abortive rising in Malvern

There are rumours that Oldcastle was involved in the Southampton Plot of this date. This sought a revival of the old alliance of Percy, Mortimer and Glyndwr, in which the young Mortimer earl of March, believed by some to be the son of Richard II's nominated heir (see page 73), would be encouraged to stake his claim to the throne. But the plot was laid bare by the earl of March himself, who had wavered in his support for the scheme. Henry acted swiftly and the ringleaders were executed on the eve of his departure for France. It was at this moment that Oldcastle emerged from hiding, sending a threatening letter to Richard Beauchamp, Lord Abergavenny at Hanley Castle, against whom, according to Walsingham, Oldcastle bore a grudge concerning the treatment of Lollards. (This may have been because Sir Richard's father, William, who had died in 1411, had been a close associate of the 'Lollard knights' prominent in Richard II's reign, and appears to have at least tacitly supported Lollard-inclined priests, his son holding different views.) In response, Sir Richard is reported to have raised the improbably large force of 5,000 men-at-arms and archers. Whatever its actual size, it forced Oldcastle to flee whilst five of his accomplices were captured. Arms and money were also discovered, apparently hidden between two walls in a house, along with banners, one of which was said to depict a chalice and a host in the shape of a loaf of bread, apparently similar to banners carried by the Bohemian Hussite armies at this time.[65] It would seem that Oldcastle had hopes of a sizeable following for this second attempted rising, with men perhaps coming from the Marches, now that he was close to the area, and also from Warwickshire and parts of Worcestershire where Lollards are known to have existed. As for where Oldcastle was hiding and

Birtsmorton Court in 1830

where these arms might have been found, a likely contender is Birtsmorton Court, five miles south of Malvern, which was then owned by the Ruyhale family.[66]

Richard Ruyhale had died in 1408, leaving as his heir a son who was to die under age. His widow then married John Philipot and, after Philipot's death, took as her third husband Richard Oldcastle, Sir John's cousin. It was probably this link that brought Sir John to the Malvern area.[67] It is unlikely, however, that Oldcastle's abortive Malvern rising was in any way connected with the Southampton Plot. In their confessions, Richard, earl of Cambridge, Henry, Lord Scrope of Masham and Sir Thomas Grey made only passing reference to any involvement of Lollard elements in their plans, Scrope inferring that Lollard participation might aid their plans and Grey referring to a potential rising by Sir Thomas Talbot.[68] Any other Lollard rising planned in Henry's absence in France may have been warned off by the burning of two notorious Lollards, William Turmyne and William Claydon (who had apparently appointed his son to be his priest), in London that September.[69]

This second abortive rising was an event of sufficient importance to have left its mark in local folklore, a source not always to be dismissed out of hand. Bed and breakfast accommodation listings, when mentioning local places of interest, say of Birtsmorton Court that 'the earliest south wing contains the great hall. Here is a secret hiding place where Sir John Oldcastle, the Lollard leader, sheltered after his escape from the Tower of London.'[71] In his historical novel *Malvern Chase*, which is set during the Wars of the Roses, Revd W.S. Symonds makes Birtsmorton Court the home of the de Brutes, and says that Oldcastle and Thomas Payne (whom Symonds describes as Oldcastle's

A wall painting of Jan Zizka leading Hussite forces, in the Bethlehem Chapel in Prague, where Jan Hus preached. When Oldcastle's force was dispersed by Richard Beauchamp, Lord Abergavenny, it is said that Oldcastle's banners were captured. These are reported by Walsingham to have depicted a golden chalice and the host in the shape of a loaf of bread, alluding to the Last Supper. The chalice had been adopted as a symbol by the reformers in Bohemia as seen in the above illustration. Another of Oldcastle's banners was described as depicting 'a sort of cross of Christ with scourges, and a spear with nails'.[70] (Author)

chaplain), sheltered there for several weeks. The book is based on the life of a fictional Hildebrand de Brute, whose grandfather, Giles, had Sir John Oldcastle as 'his dearest friend and cousin', and whose father 'was a Wycliffite, or as now termed a lollard'. Hildebrand tells the story of Oldcastle's hiding to his love, Rosamond Berew, saying that Archbishop Arundel sent bloodhounds to sniff out Oldcastle's whereabouts so that even the 'secret room in the panelled chamber was unsafe' and Oldcastle had to seek refuge in a grove of hollies. Rosamond, in turn, says that her grandfather had cut himself and spilt his blood on Oldcastle's trail to confuse another hound sent to find him when he sought refuge in a cave on the hills. In a footnote, Symonds remarks that a Mrs Webb of Ledbury, then aged 101 (the book was published in 1881), remembered the tradition of Oldcastle hiding in the chamber. In his *Historic Memories of the Manor and Parish of Almeley in the county of Hereford*, published in 1917, the Reverend Hyett-Warner adds the detail that it is believed that Oldcastle had to swim the moat to escape his pursuers, whilst other stories say that the secret chamber led to a tunnel under the moat. In correspondence in the early 2000s, Louise Fletcher, then living in Hereford, said that Walter Brut (for whom see Chapter Two) owned land at Castlemorton Common near Welland, where Louise's sister lived, and that it was believed that Oldcastle hid his 'treasure' in a stone wall there, only for it to be discovered. As for the Brut family's connections with Birtsmorton Court, a branch of the family held it from the later 1100s, the manor passing to the Ruyhales in 1301, though the Bruts still held some land nearby until at least 1361.[72]

Oldcastle on the run once more

According to the unreliable John Strecche, Oldcastle is supposed to have spent time near Shrewsbury and Welshpool. (Strecche was a canon of the Augustinian Priory at Kenilworth, who compiled a chronicle based on the writings of Ralph Higden, a monk of Chester who wrote the long *Polychronicon* – a work of both theology and history – and accounts of the priors of Kenilworth.) An accusation made by a John Fitzharry holds that Oldcastle was assisted financially by the abbot of Shrewsbury, but the latter would have been an unlikely ally given Oldcastle's views on the temporalities of the Church, and Fitzharry probably made the claim to try to gain a reprieve for his own life, a plan which failed.[73] Claims by a William Carsewell that Oldcastle was seeking support from the prior of Wenlock also proved unfounded, Carsewell likewise trying to save his own life.[74] The stories show how rumours could feast on each other to create confusion as to the realities of Oldcastle's movements and intentions. There is firmer information that by the end of 1415 Oldcastle may have returned to the Coventry area.[75]

Sometime before spring 1416 a Hereford Lollard, Thomas Cromp, was denounced by fellow citizens for 'maintaining Oldcastle', but was released after swearing not to support Lollardy or Oldcastle in future.[76] His 'maintaining' may simply have been supplying Oldcastle with wares or money rather than actually harbouring him, and it may be that the rumour that Oldcastle was sheltering at Olchon Court in the Olchon Valley along the flanks of the Black Mountains in Herefordshire relates to this time. When members of Herefordshire's Woolhope Naturalists' Field Club made a visit to the Court in the summer of 1916, they were informed that Oldcastle hid himself in the house for three or four years and were shown a window through which he apparently escaped when closely pursued. This story is a tradition that John Howells recorded in his booklet of 1886 referred to in Chapter One, which contains what are now known to be several errors, a tradition given further recent airing in *People of the Black Mountains*, a novel by Raymond Williams published in 1989.[77] As far as this tradition goes, there is one major problem – the Royal Commission of Ancient and Historical Monuments have dated the part of Olchon Court that contains the window through which Oldcastle is said to have fled, and which is the oldest part of the house, to a hundred years after Oldcastle's death. Not only that, but the window itself is probably a later insertion still.[78] Another version of the tale has it that the house concerned was once known as Walter's Court, as it had been owned by Walter Brut, but there is no record of Walter Brut having held land in this part of Herefordshire and the Walter ascribed to the house must be another of that name.[79] Even if it was from an earlier Olchon Court that Oldcastle is said to have fled, from his known whereabouts at various dates, he cannot have been in the Olchon valley for as long as three or four years. Even though the valley has a reputation for sheltering purveyors of religious nonconformity, there is no firm evidence that Oldcastle ever hid there.

Another rumour suggested that one of Oldcastle's hiding places was at Chapel Farm near Leintwardine in Deerfold Forest. There was certainly a Lollard community in the area, for both Newton, near Leintwardine, and Deerfold were places where Swynderby was recorded as preaching (as mentioned in Chapter Two). In 1869 the Woolhope Naturalists' Field Club explored the area, describing what they found as follows: 'A small promontory jutting out from high ground of the forest on its western side between Limebrook and Lingen is called "Oldcastle". A few acres of tableland surrounded to North and South sides by steep wood covered declivities. It could have been a refuge. There is no sign of building or habitation but it would make a good defensive outpost.' This spot would seem to be at OS reference 371667, Chapel Farm lying two miles to the north-east.

Rumours and tales of Oldcastle's whereabouts flourished down the years. The Elizabethan poet John Weever saw him as a hero, and in his 'Mirror of Martyrs' recounts a journey made by Oldcastle along the course of the River Weaver from Cheshire to the sea, at some point in his wanderings. Though the course of the journey is almost certainly made up so that Weever could associate his hero with a river that bears his own name (albeit with a slightly different current spelling) and with his native countryside, Weever did generally keep to historical facts as known to him from chronicles or handed down through his family. It's possible therefore that this poem remembers Oldcastle as having journeyed through the area at some point between 1414 and 1417:

Through many bywaies, many countries fled
In midst of Cheshire now I'm on a river
Her tumbling streame my guide was to Vaile Roiall
Through all the Wyches unto Ashton's chapel
Frodsham, Rockesavage, thus I had a triall
To Lancashire from thence my journey lies …
So there, through many paines and perils past
I'm safe returned back to Wales at last.[80]

Somewhat more reliably, in early October 1416 Oldcastle was rumoured to be in the London area, given shelter by Thomas Payne. Payne was described by W.S. Symonds as Oldcastle's chaplain, but it is more likely that he was his clerk and scrivener (though clerks were frequently clerics). Often referred to in the documents as a 'serviens and familiaris' of Oldcastle and in others as 'sumtyme clerk and chief conseillour' to Oldcastle, Payne appears to have escaped the debacle of St Giles's Fields.[81] On 11 November, Richard Clodesdale, an esquire of the royal household, was said to have met Oldcastle at Acton and given him £100 towards wages for men to rise against the king. Both men were subsequently acquitted of these offences, but the episodes suggest that Oldcastle was at least in contact with people in London at this time, even if probably spending most of his time in the Midlands during that autumn. A priest by the name of John Whitby was hanged at Oxford the following summer for harbouring Oldcastle at Paddington in Oxfordshire on 26 October.[82]

On 10 December 1416 Oldcastle was rumoured to have been at Hickling in Nottinghamshire, where John Howes, 'gentleman', of Hose on the Leicestershire/Nottinghamshire border is said to have taken him provisions and money. Robert Rose, a chaplain of known Lollard beliefs but not necessarily a savoury character (being accused of counterfeiting, theft, highway robbery and rape), claimed to have met Oldcastle at some date before 7 January 1417 at Swarkeston Bridge near Aston-on-Trent. However, this claim could have been a fabrication so that he could pretend to turn 'king's evidence' and escape prosecution for his other crimes.[83]

In the meantime, at Christmas a plot against Henry V at Kenilworth, organised by a 'certain esquire' of Oldcastle's, had been discovered, though what the plan was and why it failed are not reported.[84] It was followed the day after Christmas by the delivery of Lollard tracts, attacking the Church's estates, to every hostelry in St Albans, Northampton and Reading.[85] This 'plot' led to fresh proclamations being issued for the capture of Oldcastle, the 'Lollard of Lollards'. At some point between these events and Michaelmas 1419, Thomas Payne, Oldcastle's clerk, became involved in a plot to free King James I of Scotland, then a prisoner in Windsor Castle. The plot failed and Payne was himself in prison at Michaelmas 1419, staying there till May 1421 before being transferred to the Tower. The following year, on 11 April (in conjunction with another conspirator against Henry V and two French prisoners), Payne escaped from the Tower, but was back in custody by 6 June. He was still in jail at the beginning of

Henry VI's reign in 1422, and whilst tried for treason he seems never to be have been condemned as a heretic.[86]

At Easter 1417, Thomas Lucas, a former fellow of Merton College, who was believed to have been aided and abetted by Oldcastle, was tried for conspiring to kill the king. Lucas had also sent a letter to the Holy Roman Emperor Sigismund when he was on a visit to England to sign a treaty with Henry agreeing mutual defence against France. In the letter Lucas promoted the disendowment of the Church, wrongly believing that Sigismund supported this view, whilst also claiming that Richard II was still alive and in Scotland. He also scattered handbills with these views in London and Canterbury.[87]

On 8 May 1417 Oldcastle may have been in Daventry, staying with John Heywode, who apparently lived in a house that formerly belonged to Philip Turnour, with whom Oldcastle had stayed in June 1414. On 29 May Oldcastle is said to have met with Sir Thomas Talbot (who had received a pardon by September 1415) and others at Silverstone, planning to join with the Scots in a rising against the king. Talbot was arrested and charged but found not guilty by the jury, only to be held in the Tower of London on the king's orders due to his continual trouble-making. Talbot was never accused of heresy and his motives seem to have been political and directed against the House of Lancaster.[88] During 1417 rumours abounded that Oldcastle was in league with Thomas Talbot's brother, Henry, who for several years had been conspiring with assorted Scottish nobles and Thomas Warde of Trumpington, the counterfeit Richard II mentioned earlier, to organise an invasion from Scotland. This came to nothing, and there is no evidence that there was any contact between Henry Talbot and Oldcastle, even though Henry Talbot appears to have had Lollard sympathies.[89]

In June 1417 Oldcastle was reported to be near Coventry, and in July he was harboured by Hugh Frayn and his wife Joan. His presence must have been detected, for he left behind a complete suit of plate armour, presumably having to leave in a hurry (from later evidence, set out below, he may have been travelling with two horses), and sought refuge with William atte Well and his wife at Byfield, a particular centre of Lollardy, near Chipping Warden. At this time, he seems to have been accompanied by John Langacre, a mercer from London and High Wycombe, another who had taken part in the rising of 1414 but who had been pardoned. The authorities were on Oldcastle's heels, however, and whilst he escaped, Hugh Frayn, William atte Well and Langacre were all caught and hanged, their heads being displayed on the gates of Coventry and Northampton. Joan Frayn was still in custody in Northampton Castle in February 1418.[90] Thomas Walsingham also suggests that Oldcastle was in the vicinity of St Albans during 1417, probably late in the year, but no other evidence for this has come to light.

It was also in 1417 that Henry Greyndour Esq. of Clearwell in the Forest of Dean (probably the uncle of Oldcastle's companion-in-arms Sir John Greyndour) presented the king with a bill, purportedly drawn up by Oldcastle, urging him to confiscate all the temporalities of the Church. Henry promptly threw the older Greyndour into prison as a heretic.[91] It was clear that Oldcastle was still pursuing his dreams of rebellion, for in the autumn two priests (one of them Richard Wyche, whom we met in Chapter Six, sharing messengers with Oldcastle between England and Prague) were arrested in Hampshire in possession of some money belonging to Oldcastle, presumably being used to help purchase support.[92]

What must have been going through Oldcastle's mind during this time? He would have been aware that some of his close associates, such as Sir Roger Acton, his own squire John Brown and possible squire Robert Harley, had been hanged, along with several merchants, chaplains, clerks, craftsmen and labourers. He had turned down two pardons, assuming he knew of their existence, but even if he did and accepted Henry's word that he would be pardoned for treason, he would still face the charge of heresy. As the months of wandering went by, he must have been aware that several Lollards had recanted to save their lives, even if they retained their beliefs privately, and that those willing to rise up with him were becoming fewer in number. His attempted revolt at Malvern seems to have been the last time he thought to place himself at the head of an armed force. Many of those he may now have plotted with were not concerned about Lollardy, but held grudges against the House of Lancaster or were simply out for their own ends.

Oldcastle's failure and position didn't seem to produce any bitterness or change of character in him, for his friends stood by him whatever their feelings about his motives and beliefs. This suggests a stalwart character who exuded strength of mind and good companionship. He does not seem to have made any effort to contact his sons and daughters, but that may be because he thought that they were being watched (especially after the Birtsmorton escapade), and that contact would be a risk to them and himself. His wife was anyway detained in the Tower of London and only released after his death, even though she was suspected neither of any involvement in the rising, nor of holding Lollard beliefs. If he was temperamentally unable to lie quiet, as Owain Glyndwr managed to do after the eventual failure of his rising, then all Oldcastle could do was to wander and plot.

Back in Almeley

By the summer of 1417 Oldcastle was back at Almeley. Rents from the village, which should have been forfeited to the Crown once he had been declared a traitor, were still reaching him, as a result of which, in January 1419, nine men were accused of having helped him. The nine were Walter Harald, a chaplain of Wigmore, and his brother Nicholas (who might have already come to the attention of the authorities as Lollards, as they had to swear an oath against heresy in February 1418[93]); John Bally of Aymestrey; David Says of Hay; and John Carpenter, Richard Webbe, Richard Dryver, William Lydus and John Yonge of Almeley, the latter having formerly been Oldcastle's bailiff. (The Yonges appear as Almeley poll tax payers in 1379, unlike the others from Almeley.) Only five were to stand trial. Dryver said he met Oldcastle by chance on 20 August when Sir John had forced him to swear to lend his support. As a result, he had tricked Yonge into meeting Oldcastle, saying that the vicar wanted to see him at the village cross. Oldcastle then made Yonge swear to give his support, but Yonge had gone to Sir John Merbury at Weobley (just 5 miles due east of Almeley), who was then sheriff of Herefordshire, to report Oldcastle's whereabouts. Webbe, presumably a leather-worker, said he had refused to make Oldcastle a pair of shoes and other items he wanted, but had been forced to supply him with food. Says, who may have been a relation of Oldcastle through his first wife Katherine, said he had been tricked into looking after Sir John's two horses; he had initially refused but had eventually taken one, which he had not returned. Carpenter said he had not just been tricked into helping Oldcastle, but virtually kidnapped, and had gone in mid-October with Oldcastle to visit Gruffydd (though Maredudd is probably meant, see below), son of Owain Glyndwr in north Wales. Hearing them discuss treason, he had slipped away, returning to Almeley on foot. The trial of the five men took place in the court of the King's Bench, and all were cleared of the charges.[94] However, the case shows that Oldcastle was living in Almeley fairly openly, his presence presumably known to many, and that he was there from late August to early October 1417 at the very least.[95]

Others in a position of power locally made no overt moves against Oldcastle during this period. Sir John Merbury was apparently an archer in France at one time, in 1395 having enlisted in Bordeaux with John of Gaunt and receiving an annuity of ten marks, thus becoming a lifelong retainer of the house of Lancaster. Entering the service of Henry IV and then Henry V, by March 1400 Merbury was appointed chamberlain and receiver for south Wales, the chief financial officer for that part of the principality (an office he was to hold for the next 21 years). By 1402 he had been granted several more annuities, providing him with an annual income of a healthy £126. In 1400 he married Alice, the widow of Thomas Oldcastle, holding during her lifetime her castle and manor of Boughrood south of Builth Wells, the manor of Eyton near Leominster and an estate at Burghill near Hereford. During the wars against Glyndwr he served with John ap Harry, and he was sheriff of Herefordshire in 1405. In 1409 Bishop Mascall of Hereford made him steward of swathes of episcopal lands, and over the following years he was to be found in several official positions. In 1412 Prince Henry awarded him a further annuity of 100 marks in recognition of his various services. As chamberlain of south Wales, he was involved in the preparations for the invasion of France, including the mustering of 20 men-at-arms and 500 archers at Carmarthen and Brecon. Merbury himself was not destined for France, but was given joint command of a force of 60 men-at-arms and 120 archers for the defence of south Wales against any rebellion during the king's absence. One of his fellow commanders was his stepson Richard Oldcastle and another was Sir Robert II Whitney, the husband of his stepdaughter, Wintelan Oldcastle. Merbury's wife Alice died in 1415, and by March 1417 he had married the twice widowed Agnes Crophill, who brought him extensive lands spread across the Midlands, including the castle and manor of Weobley. It was here that John

A reconstruction drawing of Weobley Castle showing how it may have looked
at around the date of its occupation by Sir John Merbury.
The drawing is based on a plan made by Silas Taylor in 1655, corroborated by information
contained in Merbury's will made shortly before his death in 1437.

Yonge brought Merbury news of Sir John Oldcastle's presence in Almeley.[96] Merbury offered Yonge the sum of £100 to reveal Sir John's precise location, but Yonge refused, saying he did not know it and even if he did would refuse for fear of his life. Merbury was in receipt of news of Oldcastle's whereabouts in late August, and had command of a large force of men with which to suppress rebellion, yet Oldcastle appears to have remained in Almeley until sometime in October. It seems clear that Merbury took no further action. Was the offer of £100 to Yonge simply to give him some cover for his subsequent inaction? Perhaps the ties of family alliance through his previous wife and his stepchildren were greater than his allegiance to a king, even one who had showered wealth and appointments on him. Then again, perhaps his lowly start in life gave him an appreciation of Lollard teaching that others did not have, though there is nothing to suggest that he held Lollard views, outwardly at any event.

Even more intriguingly, staying with Merbury at the time of Yonge's report on the presence of Oldcastle in Almeley was John Brugge, then sheriff of Herefordshire, the man with the greatest responsibility in the county for arresting Oldcastle. Here, local loyalty once again seems to have played its part, and perhaps Brugge's influence weighed on Merbury. Brugge held the Herefordshire manors of Sapey, Staunton-on-Wye and Letton, and was therefore a neighbour of the Oldcastle lands at Letton. He probably stood surety for the attendance of Thomas Oldcastle at the parliament of 1390, and served in 1400 with Sir John Oldcastle under Richard, Lord Grey of Codnor on the Scottish border. In later life he was to be a feoffee, or trustee, of Richard Oldcastle.[97]

On 23 January 1417 Henry V had reiterated the reward for the capture of Oldcastle, sending out orders to the sheriffs of a number of counties, including Herefordshire, to proclaim that there was a reward of 1,000 marks for those that took him, kept him in custody and brought him before the king, together with £20 for life. If the authorities in a town should so take him, the town's citizens would be free of all taxes of a tenth or fifteenth or other taxes thereafter granted to the king and his heirs, Oldcastle being stated as 'persevering in his nefarious intent to destroy the church of England, the king and his true lieges'.[98] Despite the protestations of coercion by the five men charged with aiding and abetting Oldcastle, none of them and no other Almeley residents sought the rewards on offer for aiding Oldcastle's capture. It would seem that a mixture of loyalty to the family combined with disparate Lollard views proved the greater draw. As with Merbury's offer of a £100 reward, perhaps the tales of coercion were simply alibis.

It wasn't just local residents who stayed loyal. Despite his close associations with Sir John Oldcastle (see Chapters One and Three), John ap Harry was not suspected of any collusion with his friend in the rising of 1414, and just a month later was appointed to a royal commission to investigate an armed raid on Eardisley by Richard de la Bere. No details of this episode survive, but it is clear that in the aftermath of Glyndwr's rising, much of Herefordshire was still in a state of lawlessness, in part now caused by members of the gentry, such as de la Bere, employing their tenants and retainers in pursuit of their personal quarrels.[99] In the summer of 1417, when Oldcastle was in Almeley, ap Harry was acting as itinerant justice in the duchy of Lancaster lordships in south Wales; he had been an adherent of Henry IV before he became king and when Henry was heir to the duchy of Lancaster, accompanying him to Prussia in 1391.[100] In July, ap Harry and others associated with Oldcastle had been bound over not to lend Oldcastle support – 'nor adhere to John Oldecastelle knight late lord of Cobham for annulment or breach of the rights of holy mother church, nor go nor ride with him against the king or any of his lieges, to do no hurt contrary to the law, nor by himself or others support or aid the said John in his heretical opinion contrary to the laws and states of the realm'.[101] Ap Harry had to find people willing to provide sureties of £1,000, one of those who helped being Sir Robert II Whitney. After Oldcastle's death, the inquisition into his lands showed that ap Harry had been collecting the rents on Oldcastle's lands since 1414 and, rather than handing them to the Crown, had been passing at least some of the money to Oldcastle. When accused of this, ap Harry said that he was unaware of the forfeiture, which would seem a lame excuse for someone who acted as a justice. Ap Harry seems to have escaped any punishment as a result of his lapse, but was to receive no further commissions or appointments from the government.[102]

As mentioned above, in October 1417 Oldcastle went to north Wales to meet with Gruffydd, a son of Owain Glyndwr. If Gruffydd was then at large, this is the only reference to the fact, as otherwise records show that he was captured in 1405 and was still a prisoner in the Tower in 1411, dying there of the plague in 1412.[103] It may be that the son meant was Maredudd, the last of Glyndwr's six sons still at liberty. (Maredudd finally accepted a pardon in 1421, which is taken to mean that his father had almost certainly died by then.)

At the end of November, probably on his way back to Almeley, Oldcastle was captured in a glade, still known as Cobham's Garden, at Pant-Mawr farm at Broniarth near Welshpool, after a struggle with four tenants of Sir Edward Charlton, Lord Powys. In some accounts it is said that a few people were slain in the encounter; in another that Oldcastle's leg was broken by a stool wielded by one of the women onlookers. Whatever the nature and scale of the fracas, Oldcastle certainly seems to have been wounded.[104] He was handed over to Lord Powys and held in Welshpool Castle before being transported to London in a 'whirlecote', a fast two-wheeled carriage. The carriage might have been needed because of the extent of the wounds Oldcastle had received during his capture, or because of the need to have his case urgently heard before parliament, which happened to be sitting but was close to dissolution, or perhaps for a combination of these reasons.[105]

Whilst Oldcastle had been condemned as a heretic, he had escaped from the Tower before his case had been referred back to the secular arm of government for the

The piece of land now known as Cobham's Garden, and marked as such on current OS Explorer maps, south-east of Meifod and north-west of Welshpool (Grid ref: SJ 157117), where tradition has it that Oldcastle was captured by 'Jevan and Gruffuth, sones of Gruffuth ap Jevan ap Madoc ap Gwennoys, of Powys Londe, gentilmen, Hoel ap Gruffith ap David ap Madoc, and Dero ap Jevan ap Jorum ap Ada of the same Lond, zemen [yeomen], tenauntz to Sire Edward Charletoun knyght Lord of Powys'. In their letter reporting the capture they describe Oldcastle as 'myscreant and unboxome to the lawe of God'.[106] The area is known locally as Cae'r Brawn – Baron's Field.[107] (Author)

sentence to be confirmed and carried out. As Oldcastle was a member of the House of Lords, his case now needed to be heard before parliament, and on the orders of John, duke of Bedford (the eldest of King Henry's younger brothers, who was acting as regent in England whilst Henry was in France), on 14 December Oldcastle was duly brought before parliament. His conviction for heresy and record of outlawry were read out. Asked to show why he did not deserve to be sentenced to death, Oldcastle's reply is summarised by Walsingham: 'using a parable, he began to preach about the mercy of God and to say that all men who wished to be imitators of God should always exalt mercy above judgement. Punishment belonged to God alone and should be left to Him alone and not be exercised by his worshipper.' Oldcastle continued to discourse widely, but Bedford ordered him not to waste their time and answer the charges directly. 'With consummate arrogance and perversity he evaded the question and forthwith replied that he acknowledged no judge amongst them, while his liege lord, King Richard, was still alive in the kingdom of Scotland.'[108] So speaking words of treason, he was quickly condemned as a traitor as well as a heretic.

Death of Oldcastle as depicted in Foxe's *Actes and monuments*. Foxe says: 'Than was he hanged vp there by the middle in chaines of yron, and so consumed aliue in the fyre, praising the name of God, so long as his life lasted. In the end. he commended his soule into the handes of God, and so departed hence most christēly, his body resolued into ashes.' His execution cost 56 shillings.[110]

The record in *Rotuli Parliamentorum*, the Rolls of Parliament, gives a much drier account. Having been read the charge of treason for which he was outlawed, the Rolls state that Oldcastle was 'asked several times on behalf of the king if he had anything to say why execution should not be done on him because of the outlawry aforesaid. To this demand John said nothing to excuse him in this matter; wherefore judgement was given …'. From parliament he was returned to the Tower, where he had been lodged on arrival in London. On the same day he was drawn from there on a hurdle to St Giles's Fields, where he was hanged, and then he and the gallows were burned. Fabyan records that he was hanged 'upon a newe peyer of galowys with chaynes, after consumed with fyre'. The official records do not indicate that he was burned alive, though the Rolls of Parliament did say that he 'should be hanged and burnt hanging', and others later asserted that he was so executed.[109]

It has been suggested that, with his end in sight and perhaps as a result of his injuries, Oldcastle may have become a little unhinged. Two chroniclers assert that he claimed that after his execution he would rise again.[111] One of them, Walsingham, records that on the scaffold he begged Sir Thomas Erpingham (he of Agincourt fame in Shakespeare's *Henry V*, who may have been another friend of Oldcastle) to intercede on behalf of Lollards 'if he saw his victim rise again on the third day'. Maybe Oldcastle was desperately hoping that something good would come from the beliefs he held so deeply, but Walsingham ends his account by calling him a 'bigot'.[112]

Even so, there are signs of Oldcastle's forthcoming martyr status. In his *Historium Regum Angliae*, John Strecche, a canon of Kenilworth, says that some of Oldcastle's followers anointed their eyes with his ashes, but only to go blind.[113] Did they use the ashes when hot, or is this just some gossip that Strecche recorded, for his history is noted for being tainted with such comment? Nevertheless, both martyr and hero status awaited.

9

Traitor, Martyr, Hero and Falstaff

With Oldcastle's death, Lollardy was dealt a serious blow. Not only had the state managed to link Lollard beliefs to crimes of treason, but the most senior lay member of any perceived Lollard sect had been disgraced and killed. In truth, there had been no organised structure, no alternative Church, and now there was no potentially unifying figurehead either. The beliefs still persisted, but more in the minds of artisans, craftsmen and labourers, some members of the clergy and wandering preachers, and rarely in the expressed thoughts of esquires, knights or nobles. But Lollardy still persisted, and was still subject to persecution. In 1427 Pope Martin V ordered the bishop of Lincoln to carry out the decree that was passed at the council of Constance held between 1414 and 1418, that Wycliffe's remains should be treated as those of a condemned heretic. His body was exhumed from his grave at Lutterworth, and his bones were smashed and thrown into the River Avon. In 1425 Thomas Waweton, who seems to have been a robust character and not afraid of the law, was Speaker of the House of Commons when two petitions that were strongly Lollard in flavour were presented. One complained of absentee clergy and of the holding of livings in plurality (when priests held several livings, often scattered about the country), while the other concerned suspected heretics who had been held in prison for long periods awaiting trial. It is not known if Waweton encouraged these petitions, but he is believed to have had Lollard sympathies, being a friend of Sir John II Cheyne, who was implicated in Oldcastle's rising (see page 170).[1]

Despite the lack of any organisation or figurehead, in 1428 Archbishop Chichele (who had succeeded Arundel after the latter's death in February 1414) admitted that Lollards seemed to be as numerous as ever and that the dissemination of their views went on as vigorously as before. As can happen, persecution had in some cases hardened individual views. A Thomas Bagley is supposed to have said that if in the sacrament the priest turned the bread into God, then he had made a God that could be eaten by rats and mice. In 1431 there was another Lollard rebellion, led by a Jack Sharp, who revived the petition of 1410 (see pages 112-13) and was captured and put to death at Oxford. Two years later Lollardy flared once more in Almeley. On 27 February 1433 Bishop Spofford of Hereford appointed a commission of three men to investigate heresy in the parish, and quickly homed in on John Woodhulle, a cleric. In his notes for his history of Herefordshire Duncumb suggests that Woodhulle was the vicar of Almeley,[2] but according to official lists in the bishop's registers the vicar was Thomas Bydyn, who had been appointed in June 1430 on the death of the previous incumbent. It's more likely that Woodhulle was a cleric based in Woonton in the east of the parish. Woodhulle quickly recanted his heretical views, signing a confession on 13 April:

> Forasmuche as I, John Woodhulle, am accused of certeyn poyntes and articles that ben agaeine the byleve of holy Chirche, I am comanded be my lord the Bisshope of Hereford to knowleche my byleve in the poyntes that here put upon me or in bookes y founden wyth me to the help of myn owne sowle, restorynge of myn owne name, and that nought by me mennes sowles sholde be hyndred either empeired. Furst, ye put to me that I shuld kepe and concele wyth inne me bokes ageine the commandment of holy Churche in the whiche ar encluded dyvern erroures and heresies the whiche ben these that followeth y wretene.

There then follows a list of common Lollard heresies, including the beliefs that the bread remained material bread after the sacrament, that tithes should only be given by free will, that support should be withdrawn from prelates and priests who 'synne openly and fayles in their offis', and that John Wycliffe's opinions were commendable.[3]

Hoccleve's 'Address to Sir John Oldcastle' and the anonymous 'Against the Lollards'

These events were soon to be followed by the Wars of the Roses (1455–85), a time when discontent followed avenues other than those inspired by Lollardy. As a result Lollardy gradually faded, to be replaced by new sects with the coming of the Reformation in the sixteenth century. In the meantime, Sir John Oldcastle had become the subject of poetry. The first poem, a paean of praise as well as potentially harsh criticism, was written during his lifetime and called on him to make peace with the Church. It was written by Thomas Hoccleve (or Occleve), who at about the age of 19 became a clerk in the Office of the Privy Seal (which dealt with warrants and documents that needed the royal seal, a seal that could also be used in terms of secrecy and speed by the king, avoiding the use of the great seal and its bureaucratic processes) and continued to work there for some 35 years. In his poetry, some of which is autobiographical, Hoccleve describes himself as follows: 'Vain he may be; prodigal he may be; somewhat cowardly he may be; but he is totally human. He is an ordinary man gifted with some small ability to tell of himself and his time.'[4] He was a spendthrift who earned additional income from writing poems about individuals and hoping for reward. This paid off when in 1399 Henry IV granted him an annuity of £10 *per annum* for life, a grant that was increased to 20 marks (£13 3s 3d) in May 1409. Among the individuals listed as his patrons by Furnival in *Hoccleve's Works; The Minor Poems* are Henry IV, Henry V, Humphrey duke of Gloucester, Edward duke of York, the duchess of York, the duke of Bedford, John of Gaunt, Sir Henry

Thomas Hoccleve presenting his book, *De Regimine Principum* (Regiment of Princes), to Prince Henry shortly before his accession to the throne. The book is an elaborate homily on virtues and vices, adapted from works by earlier authors. (© The British Library Board, BL MS Arundel 38, f.37)

Somer (chancellor of the exchequer between 1410 and 1437) and 'possibly' Sir John Oldcastle.[5] It is noticeable that few of his 'patrons' commissioned further poems after receipt of the first, and the connections with Oldcastle will be examined after consideration of the poem.

The theme of Hoccleve's 'Address to Sir John Oldcastle' (also known as his 'Remonstrance against Oldcastle') is that heresy is a constant danger and that the duty of the king and his knights is to protect and support the Church and its views, not to become preachers and undermine it. The poem was written when Henry V was at Southampton preparing for the voyage to Harfleur and the subsequent Agincourt campaign, at the time of the Southampton Plot and while Oldcastle was preparing for his second attempted rising at Malvern. The poem is in 64 verses, six of which (as numbered) are reproduced below in modern English:

2
Alas! That you, who were a manly knight and shone clean in famous worthiness and stood in the favour of everyone, have lost the manner of Christian prowess among all who stand in the purity of good faith and that no man will hold with you except cursed wretches, heirs of darkness: my heart is overcome with pity for you.

3
You have made a fine change from Christ's teaching to fiendish doctrine; from honour and domination to reproof and mischievous ruin; from Christian folk to heathen carrion; from surety to insecurity; from joy and ease to war and pain; from the light of truth to dark falseness.

4
O, Oldcastle, alas, what ailed you to slip into the snare of heresy through which you are a foe to the Trinity and the blessed virgin Mary, and to the countless holy company of heaven and all holy church? Alas! Too long you have bathed in that folly! Rise up and purge yourself of your trespass.

13
O, Oldcastle! How the devil has blinded you! Where is your knightly heart? Are you his slave? You also make a foul error in declaring that the sacrament of the altar is not needed at all; it is known in many regions. Now since the fiend has given you a fall, have revenge; rise up and sling him down!

14
Rise up a manly knight out of the slough of heresy. Where you have lurked and erred as a wretch, correct it now! You may reach for mercy through humility. Go to holy church and seek the wholesome oil of absolution. If you do not take heed of your soul's damage or shame, you will lose heaven and all knightly renown.

25

Beware, Oldcastle, and for Christ's sake, stop climbing so high in holy writ!
Read the story of Lancelot of the Lake, or Vegece[6] of the Art of Chivalry, or the
Siege of Troy or Thebes. Apply yourself to things that may belong to the order
of knighthood! Hurry now to your correction, for you have been out of joint too
long!

On the surface it seems that Hoccleve may have written the poem out of pure
admiration for Oldcastle as a worthy knight or, by encouraging Oldcastle to abandon
Lollardy, to curry favour with the king and the court. Perhaps both motives played a
part, or just maybe something else is going on here.

The Keeper of the Privy Seal between 1406 and 1415, and Hoccleve's boss at this
time, was Sir John Prophete. Prophete was from Herefordshire and appears to have
been related to Oldcastle's first wife. He was elected dean of Hereford in 1393, resigning
in 1404 to become dean of York and Keeper of the Seal. He became a member of the
king's council for the first two years of Henry V's reign. That he and Oldcastle remained
in contact over the years is evidenced by a letter, written after Oldcastle's goods had
been declared forfeit in January 1414, by Prophete's nephew, Thomas Felde, who had
become a clerk of the Privy Seal, like Hoccleve. Whilst close to Oldcastle, Prophete
seems to have been orthodox in his religious beliefs, though interested in reform of the
Church at least to some extent – as dean of Hereford he was noted for his reform of St
Katherine's Hospital in Ledbury, and the overseeing of the granting of a charter to the
Vicars Choral in Hereford.[7]

Felde wrote to a bishop closely connected to Oldcastle's second wife, Joan, Lady
Cobham (believed to be Richard Courtenay of Norwich, who was her second cousin),
suggesting that he should buy the possessions due for forfeiture so as to provide Lady
Cobham with money and prevent anyone else from obtaining them. He wrote that
his uncle, John Prophete, would have intervened to prevent the sale if the king had
not been a party to the transaction (the possessions being forfeited to the Crown and
Prophete being on the king's council), as Oldcastle had, some years before, transferred
by charter ownership of all his movable possessions to his uncle (presumably fearing
that they might be forfeited at some point because of his activities). Courtenay was a
close associate of Henry V and he, like many others, was to die of dysentery at Harfleur
at the start of the Agincourt campaign. However, the letter might have reached him
in time and had some effect, for Oldcastle's Kentish possessions weren't forfeited until
November 1417.[8]

There seems to have been a strong bond of fellowship amongst those working at
the Office of the Privy Seal, Hoccleve himself talking of 'dwelling in the Privy Seal'
and of taking a boat 'home to the Privy Seal'. As one of this fellowship. Hoccleve
would probably have known of Prophete's and Felde's albeit distant relationship
to Oldcastle, and known that, at the time he wrote his 'Address', they would be

concerned about the plight of his wife. It was a time of increasing control over what was written and circulated by both Church and in secular statute, not least Archbishop Arundel's Constitutions drafted in 1407 and published in 1409, which prohibited discussion of any article of dogma if unlicensed to do so. In addition, Hoccleve seems to have been suspected of Lollardy by Thomas Walsingham. During the 1390s Hoccleve was on the fringes of Geoffrey Chaucer's circle, which included three of the Lollard knights mentioned on page 51, another of whom, Clanvowe, was a poet. It's possible therefore that Hoccleve did have some sympathy for Lollard views, and as part of that circle could have become used to writing satirical verse. Take verse 54 of his 'Address' in modern English:

> You also hold against possessions of holy church, and that is also an error; your inner eye is full of smoke and mist! While on earth, our Saviour, whom angels served and honoured, had purses. Why? So that His church should increase after; so says my authority. You have gone all amiss; all you believe is wrong!

The purse referred to here is the 'common purse' that Christ gave to Judas Iscariot to look after, and from which payments were made to the poor (John 12:6). The possession of purses by Christ became a justification as to why the Church should have possessions, but in this verse Hoccleve has turned the argument round, making the fact that the Church has possessions as the reason for Christ having purses. In other places Hoccleve exaggerates his eulogies and praise for certain people with ironic intent, if this reading of the poem is correct. He also repeats accusations against the Lollards, which were apparently well known at the time to be false, such as succumbing to lust 'as you don't care whose wife you take and hold'.

With other references to darkness and light (including a reference to 'lanterns of darkness' which could be a play upon the Wycliffite tract the *Lantern of Light*, possession of which could lead to death as a heretic), perhaps Hoccleve is encouraging people to look closely at Christianity and to consider Lollard views.

A poem of a rather different tone was written around the same time. Called 'Against the Lollards',[9] it targets not just Lollardy but Oldcastle himself. Its writer is unknown. It comprises 19 verses, verses 4 and 5 of which are reproduced here in their old English:

> Hit is unkyndly for a knizt,
> That shuld a kynges castel kepe,
> To bable the Bibel day and nizt
> In restyng tyme when he shuld slepe;
> And carefoly awey to crepe,
> For alle the chief of chivalrie.
> Wel aught hym to waile and wepe,
> That suyche lust hath in lollardie.

An old castel, and not repaired,
With wast walles and wowes wide,
The wages ben ful yvel wared
With suiche a capitayn to abide;
That rerethe riot for to ride
Agayns the kynge and his clergie,
With privé peyne and pore pride;
Ther is a poynt of lollardie.

Oldcastle as martyr, traitor and stage character

The first recorded description of Oldcastle as a martyr resulted from the trial of William Emayn of Bristol in 1429. Emayn had been a resident of Byfield in Northamptonshire, where Oldcastle sought refuge during 1417, and Byfield and nearby Chipping Warden appear to have been centres of Lollardy. Emayn had moved to Buckingham, where he spread Lollard ideas and soon found himself in the bishop's gaol, in which he spent two years. Eventually he successfully convinced the church authorities that he had purged himself of heretical beliefs, but he next appears in Bristol, once again espousing Lollard doctrines. He was brought before Bishop Stafford of Bath and Wells for trial for heresy on 10 March 1430. Of the 16 heretical articles he was charged with, one was:

> the opinions that Sir John Oldecastel, called the lord Cobham … [together with six others, including Wycliff], which persones for their errours and heresies that they pertinatlich defended were convicted and demed for heretikes, and so take to secular pouer and punisshed to the deth, were holy men and thair doctrine and opinions were trewe and catholik, and therfor thay be worshipped in heven as holy martirs.[10]

Presumably Emayn was not the only Lollard to hold such views, but after this trial Oldcastle seems to drop out of sight, at least in the written record, until around a century later when *A Boke of Thorpe or of John Oldcastelle*, believed to have been written by George Constantine, was published in Antwerp in 1530. The book is a record of the examinations for heresy under Archbishop Arundel of John Thorpe in 1407 and of Oldcastle in 1413. It was condemned in 1531 by John Stokesley, bishop of London, a staunch Catholic and opponent of Protestant-inspired heresies.[11] As covered in Chapter Seven, this book became one of the main sources first for Bale's *Brefe Chronicle* in the 1540s (which also sought to have Thomas à Becket replaced by Oldcastle as a hero for emulation) and then for Foxe's *Book of Martyrs*, first published in English in 1563. In his preface Bale refers to Oldcastle as 'one of those godly and valiant warriors … Of whose gracious number a very special member, and a vessel of God's election, was that virtuous knight Sir John Oldcastle, the good lord Cobham', Foxe calling him 'a man of extraordinary merit, … who left the world with a resolution and constancy'. The Lollard rejection of transubstantiation, pilgrimages and the veneration of images, coupled with their call for the reform of the clergy and their view that the pope was the Antichrist, would have appealed to those seeking to bolster the nascent Protestantism in England. In this view of the early days of Protestantism, Oldcastle provided a valuable figure in a suggested continuity of the clamour for reform that began with Wycliffe. The scene was therefore set for a tussle between those who wished to vilify Oldcastle as a traitor and heretic, and those who sought to put him on a pedestal as a martyr and example of a Christian knight.

Oldcastle was to appear in a rather different light to that propounded by Foxe in *The Famous Victories of Henry the fifth*, a play written sometime before 1594 – when it was entered by the printer Thomas Creede in the Stationers' Register – and possibly as early as the late 1570s. (The Stationers' Register was operated by the Stationers' Company, a trade guild established in 1577 which allowed printers and playwrights to gain a form of copyright by registering their works.) The earliest surviving edition of the play dates to 1598 and covers the same ground as Shakespeare in his three plays *Henry IV Parts I* and *II* and *Henry V*, but in much less detail. There are numerous elements of the play that reappear in Shakespeare's trilogy: the robbery at Gad's Hill,

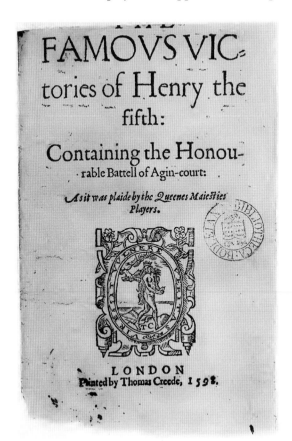

The title page of
The Famous Victories of Henry the fifth.

the meeting of the robbers in an inn at Eastcheap, the 'borrowing' of the crown by Prince Hal while Henry IV is asleep, the reconciliation of the prince with the chief justice on becoming king, the rejection by the king of his former dissolute friends, the gift of tennis balls from the Dauphin, and the wooing of Katherine by Henry following his victory at Agincourt.

The Famous Victories contains next to nothing that equates with the known history of Oldcastle, but there are several scenes in which Oldcastle plays a role similar to that later played by Falstaff in Shakespeare's trilogy. The play opens with a scene in which Prince Henry and two companions, who have stolen money from two royal receivers, meet Oldcastle, who is addressed as Jocky in the text. The money is spent on carousing in an inn, which leads to a brawl and the prince's arrest. Henry IV despairs of his son and asks that he be brought to see him. In the meantime, the prince has been released, angry at his treatment by the chief justice, and tells Jocky and his companions that they will have major positions of state when he is king. Meeting the chief justice, the prince assaults him. Brought before his father, the prince promises to reform his lifestyle. As King Henry lies dying, the prince picks up the crown, but the king revives and upbraids him once more, the prince promising to do well as king. Henry dies and the prince dismisses his old companions. The play continues into the prince's reign as Henry V with no mention of the Southampton Plot, but includes discussions with the archbishop about his claim to the throne of France, the arrival of the tennis balls from the Dauphin (called Dolphin in the play, as Exeter also calls him in Shakespeare's *Henry V*), the capture of Harfleur, the Battle of Agincourt and the wooing of Katherine of France. There is also a subplot of low life soldiery, akin to the tales included by Shakespeare.

Who wrote *The Famous Victories* is unknown, but several names have been suggested. Some say it was Richard Tarleton, the actor who is said to have played Dericke, a tradesman and clown, when the play was first performed.[12] Others name Edward de Vere, 17th earl of Oxford – or at least the play is said to be based on a court masque that he had written, or to be by someone who wished to flatter the earl, as his ancestor, the 11th earl, plays an overly prominent role.[13] Another contender is a very young Christopher Marlowe, on the basis that one of the characters is called John Cobler, the name of Marlowe's shoemaker father, and another is called Lawrence Applegate, the name of a friend and neighbour of his. It has also been proposed that the author could have been a young Shakespeare, though this suggestion has been largely rejected due to the flatness of the dialogue compared with Shakespeare's usual writing. To counter this latter point, some say that the surviving record of *The Famous Victories* was written down by someone other than Shakespeare from memory, having seen it performed.

The play's precise location in the chronological order of plays written around this time is equally uncertain. There have been suggestions that the first performance took place sometime between 1576 and 1583, and one record states that William Knell, who died in 1587, played Henry, and that Richard Tarleton, who died in 1588, played Dericke. If this is accurate, *The Famous Victories* clearly predated Shakespeare's trilogy, which was written in the late-1590s as will be detailed later. The edition of *The Famous Victories* published in 1598 states that it was performed by the company of actors known as the Queen's Men; at that time Shakespeare was with the company known as the Lord Chamberlain's Men. The play was republished in 1617, when it was said to be acted 'by the Kinges Maiesties Seruants', or the King's Men, which the Lord Chamberlain's Men had by then become. It is possible that Shakespeare had acquired the rights to *The Famous Victories* by the time he wrote his trilogy, but in any case he must have been familiar with the play, for he clearly used its structure in his own work.

It has been suggested that the Oldcastle character that first saw light of day in *The Famous Victories* was in part based upon Sir Nicholas Dawtrey, who served Queen Elizabeth throughout his life; however, this is unlikely. Dawtrey was apparently corpulent and hated work, so at least in those characteristics he was Falstaffian, but his career was spent partly in Ireland and partly laying claim to a potential inheritance, nothing that would suggest substituting the name Oldcastle in place of Dawtrey, the real Oldcastle at best spending a little over a year in Ireland with no surviving records as to what he did whilst over there.[14]

Foxe's *Martyrs* had been published in English in 1563, and the Church of England, as it now was following the break with Rome, ordered all cathedrals to have a copy available for public reading, with some parish churches following suit. In 1565 Thomas Stapleton's translation of Bede's *Ecclesiastical History of the English People* was published; this included a preface setting out how Queen Elizabeth's predecessors had countered heresy, drawing particular attention to Henry V's suppression of Oldcastle's rising.[15] This was followed by a publication written by Nicholas Harpsfield which questioned the accuracy of Foxe's work, and later editions of Foxe's book included a refutation of Harpsfield's criticisms. Foxe mounted a strong defence of the charge of treason against Oldcastle, for if Oldcastle could be cleared of such a charge and that of sedition, his strong support of much of the status quo during his trial and his position in the nobility lent him credibility as an ideal Protestant martyr. For, as Foxe sought to counter Harpsfield's criticisms, he learned more about the Lollards and came to appreciate the wide variety of views they held, not all of which he or other reformers would have supported. This defence was necessary not only due to Harpsfield's attack on his first edition, which pointed out several errors of detail, but to counter a work by Sir Thomas More that had been published in 1529. In responding to an Evangelical tract that had suggested that the Catholic Church tended to usurp princely authority, More pointed out the various times in history that it was actually those deemed heretics by the Church who had encouraged sedition and challenged such authority, citing as the most recent example a peasants' revolt in Germany that had followed on publication of works by Martin Luther.[16] Thus, in his later editions, Foxe heaped doubt on the motives of the Catholic chroniclers who recorded Oldcastle's life. He made much of the fact that there is no evidence that Oldcastle was present at the gathering on St Giles' Fields, that it is not known for certain what was intended by the gathering, and that treason shouldn't be imputed to unknown intentions. He also explained Oldcastle's escape from the Tower as the providential work of God. (As is now understood from records, of which Foxe would not have known and which have been explored in the previous chapter, the intentions and treasonable nature of the rising do now seem clear.)

In sixteenth- and seventeenth-century England, ecclesiastical history was seen as the next best thing to read after the Bible and, despite the relatively small numbers printed, as Foxe's *Martyrs* was comparatively freely available it soon spawned ideas for subjects as disparate as household decoration and ballads.[17] Thus, it is not surprising that it also brought Oldcastle's name to a wider public. As a companion-in-arms with Prince Henry, Oldcastle therefore became an obvious choice for a character in *The Famous Victories*, a character with whom the audience could identify.

Perhaps the author of *The Famous Victories* was inclined to Catholicism and simply wanted to prick the Protestant bubble in a fairly gentle way, and certainly in a way that did not trouble Sir Edmund Tilney, the Master of Revels and censor of plays from 1579 (see below).

Shakespeare and Falstaff join the fray

Shakespeare certainly gained much inspiration from *The Famous Victories* for his plays about Henry IV and V, not just in regards to the history of the period but also for the juxtaposition of comic and tragic scenes. In addition he used *Holinshed's Chronicles*, which were first published in 1577, with a revised and extended edition published ten years later, after Holinshed's death. Holinshed wrote in English, compiling his work from a number of sources. He devoted considerable space to the early history of Britain (including Ireland, Scotland and Wales along with England), but even so the passage covering the reigns of Henry IV and V is quite detailed. Regarding Oldcastle he wrote:

> Also in this first yeere of this kings reigne [that of Henry V], sir Iohn Oldcastell, which by his wife was called lord Cobham, a valiant capteine and a hardie gentleman, was accused to the archbishop of Canturburie of certeine points of heresie, who knowing him to be highlie in the kings fauour, declared to his high-nesse the whole accusation. The king first having compassion of the noble man, required the prelats, that if he were a straied sheepe, rather by gentlenes than by rigor to reduce him to the fold. And after this, he himselfe sent for him, and right earnestlie exhorted him, and lovinglie admonished him to reconcile himselfe to God and to his lawes. The lord Cobham not onelie thanked him for his most favourable clemencie, but also declared first to him by mouth, and afterwards by writing, the foundation of his faith, and the ground of his beliefe …[18]

Holinshed then goes on to record fairly faithfully, over several pages, the events leading up to Oldcastle's trial, the trial itself, his escape from the Tower and subsequent capture and execution. There is no sign of the low-fallen, witty knight of Shakespeare's Oldcastle/Falstaff, although in other ways Shakespeare follows Holinshed almost to the letter, and keeps extremely close to what were then believed to be historical facts.

In Chapter Five (pages 112-13) it was seen how closely the opening scene of Shakespeare's *Henry V* follows the actual history of the Church's concern that the Lollard petition presented to parliament in 1410 was seeking to take the Church's wealth for the benefit of the kingdom. See now how closely Shakespeare, in putting words into Archbishop Arundel's mouth, follows Holinshed's story of the archbishop of Canterbury's attempt to divert Henry's attention from matters concerning the Church to those concerning France. Holinshed writes:

> Herein did he [the archbishop] much inveie against the surmised and false fained law Salike, which the Frenchmen alledge ever against the kings of England in barre of their iust title to the crowne of France. The verie words of that supposed law are these, *In terram Salicam mulieres ne succedant*, that is to saie, Into the Salike land let not women succeed. Which the French glossers expound to be the realme of France, and that this law was made by king Pharamond; whereas yet their owne authors affirme, that the land Salike is in Germanie, betweene the riuers of Elbe and Sala; and that when Charles the great had overcome the Saxons, he placed there certeine Frenchmen, which having in disdeine the dishonest maners of the Germane women, made a law, that the females should not succeed to any inheritance within that land, which at this daie is called Meisen, so that if this be true, this law was not made for the realme of France, nor the Frenchmen possessed the land Salike, till foure hundred and one and twentie yeares after the death of Pharamond, the supposed maker of this Salike law, for this Pharamond deceassed in the yeare 426, and Charles the great subdued the Saxons, and placed the Frenchmen in those parts beyond the river of Sala, in the yeare 805.[19]

Shakespeare puts almost the exact words into the mouth of the archbishop in *Henry V*, Act I, Scene II:

> ....There is no bar
> To make against your highness' claim to France
> But this, which they produce from Pharamond,
> '*In terram Salicam mulieres ne succedant:*'
> 'No woman shall succeed in Salique land:'
> Which Salique land the French unjustly gloze
> To be the realm of France, and Pharamond
> The founder of this law and female bar.
> Yet their own authors faithfully affirm
> That the land Salique is in Germany,
> Between the floods of Sala and of Elbe;

Where Charles the Great, having subdued the Saxons,
There left behind and settled certain French;
Who, holding in disdain the German women
For some dishonest manners of their life,
Establish'd then this law; to wit, no female
Should be inheritrix in Salique land:
Which Salique, as I said, 'twixt Elbe and Sala,
Is at this day in Germany call'd Meisen.
Then doth it well appear that Salique law
Was not devised for the realm of France:
Nor did the French possess the Salique land
Until four hundred one and twenty years
After defunction of King Pharamond,
Idly supposed the founder of this law;
Who died within the year of our redemption
Four hundred twenty-six; and Charles the Great
Subdued the Saxons, and did seat the French
Beyond the river Sala, in the year
Eight hundred five. ....

If Shakespeare was happy to use Holinshed so freely, what made him decide to dramatise the buffoon Oldcastle of *The Famous Victories* as opposed to the 'valiant capteine and a hardie gentleman' of Holinshed? The answer is probably simple. Henry V was to be seen as the pinnacle of English kingship, so there was no room in the play for another 'valiant capteine'. Shakespeare needed a clown character. Who better than the embryonic figure of *The Famous Victories*, made fat for the purpose? In Shakespeare's day fatness was seen as a sign of ill health and fat people were believed to die young, so the mere presence of a fat old man actually surviving already lent itself to mirth, and giving him a character full of life developed the theme. The idea was to have the part played by an actor with stuffing inside his doublet, giving Shakespeare the excuse to add to the comedy by describing Falstaff as a 'woolsack', a 'stuffed cloakbag of guts' and a 'creature of bombast'. Falstaff has a hearty dislike of authority, which Oldcastle certainly had in respect to the Church, though not obviously in other aspects of life – indeed he was appointed as a justice of the peace and commissioner into various concerns on several occasions. A character poking fun at authority would have appealed to Shakespeare, as to many a playwright. But why call him Falstaff and not Oldcastle?

That Shakespeare originally wrote *Henry IV Part I* with Oldcastle as the name of the 'fat knight' is known in part from textual evidence set out later in this chapter, and also from a letter from a Dr Richard James to Sir Henry Bourchier, probably dated either 1634 or 1635. James had gained a Bachelor of Divinity degree at Oxford and subsequently moved in literary circles, becoming a friend of Ben Jonson and librarian to Sir Robert Cotton, owner of an extensive library. His letter to Bourchier accompanied a copy of Hoccleve's 'Address to Sir John Oldcastle' and in it he says:

Wherefore to you I dedicate this edition of Occleve, where Sr Jhon Oldcastell apeeres to have binne a man of valour and vertue, and onely lost in his owne times because he would not bowe vnder the foule superstition of Papistrie …. That in Shakespeare's first shewe of Harrie ye fift, ye person with which he undertook to playe a buffone was not Falstaffe but Sir Jhon Oldcastle, & that offence being worthily taken by personages descended from his title, as peradventure by manie others allso whoe ought to haue him in honourable memorie, the poet was putt to make an ignorant shifte of abusing Sr Jhon Fastolphe, a man not inferior of vertue though not so famous in pietie as the other, whoe gaue witness vnto the truth of our reformation with a constant & resolute martyrdom, vnto which he was pursued by the Priests, Bishops, Moncks, & Friers of those dayes.

Richard James's reference to 'Shakespeare's first shewe of Harrie ye fift' is taken to mean the trilogy of plays spanning the king's life, rather than the single play *Henry V* in which only Falstaff's death appears. James mentions that the change of name now cast a slur on that of Sir John Fastolfe, one of King Henry's V's commanders in the war in France.

At this date plays had to go through a form of censorship at the hands of the Master of the Revels, a post that carried two prime duties: planning and conducting royal entertainments, and prohibiting the discussion of anything controversial in theatrical performances. Any play to be performed had to carry his signature, and the decision as to whether it could be performed was his alone. Between 1579 and 1610 the post was held by Sir Edmund Tilney, and he must have read and passed *Henry IV Part I*, wherein the name Oldcastle is given to the character who was to be renamed Falstaff, the play being first performed during 1596. Yet on 25 February 1598 *Henry IV Part I* was entered in the Stationers' Register with the name Falstaff. So, what had happened between the first performance of the play and its entry in the Stationers' Register?

Those who held the title of Lord Cobham – 'personages descended from his [Oldcastle's] title' as described in James's letter – during Shakespeare's lifetime were successively Sir William and Sir Henry Brooke, 10th and 11th Lords Cobham. Oldcastle would have been the stepfather of William's great-great-great-grandmother. Discussion of the precise details as to what happened have engendered a series of articles down the years, but the key details as far as the story of Oldcastle are concerned are broadly as follows.[20]

Falstaff appears not just in *Henry IV Parts I* and *II*, but also in *Henry V* (in the report of his death) and more particularly in *The Merry Wives of Windsor*. *Merry Wives* must post-date *Henry IV Part I*, as the character of Oldcastle/Falstaff has been established, and it is generally accepted that *Merry Wives* was written at the request of Queen Elizabeth after she had seen Falstaff on stage. The Lord Chamberlain, Henry Carey (Lord Hunsdon, the founder of the Lord Chamberlain's Men) died during July 1596. His successor in the post, appointed on 8 August, was William Brooke, the 10th Lord Cobham. Brooke apparently took on the role of Lord Chamberlain reluctantly, and

The Lord Chamberlain, Henry Carey,
Lord Hunsdon, who died in 1596.

William Brooke, 10th Lord
Cobham, who succeeded Henry
Carey as Lord Chamberlain.

some have suggested that he was no lover of plays, but as Lord Warden of the Cinque Ports he was a patron of a group of actors that performed in the south of England in the 1560s. He also hadn't complained, when others had, of the potential nuisance that would be caused by the refurbishment of a property in Blackfriars that was to become a theatre, even though the property was next to his.[21] It would seem he did enjoy and support the theatre.

Given that it was the Cobhams who took exception to the use of the Oldcastle name (although, as James says in his letter, they weren't the only ones, there being 'manie others allso whoe ought to haue him in honourable memorie'), *Henry IV Part I* must have been passed by Tilney while Lord Hunsdon was still Lord Chamberlain, and so must have been completed by 23 July 1596 at the latest, the day that Hunsdon died. Tilney (or his predecessor, depending precisely when it had been written) had already passed *The Famous Victories of Henry the fifth* with its caricature of Oldcastle, about which Brooke had not complained (though, as Oldcastle is largely referred to as Jocky throughout, Brooke might not have seen this as a concern), so saw no problem with licensing *Henry IV Part I*. The play might have been completed earlier in 1596, and performed in London before the theatres were closed on 22 July, due to worries about the spread of an outbreak of plague, and then taken on tour until the London theatres reopened in October. Alternatively, at the very least it would have been put on when the theatres opened again if, as events suggest, the play was to be performed at Court during the Christmas festivities, for the company would have wanted to have perfected it in advance. It is unlikely that William Brooke would have gone to a performance of the play in Shoreditch during these months: he was nigh on 70 years old and had multifarious duties as Lord Warden of the Cinque Ports, privy councillor and Lord Lieutenant of Kent. If he had seen the play, or got word that what he was to see was a slur, then the performance that did take place at Court and which he witnessed, would presumably have not gone ahead with the name Oldcastle.[22]

The occasion Brooke saw the play seems to have been during the Christmas festivities of 1596, when the Lord Chamberlain's Men performed a play at Court. Though it is not recorded which play it was, a letter written by Tilney in subsequent years refers to what would seem to be an incident that followed shortly afterwards. In this, he refers to a letter he had received on another matter as the 'most Arrogantist letter that Euer I receiued only for findinge fault therwith, and yett I have receuid diuerss braue letters from the last Lord Chamberlain When he and I were att odds'.[23] This letter was dated 25 January, and references to people in certain positions within it pin down the date of its writing it to either 1599 or 1600. This makes William Brooke, Lord Cobham, 'the last Lord Chamberlain' referred to. A degree of analysis suggests that the episode referred to was in connection with the performance of *Henry IV Part I* and that Tilney was severely rebuked for not having censored the name of Oldcastle and was asked to take immediate steps to do so. Surprised at the vehemence of William Brooke's feelings, Tilney evidently immediately requested a revised copy of the play with the names changed that he could show to Brooke. As the writing of *Henry IV Part II* was at least underway, and possibly well advanced, he would have required the change of name in this play as well. Brooke seems to have been touchy on the subject of Oldcastle not for the slur of lampooning a very distant relative, but for fear it would raise associations in the mind of the Court (and Elizabeth I in particular) with his own treason. For Brooke had been involved on the margins of the Ridolfi Plot of 1571 which sought to put Mary, Queen of Scots on the throne and restore Catholicism to England, when he had handled and passed on treasonous correspondence when trying to protect his brother.[24]

This train of events seems to fit with what we know about the plays and their various versions. During Shakespeare's time, plays were usually printed as quartos: four leaves (and so eight pages) made from one large sheet of paper folded down. Plays were often revised, and so different quartos can represent different editions. The printing of the first quarto of *Henry IV Part I* is considered to be tidier than its equivalent for most plays, suggesting that someone had copied out the original manuscript from which the play was first performed, in this case perhaps to incorporate the fresh name of Falstaff in the version that was then printed. This surmise is supported by the fact that all the characters' prefixes in *Part I* are more uniform than in *Part II*, where (in early, untidied copies) Falstaff appears variously as John, sir John, Fa., Fal., Falst., and in one instance as Old., presumably where Shakespeare reverted to the original name for the character without realising it. This also supports the idea that Shakespeare was still writing *Part II* when the requested change came through.

The text in *Part II* also makes a link for those who had seen the original *Part I* before the change of name, confirming that the character they saw on stage in *Part II*, now named Falstaff, was the same as the character called Oldcastle in *Part I*. The link to events in *Part I* – the robbery at Gad's Hill and the Battle of Shrewsbury – is made in Act I, Scene II of *Part II*:

> Lord Chief-Justice: What's he that goes there?
> Servant: Falstaff, an't please your lordship.
> Lord Chief-Justice: He that was in question for the robbery?
> Servant: He, my lord: but he hath since done good service at
>   Shrewsbury; and, as I hear, is now going with some
>   charge to the Lord John of Lancaster.
> Lord Chief-Justice: What, to York? Call him back again.
> Servant: Sir John Falstaff!

There is a more direct link in the epilogue which says:

> One word more, I beseech you. If you be not too much cloyed with fat meat, our humble author will continue the story, with Sir John in it, and make you merry with fair Katharine of France: where, for any thing I know, Falstaff shall die of a sweat, unless already a' be killed with your hard opinions; for Oldcastle died a martyr, and this is not the man.

It is probable that those last 11 words were added at the request of Tilney to make it absolutely clear that the character of the now totally fictitious Falstaff bore no relation to the real-life Oldcastle. Yet hints remain, some subtle, some less so. For instance, in *Part I* Oldcastle/Falstaff talks about repentance, which would fit with the real Oldcastle's views on contrition. In Act III, Scene III, Falstaff says to Bardolph: 'Well, I'll repent, and that suddenly, while I am in some liking; I shall be out of heart shortly, and then I shall have no strength to repent. An I have not forgotten what the inside of a church is made of, I am a peppercorn, a brewer's horse: the inside of a church! Company, villainous company, hath been the spoil of me.'

Then there are the oft-quoted lines concerning the Oldcastle link with Falstaff, in *Part I*, Act I, Scene II:

> Falstaff: … And is not my hostess of the tavern a most sweet wench?
> Prince Henry: As the honey of Hybla, my old lad of the castle. And
>   is not a buff jerkin a most sweet robe of durance?'

Shakespeare may have left this quip in, having changed the name, without remembering the link between the two, or, possibly, purposely left it in to remind those already familiar with the play of the character's real name or as a camouflaged symbol of annoyance with William Brooke. On the other hand he might have added the quip when making the name change as a form of revenge. If revenge was in his mind, a further barb comes in the same scene when Falstaff says to Henry, reflecting Oldcastle's life:

> By the Lord, I'll be a traitor then, when thou art king.

Falstaff is depicted as an old warrior, now rather disdainful of warfare, deriding honour and favouring life over death. Is there a hint in this of the pacifist views of John Clanvowe and of the *Twelve Conclusions* put to parliament in 1395? But that is probably trying to find too much of Lollardy in the Oldcastle/Falstaff character. It would seem more likely that Shakespeare's inclusion of the name Oldcastle was purely accidental and had no ulterior motive. The outline of the character Oldcastle came from *The Famous Victories of Henry the fifth*, and as such a person did exist at the time and was mentioned in Holinshed, that would have provided some additional details to conjure with: a 'valiant capteine' / 'brave Jack Falstaff' who was a close companion of Hal, if not the boon companion that he became in the play. Nevertheless, the enforced name change may have riled him, leading to the insertion of those few additional jibes in the text.

Whilst Shakespeare was engaged in amending *Henry IV Parts I* and *II*, Sir William Brooke died. On 24 January 1597, his daughter Elizabeth, wife of Sir Robert Cecil, died in childbirth. Sir William then withdrew in mourning to his house in Blackfriars, so upset by the circumstances that he himself died on 6 March. On 17 April, George

Carey, 2nd Lord Hunsdon, was appointed Lord Chamberlain, and five days later he was elected a Knight of the Garter. Now patron of the Lord Chamberlain's Men, he requested a new entertainment to accompany the installation of new Garter knights on 23 May. This supports the tradition of the hasty compilation of *The Merry Wives of Windsor*, supposedly written in 14 days at the queen's command. The name Falstaff would, of course, have been used for the character in this play from the start.

As for the name Falstaff, it is widely thought that Shakespeare adapted the name of Sir John Fastolfe. Shakespeare had already written his *Henry VI* trilogy, in *Part I* of which Sir John Fastolfe makes a small appearance (in Act II, Scene II and Act IV, Scene I). This Sir John saw much service in France under John, duke of Bedford, in whose household he served. He was discredited for perceived cowardice at the Battle of Patay, when the rearguard of the English army retreating from the siege of Orléans was overwhelmed, essentially with only the van, led by Fastolfe, evading death or capture by a rapid retreat. Until then Fastolfe had been trusted with many commands, giving distinguished service in the victory of Verneuil, being one of the commanders of the force that took Le Mans and being victorious at the Battle of Rouvray (also known as the 'battle of the herrings' as he used barrels of the fish as a stockade). Nevertheless, the charge of cowardice was to pursue him for many years – the case against him was still being aired in the 1440s – until he was finally vindicated. It is the accusations of cowardice that shape his character in *Henry VI Part I* and it is the story of cowardice that is easily transferable from Fastolfe to Falstaff, who utters the words 'The better part of valour is discretion', much as Fastolfe would have defended his actions at Patay (and the phrase is now deemed to express good sense, of course). All other comparisons between the actual Fastolfe and fictitious Falstaff show no relation between the two;

Eastcheap Market as depicted in 1598.

The original Boar's Head Tavern in Eastcheap was destroyed during the Fire of London in 1666. When it was rebuilt in brick, this carved stone bas-relief of a boar's head was set above its first-floor windows. This replacement building was itself demolished in 1831 in preparation for the rebuilding of London Bridge, but the sign was retained and ended up in the Museum of London. Since 2010 it has been installed in the Globe Theatre, but this may change during 2021 when the exhibition space could be reduced as part of alterations to the building, and the inn sign may return to the Museum of London. (© Museum of London)

33–35 Eastcheap (slightly to the west of where the Boar's Head Tavern would have stood) was built in a gabled gothic style to the design of R.L. Roumieu in 1868, incorporating a roundel above its central window that pays homage to the earlier tavern. (Author)

Fastolfe was never numbered among Henry V's close friends when either prince or king. When Fastolfe returned to England in 1439 he did, however, acquire the Boar's Head Tavern in Southwark, where he also built himself a residence.[25] In *Henry IV Part I* Shakespeare named the inn in Eastcheap, in which he set the scenes of revelry for the young prince and his cohorts, the Boar's Head, using Stow's story (mentioned on pages 94-95) to give added historical weight. The further use of the name Fastolfe as the basis for that of Falstaff is just the next step.

As for the inn, Stow says 'there was no tauerne then [in Prince Henry's time] in Eastcheape',[26] but a Boar's Head Tavern did exist in Eastcheap by 1537,[27] so would have been in existence by Shakespeare's time. This may have led him to conflate Sir John Fastolfe's inn in Southwark with this one, allowing him to assign the various pieces of information and action to a Boar's Head in Eastcheap, whether extant at the requisite date of 1410 or not. The Elizabethan inn in Eastcheap was burned down in the Fire of London in 1666, but was rebuilt two years later, when it acquired a stone-carved boar's head as its sign.

But there was another Sir John Fastolf (no final 'e' in this case) who might have provided the inspiration for the name of Falstaff. In Chapter Four it was mentioned that in the story of Prince Henry's contretemps with a judge (as related by Thomas Elyot in *The Governor* of 1531) there are similarities to a recorded case. In 1380 'Hugh Fastolf and John Organ, citizens of London', acknowledged that they owed John Cobham, Lord Cobham, 800 marks (this would technically be Sir John Oldcastle's father-in-law, though he had died by the time Oldcastle married his daughter, Joan). The money was to be 'raised from their lands and chattels in London, and in the counties of Essex, Norfolk and Suffolk, and elsewhere'. The case clearly rumbled on, for some 20 years later both Hugh Fastolf and John Organ had died, but Cobham was still seeking the money due to him. The case went to court again, to ascertain if Sir John Fastolf, of Nacton (near Ipswich), the heir of Hugh Fastolf, owned or had certain manors from which the money could be raised. But the jury never reached a decision because Sir John Fastolf, or someone acting on his behalf, prevented the jury from giving their verdict. Apparently, a brawl took place during which some of the jurors were evicted from the court. Fastolf was then tried for this offence and four of his friends had to stand surety for his good behaviour in future, Fastolf pledging not to do or cause to be done any injury to the jurors of his case by 'threats, assaults, insults, or any other means which might in any manner tend to a lesion or disturbance of the peace …'.[28]

The contempt of court in the above case is never mentioned as such in the roll of the court proceedings, so it is possible that a similar occurrence took place in the story concerning Prince Henry and a judge. Perhaps the prince, after one of his escapades against the king's receivers (as recounted in Chapter Four), did get into legal difficulty and one of his comrades did threaten members of the jury. The judge, be it Gascoigne or another, determines to see the law complete its course; the prince gets angry but then realises he has done wrong, makes a submission, and his jury-threatening comrade is bound over to keep the peace, much as Sir John Fastolf is in the above case – leaving no record of the prince's actions in the court roll. That could mean that Elyot's story is true. But whether true or not, the case involving Sir John Fastolf of Nacton and Oldcastle's future father-in-law does create the possibility that it is this Fastolf that Shakespeare had in mind when making the name-change. If Shakespeare was annoyed at having to do this, he could at least take the opportunity of choosing a name similar to Fastolf to show his irritation, without provoking a further response.

The Oldcastle Play

And then there is the play called *The First Part of the true and honorable historie, of the life of Sir John Oldcastle, the good Lord Cobham*. The diary entry for 16 October 1599 of Philip Henslowe, manager of the Admiral's Men (a rival of the Lord Chamberlain's Men), says, 'to pay Mr Monday, Mr Drayton, and Mr Wilson and Hathway, for the first pte of the lyfe of Jhon Ouldcasstell, and in earnest of the second part' the sum of £10. The play was first performed sometime between 1–8 November that year and obviously proved a success, for on the latter date Henslowe recorded in his diary that he made a gift of 10 shillings to the playwrights. One version of the play, printed in 1600, claims it was written by William Shakespeare, but on the page that records Shakespeare's authorship, the phrase 'As it hath bene lately acted by … Lord High Admiral Of England, His Servants' has been retained, as it also appears in the other version printed in 1600, and this was not Shakespeare's company of actors. The printer, William Jaggard, was trying to retain printing rights to a number of plays which had similarities, so preventing anyone else claiming they had rights.

With the various companies of actors each trying to outdo their competitors by having the most popular plays, or the most popular version of a play, playwrights often wrote 'improved' versions of their plays, often taking ideas from others. This is essentially what Shakespeare had done with *The Famous Victories of Henry the fifth*. Actors, meanwhile, would seek to include authors' names on versions of texts, with the intent of denying that their text was similar to one carrying another author's name. Printers, meanwhile, needed to try to retain rights to plays they had printed in order to sell their print run, otherwise they would make a loss. So, anything that bore resemblance to Oldcastle, Falstaff, Henry IV or Henry V would have been in Jaggard's sights as a play to which he should try to lay a claim. (Shakespeare's name was attached to several other plays written around these years, by managers and playwrights wishing to cash in on his success and aiming to gild their own work or forthcoming performances with his name.) Jaggard's edition of the play made a false claim not only to Shakespeare's authorship, but also to the date of printing, for it was in fact printed in 1619. The false date was, in part, an attempt to get round an edict of the Lord Chamberlain of May 1619 that sought to prevent any further printing of plays written for the King's Men without the company's permission. In essence, printers, stationers, actors and

The first part

Of the true & hono-
rable hiftory, of the Life of
Sir Iohn Old-caftle, the good
Lord Cobham.

As it hath bene lately acted by the Right
honorable the Earle of Notingham
Lord High Admirall of England,
his Seruants.

Written by William Shakefpeare,

London printed for T. P.
1600.

The firft part

Of the true and hono-
rable hiftorie, of the life of Sir
John Old-caftle, the good
Lord Cobham.

As it hath been lately acted by the right
honorable the Earle of Notingham
Lord high Admirall of England his
feruants.

L O N D O N
Printed by V.S. for Thomas Pauier, and are to be folde at
his fhop at the figne of the Catte and Parrots
neere the Exchange.
1 6 0 0.

Title pages from two printings in 1600 of The First Part of the true and honorable historie(y), of the life of Sir John Oldcastle, the good Lord Cobham, one claiming it to be written by Shakespeare.

playwrights had conflicting interests when it came to protecting intellectual property rights in the absence of any detailed law on the subject.[29]

The versions of *Sir John Oldcastle*, to give it a shorter title, are slightly different, the later version being longer, but the differences between them do not concern us; what does is why the play was written and what, if anything, it tells us about Oldcastle or perceptions of him. It is only the first part that we can consider, for the promised second part, which would have had to deal with Oldcastle's death, has not survived.

In the late 1500s the Admiral's Men were performing at the Rose Theatre, close to the Globe where the Lord Chamberlain's Men performed. It is likely, therefore, that Henslowe wanted to have a play that would respond to Shakespeare's *Henry IV*, and if it might also embarrass the Lord Chamberlain's Men over the enforced name-change of one of the main characters, so much the better.[30] It could also be that Henslowe saw that those of a more Protestant disposition would enjoy a play in which Oldcastle was a hero and an upholder of Protestant ideals, rather than one which might be said to slander Oldcastle's memory in the shape of a licentious clown. After its first performance in early November 1599, the Admiral's Men performed their Oldcastle play twice more: once later in November and once in December. However, when they left the Rose for their new theatre – the Fortune in London's then northern suburbs just beyond the boundaries of the City of London – they passed both the Rose and the play onto Worcester's Men, presumably the play losing part of its relevance for the company if it wasn't standing in competition with Shakespeare's *Henry IV.* Worcester's Men performed the play twice, in August and September 1602, then allowed it to lapse. It has nevertheless been printed 18 times (sometimes as part of a collection of plays attributed to Shakespeare), including twice in the eighteenth century, five times in the nineteenth and four times in the early twentieth. Those organising some of these later printings took the opportunity to slightly 'tidy' the text of errors of one kind or another. The play has also been translated into German and Danish.[31]

The Lord Chamberlain's Men are recorded as playing 'Sir John Old Castle' in March 1600, at the Blackfriars home of their patron. It was very rare for a company to perform the play of another company, and this record therefore probably refers to a play whose main character, it was well known, had originally been called John Oldcastle – that is either *Henry IV Part I* or *Part II*. If so, it would be just one example, it would seem, of how audiences saw through the disguise of Falstaff to Oldcastle at this time and for at least a few decades thereafter.[32] For example, there is a record of a performance of a play simply called 'Olde Castell' performed at Court on 29 May 1638, which is thought to have been one of Shakespeare's 'Falstaff' plays.[33] And it would seem that *Henry IV Part I* at least was a popular play. Having been first printed in 1598, it required reprinting that same year (only a single fragment of eight pages survive from the first printing), with five further editions between then and 1623. As Stanley Wells says in *Shakespeare For All Time*, 'The printing of two editions within a few months, and the fact that one of them was read almost out of existence, reflect the great interest in the play both in itself and as a topic of scandal centring on its main comic character.'[34]

It appears that the poet and playwright Michael Drayton supplied much of the dialogue for the lighthearted parts of *The First Part of the true and honorable historie, of the life of Sir John Oldcastle, the good Lord Cobham.* Anthony Munday, who was often behind ferocious wordy attacks on Catholics, probably crafted at least the core of the scenes bearing on religious and political issues, with Richard Hathway, who appears to have been a comedy writer, and Robert Wilson, who collaborated on several plays for Henslowe in this period,[35] filling in the gaps and smoothing out the whole. The play was clearly intended to restore the reputation of the real Sir John Oldcastle, for the prologue states:

> It is no pampered glutton we present,
> Nor aged Councellor to youthful sinne,
> But one, whose vertue shone above the rest,
> A valiant Martyr and a vertuous peere,
> … Let fair Truth be grac'te,
> Since forg'de inuention former time defac'te.

The play in fact has two Sir Johns, one being Oldcastle and the other a fat priest by the name of Sir John of Wrotham. This latter Sir John, along with William Murley, the Dunstable brewer who in real life (as William Morley) was arrested and hanged for his part in the St Giles's Fields rising, are the two comic parts in the play. The priestly 'Sir John', then a common name for a parson, becomes a highwayman who, it becomes clear, has himself been robbed in the days of Hal's association with Falstaff (differentiated in this play from Oldcastle). Wrotham travels with a 'Doll', the same name given by Shakespeare to the whore in *Henry IV Part II*, and at that time a common name for a lady of the night. As for Oldcastle's reputation, the aim of the play is to show that he was anything but a traitor whilst maintaining his good 'Protestant' views. To this end the play tells a story in which not only is Oldcastle unaware of the rising on St Giles's Fields (which is planned by, amongst others, Sir Roger Acton and the brewer Murley), but also betrays the Southampton Plot to Henry. The bishop of Rochester becomes Oldcastle's clerical adversary in place of Archbishop Arundel, constantly trying to get Oldcastle declared a traitor, only for Henry to keep pardoning him, with the two often acting in parallel. Thus, although Oldcastle has been pardoned by Henry as a result of betraying the Southampton Plot, the bishop is still out to arrest Oldcastle for perceived treachery, believing him to have been present at the rising on St Giles's Fields. Henry is embarking for France by the time the bishop arranges for Oldcastle and Lady Cobham to be detained in the Tower of London. They escape by tying up the bishop when he comes to visit them, and taking his clothes. After they have managed to prove their innocence of a murder for which they have been stitched up during their flight, the play ends with Lord Powis, on whose part Oldcastle has earlier gained a pardon from Henry for an inadvertent murder he committed, escorting Oldcastle and his wife towards his castle for their safekeeping. One presumes that this is setting up a sting in the tail for the lost *Part II*, as it was Powis's men who captured the historical John Oldcastle and sent him to London and his death.

There are several points in the play where Oldcastle is shown in a good light, once more the 'valiant capteine and a hardie gentleman' of Holinshed, as well as the Protestant martyr of Bale and Foxe. The bishop of Rochester, speaking with the earl of Suffolk, says of Oldcastle (lines 137–42):

> Greevous complaints have past betweene the lips
> Of envious persons to up braide the Clergy,
> Some carping at the livings which we have;
> And others spurning at the Ceremonies
> That are of ancient custome in the Churche.
> Amongst the which, Lord Cobham is a cheefe; …

Suffolk then reports the bishop's concerns to King Henry (lines 209–20):

Suffolk:
　　… and suppresse
All such malicious errors as begin
To spot their calling, and disturbe the Church.

King Henry:
God else forbid: why Suffolke,
is there any new rupture to disquiet them?

Suffolk:
No new my Lord, the old is great enough,
And do increasing, as if not cut downe
Will breede a scandall to your Royall State,
And set your kingdome quickly in an uprore.
The Kentish Knight, Lord Cobham in despight
Of any Law, or spirituall discipline,
Maintaines this upstart new Religion still, …

Later in this conversation, Henry says to Suffolk (lines 243–45):

But he [Oldcastle] hath always been reputed loyall,
And in my knowledge I can say this much,
That he is vertuous, wide, and honourable.

Elsewhere in the play, Sir Roger Acton and others are questioned as to whether they knew Oldcastle was to join them at St Giles's Fields aside from hearsay, Acton replying (lines 1,756–58):

I must confesse we have no other ground
But onely rumour to accuse this Lord,
Which now I see was meerely fabulous

In a gathering of poor people, old soldiers and old men, one of the old men remarks (lines 328–330):

Ha, were I but as lusty as I was at Shrewsbury battel,
I would not de as I do: but we are now come to the good
Lord Cobham, the best man to the poore in al Kent.

Here is seen a combination of building up the good (Protestant) Christian knight, and also combatting the story of Oldcastle/Falstaff at the Battle of Shrewsbury, as depicted in Shakespeare's *Henry IV Part I* (the real Oldcastle not having been present at that battle, of course).

Sir John Oldcastle: one of a set of 46 illustrations engraved by Michael Vandergucht to accompany Shakespeare's plays edited by N. Rowe (in which *The First Part of the true and honorable historie, of the life of Sir John Oldcastle* was numbered amongst those credited to Shakespeare) and published in 1709. The illustration was used as a frontispiece. It shows the scene when Oldcastle has been imprisoned on the orders of the Bishop of Rochester and is about to escape by wearing the bishop's clothes. The text from the play which this drawing illustrates is given below. (© V&A Museum; Dyce Coll. No.2381)

The History and Legends of Old Castles and Abbeys, published in 1875,[36] tells a story of the serving of the summons on Oldcastle, when he was at Cooling Castle, to appear before Archbishop Arundel. In this tale, Harpool, Oldcastle's servant, makes the summoner eat the parchment on which the summons was written and the wax with which it was sealed, a story taken straight from the play.

Oldcastle: My lord of Rochester on good advice
    I see my error; but yet understand me,
    I mean not error in the faith I holde,
    But error in submitting to your pleasure,
    Therefore your Lordship without more to do,
    Must be a meanes to helpe me to escape.

Bishop: What means thou heretike?
    Darst thou but lift thy hand against my calling?

Oldcastle: No not to hurt you, for a thousand pound.

Harpool [Oldcastle's servant]: Nothing but to borrow your upper garments
    a little not a word more, peace for waking the children; there, put them on,
    dispatch my lord, the window that goes out onto the Leads is sure enough:
    and as for you, I'll bind you surely in the inner room.

As mentioned above, *Sir John Oldcastle* was possibly written for the Admiral's Men performing at the Rose Theatre, to make use of the popularity of Shakespeare's *Henry IV* performed by the Lord Chamberlain's Men in the nearby Globe, and embarrass them over the enforced change of name of the Oldcastle character to Falstaff. It has also been suggested that the play may have been written to pander to the tastes of a Protestant-inclined audience who favoured a view of Oldcastle as valiant knight and martyr. Whilst commercial considerations underlie the first two premises, there is an alternative political motive for the third. The story of Sir John Oldcastle in the play bears little relation to what is known about his life. There are, however, parallels between his life as portrayed, and events some three decades before the play was written surrounding Thomas Howard, 4th duke of Norfolk. Norfolk was born in 1536, a second cousin to Queen Elizabeth, and though he had Catholic leanings he was initially a loyal supporter of the queen. After the death of his third wife, he schemed to marry Mary, Queen of Scots. Drawn into the Northern Rebellion which sought to free Mary, he was arrested, but released after spending nine months in prison. Norfolk was then involved in the Ridolfi Plot with Philip II of Spain (in which William Brooke had also been involved, as recounted above), which sought to put Mary on the throne and restore Catholicism to England. For the much larger part that Norfolk played in this, he was executed.

Much prominence is given in the play to Oldcastle's alerting of King Henry to the Southampton Plot. As we saw in Chapter Eight, Oldcastle was not involved, although the plotters may have had some vague hope of him aiding their cause. Probably coincidentally, he in fact used the time of Henry's departure for France to try to instigate his own rising in Malvern, although this was broken before it started. However, for someone trying to clear Norfolk's name of acts of treason, and perhaps trying to distance him from the Ridolfi Plot, the play's story could be a useful parallel. Certainly, the Oldcastle play aims to clear Sir John's name of treason. No mention is made of any trial for heresy, and there are only allusions via hearsay to his views on religion. However, in the play's rewriting of the Southampton Plot, the earl of Cambridge refers to the earlier removal of two of 'his wild race' when talking of a stag, a metaphor for the king. Henry V had loyal brothers, and no direct heirs at the time of the Southampton Plot, but at the time of the Ridolfi Plot two of Henry VIII's offspring had died – Edward VI and Queen Mary. There are other aspects of the play that fit the theory of it being an attempt to rehabilitate Norfolk. For example, Oldcastle's nemesis, Archbishop Arundel, is replaced by the bishop of Rochester. Why? At the time of the Ridolfi Plot the earl of Arundel was suspected of Catholic sympathies and had been under house arrest, so any mention of the name Arundel would not have served the rehabilitative cause well. And much of the last part of the play is concerned with a murder for which Oldcastle is blamed, but of which he is innocent. This could be a parallel for either the real Oldcastle's trial for heresy, of which Protestants would feel he was not guilty, or for Norfolk's charge of treason, for which this reading of the play makes the case that

Norfolk is innocent. Certainly, there is little relation to Oldcastle's real life in the play, but is it right to see it in relation to Norfolk's life? If so, then perhaps Edward de Vere, 17th earl of Oxford, (seen by some as a contender for the authorship of Shakespeare's plays), provided some impetus for this play and its content, for Norfolk was his cousin.[37] To most theatre goers, unaware of these potentially deeper meanings, the play would have been clear in its defence of Oldcastle.

Martyr or Traitor?

In between the three performances of *Sir John Oldcastle* by the Admiral's Men and the two by Worcester's Men appeared John Weever's poem, 'Mirror of Martyrs or the life and death of that thrice valiant capitaine, and most godly martyre Sir Iohn Old-castle knight Lord Cobham'. It was published in 1601, but Weever said it was finished two years previously (though presumably after 10 January 1599, the date of Edmund Spenser's death, which is mentioned in the poem). The first half of the poem is polemical, and then it turns to Oldcastle, covering his trial, escape from the Tower and subsequent flight. It is full of inaccuracies, for example giving Oldcastle's father as Reignold Cobham. However, what is most interesting in terms of interpreting the changing view of Oldcastle's life is that although Weever – writing at about the same time as Munday, Drayton, Hathway and Wilson – differs from their plot-line in many details, like them he suggests that Oldcastle played no part in the rising at St Giles's Fields. It can, of course, be argued that Oldcastle did not in fact take any part in that gathering, for it is almost certain that he never left the walled city of London to reach St Giles's Fields on the night of the abortive revolt.

This becomes the key point in the arguments that follow between those calling Oldcastle a martyr and those denigrators calling him a rebel: if it cannot be proved that Oldcastle attended the gathering at St Giles's Fields, nor that he was the master-mind behind the rising, then he cannot be accused of treason. His death was therefore martyrdom for the new religion that became Protestantism in the years that followed. In this scenario the supporters of Oldcastle's martyrdom untainted by treason, suggest that all the chroniclers who talk of Oldcastle as the leader of the rising have fallen for the government propaganda put about to justify the actions taken against Lollards. They have swallowed the authorities' line that it was planned for the king and his family to be imprisoned at the very least, and possibly put to death, for Oldcastle to become regent, and for the property of the Church to be seized. Some holding this view even go on to suggest that the gathering at St Giles's Fields was solely religious in intent. Foxe himself suggests 'Yet might they not come to those thickets near to the fielde of Saint Giles, hauing Beuerley their Preacher with them … as well to pray & to preach in that woody place', though admitting that they might go on 'to fight'.

Foxe included a 'Kalender' that suggested days on which various saints and martyrs should be honoured. Oldcastle was listed for 6 February, the day on which Foxe mistakenly believed he had been killed, with Sir Roger Acton on 6 January, the preacher John

Beverley on the 7th and John Brown, Oldcastle's squire, on the 8th, all close to the date of the rising. In doing so, Foxe displaced some saints from the existing Calendar, leading some to suggest he was proposing that saints be made of Oldcastle and the others. Foxe robustly rejected this claim: 'I so diligently and expressely do warne all men before, first that I make here no Calendare purposely of any Saintes, but a Table of good and godly men that suffered for the truth, to shew the day and moneth of their suffering', going on to consider some of those he had displaced:

> And nowe to consider what Saintes these were, or what were the causes of their sancting: … commonly he was either some Pope, or some rich Bishop and Prelate, or some fat abbat, or some blind Frier, some Monke, or Nunne, some superstitious regulare, or some builder of monasteries, or some geuer and benefactour to the popish clergy, or mainteiner agonising for the dignities and liberties of the Popyshe church? What poore lay man or lay woman, were their liues neuer so Christian, their faith and confession neuer so pure, their death neuer so agonising for the witnes of Christ, and truth of his word, shall finde any place or fauour …[38]

All strong stuff, but those wishing to cleanse Oldcastle of any taint of treason never suggest who it was that did plan the gathering at St Giles's Fields. It is difficult to think that anyone other than someone with the stature of Oldcastle could have done so, given the disparate Lollard views that abounded. They also often overlook the arms that many bore, the belief that people like the brewer Morley had in the role and position he might hold (unless he and many others were deceived, of course). They also overlook Oldcastle's second abortive rising in Malvern, an event mentioned neither in Weever's poem nor in the *Oldcastle* play. Nor do the poem, the play or the supporters of an 'untreasonable' Oldcastle mention any of the other plots in which he might have been involved.

But in the meantime, what had become of Oldcastle's family, and what other twists were still to occur in the perception of his life?

Afterword

Only three days after Oldcastle's execution, Lady Cobham was released from the Tower of London, (where she had been held since Oldcastle's failed rising), and the Cobham lands were restored to her.

Oldcastle's children were all by his first wife.[1] John, the eldest, inherited his maternal grandmother's lands in Buckinghamshire, but died in 1420. In 1429 Henry Oldcastle, Sir John's younger son, started the process of obtaining possession of the forfeited manor of Almeley. One of those sitting on the commission of inquiry set up to investigate the issue was Robert II Whitney, the son of the man whose patronage of Whitney Church had brought William Swynderby to preach his sermon on 1 August 1390.[2] Henry finally obtained restoration of the Herefordshire estates c.1444 after a series of court cases. He was a member of parliament for Herefordshire in the parliaments of 1427–28, 1442 and 1453–54, and a justice of the peace between 1456 and 1458. In a commission appointed in 1433 to list the principal inhabitants of each county, Henry is listed as one of 45 esquires.[3] He had married Elizabeth Milbourne and was sometimes described in documents as 'of Tillington', a manor he came into through his wife and where he lived at least until he had inherited the Almeley estate.[4] Neither son produced any heirs. Henry lived till c.1460, and was buried at Blackfriars Monastery in Hereford.[5] Almeley manor then passed into the hands of the Milbournes.

Whilst nothing is known of two of Oldcastle's daughters, Katherine/Catherine and Joan (perhaps because they died young), his third daughter, Maud, married Roger Clitherow. They must have married sometime before August 1414, for it was then that Lady Cobham, still imprisoned in the Tower following Oldcastle's rebellion, asked for Roger's father, Richard, and Thomas Brooke, her son-in-law, to be allowed to manage the estates forfeited by Sir John, a wish granted by Henry V. In 1404–05 Richard Clitherow had been sheriff of Kent, and between April 1405 and December 1406 'Admiral of the Seas from the Thames westwards'. In 1410 he had been appointed victualler of Calais, and was twice summoned to clarify use of public funds, some evidence of fraud having been found. Despite this, and perhaps because it involved no personal gain, he continued in office. His religious views appear to have been orthodox. It is not known when Maud died, although it could have been c.1435, the date ascribed to a memorial brass commemorating her in the church at Ash-by-Sandwich in Kent. Only the upper part of the brass now remains, whilst the figures of Roger and their six

Looking along the nave to the chancel in Ash-by-Sandwich Church in Kent, with the brass of Maud Clitherow, née Oldcastle, in the foreground, with a detail of the brass on the right. (Author)

children, which once formed part of the memorial, have completely disappeared.[6] The heraldic detail was, however, recorded in 1613 by Peter Le Neve, who noted a triple-towered castle representing Oldcastle's arms. Stained glass windows, since lost, also depicted Clitherow arms impaling those of Oldcastle.[7]

Following Oldcastle's death, Joan, Lady Cobham, married Sir John Harpenden as her fifth husband, she dying in 1434 and Harpenden in 1458. She is commemorated by a brass in Cobham Church in Kent, as are many of her forebears and earlier husbands, though not Oldcastle. Her image on the brass shows her in the garb of a widow, and at her feet are represented her six sons and four daughters, together with a pet dog, the symbol of rank. The shields surrounding her show the arms of her ancestors, her second husband Sir Reginald Braybrooke, and Thomas Brooke, her son-in-law. The inscription at her feet states 'The Lady of Cobham and wife of Sir Reginald Braybrooke'; no mention is made of any other husband.[8]

Thomas Brooke, who had married Oldcastle's stepdaughter, Joan, spent some months in the Tower after his arrest following the failed Oldcastle rising. It is not known when he was released, but it must have been by 24 August 1414, when he and

Brass commemorating Joan, Lady Cobham, Oldcastle's second wife, in Cobham Church, Kent. (Author)

Roger Clitherow were granted custody of all the Cobham lands. Brooke may have stayed in contact with Oldcastle during his period on the run, for he and his half-brother, Richard Cheddar, had to provide a surety of £1,000 that they would not support him. Both Brooke and Cheddar were returned as MPs for Somerset in the parliament of late 1417, to which the wounded Oldcastle was brought and which confirmed his sentence of death. Brooke appears to have retained his Lollard views throughout the rest of his life.[9]

We briefly met Sir John Oldcastle's cousin Richard, son of Sir Thomas Oldcastle, in relation to Birtsmorton Court at the time of Sir John's second attempted rising at Malvern. Richard was married to Elizabeth, the widow of Robert Ruyhale. On 26 October 1416, together with 30 armed servants, Richard ambushed Guy Whittington (who is believed to have fought at Agincourt) and his father near Mordiford outside Hereford, and took them to Dinmore Hill, north of the city, where he imprisoned them in a chapel overnight. This action is thought to have concerned an unpaid debt that Richard believed he was owed. The two men were released, having signed bonds for part of the sum in question, the Whittingtons presenting a petition for redress in the parliament then sitting, though the outcome is not known. Presumably matters were patched up, for after Richard died in 1422 his widow named Guy Whittington as one of her executors.[10] In 1419 John Merbury and two others settled an estate at Woonton in Almeley parish on Richard and Elizabeth, obtaining pardon for alienating the estate from them.[11] On Richard's death Birtsmorton Court, his then home, reverted to the Ruyhales, his Ruyhale widow living there for another six years.[12] He was also survived by two daughters, but no sons.

Yet, if Oldcastle's family name was to die out with his sons and his nephew, there is a mystery concerning a Hugh and William Oldcastle (or Oldecastell in the records), who make an appearance in the lists of chancery proceedings in cases addressed to Sir Thomas Audley, Lord Chancellor, in 1533–38. In these, Hugh is described as a 'kinsman and heir of John Oldecastell, knight' and grandson of William Oldecastell.[13] In Chapter One a Willelmo Oldecastile is mentioned as paying 4d in the poll tax of 1379, and even if he was aged just 14, the youngest age to have to pay the tax, it is virtually impossible for him to be the grandfather of a Hugh Oldcastle over 150 years later. Were these Oldcastles of 1379 and the 1530s somehow related to Sir John, and if so how? No leads have been found to discover anything more about them.

If his name has indeed died out, his heraldic arms have at least survived in a couple of locations, one of them more hidden from public view than the other.

Maud and Roger Clitherow's eldest daughter, Eleanor, married Sir John Norreys as his second wife. Norreys, an Esquire of the Body and Master of the Wardrobe to Henry VI, successfully transferred his allegiance to Edward IV in the Wars of the Roses, and rebuilt Ockwells, the family's manor house west of Maidenhead in Berkshire. The east window of the hall displays some heraldic glass, one shield showing the arms of

Ravenscroft (for Norreys) impaling Clitherow quartered with Oldcastle; there is also a corbel which shows the same device.

Archbishop Arundel died on 19 February 1414 following a sudden attack of some complaint of the throat. A legend of a later age tells how, just before his death, he was struck dumb for preventing the preaching of the word of God; Oldcastle might have approved. New cloisters were built at Canterbury Cathedral between the years 1397 and 1411 or 1414, under the auspices of Arundel, who was archbishop from 1396 until his death. The bosses in the cloisters display a huge number of heraldic devices including those of Cobham quartering Oldcastle and separately of Oldcastle alone. The cloisters were completed before Oldcastle's execution, but at the time the heraldic devices were commissioned Oldcastle's heresy was probably not publicly known. Nevertheless, Arundel did not take the opportunity to have the arms replaced with those of anyone else.

Meanwhile, both denigration and praise of Oldcastle continued beyond the Elizabethan period, whilst the image created by Shakespeare's Falstaff, under the name of Oldcastle, also kept appearing or being alluded to in later plays. In 1603 the Jesuit

Ockwells Manor: A corbel together with stained glass in the east window of the hall showing the arms of Ravenscroft (for Norreys) impaling Clitherow quartered with Oldcastle.

The bosses in the cloisters at Canterbury Cathedral, showing the arms of Cobham quartering Oldcastle (left) and of Oldcastle on its own (right). To reach the bay in which these appear (Bay no.20 according to the numbering given in 1827 by Thomas Willement, a writer on heraldry and a stained-glass artist), enter the cloisters by the door from the north transept and turn left to walk along the south cloister and then along the west cloister to reach the point diagonally opposite where you entered the cloisters. Bay 20 is then the first bay reached along the north cloister. (Author)

Robert Parsons wrote that Oldcastle was 'a Ruffian-knight as all England knoweth, & commonly brought in by comediants on their stages: he was put to death for robberyes and rebellion under the foresaid K. Henry the fifth'. This brought a riposte from John Speed, author of a *Historie of Great Britaine* published in 1611, who inveighed against Parsons for making 'Ouldcastle a Ruffian, a Robber and a Rebell, and his authorities taken from the Stage-plaiers', a slander 'only grounded from this Papist and his Poet, of the like conscience for lies, the one ever fairing, and the other ever falsifying the truth …'.[14] In *The meeting of Gallants* (author unknown, written about 1604) are the words: 'and if you chaunce to talke of fatte Sir John Oldcastle, he will tell you, he was his great Grandfather, and not much unlike him in paunch, if you marke him well by all descriptions', while the following appears in a speech in *Amends for Ladies* written about 1611 by Nathan Field, an actor in Shakespeare's company:

> I doe heare
> Your Lordship this faire morning is to fight,
> And for your honor: Did you never see
> The Play, where the fat knight hight Old-castle
> Did tell you truly what his honor was?

The popular image of Falstaff, this painting being by Eduard von Grützner in 1906.

This appears to refer to the words of Falstaff in *Henry IV Part I*, Act V, Scene I:

> … Well, 'tis no matter; honour pricks me on. Yea, but how if honour prick me off when I come on? how then? Can honour set to a leg? no: or an arm? no: or take away the grief of a wound? no. Honour hath no skill in surgery, then? no. What is honour? a word. What is in that word honour? what is that honour? air. A trim reckoning! Who hath it? he that died o' Wednesday. Doth he feel it? no. Doth he hear it? no. 'Tis insensible, then. Yea, to the dead. But will it not live with the living? no. Why? detraction will not suffer it. Therefore I'll none of it. Honour is a mere scutcheon: and so ends my catechism.

The Wandering Jew telling Fortunes to Englishmen, written about 1630, contains the following:

> All that I say is this, – I'me a fat man. It has been a West Indian voyage for me to come reeking hither. A kitchen-stuffe wench might pick up a living by following me for the fat which I lose in stradling. I doe not live by the sweat of my brows, but am almost dead with sweating. I eate much, but can talke little. Sir John Oldcastle was my great-grandfather's uncle, – I come of a huge kindred!

Clearly, although Shakespeare had been forced to shroud Oldcastle by changing his name to Falstaff, the image of the fat Sir John Oldcastle embodied in the early success of *Henry IV Part I* lived on.

In 1665 Thomas Fuller wrote in his *Church History:*[15]

> Stage-poets have themselves been very bold with, and others very merry at, the Memory of Sir John Oldcastle, whom they have fancied a boon companion, a jovial roister, and yet a coward to boot, contrary to the credit of all chronicles, owning him a martial man of merit. The best is, Sir John Falstaff hath relieved the memory of Sr John Oldcastle, and of late is substituted buffoon in his place; but it matters as little what petulant poets, as what malicious papists have written against him.

In the early 1700s the record of Oldcastle's trial was still being repeated in various publications. For example, in *The History of the Most Remarkable Trials in Great Britain*, printed for A. Bell in 1715, one of the trials recounted is that of Oldcastle, the text essentially drawing on that of Bale and Foxe. In the grandly named *Magna Britannia Antiqua & Nova, Or, a New, Exact, and Comprehensive Survey of the Ancient and Present State of Great Britain*, printed for the booksellers Caesar Ward and Richard Chandler in 1738, within the entry for Herefordshire is again a summary of the trial based on the same texts.

But over time the jovial 'fat knight' relinquished the name of Oldcastle in the popular imagination to be replaced by that of Falstaff. Indeed, in the 1700s the name

Oliver Goldsmith,
by Sir Joshua Reynolds.

of Oldcastle appears to have become vilified. In about 1760, in an essay entitled 'A Reverie at the Boar's Head Tavern, Eastcheap' (in which he overlooks the fact that the original tavern had been destroyed in the Fire of London, see pages 206 and 207), Oliver Goldsmith enters into a reverie conversation with the ghost of Mistress Quickly, the innkeeper of *Henry IV Parts I* and *II*. In this, Mistress Quickly says of Wycliffites that

> 'Tis certain that, if what was alleged against them be true, they deserved no mercy; they were magicians or witches every one of them; they were sometimes seen eating dead bodies torn from the grave. Sir John Oldcastle, one of the chief of the sect, was particularly fond of human flesh. I need not mention their promiscuous copulations, their cursings, and their treasons; these are written in all the books of those times: the laws took every method to extirpate them, promised them life in order to make them repent; and then burned them to prevent a relapse. Acton, Brown, and Beverly, men of distinction, and who, till they were detected of heresy, were famed for having lived virtuous and pious lives, were the three that were tied to the stake, to give solemnity to the present rejoicing.[16]

Unpleasant views about Oldcastle seem to have taken root, to the extent that John Wesley, in his abridgement of Foxe's *Book of Martyrs* published in 1750, omitted all reference to Oldcastle, referring editorially to 'trash which that honest unjudicious writer has heaped together and mingled with those venerable records which are worthy to be had in everlasting remembrance'.[17] In 1826, William Eusebius Andrews in his *Review of Fox's* [sic] *Book of Martyrs* says that '… sir John Oldcastle was, among our more ancient dramatists, the debauched but facetious knight who now treads the stage under the name of sir John Falstaff. Thus we have the same personage pourtrayed by Fox as a "godly martyr," and by Shakespeare as a "beastly debachee." What an edifying saint to grace the martyrology of John Fox.'[18]

Thus in the 125 years since the first performance of *The Famous Victories of Henry V*, if we take the earliest suggested date of 1576, Oldcastle had become several different characters. To some he seemed a scorned comic figure, to others a wise sage of joviality and life (depending upon your view of Falstaff) and a father figure to the young Prince Hal (albeit that the prince subsequently rejects him), and to a third group a noble hero shorn of the taint of treason and a valiant early upholder of the new Protestant faith. In the years that followed, Oldcastle then became a figure of opprobrium once more, harking back to the Catholic chroniclers of history at the time of his death.

In 1704 Thomas Goodwin's *The History of the Reign of Henry the Fifth* was published. This has been adjudged an early example of a history that can still largely be relied upon. It makes use of more sources that were becoming available from collections of manuscripts, from which Goodwin sometimes gives two points of view, asking the reader to make up their own mind. In considering Oldcastle, Goodwin clearly admires the man, not least for his religious views. In defending his positive view of Henry, he adopts the line that it was the Church that was responsible for hunting down Oldcastle.[19] As we have seen, it was the Church that instigated the moves against Oldcastle for heresy, moves which Henry reluctantly pursued, giving Oldcastle occasion to recant and save himself. But once Oldcastle was implicated in treason, Henry made moves which quickly quashed the revolt, and offered a high reward for his capture. It is nevertheless arguable that it was the Church that was finally responsible for Oldcastle's death, for Henry subsequently issued pardons, but these would presumably have only covered charges of treason; the charge of heresy lay with the Church. Goodwin wishes to support what he sees as the good sides of both Henry and Oldcastle.

As a slight aside, analysis of Henry's actions in pursuing Lollards after Oldcastle's rising sheds a slightly different light on the view generally held about Henry's support for a fair administration of justice. A paid jury was picked for the trials that followed the day after the arrests at St Giles's Fields, albeit that most of those charged were caught 'red-handed'. More critically, several Lollards were thrown into gaol without proper charges being levelled and so with no recourse to mounting a defence, and were often so held for several months. This happened notably in the second half of 1417 when Oldcastle was still at large and Henry was absent in France, increasing Henry's concern

Alfred, Lord Tennyson
in a photograph of c.1860.

that Oldcastle might instigate another Lollard rising. This saw the arrest and imprisonment of 13 Lollards in the Marshalsea in London, on mere suspicion of Lollardy and of aiding Oldcastle (but never charged with either heresy or treason). It was only after Oldcastle's capture and execution that they were able to petition for their release, having to provide extortionate bonds for their future good behaviour or, in one case at least, to agree to serve with the king in France. Further such arrests and detentions continued throughout the rest of Henry's reign. Richard II had also been accused of imprisoning people without charge, a practice that Henry IV had sought to end. But Henry V's abuse of power in this area was to set a sorry precedent for his son's reign.[20]

In 1880 a more romantic view of Oldcastle is portrayed in Tennyson's poem 'Sir John Oldcastle, Lord Cobham (in Wales)'. The poem is set in a period when Oldcastle is on the run in Wales and is pondering on recent events – his friendship with Hal, his trial, the friends he has lost since the rising, the actions of Arundel and others in pursuing 'heresy'. It considers his fears for his own future, coupled with determination to stand firm in his beliefs. Tennyson seems to have chosen Oldcastle as the subject for a poem as a representative of those whom he saw as unjustly treated by the establishment. He was writing at a time of social upheaval in the wake of the Paris Commune of 1871, of Reform Acts extending the Parliamentary franchise (and with another to come in 1884), of agricultural depression, and at a time when unions were being formed that sought to improve conditions for workers.[21]

As the poem covers ground that has been discussed in previous chapters, most of it is reproduced below to show the light in which Tennyson wished to depict Oldcastle.

MY FRIEND should meet me somewhere hereabout
To take me to that hiding in the hills.

    I have broke their cage, no gilded one, I trow –
I read no more the prisoner's mute wail
Scribbled or carved upon the pitiless stone;
I find hard rocks, hard life, hard cheer, or none,
For I am emptier than a friar's brains;
But God is with me in this wilderness,
These wet black passes and foam-churning chasms –
And God's free air, and hope of better things.
    I would I knew their speech; not now to glean,
Not now – I hope to do it – some scatter'd ears,
Some ears for Christ in this wild field of Wales –
But, bread, merely for bread. This tongue that wagg'd
They said with such heretical arrogance
Against the proud archbishop Arundel –
So much God's cause was fluent in it – is here
But as a Latin Bible to the crowd;
'Bara!' – what use? The Shepherd, when I speak,
Vailing a sudden eyelid with his hard
'Dim Saesneg' passes, wroth at things of old –
No fault of mine. Had he God's word in Welsh
He might be kindlier: happily come the day!

    Not least art thou, thou little Bethlehem
In Judah, for in thee the Lord was born;
Nor thou in Britain, little Lutterworth,
Least, for in thee the word was born again.

            …

What did he say,
My frighted Wiclif-preacher whom I crost
In flying hither? that one night a crowd
Throng'd the waste field about the city gates:
The king was on them suddenly with a host.
Why there? they came to hear their preacher. Then
Some cried on Cobham, on the good Lord Cobham;
Ay, for they love me! but the king – nor voice
Nor finger raised against him – took and hang'd,
Took, hang'd and burnt – how many – thirty-nine –
Call'd it rebellion – hang'd, poor friends, as rebels
And burn'd alive as heretics! for your Priest
Labels – to take the king along with him –

All heresy, treason: but to call men traitors
May make men traitors.

…

So to this king I cleaved: my friend was he,
Once my fast friend: I would have given my life
To help his own from scathe, a thousand lives
To save his soul. He might have come to learn
Our Wiclif's learning: but the worldly Priests
Who fear the king's hard common-sense should find
What rotten piles uphold their mason-work,
Urge him to foreign war. O had he will'd
I might have stricken a lusty stroke for him,
But he would not; far liever led my friend
Back to the pure and universal church,
But he would not: whether that heirless flaw
In his throne's title make him feel so frail,
He leans on Antichrist; or that his mind,
So quick, so capable in soldiership,
In matters of the faith, alas the while!
More worth than all the kingdoms of this world,
Runs in the rut, a coward to the Priest.

Burnt – good Sir Roger Acton, my dear friend!
Burnt too, my faithful preacher, Beverley!
Lord give thou power to thy two witnesses!
Lest the false faith make merry over them
Two – nay but thirty-nine have risen and stand,
Dark with the smoke of human sacrifice,
Before thy light, and cry continually –
Cry – against whom?

Him, who should bear the sword
Of Justice – what! the kingly, kindly boy;
Who took the world so easily heretofore,
My boon companion, tavern-fellow – him
Who gibed and japed – in many a merry tale
That shook our sides – at Pardoners, Summoners,
Friars, absolution-sellers, monkeries
And nunneries, when the wild hour and the wine
Had set the wits aflame.
Harry of Monmouth,
Or Amurath of the East?
Better to sink
Thy fleurs-de-lys in slime again, and fling

Thy royalty back into the riotous fits
Of wine and harlotry – thy shame, and mine,
Thy comrade – than to persecute the Lord,
And play the Saul that never will be Paul.

          …

    Eh! how I anger'd Arundel asking me,
To worship Holy Cross! I spread mine arms,
God's work, I said, a cross of flesh and blood
And holier. That was heresy. (My good friend
By this time should be with me.) 'Images?'
Bury them as God's truer images
Are daily buried.' 'Heresy. – Penance?' 'Fast,
Hairshirt and scourge-nay, let a man repent,
Do penance in his heart, God hears him.' 'Heresy –
Not shriven, not saved?' 'What profits an ill Priest
Between me and my God? I would not spurn
Good counsel of good friends, but shrive myself
No, not to an Apostle.' 'Heresy.'
(My friend is long in coming.) 'Pilgrimages?'
'Drink, bagpipes, revelling, devil's-dances, vice.
The poor man's money gone to fat the friar.
Who reads of begging saints in Scripture?' – 'Heresy' –
(Hath he been here – not found me – gone again?
Have I mislearnt our place of meeting?)

'Bread –
Bread left after the blessing?' how they stared,
That was their main test-question – glared at me!
'He veil'd Himself in flesh, and now He veils
His flesh in bread, body and bread together.'
Then rose the howl of all the cassock'd wolves,
'No bread, no bread. God's body!' Archbishop, Bishop,
Priors, Canons, Friars, bellringers, Parish-clerks –
'No bread, no bread!' – 'Authority of the Church,
Power of the keys!' – Then I, God help me, I
So mock'd, so spum'd, so baited two whole days –
I lost myself and fell from evenness,
And rail'd at all the Popes, that ever since
Sylvester shed the venom of world-wealth
Into the church, had only prov'n themselves
Poisoners, murderers. Well – God pardon all –
Me, them, and all the world – yea, that proud Priest,
That mock-meek mouth of utter Antichrist,

That traitor to King Richard and the truth,
Who rose and doom'd me to the fire.
                                        Amen!
Nay, I can burn, so that the Lord of life
Be by me in my death.

                         …

                    So, caught, I burn.
Burn? heathen men have borne as much as this,
For freedom, or the sake of those they loved,
Or some less cause, some cause far less than mine;
For every other cause is less than mine.
The moth will singe her wings, and singed return,
Her love of light quenching her fear of pain –
How now, my soul, we do not heed the fire?
Faint-hearted? tut! – faint-stomach'd! faint as I am,
God willing, I will burn for Him.
                    Who comes?
A thousand marks are set upon my head.
Friend? – foe perhaps – a tussle for it then!
Nay, but my friend. Thou art so well disguised,
I knew thee not. Hast thou brought bread with thee?
I have not broken bread for fifty hours.
None? I am damn'd already by the Priest
For holding there was bread where bread was none –
No bread. My friends await me yonder? Yes.
Lead on then. Up the mountain? Is it far?
Not far. Climb first and reach me down thy hand.
I am not like to die for lack of bread
For I must live to testify by fire.

In 1986 the Oxford edition of Shakespeare's *Henry IV Part I* reinstated the name of Oldcastle in place of Falstaff, as it was felt that there should be one edition, at least, in which the character had his original name.[22]

Villain, hero (Romantic or otherwise), or somewhere in between?
The chronicler Walsingham attended Oxford at the time Wycliffe was there, and long afterwards, in his chronicle, turned his pen against Wycliffe and his followers, often calling his words 'rants' and his followers 'mad'.[23] In other respects Walsingham's records are a model of rectitude: for example, he notes where his information is only partial or records are incomplete. His chronicle is one of the most important records of English history during the reigns of Richard II, Henry IV and Henry V (as well as of events happening on the Continent, especially where it affected the Church). He probably obtained much of his information from the abbots of St Albans (where he

was a monk), who were often called to parliament, Court or meetings of the king's council.[24] He seems to have been a modest man, unlike some other chroniclers, but a patriotic Englishman who would celebrate the deeds of Englishmen whilst ignoring the morality of the men or their actions, unlike in his recording of deeds committed by the French. He also did not hold back on the corruption and crisis in the Church that led to the Schism. He was nevertheless a reliable supporter of the established Church and would attack those he saw as heretics at every opportunity, yet he also described Oldcastle as 'strong and brave and very suited to the deeds of war'.[25]

There are no family archives to help us shape our own view, and parliamentary records essentially state what was agreed and little more – certainly nothing about who said what, or the degree of debate over any one item as opposed to another. The chroniclers of the period often had their own agenda or viewpoint over and above recording the events of the time. Walsingham wanted to protect the Church, as did the writer of *Gesta Henrici Quinti*, who saw Oldcastle as a 'man of sedition' and 'follower of Satan'. On the other side, Hoccleve was possibly a friend or at least a supporter of Oldcastle, whilst Weever in his 'Mirror of Martyrs', Bale in his *Brefe Chronicle*, and Foxe in his *Acts and monuments*, all writing later, were writing with the intention of promoting Oldcastle when the pendulum had swung from villain to hero. The nearest we have to a truthful record that says something deeper about the man is Arundel's account of the proceedings of Oldcastle's trial for heresy – and this was by someone who waged a long campaign against views that were then seen as heretical, and who saw Oldcastle as one of their key promoters.

Through all this material, what can we hazard as to Oldcastle's character? He clearly became well practised in the arts of war, presumably gaining his knighthood in Ireland for some military deed, and later being given notable commands of men and castles in the wars against Glyndwr, followed by a senior command in the army that Prince Henry sent to France in 1411. He seems to have been learned, possessing books and able to argue his case well in front of Archbishop Arundel, and to have communicated with Hus, Wenceslas and others in Bohemia. He may have played an important part in some of the Lollard-inspired discussions in parliament, and in supporting the move to appoint treasurers of war in the parliament of 1404. He appears to have inspired loyalty in a range of people, from relatively humble craftsmen who sheltered him after the abortive rising at risk to their own lives, to esquires who acted as messengers, knights who rode with him in his rising or supported him thereafter (or at least failed to carry out the king's orders to arrest him when he must have been in their grasp), and King Henry himself, who included Oldcastle in his household for a while and tried to protect him from the Church until his political aims and need for money for war in France became the more compelling.

Though seemingly orthodox in his views, Henry, once any immediate danger had been dealt with, was known more for clemency than retribution, and does not seem to have sought out Lollards with any great zeal. Indeed, Netter inveighed against him for his great negligence in regard to the duty of punishing heretics. Henry sought to save Badby from the flames, and once the immediate threat of Oldcastle's rebellion was past, made him an offer of pardon. In the case of Oldcastle, the sense of loyalty to an old friend might derive from the bond often shared by old soldiers who have campaigned together and been through events that are not easily communicated to others. In addition, Henry seems to have shared at least some views with Oldcastle regarding the need for reform in the Church, but he was more focused on controlling papal authority than stripping the Church of the bulk of its worldly possessions, for he was orthodox in his religious views. Henry founded two new religious establishments close to London, at Sheen and Syon on the Thames, which had severely austere rules, with the monks and nuns being urged to offer prayers to help secure what he saw as just, including his claims in France – Henry had a deep belief in the efficacy of prayer. He sent a hand-picked set of clerics to the Church council held at Constance, which started its proceedings in 1414 and saw, amongst other things, the conviction and burning of Jan Hus for heresy and, eventually, the ending of schism in the Church and the election of Martin V as the one pope. The English delegation voted *en bloc* for Pope Martin from the start of the election process, so ensuring a greater degree of English influence at the papal court than had been the case for a while. At the same time Henry used the council to help form an anti-French alliance which he hoped would aid him in his campaigns in that country.[26] Yet it could be argued that the power that Henry sought to exercise in his relations with the papacy and Archbishop Arundel – an approach that sprang from Wycliffe's views on the power of a king over the Church – owed something to his friendship with and the views of Oldcastle and others who had presented petitions to parliament, and ultimately could be said to be what led to Henry VIII becoming head of the Church of England.

Yet Oldcastle was to be disappointed in Henry. In his letter to Wenceslas (see pages 134-35) he praised the actions that the king – 'an example and mirror and first-fruits of other kings' – was taking in supporting Hus and the reformers: 'O what a delightful thing so excellent a prince, so excellent a solider of Christ has been made! O how remarkable and inexpressible but unsurprisingly laudable it is that a king carry out the duty of his position in modern times!' His disappointment was to lead to rebellion, his devotion to what he believed to be the true course of Christianity proving to be greater than his loyalty to his companion-in-arms and someone who was almost certainly a good friend, if not the boon companion created by Shakespeare.

He must have held his religious views deeply. The views about the Church expressed in Chaucer's *Canterbury Tales*, written between 1387 and 1400, appear to have mirrored widespread dissatisfaction with the Church's performance and organisation but was not subject to any action by Church or state; indeed many members of the Church and state shared those feelings of dissatisfaction. The Statute of *De Haeretico Comburendo* of 1401 (enacted shortly after the burning of William Sawtre for heresy as mentioned on page 142) only applied to those who refused to recant or were charged a second time with heresy. As Lollards set no store by swearing oaths, their conscience could allow them to safely offer to swear to recant, only to retain their views but keep them more to themselves thereafter. Clearly Oldcastle, and others, felt the need to assert and expound their views more forcibly.

Oldcastle's support of Lollardy might also have helped embed nonconformity in north-western Herefordshire. Oldcastle's rising, an act of treachery, allowed the government to equate Lollard views with treason and would have dampened the reformist spirit. Certainly there is no evidence for any lordly support thereafter for religious reform by the equivalent of a John of Gaunt, a substantial group of 'Lollard knights' (one of whom, John Montagu, was to become earl of Salisbury), or a Lord Cobham. In Chapter Eight it was mentioned how the Wars of the Roses subsequently became the vehicle for expressing discontent (though discontent that was political rather than religious in nature), yet Lollardy survived, near Almeley at least. Bishop Mayhew of Hereford's register for 1505 includes the cases of three men in Eardisley, the neighbouring parish to the south-west of Almeley, who abjured their heresies, one at least seeming to have preached views akin to those of the Lollards of Oldcastle's time.[27] And Almeley was to be the place of birth for some of those Quakers who helped found the commonwealth of Pennsylvania in the late 1600s, and there is still an active Quaker Meeting in the village.

From what we can tell, Oldcastle's family seems to have meant little to him. There is no evidence that he was close to either his sons John and Henry or his daughters, or supportive of their affairs, and they do not seem to have shared his Lollard views. Neither did his second wife, Joan. She spent several years in the Tower between Oldcastle's rising and his execution, and there is no indication that letters were smuggled to her by his friends in London. It is possible, of course, that Oldcastle did not want to put his direct family members at risk due to his own views, yet he seems to have arranged the marriage of his stepdaughter to a family that shared those beliefs.

Considering Oldcastle as a strategist, something might be left to be desired. Given a command and an objective he seems to have done as well as anybody, and possibly better than most, but his plan for the rising – and it seems logical to assume that it was his plan, for no one else would have managed to garner even the limited support that he achieved – would seem to be wanting. Did he really think that a group of Lollards disguised as mummers would be able to capture the king and his brothers, warriors all, whilst celebrating in one of the royal palaces where all the other family retainers and guards would have been around? And did he think that several hundred Lollards, perhaps a few thousand at best and probably not well armed, would have been able to affect a putsch? Did he really think the figure of 25,000 that was bandied about by the chroniclers would be the number he could have led at the field of St Giles? Would he not have done better to lie low having escaped from the Tower rather than risk all, and the lives of so many others (though thankfully few were actually lost)? And yet, in passing ownership of his movable possessions by charter to John Prophete some years before his clash with Henry and his trial for heresy (see page 191), he appears to have foreseen that he might well be declared a traitor for actions he might need to take due to his beliefs.

As for the evidence from his trial, his initial confession of faith was typical of the times, in that he left critical questions regarding common Lollard heretical views unanswered, but once forced to choose between denying them or standing by what he believed, he admitted them, and appears to have done so both forcefully and with well-judged (from a later standpoint at least) argument. But his heresies were confined to the taking of the sacrament, to the structure of the Church, to views on pilgrimage and confession, and to the use of the wealth of the Church for the better government of the realm. They did not include views on, for example, pacifism. The trial records show that he may also have been somewhat intemperate, not least in his flight to Cooling Castle, but also in his final exclamations to the trial judges.

As to what gave him pleasure, we have almost no information. We know of nothing definite about any sense of humour or jollity, and certainly nothing that would get us at all close to the character of Falstaff, though we can guess that he probably enjoyed a good feast as much as any other man, such as that provided after his jousting tournament at Lille.

We are left with a picture of a relatively learned man, a staunch and good friend of deeply held religious convictions, but perhaps not a great family man and perhaps given to outbursts of anger. The one quality it seems we can be sure of is that he was a good military commander. He was quite possibly supported in seeking the hand in marriage of Joan, Lady Cobham by two other able military commanders of the day, Richard, Lord Grey of Codnor, and Prince Henry himself, thus becoming Lord Cobham, one of an elite group of nobility. Not only that, it is possible that Henry proposed him for the tournament at Lille and the associated handling of diplomatic affairs with Burgundy, and certainly the prince appointed him to a senior command in the army sent in support of Burgundy in 1411.

Thus, the details of Oldcastle's life that can be gleaned from the historical records show that it is 'the valiant knight' that is closest to the truth of his character. Even his poet and chronicler critics, who took him to task over what they saw as his heresy, largely applauded him as such. He was also clearly staunch in his views about the Church, views that garnered him support from a number of England's citizens prepared to risk their lives for him. He must have been a good friend too, as evidenced by those in Herefordshire who chose not to apprehend him in 1417 but to allow him to live in peace, some even providing him with funds rather than claiming a large reward for betraying him.

But what about the sack-drinking Falstaff who led the young Prince Henry astray? The impression is that the prince may well have taken part in some lively jaunts in his youth – few teenagers haven't – but that once he became king he set himself upon the path of the uniter of the country and a seeker for what he saw as justice owed to the English Crown in France, establishing a positive and hardworking role for the monarch. That this was so very different to the clique-ridden reign of Richard II and the somewhat dithering reign of his father (hampered as Henry IV was by ill-health and beset by financial issues) would have been noted by chroniclers. It may be this clear difference between Henry and his immediate predecessors that encouraged apocryphal stories about his youth, stories that were subsequently exaggerated.

Henry sought to trust people and sought their trust in him. In this respect he must have felt Oldcastle's treason as a personal blow, just as Shakespeare writes about Henry's feelings when another close colleague, Lord Scrope of Masham, is found to have committed treason in the Southampton Plot.

As the perceived 'good friend', it would be enjoyable to sit down with Oldcastle in Almeley's village inn and resolve some of the outstanding mysteries: who were the Isabella and Willelmo 'Oldecastile' of the 1379 poll tax return? Did Lewis Clifford help him obtain a place as an esquire in the duke of Norfolk's household or did his uncle help him out? It would be interesting to find out more about his family, including the two daughters of whom nothing is known, and his feelings for Henry, prince and king and especially what he felt when organising his rising at St Giles's Fields. That might be a difficult part of the evening. One imagines he would be pleased by some of the changes that have happened in the intervening centuries in what is now the Church in England, but displeased by others. But hopefully chatting about his wider life, his friends and his possible enjoyment of jousting might lead to a convivial occasion. I fear, however, that that is the closest we would get to Falstaff.

Bibliography

Adam of Usk, *Chronicon 1377-1404* (ed. Edward Maunde Thompson), (John Murray, 1876)

Allmand, Christopher, *Henry V* (University of California Press, 1992)

anon., *The Famous Victories of Henry the fifth*, (Tudor Facsimile Text, accessed online via Hathitrust)

Bale, John, *Select Works containing the examinations of Lord Cobham ...*, (Parker Society, Cambridge, 1849)

Barbett-Smith, C., *History of the English Parliament*, Vol. 1, (Ward Lock, 1892)

Bevan, Bryan, *Henry IV*, (Rubicon Press, 1994)

Brown, Andrew Morton, *The Leader of the Lollards, Sir John Oldcastle*, (1848)

Capes, William (ed), *The register of John Trefnant, Bishop of Hereford (A.D. 1389-1404)*, (Hereford, 1914)

Capgrave, John, *The Chronicle of England*, (Elibron Classics, 2005)

Cole, C.A., *Memorials of Henry V, King of England*, (Longman & Co 1858)

Coulton, George C., *Chaucer and his England*, (Methuen & Co, 1908, reprinted Senate, 1988)

Copeland, Rita, *Pedagogy, Intellectuals, and Dissent in the Later Middle Ages; Lollardy and Ideas of Learning*, (CUP, 2001)

Curran, Susan, *The Wife of Cobham*, (Lasse Press, 2016)

Davies, R.R., *The Revolt of Owain Glyn Dwr*, (OUP, 1997)

Dockray, Keith, *Henry V*, (Tempus, 2004)

Dodd, Gwilym (ed), *Henry V: New Interpretations*, (York Medieval Press, 2018 [paperback])

Dodd, Gwilym and Douglas Biggs (eds), *The Reign of Henry IV, Rebellion and Survival, 1403-1413*, (York Medieval Press, 2008)

Drayton, Michael, Anthony Munday, Richard Hathway & Robert Wilson, *The First Part Of Sir John Oldcastle* (with extensive introductory chapters by John Robertson Macarthur), (Scott, Foresman and Company, Chicago, 1907)

Dutton, Richard, *William Shakespeare, a Literary Life*, (Macmillan, 1989)

Ellis, Sir Henry *Original Letters*, (London, 1846)

Elmham, Thomas, *Liber Metricus* or *Memorials of Henry the Fifth, king of England*, (ed. Charles Augustus Cole), (Longmans, 1858)

Elmham, Thomas, *Vita & gesta Henrici Quinti, Anglorum regis*, (Oxford, 1727)

Fehrenbach, R.J., 'When Lord Cobham and Edward Tilney were at odds; Oldcastle, Falstaff and the Date of 1 Henry IV' in *Shakespeare Studies*, Vol. 18 (1986)

Fiehler, Rudolph, *The Strange History of Sir John Oldcastle*, (American Press, 1965)

Foxe, John, *The acts and monuments of John Foxe: a new and complete edition: with a preliminary dissertation, by the Rev. George Townsend ...* (London, 1837–41). Editions of Foxe's work of 1563, 1570, 1576 and 1583 can be read online at www.dhi.ac.uk/foxe/

Furnivall, F.J., (ed), *Hoccleve's Works, 1. The Minor Poems*, Early English Text Series, Extra Series LXI, (1892)

Gaspey, Thomas, *The life & times of the Good Lord Cobham*, (London, 1844)

Griffiths, R.A., *Conquerors and Conquered in Medieval Wales*, (Alan Sutton, 1994)

Griffiths, W.R.M., 'Prince Henry, Wales and the Royal Exchequer' in *Bulletin of the Board of Celtic Studies* 32, (1985)

'Prince Henry's War: armies, garrisons & supply during the Glyndwr Rebellion' in *Bulletin of the Board of Celtic Studies* 34, (1987)

'The military career and affinity of Henry Prince of Wales', (Unpub. Ox. Univ. M.Litt thesis, 1980)

Halliwell, James Orchard, *On the Character of Sir John Falstaff*, (1841)

Harris, Gerald, *Shaping the Nation, England 1360-1461*, (Clarendon Press, 2005)

Hay, Denys, *Europe in the Fourteenth and Fifteenth Centuries*, (Longmans, 1966)

Heath, Peter, *Church and Realm 1272-1461*, (Fontana, 1988)

Hodges, Geoffrey, *Owain Glyn Dwr & the War of Independence in the Welsh Borders*, (Logaston Press, 1995)

Holder, Anthony, *William Shakespeare, his life and work*, (Abacus, 1999)

Holinshed, *Chronicles as used in Shakespeare's plays*, Everyman's Library no.800, (Dent 1927)

Holinshed's Chronicles, Richard II 1398-1400 and Henry V, (eds R.S. Wallace and Alma Hansen), (Clarendon Press, 1917)

Howells, John, *The History of the Old Baptist Church at Olchon together with the Life and Martyrdom of Sir John Oldcastle, The Lord Cobham*, (South Wales Printing Works, 1996)

Hyett-Warner, Revd R., *Historic Memories of the Manor and Parish of Almeley in the county of Hereford*, (Jakeman & Carver, 1917)

Jacob, E.F., *Henry V and the Invasion of France*, (Hodder and Stoughton, 1947)

The Fifteenth Century, 1399–1485, (OUP, 1961)

James, Richard, *Iter Lancastrene*, (Chetham Society, 1845)

Jolliffe, J.E.A. *The Constitutional History of Medieval England, from the English Settlement to 1485*, (Adam and Charles Black, 1961)

Jurkowski, Maureen 'Henry V's Suppression of the Oldcastle Revolt', Chapter 4 in *Henry V: New Interpretations* (ed. Gwilym Dodd,) (Boydell & Brewer, 2018 [paperback]), pp.103-28.

Keen, M.H., *England in the Later Middle Ages*, (Routledge, 2004)

Kingsford, C.L., *Henry V, the typical medieval hero*, (G.P. Putnam's Sons, 1901)

Kightly, Charles, 'The Early Lollards, A survey of Popular Lollard Activity in England, 1382-1428', (University of York thesis, 1975)

Labarge, Margaret Wade, *Henry V, The Cautious Conqueror*, (Secker and Warburg, 1975)

Leff, Gordon, *Heresy in the Later Middle Ages; The relation of Heterodoxy to Dissent c.1250-c.1450*, (Manchester University Press, 1967, edition of Sandpiper Books, 1999)

Marino, James J. 'William Shakespeare's *Sir John Oldcastle*', in *Renaissance Drama*, New Series, Vol.30 91999-2001), pp.93-114

McFarlane, K.B., *John Wycliffe and the beginning of English Nonconformity*, (English Universities Press, 1952)

Lancastrian Kings and Lollard Knights, (Clarendon Press, 1972)

McGettigan, Darren, *Richard II and the Irish Kings*, (Four Courts Press, 2016)

McKeen, David Bruce, "A Memory of Honour', A Study of the House of Cobham in Kent in the reign of Elizabeth I', (University of Birmingham thesis, July 1964)

McKissack, May, *The Fourteenth Century, 1307–1399*, (OUP, 1959)

Patterson, Annabel, 'Sir John Oldcastle as Symbol of Reformation Historiography' in *Religion, Literature, and Politics in Post-Reformation England, 1540-1688*, (eds Donna B. Hamilton & Richard Strier), (CUP, 1996), pp.6-26.

Powicke, Michael R., 'Distraint of Knighthood and Military Obligation under Henry III' in *Speculum*, Vol. 25, No. 4 (Oct., 1950), pp.457-470

Pugh, T.B., *Henry V and The Southampton Plot*, (Sutton Publishing, 1988)

Rees, R., *South Wales and the March, 1284-1415*, (Oxford, 1924)

Rittenhouse, John (ed) *A Critical Edition of I Sir John Oldcastle*, The Renaissance Imagination, Vol. 9, (Garland Publishing, 1984)

Royal, Susan Ann, JohnFoxe's'ActsandMonuments'andtheLollardLegacyintheLongEnglishReformation,Durhamtheses,DurhamUniversity.AvailableatDurhamE-ThesesOnline:http://etheses.dur.ac.uk/10624/ (2014)

The Brut or Chronicle of England

Scattergood, V.J. (ed), *The Works of Sir John Clanvowe*, (Cambridge, 1975)

Scott Robertson, W.A., 'Couling Castle' in *Archaeologia Cantina*, Vol.11, (1877)

Shakespeare, William, *Henry IV Parts I and II*

Skidmore, Ian, *Owain Glyndwr, Prince of Wales*, (Christopher Davies Publishers, 1992)

Smith, J. Beverley, 'The last phase of the Glyndwr rebellion', *Bulletin of the Board of Celtic Studies*, Vol. 22, (1966-68)

Solly-Flood, F., 'The Story of Prince Henry of Monmouth and Chief-Justice Gascoign' in *Transactions of the Royal Historical Society*, Vol. 3 (1886), pp.47-152

Taylor, Garry, 'William Shakespeare, Richard James & the House of Cobham', *Review of English Studies* N.S. 38 (1987), pp.354-54

Thomson, John A.F., *The Later Lollards 1414–1520*, (OUP, 1965)

The Transformation of Medieval England, 1370–1529, (Longmans, 1983)

Trevelyan, G.M., *England in the age of Wycliffe*, (Longmans, 1899 with several subsequent reprints)

Tyrell, E. & N.H. Nicolas, *Chronicle of London 1089-1483*, (London, 1827)

Walpole, Horace, *A Catalogue of the Royal and Noble Authors of England: With Lists of Their Works*, (Cambridge, 1759)

Waller, J.G., 'The Lords of Cobham, their Monuments and the Church', *Archaeologia Cantiana*, Vol.11 (1877)

Walsingham, Thomas, *The Chronica Maiora of Thomas Walsingham 1376–1422*, trans. David Priest with introduction and notes by James G. Clark, (Boydell, 2005)

Waugh, W.T., 'Sir John Oldcastle' in *English Historical Review*, Vol. 20, (1905), pp.434-56, 637-58

Weever, John, *The Mirror of Martyrs*, (1601)

Wiles, David, *Shakespeare's Clown - Actor & Text in the Elizabethan Playhouse*, (Cambridge University Press, 1987)

Wilkinson, B., *Constitutional History of England in the Fifteenth Century, 1399-1485*, (Longmans, 1964)

Wright, Thomas (ed.), *Political Poems and Songs relating to English History composed during the period from the Accession of EDW. III to that of Ric. III*, Vol II (Longmans, 1859–61)

Wylie, James Hamilton, *History of England under Henry the Fourth*, (Longmans, 1884), 4 volumes

References

Abbreviations used

BENC	K.B. McFarlane, *John Wycliffe and the Beginning of English Nonconformity*, (English Universities Press, 1952)
CCR	Calendar of Close Rolls
CPR	Calendar of Patent Rolls
Foxe	*The acts and monuments of John Foxe: a new and complete edition: with a preliminary dissertation, by the Rev. George Townsend …* (London, 1837–41)
Hodges	Geoffrey Hodges, *Owain Glyn Dwr & the War of Independence in the Welsh Borders*, (Logaston Press, 1995)
Hyett-Warner	Revd R. Hyett-Warner, *Historic Memories of the Manor and Parish of Almeley in the county of Hereford* (Jakeman & Carver, 1917)
Kightly	Charles Kightly, 'The Early Lollards, A survey of Popular Lollard Activity in England, 1382-1428', (University of York thesis, 1975)
Leff	Gordon Leff, *Heresy in the Later Middle Ages, the relation of Heterodoxy to Dissent c.1250–1450*, (Manchester University Press, 1967, edition of Sandpiper Books, 1999)
McFarlane	K.B. McFarlane, *Lancastrian Kings and Lollard Knights*, (Clarendon Press, 1972)
Reg. Trefnant	William Capes (ed), The register of John Trefnant, Bishop of Hereford (A.D. 1389–1404), (Hereford, 1914)
Thomson	John A.F. Thomson, *The Later Lollards 1414–1520*, (OUP, 1965)
TNA	The National Archives
Walsingham	*The Chronica Maiora of Thomas Walsingham 1376–1422*, trans. David Priest with introduction and notes by James G. Clark, (Boydell, 2005)
Wylie	James Hamilton Wylie, *History of England under Henry the Fourth*, (Longmans, 1884), 4 volumes

Chapter 1   Family Background and Early Life

1. From discussions with Keith Ray, former county archaeologist for Herefordshire and his book *Offa's Dyke, Landscape and Hegemony in Eighth-Century Britain*, (Oxbow Books, 2016).
2. Hyett-Warner, p.56.
3. *ibid*, p.56.
4. P. Schofield, *Peasant and Community in Medieval England, 1200-1500*, (Palgrave Macmillan, 2003), p.30.
5. *ibid*, p.44.
6. TNA, C 143/394/8; *CPR, 1377–1381*, p.528.
7. Revd C.J. Robinson, *A History of the Mansions and Manors of Herefordshire* (1872, republished Logaston Press, 2009) under the entries for Brinsop and Wormsley.
8. Hyett-Warner, pp.75–77.
9. W.T. Waugh, 'Sir John Oldcastle', EHR, Vol. XX, (1905), p.436. n.17; Revd C.J. Robinson, *A History of the Castles of Herefordshire and their Lords* (1869, republished Logaston Press, 2002), p.2.

10. Hyett-Warner, p.57.
11. Thomas Elmham, *Liber Metricus* or *Memorials of Henry the Fifth, king of England*, (ed. Charles Augustus Cole), (Longmans, 1858), p.156.
12. Rudolph Fiehler, 'Sir John Oldcastle Reconsidered' in *Concordia Theological Monthly*, August 1957, p.580, for *Chronica Regum* BM Cotton MS. Claud. E IV, f.32.
13. For example *Archaeologia Cambrensis*, 1st series, i, p.47; 4th series, viii, p.125. See also the entry for John Oldcastle in the *Dictionary of National Biography*, 1885-1900, Volume 42 by James Tait. That Oldcastle was known by this Welsh name is also stated in John Howells' booklet, for which see note 18 for this chapter. For other errors in Howells's booklet see page 176.
14. Vernon M. Norr, *Some Early English Pedigrees: Combined from Most Available Sources* (Pennsylvania State University, 1968).
15. Herefordshire SMR 1704.
16. W.T. Waugh, 'Sir John Oldcastle', EHR, Vol. XX, (1905), p.434.
17. Revd C.J. Robinson, *A History of the Castles of Herefordshire and their Lords* (1869, republished Logaston Press, 2002), p.1.
18. John Howells, *The History of the Old Baptist Church at Olchon together with the Life and Martyrdom of Sir John Oldcastle, The Lord Cobham*, (South Wales Printing Works, 1996), a photocopy of which was kindly lent me by the Longtown & District Historical Society. For example, when discussing the claims of Almeley or the Olchon Valley to be the place of his birth, Howells says "Tradition preponderates in favour of the latter', showing he was either ignorant of or chose to ignore both Almeley's traditions and, more importantly, the evidence contained in Close Rolls and elsewhere. Howells states that 'Sir John owned a large estate in and around this [the Olchon] valley', but gives no sources and none have come to light. Howell's' belief in the traditions told him by 'old hoary-headed men and women, gifted with retentive memories' (page 23 of his booklet) is, at one level, to be applauded, for traditions can sometimes hold a grain of truth. But his belief seems excessive as when, for example, recounting a story (unconnected with Oldcastle) he says 'Dr. Samuel Stennett, on whose authority it was related, had it from Dr. Joseph Stennett, his father, so that its truth is beyond doubt.'
19. *CCR*, 22 September 1231.
20. Revd Charles J, Robinson, *A History of the Castles of Herefordshire and their Lords* (Logaston Press reprint, 2002), p.1.
21. The inquisition is detailed in *CPR, 1422–29*, 14 July 1429, pp.546–48.
22. *CPR, 1429–36*, pp.178–79.
23. Early title deeds for Hereford show that Henry Oldcastle had interests in a house in Northgate (presumably referring to what is later called Widemarsh Gate) in Hereford, but whether that is the same as any of the properties mentioned into the inquisition post mortem on John Oldcastle's lands is unknown, *The Manuscripts of Rye and Hereford Corporations, Etc. Thirteenth Report, Appendix: Part IV* (HMSO, 1892) accessed at www.british-history.ac.uk/hist-msss-comm/vol31/pt4/pp290-292.
24. *CCR, 1405–09*, pp.344–46.
25. *CCR, 1405–09*, p.470.
26. *CPR, 1436–41*, p.309.
27. *CPR, 1441–46*, p.249.
28. *CCR, 1402–1403*, p.111 for 8/9/1403.
29. Hyett-Warner, pp.106–07 mentions that a house standing here is listed in the taxation records of Edward III.
30. *Calendar of Close Rolls, Edward III: Volume 8, 1346–1349*, ed. H.C. Maxwell Lyte (London, 1905), pp.278, 279. For 18 June 1347 the Close Rolls record: 'To Roger Hillary and his fellow justices of assize in county Hereford for John de Veer, earl of Oxford, who is staying in the King's service in parts beyond the sea in the company of Henry, earl of Lancaster, for the assize of novel disseisin [and action to reclaim lands of which the owner had been dispossessed] which Richard son of Richard de Hopton arrames against him and others for tenements in Neuport [Newport], Home

[?Holmes Marsh], Wolston, Ellesdon [Elsdon, the old centre for the Hundred] More in Lunhales [Lynhales, part of Lyonshall], Yaydon, Wassayl, Hope in Lunhales and Kyngeswood in Lunhales'. The order is repeated on 8 September when Lunhales becomes Leonhales and Wassayl becomes Bassayl (?).

31. These are listed across the following membranes of the record: E179/117/16/3d c.1 and c.4 and E179/117/16/3d c.1, reproduced in Carolyn C. Fenwick (ed.), *The poll taxes of 1377, 1379, and 1381 Part I Bedfordshire - Leicestershire*, published for the British Academy by Oxford University Press 1998.
32. TNA, E179/117/16/3d c.1 as listed in Carolyn C. Fenwick (ed.) *ibid*.
33. M. Jurkowski, C.L. Smith and D. Crook, *Lay Taxes in England and Wales, 1188-1688*, (PRO Publications, 1998).
34. www.historyofparliamentonline.org/volume/1386-1421/member/oldcastle-thomas-13989.
35. *CCR, 1374–77*, p.258.
36. *The Peerage of Ireland*, Vol. 2 (London, 1768), p.238; http://celtic2realms-medievalnews.blogspot.com/2016/06/john-bromwich-justiciar-of-ireland_14.html.
37. The History of Parliament online entries for both Thomas Oldcastle and Thomas II Walwyn suggests that they returned in January 1398, but no date is given for John Oldcastle's return.
38. McFarlane, pp.115–20; Christopher Allmand, *Henry V*, (The University of California Press, 1992), p.10.
39. McFarlane, pp.162, 165, 169, 181 and 187.
40. Mowbray was to be banished from the kingdom in 1398, along with Henry Bolingbroke, and died abroad.
41. Nigel Saul, *English Church Monuments in the Middle Ages, History and Representation*, (OUP, 2009), pp.245–46, 284.
42. Anglo-Norman Studies III: *Proceedings of the Battle Conference 1980*, (ed. R. Allen Brown), Boydell Press, 1981), p.104. For the duties of a custodian of an alien priory see Carole A. Hutchinson, *The Hermit Monks of Grandmont*, (Cistercian Publications, 1989).
43. www.historyofparliamentonline.org/volume/1386-1421/member/oldcastle-thomas-13989.
44. www.historyofparliamentonline.org/volume/1386-1421/member/oldcastle-thomas-13989. This states that the chantry chapel was established at Castle Frome rather than Norton Canon.
45. Details of the parish church of St Nicholas at Norton Canon found at http://www.weobleyands-taunton.co.uk/archive/nortoncanon/nortoncanon2.htm.
46. www.historyofparliamentonline.org/volume/1386-1421/member/nash-(ash)-richard-13945.
47. www.historyofparliamentonline.org/volume/1386-1421/member/holgot-philip-14034.
48. Revd Charles J, Robinson, *A History of the Castles of Herefordshire and their Lords*, (Logaston Press reprint, 2002), p.109.
49. www.historyofparliamentonline.org/volume/1386-1421/member/bere-kynard-de-la-1402.
50. https://www.britannica.com/biography/Charles-II-king-of-Navarre.
51. www.historyofparliamentonline.org/volume/1386-1421/member/whitney-sir-robert-i-1402.
52. www.historyofparliamentonline.org/volume/1386-1421/member/whitney-sir-robert-ii-1443.
53. www.historyofparliamentonline.org/volume/1386-1421/member/walwyn-thomas-ii-1415.
54. www.historyofparliamentonline.org/volume/1386-1421/member/devereux-sir-walter-1402.
55. In Richard Parry's *History of Kington*, (Kington, 1845), p.217, there is a footnote: 'It is supposed that Hergest Court at the time of the Norman Conquest, or soon after, was a place of considerable note; and that Phillip de Clavinogh who was the owner of the Manor of Hergest in 1330 and his ancestors lived and flourished there for several generations before the property was enjoyed by Thomas Vaughan.'
56. www.historyofparliamentonline.org/volume/1386-1421/member/clanvowe-thomas-1410.
57. J.E.A. Jolliffe, *The Constitutional History of Medieval England*, (Norton & Co., 1937), pp.440–41.
58. Jolliffe, *ibid*, pp.431–33.
59. *ibid*, p.448; en.wikisource.org/wiki/Portal:Acts_of_the_Parliament_of_England/Henry_IV and Henry_V.

60. For more on the role of sheriffs see *English Historical Documents*, Vol. IV, 1327-1485 (ed. David C. Douglas), (Eyre & Spottiswoode, 1969), pp.384–85.

61. For more on the role of justices see *ibid*, pp.386–87.

62. TNA, 8/132/6582, 8/213/10624 and David H. Williams, 'The Abbey of Dore' in *A Definitive History of Dore Abbey*, (eds Ron Shoesmith & Ruth Richardson), (Logaston Press, 1997), p.27 and also Ruth Elizabeth Richardson, *Mistress Blanche, Queen Elizabeth's Confidante*, (Logaston Press, 2007, revised edition 2018), pp.9–10.

63. gw.geneanet.org/dgill?lang=en&pz=douglas+r.&nz=gill&p=john&n=oldcastle.

64. Details of the will come from *CCR, 1402–1405*, p.306.

65. Hyett-Warner, p.82, follows Robinson and the herald's visitation of 1569 in saying that Catherine was sister of Sir John Oldcastle. For the herald's visitation of 1569, see *Visitation of Herefordshire made by Robert Cooke, Clarencieux* (ed. Frederic Weaver) (Exeter, 1886). For reference to the visitation of 1619 and its correction to the Oldcastle pedigree, see *Memorials of Old Herefordshire*, (ed. Revd Compton Reade, (London, 1904), p.189. For details of the life of John Bromwich, justiciar in Ireland, see http://celtic2realms-medievalnews.blogspot.com/2016/06/john-bromwich-justiciar-of-ireland_14.html.

Chapter 2   Oldcastle and Lollardy

1. BENC, pp.129–30; Foxe, Vol. III, pp.111–12; Kightly, p.168 for the name of Lebyot. It is possible that the place of worship used by Swynderby in Deerfold Forest was a chapel adjacent to Chapel Farm (SO39426842), In 1873 during repairs to the property several slabs of reworked sandstone were found to have been used as part of the foundations, three of which formed part of a small Norman window. Chapel Farm is thought to have formed part of a grant of land made by Roger Mortimer *c*.1250 to Limebrook Priory and which included 'the church of the Blessed Mary and St Leonard', to which the name of the farm presumably refers: Hereford Archaeological Service report 356, Watching Brief at Chapel Farm, Wigmore (HWCM 1678). In addition, the Woolhope Naturalists' Field Club noted in a paper on *Lollardism in the diocese of Hereford from the Fourteenth to the Sixteenth Century* by the Rt Revd Martin Linton-Smith, bishop of Hereford, read on 24 June 1930 that Chapel Farm is 'popularly known as Swynderby's Chapel'.

2. Foxe, Vol. III, pp.111–12, 117.

3. Maureen Jurkowski 'Henry V's suppression of the Oldcastle revolt', chapter 4 in *Henry V: New Interpretations*, (Boydell & Brewer, 2013), p.104.

4. BENC, pp.15–17.

5. BENC, pp.20–21.

6. 'The Lollards; Wycliffe's Personality' in *Religious Movements in the Fourteenth Century*, www.bartleby.com/212/0217.html.

7. Leff, pp.511–12.

8. BENC, p.91.

9. Leff, p.516.

10. Leff, pp.517–18.

11. Leff, pp.527, 531.

12. John Wyclif, *Tractatus De Officio Regis*, (ed. Alfred Pollard and Charles Sayle), (Wyclif Society, 1887), p.149.

13. Leff, pp.519–20.

14. G.M. Trevelyan, *England in the Age of Wycliffe*, (Longmans, 1899 with numerous reprints), p.40 referencing Thomas Arnold, *Select English Works of Wyclif*, (Oxford, 1869-71), Vol. III, pp.216–17.

15. Walsingham, pp.29–30.

16. *Fasciculi Zizaniorum Magistri Johannis Wyclif cum tritico*, (ed. Walter Waddington Shirley), The Rolls Series, 5 (Longmans, 1858).

17. BENC, p.42.

18. *Chronicon Henrici Knighton*, (ed. J.R. Lumby), Rolls Series (1895), Vol. II, p.193.

19. BENC, pp.62–65.

20. BENC, p.55; https://biblicalstudies.org.uk/pdf/churchman/043-01_032.pdf.
21. BENC, p.45; William E. Farr, *John Wyclif as Legal Reformer*, Studies in the History of Christian Thought, vol. 10.(E.J. Brill, 1974), p.157.
22. BENC, pp.59–61.
23. BENC, pp.69–81.
24. *CPR, 1401–05*, p.17.
25. Walsingham, pp.117–18.
26. *ibid*, p.118.
27. *ibid*, p.125.
28. G.M. Trevelyan, *England in the Age of Wycliffe*, (Longmans, 1899 with numerous reprints), p.174.
29. *Chronicon Henrici Knighton*, (ed. J.R. Lumby), Rolls Series (1895), Vol. II, pp.180–81.
30. Kightly, pp.55–56.
31. Leff, p.591.
32. Whilst some 30 manuscript copies of the first version written over the next 40 years remain in existence, 140 manuscripts of the latter version remain, indicating the comparative popularity of the latter.
33. Leff, p.576.
34. By 1401 he was tried for heresy and, unable to face death by burning (the Statute of *De Haeretico Comburendo* by then having been enacted), returned to orthodoxy.
35. Kightly, pp.180–84.
36. For what follows, McFarlane, pp.148–206.
37. After Neville's death, Hereford may have spent some time at Montagu's manor of Shenley, according to Walsingham, or in Courtenay's prison according to Knighton.
38. McFarlane, p.200, note 1.
39. J.S. Roskell, *The Commons and their Speakers in English Parliaments, 1376-1523*, (Manchester University Press, 1965), pp.136-7; https://www.historyofparliamentonline.org/volume/1386-1421/member/cheyne-sir-john-i-141314.
40. A.T. Bannister 'Visitation Returns of the Diocese of Hereford in 1397' in *EHR*, XLIV, pp.279 ff, 287, 444 ff, XLV, pp.92, 444, 447, 934.
41. Reg.Trefnant, pp.v-vi. The following details of Swynderby's and Brut's movements and responses are all taken from the register.
42. Reg. Trefnant, pp.238–50.
43. Kightly, p.172.
44. Reg. Trefnant, p.284.
45. *CCR, 1405-09*, pp.169, 272.
46. Maureen Jurkowski, 'Who was Walter Brut' in *English Historical Review*, vol.127, no.525, p.300.
47. Reg. Trefnant, p.291. That this theory is astrological in its basis suggests that Walter Brut the preacher was not also the author of *Theorica Planetarum* as that is a work of pure astronomy, and free of the 'heresy' of astrology! See the entry for Walter Bryt in the *Dictionary of National Biography* by Olaf Pedersen, (2004).
48. Reg. Trefnant, p.294.
49. Maureen Jurkowski, 'Who was Walter Brut' in *English Historical Review*, vol.127, no.525, pp.291–92.
50. Foxe, pp.149, 153.
51. Kightly. pp.173–77.
52. Maureen Jurkowski, 'Who was Walter Brut' in *English Historical Review*, vol.127, no.525, pp.297–98.
53. *Pierce the Ploughman's Crede*, (ed. W.W. Skeat), Early English Text Society, vol. xxx, pref, p.16.
54. Roger Dymock's text of The Twelve Conclusions set out in Middle English from his *Determinationes contra XII haereses Lollardorum* (London, *c*.1395) at http://sites.fas.harvard.edu/~chaucer/special/varia/lollards/lollconc.htm.
55. Bale's Chronicle in Harleian Miscellany or a collection of scarce, curious and entertaining Pamphlets and Tracts, (London, 1808), p.282; Tanner, p.561; Walpole, p.58.

Chapter 3 The Military Life

1. Maureen Jurkowski, 'Who was Walter Brut' in *English Historical Review*, vol.127, no.525, p.289.
2. TNA, E101/40/33, m1, m1d and m10; E101/40/34, m21, m2i and m2ii. For Brut's lands see Maureen Jurkowski, 'Who was Walter Brut' in *English Historical Review*, vol.127, no.525, pp.285–302.
3. http://www.histparl.ac.uk/volume/1386-1421/member/dallingridge-sir-edward-1346-1393.
4. https://www.medievalists.net/2018/02/medieval-england-almost-invaded/
5. For this see Dan Spencer, 'Edward Dallingridge: Builder of Bodiam Castle' in *Ex Historia*, Vol. 6, pp.81–98.
6. For details of warfare at sea at this time, see Christopher Allmand, *The Hundred Years War: England and France at War c.1300-c.1450*, (Cambridge Medieval Textbooks, 2008) and Ian Mortimer, *The Time Traveller's Guide to Medieval England*, (Vintage Books, 2009).
7. Much of the story of this expedition is taken from Walsingham, pp.246–47 and associated notes, and also www.historyofparliamentonline.org/volume/1386-1421/member/dallingridge-sir-edward-1346-1393.
8. *CPR, 1396–99*, p.170.
9. The information on the campaigns and warfare in Ireland in these years is taken from Darren McGettigan, *Richard II and the Irish Kings*, (Four Courts Press, 2016), pp.84–164.
10. Wylie, Vol. I, p.120.
11. *ibid*, p.127.
12. Ian Mortimer, *The Greatest Traitor, The life of Sir Roger Mortimer ruler of England 1327–1330*, (Pimlico, 2004), p.175; *Chronicon de Lanercost*, trans. Sir Herbert Maxwell reproduced in *English Historical Documents*, Vol. IV, 1327–1485 (ed. David C. Douglas), (Eyre & Spottiswoode, 1969), pp.48–50.
13. Wylie, Vol. I, pp.131-33; *English Historical Documents*, (ed. A.R. Myers), Vol. V 1327–1485, Chronicon de Lanercost, pp.49–50.
14. TNA, E101/42/40, m1.
15. Maureen Jurkowski 'Henry V's Suppression of the Oldcastle Revolt', Chapter 4 in *Henry V: New Interpretations* (ed. Gwilym Dodd), (York Medieval Press, 2018 [paperback]), p.104 referencing BL Ms Lansdowne 259, fol.35r.
16. For general news of the campaign see Wylie, Vol. I, pp.138–40.
17. www.historyofparliamentonline.org/volume/1386-1421/member/oldcastle-sir john-1370-1417.
18. Walsingham, p.318.
19. Hodges, pp.38–39; *An English Chronicle of the Reigns of Richard II, Henry IV, Henry V and Henry VI written before the year 1471*, (ed. John Silvester Davies), (Camden Society, 1861), p.22.
20. Hodges, pp.22, 38–40.
21. Hodges, p.41.
22. *CPR, 1399–1401*, p.518.
23. www.historyofparliamentonline.org/volume/1386-1421/member/lucy-sir-william-1353-1401.
24. Hodges, pp.49–52; Adam of Usk, *The Chronicle of Adam of Usk 1377–1421*, Oxford Medieval Texts (Oxford, 1997) pp.144–145.
25. *Proceedings and Ordinances of the Privy Council*, (ed. Sir Harris Nicholas), (Eyre and Spottiswoode, 1834), Vol. I, p.174.
26. Walsingham writes: '… after the battle the Welsh Women cut off the genitalia of the dead, put the member of each dead man in his mouth, and hung his testicles from his chin. They also cut off their noses and stuck them up their arses'. Walsingham, p.322. For a very full analysis of this battle and why it occurred where it did, see Hodges, Chapter 6.
27. Christopher Allmand, *Henry V*, (University of California Press, 1992), p.25.
28. R.A. Griffiths, 'Prince Henry's War: Armies, Garrisons and Supply during the Glyndwr Rising' in *Bulletin of the Board of Celtic Studies*, 34 (1987), p.171.
29. Hodges, p.108.
30. Ian Mortimer, 'Richard II and the Succession to the Crown' in *History*, Vol. 91, issue 303, July 2006, pp.320–336.

31. Holinshed's *Chronicles*, (London, 1808), Vol. III, p.22.

32. Hodges, pp.90–91.

33. *Proceedings and Ordinances of the Privy Council*, (ed. Sir Harris Nicholas), (Eyre and Spottiswoode, 1834), Vol. II, pp.61-2; TNA, SC 6/774/15, mm. 1d, 2d.

34. Christopher Allmand, *Henry V*, (University of California Press, 1992), pp.384–5.

35. R.W.M. Griffiths, 'Prince Henry, Wales, and the Royal Exchequer', *Bulletin of the Board of Celtic Studies* 32 (1985), p.205.

36. Hodges, p.107.

37. *Proceedings and Ordinances of the Privy Council*, (ed. Sir Harris Nicholas), (Eyre and Spottiswoode, 1834), Vol. II, p.68.

38. *CPR, 1405-1408*, p.6.

39. R.A. Griffiths, 'Prince Henry's War: Armies, Garrisons and Supply during the Glyndwr Rising', *Bulletin of the Board of Celtic Studies* 34 (1987), p.166.

40. Eliis, *Original Letters*, 2nd Series, 1, 33, reproduced in *English Historical Documents*, Vol. IV, 1327–1485 (ed. David C. Douglas), (Eyre & Spottiswoode, 1969), pp.195–96.

41. M.R. Powicke, *Military Obligations in Medieval England*, (Oxford, 1962), p.26.

42. Philippe Contamine (trans. Michael Jones), *War in the Middle Ages*, (BCA 1984), p.68.

43. M.R. Powicke, 'Distraint of Knighthood and Military Obligation under Henry III' in *Speculum* Vol. 25, No. 4 (Oct., 1950), pp.457–70.

44. Philippe Contamine (trans. Michael Jones), *War in the Middle Ages*, (BCA 1984), pp.70–71.

45. *ibid*, p.129.

46. *ibid*, pp.132–33.

47. TNA, E. 404/31/359, E. 101/69/381.

48. Philippe Contamine (trans. Michael Jones), *War in the Middle Ages*, (BCA 1984), pp.94–95.

49. *ibid*, p.239.

50. *CPR, 1401-1405*, p.299.

51. www.historyofparliamentonline.org/volume/1386-1421/member/harry-john-ap-1420.

52. *CPR, 1401-1405*, pp.312–13.

53. Rudolph Fiehler, *The Strange History of Sir John Oldcastle*, (American Press, 1965), p.27; www.history-ofparliamentonline.org/volume/1386-1421/member/oldcastle-sir-john-1370-1417.

54. R.W.M. Griffiths 'Prince Henry, Wales, and the Royal Exchequer', *Bulletin of the Board of Celtic Studies* 32 (1985), p.203.

55. *Proceedings and Ordinances of the Privy Council*, (ed. Sir Harris Nicholas), (Eyre and Spottiswoode, 1834), Vol. I, p.237.

56. R.W.M. Griffiths, 'Prince Henry, Wales, and the Royal Exchequer', *Bulletin of the Board of Celtic Studies* 32 (1985), p.210.

57. Rudolph Fiehler, *The Strange History of Sir John Oldcastle*,(American Press, 1965), p.27. I have not been able to find an original source for Oldcastle's appointment to this role.

58. Proc. Privy Council, i, 230; Cal. Close Rolls, 1402–05, 478–9; Anglo-Norman Letters and Petitions, ed. M. Dominica Legge (Oxford, 1941), 359–60.

59. *CPR, 1401-1405*, p.464.

60. Wylie, Vol. II, p.5; *CPR, 1401-1405*, p.504 dated 2 October.

61. TNA, E.101/44/1.

62. TNA, C.47/2/49, no.17.

63. Hodges, p.125.

64. *ibid*, pp.125–28.

65. *ibid*, pp.129–40.

66. *CCR, 1402-05*, p.256.

67. *CPR, 1405-08*, p.149.

68. Hodges, pp.141–46.

69. Wylie, Vol. III, p.293 referencing Pat, 9, H. IV, 1, 6.

70. Wylie, Vol. III, pp.111–12.
71. *CCR, 1405–1409*, pp.277–78.
72. Rymer's *Foedera* July-December 1407 for September 12 accessed at www.british-history.ac.uk/rymer-foedera/vol8/pp490-509.
73. Wylie, Vol. III, pp.113, 117–18.
74. *CPR, 1405–08*, p.407.
75. TNA, E.101/405/17.
76. H.B. Workman, *The Dawn of the Reformation*, (Charles Kelly, 1901).
77. *Calendar Fine Rolls*, Vol. XIII, p.66.
78. *ibid.*

Chapter 4   Wilder Days?

1. Michael Bennett 'Henry IV, the Royal Succession and the Crisis of 1406' in *The Reign of Henry IV, Rebellion and Survival, 1403–1413*, (ed. Gwilym Dodd and Douglas Biggs), (York Medieval Press, 2008), p.10.
2. McFarlane, pp.102–09.
3. Christopher Allmand, *Henry V*, (California University Press, 1992), p.249.
4. TNA, SC 6/1222/10, m.3 and Christopher Allmand, *Henry V*, (University of California Press, 1992), p.354; www.historyofparliamentonline.org/volume/1386-1421/member/hay-thomas-de-la-1440.
5. Rot. Claus. 5 Hen V, m.14; GEC, *Complete Peerage*, Vol. VI, p.119; re the unreliability of John Philipot: http://www.hughevelynprints.com/medievil-knights/sir-john-oldcastle-lord-cobham-1370-1417. The function of heralds was to initially organise tournaments and issue the associated proclamations. As the knights taking part in tournaments were recognisable by their coats of arms, heralds soon became experts in the field and soon became responsible for first recording coats of arms, and then regulating their use.
6. G.E. Cockayne, *The Complete Peerage of England, Scotland, Ireland, Great Britain and the United Kingdom* (1895) accessed at https://archive.org/details/completepeerage06cokahrish/page/n119. See also J.H. Wylie, Vol. III, p.293.
7. Rudolph Fiehler, *The Strange History of Sir John Oldcastle*, (American Press, 1965), p.30.
8. The former date is when Joan is mentioned alone in a property matter, the latter when Ralph de Hemenhall of Suffolk, cousin and heir of Sir Nicholas Hawberk, granted by quitclaim (i.e. eschewing all rights) his manor of Burnham, Norfolk, to Oldcastle and his wife, Joan. Rudolph Fiehler, *The Strange History of Sir John Oldcastle*, (American Press, 1965), p.30.
9. For example J.G. Waller in 'The Lords of Cobham, their Monuments and the Church' in *Archaeologia Cantiana*, Vol. XI, 1877, p.84 suggests he was 92.
10. W.T. Waugh, 'Sir John Oldcastle', *EHR*, Vol. XX, p.438; *The Calendar of Inquisitions Miscellaneous*, Vol. 7, 1399–1422, pp.318–25 name the known manors as Cooling, Cobham, Pole, Stone, Beckley and Bekesbourne in Kent (noting that stone formed part of Pole); Burnham Westgate in Norfolk; Castle Ashby (along with its castle) and Chadstone in Northamptonshire; and Chisbury and Bincknoll in Wiltshire. In Essex, Oldcastle seems to have held the manor of Radwinter, east of Saffron Walden, as recorded in an Inquisition Post Mortem held in 1420 regarding William Wynselowe, www.inquistionpostmortem.ac.uk/view/inquisition/21-238/.
11. Edward Hasted, The *History and Topographical Survey of the County of Kent*, Vol. IV, p.5.
12. Gwilym Dodd, 'Patronage, Petitions and Grace: The 'Chamberlains' Bills' of Henry IV's Reign' in *The Reign of Henry IV, Rebellion and Survival, 1403-1413*, (York Medieval Press, 2008), p.119 and Rhoda L. Friedrichs, 'The Remarriage of Elite Widows in the Later Middle Ages' in *Florilegium*, 23(1), pp.76–77.
13. www.historyofparliamentonline.org/volume/1386-1421/member/oldcastle-sir-john-1370-141; N. Saul, *Death, Art and Memory in Medieval England: The Cobham Family and their Monuments, 1300-1500* (Oxford, 2001), p.29.
14. On page 52.

15. Information on The Cobham's Head from the history of Farringdon Road on www.british-history. ac.uk/survey-london/vol46/pp358-384#p1 and on Sir John Oldcastle's Field from www.british-history. ac.uk/survey-london/vol47/pp22-51#h3-0004, with other information from the website for the current Sir John Oldcastle and Islington Council's 'Streets with a story' website.
16. Walsingham, p.318 The St Albans Chronicle, p.389.
17. Thomas de Elmham, *Vita & gesta Henrici Quinti, Anglorum regis*, (Oxford, 1727), pp.14–17, and see Christopher Allmand, *Henry V*, (University of California Press, 1992), p.63.
18. C.L. Kingsford, *English Historical Literature in the Fifteenth Century*, (The Clarendon Press, 1913), pp.125–26; *The Brut Chronicle* (ed. F.W.D. Brie), (Early English Text Society, 1906, 1908, original series, Nos. 131, 196), 595 (English) reproduced in *English Historical Documents*, Vol. IV, 1327–1485 (ed. David C. Douglas), (Eyre & Spottiswoode, 1969), pp.207–08.
19. *The Brut or The Chronicle of England*, (ed. F.W.D. Brie, 2 vols, Early English Text Society, OS 131 and 136 (London, 1908), II, pp.594–95.
20. Antonia Grandsen, *Historical Writing in England: c.1307 to the early sixteenth century*, (Psychology Press, 1996), pp.217–18; Bryan Bevan, *Henry IV*, (Palgrave Macmillan), p.147.
21. Rymer's Foedera January–March 1410 for March 18 accessed at www.british-history.ac.uk/ rymer-foedera/vol8/pp617-630.
22. John Stow, *A Survey of London*, (ed. William J. Thoms), (Whittaker & Co, 1842), p.89.
23. J. Dover Wilson, *The Fortunes of Falstaff*, (CUP, 1964), pp.25–26; *Henry IV Part I*, Act II, scene IV.
24. http://www.manningtreetowncouncil.org.uk/manningtree.
25. John Stow, *A Survey of London*, (ed. William J. Thoms), (Whittaker & Co, 1842), p.82.
26. *A Chronicle of London from 1089 to 1483*, (Longmans, 1827), p.93.
27. John Stow, *A Survey of London*, (ed. William J. Thoms), (Whittaker & Co, 1842), pp.90–91.
28. *The Historical Collections of a Citizen of London in the Fifteenth Century*, the bulk of which is formed by Gregory's Chronicle. Originally published by Camden Society (London, 1876), now available on line at www.british-history.ac.uk/camden-record-soc/vol17, pp.103–28.
29. BM Egerton MS Roll 8746.
30. Wylie, Vol. IV, p.93, n.11.
31. Thomas Elyot, *The Boke Named The Governour*, (J.M. Dent & Co, 1907), Book II, pp.139–41.
32. Wylie, Vol. IV, pp.96–97.
33. Wylie, Vol. IV, pp.98–99.
34. Wylie, Vol. II, p.189.
35. Wylie, Vol. II, p.185.
36. McFarlane, pp.130–31.

Chapter 5   Oldcastle near the Centre of Government
1. The mixture of Latin, French and nascent English in the documents of the time is very common, and shows the gradual move away from the Continent and a closer attention to English affairs. At the beginning of the 1400s letters and documents in Latin or Anglo-French are most common. By the middle of the century private individuals, politicians and statesmen corresponded in English; Latin and French were restricted to foreign diplomacy. During Henry V's reign, the fact that Richard Beauchamp, earl of Warwick, could speak French fluently was regarded as something of an achievement.
2. G.E. Cockayne, *The Complete Peerage of England, Scotland, Ireland, Great Britain and the United Kingdom* (1895) accessed at https://archive.org/details/completepeerage06cokahrish/page/n119.
3. *CCR, 1402–05*, p.367.
4. For more on the loyal nature of Henry's Parliaments and the use of patronage, see *The Reign of Henry IV, Rebellion and Survival, 1403–1413*, (ed. Gwilym Dodd and Douglas Biggs), (York Medieval Press, 2008), Chapters 5 and 8.
5. R.G. Davies & J.H. Denton (eds.), *The English Parliament in the Middle Ages*, (Manchester University Press, 1981), pp.110–12.

6. A.K. McHardy, 'Henry IV: The Clergy in Parliament' in *The Reign of Henry IV, Rebellion and Survival, 1403–1413*, (ed. Gwilym Dodd and Douglas Biggs), (York Medieval Press, 2008), pp.138–39, 157.

7. This was the Henry Beaufort who subsequently became bishop of Winchester and who was one of those at the trial of Oldcastle in 1413. He later became a cardinal.

8. https://www.historyofparliamentonline.org/volume/1386-1421/member/oldcastle-sir-john-1370-1417.

9. For more on this parliament and the limitations within which parliament in general had to work, see McFarlane, Chapter 5.

10. Thomas Walsingham, *Annales Ricardi II et Henrici IV*, (ed. H.T. Riley), (Rolls series, 1866), p.391.

11. Wylie, Vol. I, p.373.

12. John Capgrave, *The Chronicle of England* (ed. Rev. F.C. Hingeston), (Longmans, 1858), p.284.

13. *Rotuli Parliamentorum*,, (London, 1767–77), Vol. III, (ed. John Strachey), pp.583–84.

14. B. Wilkinson, *Constitutional History of England in the Fifteenth Century 1399–1485*, (Longmans, 1964), p.381.

15. For more on the political crisis of 1406, see Michael Bennett 'Henry IV, The Royal Succession and the Crisis of 1406' in *The Reign of Henry IV, Rebellion and Survival, 1403–1413*, (ed. Gwilym Dodd and Douglas Biggs), (York Medieval Press, 2008), pp.15–18, 22–23.

16. Walsingham, pp.340–41, 343 and note 8 p.340.

17. Wylie, Vol. III, pp.427–28.

18. W.A. Scott Robertson, 'Coulyng Castle' in *Archaeologia Cantina*, Vol. XI, (1877), pp.128–40.

19. Wylie, Vol. III, p.293.

20. For a history of Anglo-French jousting at this period, see Chris Given-Wilson 'The Quarrels of Old Women' in *The Reign of Henry IV, Rebellion and Survival, 1403–1413*, (ed. Gwilym Dodd and Douglas Biggs), (York Medieval Press, 2008), Chapter 2.

21. For the record of the event: E. Petit, *Itinéraires de Philippe le Hardi et de Jean sans Peur*, (Paris, 1888), p.373; also W.T. Waugh , 'Sir John Oldcastle', *EHR*, Vol. XX, p.439; Wylie, Vol. III, p.293. For general information on tournaments at Lille: Steven J. Gunn, & A. Janse (eds), *The Court as a Stage: England and the Low Countries in the Later Middle Ages*, Boydell (2006), pp.39–40. For the identification of Umfraville as Gilbert of that family, see See Gwilym Dodd 'Henry V's Establishment: Service, Loyalty and Reward in 1413' in *Henry V: New Interpretations* (ed. Gwilym Dodd), (York Medieval Press, 2018 [paperback]), p.45.

22. G. Barnett Smith, *History of the English Parliament*, (Ward Lock, 1892), Vol. I, p.246; McFarlane, p.61.

23. McFarlane, p.92.

24. *ibid*, pp.102–09.

25. See for example Gerald Harris, *Shaping the Nation, England 1360–1461* (Clarendon Press, 2005), p.393 and Susan Curran, *The Wife of Cobham*, (Lasse Press, 2016) which tells the story of Joan Cobham, Oldcastle's wife, where Curran surmises that Cobham's Inn would have been a hive of activity in the days leading up to the parliament as Oldcastle worked to gain support for the petition.

26. C.L. Kingsford, *Chronicle of London*, (Clarendon Press, 1905), p.65, erroneously given under 1407.

27. Wylie, Vol. III, pp.310–11.

28. *Rotuli Parliamentorum*, (London, 1767–77), Vol. III, (ed. John Strachey), p.627.

29. Much of this background is derived from Anne Curry, 'France, England and the Political Climate, 1400–1415', in The Online Froissart, ed. by Peter Ainsworth and Godfried Croenen, v. 1.5 (Sheffield: HRIOnline, 2013), http://www.hrionline.ac.uk/onlinefroissart/apparatus.jsp?type=intros&intro=f. intros.AC-PoliticalClimate, first published in v. 1.0 (2010).

30. Most of what follows in this chapter is derived from Wylie, Vol. IV, pp.54–65 and from Anthony Tuck 'The Earl of Arundel's Expedition to France, 1411' in *The Reign of Henry IV, Rebellion and Survival, 1403–1413*, (ed. Gwilym Dodd and Douglas Biggs), (York Medieval Press, 2008), Chapter 11, each of which use as their source the accounts of the Receivers-General of John the Fearless duke of Burgundy held in the archives of the Department of the Côte-d'Or at Dijon.

31. *The Brut; or, The chronicles of England* (ed. Friedrich W.D. Brie) (Early English Texts Society, 1906), p.371.

32. Held in Hereford Archive and Records Centre, CF50/242.
33. My thanks to James Pattinson for his help in deciphering Oldcastle's heraldry. For discussion on the Rouen Roll see Sir Anthony Wagner, *A Catalogue of English Medieval Rolls of Arms*, (OUP, 1950), Vol. I.
34. The details regarding the prisoners comes from Jonathan Sumption, *The Hundred Years War, Volume 4: Cursed Kings*, (University of Pennsylvania Press, 2017), p.296. The wider account of the battle of St Cloud in this book makes no mention of Sir John Oldcastle, and also says that the return of the majority of the English force occurred before the siege of Étampes.
35. The quote is from Walsingham, p.383, referring to how prisoners were treated following the battle of St Cloud.
36. Thomas Gaspey, *The Life and Times of the Good Lord Cobham* (London, 1844), Vol. I, p.155.
37. Michael Bennett 'Henry IV, the Royal Succession and the Crisis of 1406' in *The Reign of Henry IV, Rebellion and Survival, 1403–1413*, (ed. Gwilym Dodd and Douglas Biggs), (York Medieval Press, 2008), pp.18–19.
38. McFarlane, p.108; Wylie, Vol. IV, p.40.
39. McFarlane, pp.93, 108–09.
40. See Gwilym Dodd 'Henry V's Establishment: Service, Loyalty and Reward in 1413' in *Henry V: New Interpretations* (ed. Gwilym Dodd), (York Medieval Press, 2018 [paperback]), pp.51-52.
41. Walsingham, pp.386–87.
42. McFarlane, pp.109–111 referring to *A Chronicle of London from 1089 to 1483*, ed Sir N.H. Nicolas and E. Tyrell, (London, 1827), pp.94 and 95. The scale of his retinue is also referred to in Walsingham, p.387.
43. Christopher Allmand, *Henry V*, (University of California Press, 1992) pp.57–58.

Chapter 6   Oldcastle's increasing commitment to Lollardy

1. These regulations can be found in Archbishop Arundel's Register, vol. 2, f.20, printed in D. Wilkins, *Concilia Magnae Britanniae*, III, p.314 (in Latin) and reproduced (in English) in *English Historical Documents*, Vol. IV, 1327–1485 (ed. David C. Douglas), (Eyre & Spottiswoode, 1969), pp.855–87.
2. *Concilia Magnae Britttaniae et Hiberniae*, (ed. David Wilkins), (London, 1737), Vol. III, pp.329–31.
3. Kightly, p.374.
4. www.historyofparliamentonline.org/volume/1386-1421/member/brooke-sir-thomas-1355-1418, www.historyofparliamentonline.org/volume/1386-1421/member/brooke-thomas-1391-1439; Wylie, Vol. III, p.294; *CCR, 1413–19*, p.116.
5. Denys Hay, *Europe in the Fourteenth and Fifteenth Centuries*, (Longmans, 1966), pp.323–24.
6. 'Wycliffe's influence upon Central and Eastern Europe' in *The Slavonic and East European Review*, vol. 7, No. 21, p.634.
7. Craig D. Atwood, *The Theology of the Czech Brethren from Hus to Comenius*, (Pennsylvania State University Press, 2009), pp.35–36.
8. Herbert B. Workman & R. Martin Pope, *Letters of John Hus with introductions and explanatory notes*, (Hodder and Stoughton, 1904), p.34.
9. Translated for this book by Richard Ashdowne.
10. It can be viewed at http://www.manuscriptorium.com/apps/index.php?direct=record&pid=AIPDIG-NKCR__XIII_F_21___1GP7AJ9-cs.
11. For brief time around 1400 Wyche had been a priest in the Hereford diocese, then preached in Northumberland in 1401–02 where he was examined for heresy by Bishop Skirlaw of Durham and was both excommunicated and held in prison until he recanted sometime between 1404 and 1406. In 1419 he was summoned by Archbishop Chichele of Canterbury once again under suspicion of heresy, admitted his earlier condemnation, and was sent to the Fleet prison. He was released in 1420 and then served as a rector in several churches in Kent and Middlesex in the 1420s and '30s. In 1440 he was once again arrested and this time burned as a heretic in London, a death that seems to have stirred up support for Lollardy in the capital and saw him gain the status of a martyr. Rita Copeland,

Pedagogy, Intellectuals, and Dissent in the Later Middle Ages; Lollardy and Ideas of Learning, (CUP, 2001), pp.152–53, 187–88.

12. Herbert B. Workman & R. Martin Pope, *Letters of John Hus with introductions and explanatory notes*, (Hodder and Stoughton, 1904), p.35 (can be accessed at https://oll.libertyfund.org/titles/huss-the-letters-of-john-hus); Rita Copeland, *Pedagogy, Intellectuals, and Dissent in the Later Middle Ages; Lollardy and Ideas of Learning*, (CUP, 2001) pp.186–87.

13. W.T. Waugh, 'Sir John Oldcastle', *EHR*, Vol. XX, p.444.

14. The full title of the work is: *Doctrinale antiquitatum fidei catholicae ecclesiae contra Wiclevistas et Hussitas.*

15. Detailed information on the transmission of information and letters between England and Bohemia, and the individuals who might have been involved in this, are contained in Michael Van Duessen's *From England to Bohemia; Heresy and Communication in the later Middle Ages* (CUP 2012), notably, for Oldcastle and Wyche, pp.81–85, and in Van Duessen's 'Conveying Heresy: "A Certayne Student" and the Lollard-Hussite fellowship' in *Viator* 38.2 (2007), pp.217–34.

16. W.T. Waugh, 'Sir John Oldcastle', English Historical Review, XX (1905), pp.453, 657–58.

17. Thomas Wright (ed), *Political Poems and Songs relating to English History composed during the period from the Accession of EDW. III to that of Ric. III*, Vol. II (Longmans, 1859–61), p.128, stating it is taken from MS Cotton Vespasian D, ix, fol. 51r. In Wright the verse is followed by another:

> *Versus quidam catholici contra eosdem Lollardos*
> *Gens Lollardorum gens est vilis Sodomorum,*
> *Errores eorum sunt in mundo causa dolorum.*
> *Hii sunt ingrati, maledicti, daemone nati,*
> *Quos vos, praelati, sitis damnare parati;*
> *Qui pugiles estis fidei populisque praeestis,*
> *Non horum gestis ignes prohibere potestis.*

18. Bale's Chronicle in *Harleian Miscellany or a collection of scarce, curious and entertaining Pamphlets and Tracts*, (London, 1808), p.282.

19. Thomas Gaspey, *The Life and Times of the Good Lord Cobham*, (London, 1844), Vol. I, pp.130–31.

20. Michael Van Duessen's *From England to Bohemia; Heresy and Communication in the later Middle Ages* (CUP 2012), notably, for Oldcastle and Wyche, pp.81–85, and in Van Duessen's 'Conveying Heresy: "A Certayne Student" and the Lollard-Hussite fellowship' in *Viator* 38.2 (2007), pp.217–34.

21. S.A. Swaine, *Faithful Men; or, memorials of Bristol Baptist College and some of its most distinguished alumni*, (London, 1884), pp.5–6.

22. Hyett-Warner, p.104.

23. I am indebted to Michael Brealey, Librarian at Bristol Baptist College for ferreting out this information.

24. https://www.historyofparliamentonline.org/volume/1558-1603/member/lambarde-william-1536-1601.

25. STC 20036. The specific suggestion of this text was made in correspondence by Matthew Holford of the Bodleian Library.

26. Dr Mike Rodman Jones, *Radical Pastoral, 1381–1594: Appropriation and the Writing of Religious Controversy*, (Ashgate, 2011), p.104.

27. The date is given on page 515, which also has the commencement of *The Praier and complaynte of the ploweman unto Christe.*

28. For example see Rev. Robert Vaughan (ed), *Tracts and Treatises of John de Wycliffe, D.D. with selections and Translations from his Manuscripts, and Latin Works*, (London, 1845). Due to Covid-19 restrictions in the last few months of completing this book I wasn't able to consult some more recent works such as W.R. Thomson, *The Latin Writings of John Wyclif: An Annotated Catalog*, Pontifical Institute of Medieval Studies, *Subsidia Mediaevalia*, 14, (Toronto, 1983).

29. John N. King, '"The Light of Printing": William Tyndale, John Foxe, John Day, and Early Modern Print Culture' in *Renaissance Quarterly*, Vol. 54, (2001).

30. Kightly, p.136.

31. Susan Ann Royal, (2014) John Foxe's 'Acts and Monuments' and the Lollard Legacy in the Long English Reformation, Durham theses, Durham University. Available at Durham E-Theses Online: http://etheses. dur.ac.uk/10624/ referencing John Leland, *The laboryouse iourney [and] serche of Iohan Leylande, for Englandes antiquitees* (1549), sigs. E8r-F3r, quote at F3r.

Chapter 7   The Trial

1. Lambeth Palace Record Office, Reg. Arundel, ii, ff.18–19.
2. Walsingham, p.390.
3. Thomas de Elmham, (ed) Hearne pp.30–31. Thomas Hearne was an editor of many English chronicles and, it was later determined, wrongly ascribed this chronicle to Thomas Elmham (who did compose other works) and this chronicle is now usually referred to as the Pseudo-Elmham.
4. Gwilym Dodd 'Henry V's Establishment: Service, Loyalty and Reward in 1413' in *Henry V: New Interpretations* (ed. Gwilym Dodd), (York Medieval Press, 2018 [paperback]), pp.35–74.
5. J.S. Roskell and F. Taylor, 'The Authorship and Purpose of the *Gesta Henrici Quinta*' accessed at https://www.escholar.manchester.ac.uk › api › datastream.
6. Foxe, *Acts and Monuments of the Church*, (1563 edition), Book 2, p.330.
7. *Concilia Magnae Brittaniae et Hiberniae*, (ed. David Wilkins), (London, 1737), Vol. II, p.338.
8. Rudolph Fiehler, 'Sir John Oldcastle Reconsidered' in *Concordia Theological Monthly*, August 1957, p.584; C.L. Kingsford, *Chronicle of London*, (Clarendon Press, 1905), p.101.
9. *Concilia Magnae Brittaniae et Hiberniae*, (ed. David Wilkins), (London, 1737), Vol. III, pp.351–52; Rudolph Fiehler, 'Sir John Oldcastle Reconsidered' in *Concordia Theological Monthly*, August 1957, p.584.
10. Walsingham, p.390.
11. James Endell Tyler, *Henry of Monmouth: or, Memoirs of the life and character of Henry the fifth*, (London, 1838), 2 volumes, p.361, n.1 referring to Arundel's account of the proceedings.
12. Regarding Richard II, in whose household Henry had been kept as surety for his father's good behaviour during the latter's period of banishment, Henry seems to have felt aggrieved by his father's treatment of the king. When Richard went to Ireland in May 1399, Henry went with him and is said to have been knighted by Richard whilst there, though aged only 12. When Bolingbroke landed in England and Richard returned to confront him, Henry was left at Trim in Ireland. Once Bolingbroke had Richard in his hands, he sent for his son, but on landing, the young Henry sought out Richard in Chester and took his place back in the king's household. He had been in Richard's care since Bolingbroke's banishment and had not seen his father for over a year. When Bolingbroke summoned his son to leave Richard's service and rejoin him, the story goes that Richard said: 'Good son Henry, I give thee leave to do thy father's commandment, but I know well there is one Henry shall do me much harm and I suppose it is not thou. Wherefore I pray thee be my friend, for I wot now how it will go.' It is said that the young Henry left the king with a heavy heart. (McFarlane, p.121 referencing *The Brut; or, the Chronicles of England*, [ed. F. Brie], [Early English text Society, 1908], Part II, p.545.) This was written by a source partisan to Richard, but Richard is known to have had an easy affinity with children (as well as with peasants) and it does seem congruent with the estrangement from his father that Henry felt as the years passed. After Richard's murder, his body was buried in the church of the Black Friars in Langley in Hertfordshire, the tomb for himself beside that of his wife at Westminster Abbey lying empty. But once Prince Henry became Henry V, he had Richard's body reburied in Westminster Abbey.
13. McFarlane, p.128.
14. Christopher Allmand, 'Writing History in the Eighteenth Century', Chapter 11 in *Henry V: New Interpretations* (ed. Gwilym Dodd), (York Medieval Press, 2018 [paperback]), p.280.
15. *CPR, 1413–16*, p.73.
16. *Concilia Magnae Brittaniae et Hiberniae*, (ed. David Wilkins), (London, 1737), Vol. III, pp.352–53.
17. Walsingham, p.391; *Fasciculi Zizaniorum Magistri Johannis Wyclif cum tritico*, (ed W.W. Shirley, The Rolls Series, 5 (Longmans, 1858), p.436 (online at archive.org/stream/englishhistoryi103warnuoft/ englishhistoryi103warnuoft_djvu.txt, pages 69–70).

18. Foxe gives his name as Henry 'Bolingbrook'. This is indirectly correct as he was an illegitimate son of John of Gaunt by his mistress Katherine Swynford, a birth subsequently legitimised.

19. Rudolph Fiehler, 'Sir John Oldcastle Reconsidered' in *Concordia Theological Monthly*, August 1957, p.587.

20. *Dictionary of National Biography, 1885–1900*, Vol. 3 by Mandell Creighton https://en.wikisource.org/wiki/Bale,_John_(DNB00).

21. https://www.britannica.com/biography/John-Foxe.

22. Foxe, Vol. III, pp.324–25.

23. University College MS. (Coxe) 97, fos.114r–124v and McFarlane, pp.201–05.

24. McFarlane, p.205.

25. This form of words is taken from the letter of Archbishop Arundel to the Bishop of London reporting on the case as reproduced in *English Historical Documents*, Vol. IV, 1327–1485 (ed. David C. Douglas), (Eyre & Spottiswoode, 1969), p.860. The wording is almost identical to that reproduced by Foxe, p.327.

26. This and what follows, apart from references to Arundel's own account and the part taken from Walsingham's account, is taken from Foxe, pp.329–35, some of it taken verbatim from Bale.

27. *Fasciculi Zizaniorum Magistri Johannis Wyclif cum tritico*, ed. by Walter Waddington Shirley, The Rolls Series, 5 (London: Longman, Brown, Green, Longmans, and Roberts, 1858), pp.433-50.

28. Walsingham, p.392.

29. Foxe p.334; C.L. Kingsford, *Henry V, the typical medieval hero*, (G.P. Putnam's sons, 1901), p.103 for the attribution of the question to Thomas Netter. Netter went on to collect together a set of measures passed against Lollards which forms the *Fasciculi Zizaniorum Magistri Johannis Wycliff cum Tritico* (ed W.W. Shirley, London: Rolls Series, 1848).

Chapter 8   Rising, Flight and Capture

1. Walsingham, p.393; John Capgrave, The Chronicle of England, (ed. F.C. Hingeston), (Elibron Classics, 2005 being a facsimile of the 1858 Longmans edition), p.306.

2. The Royalist General John Middleton, for example, escaped wearing his wife's clothes in 1651, Christopher Hibbert, *Cavaliers and Roundheads* (Harper Collins, 1993), p.278.

3. Ian Mortimer, *The Greatest Traitor, The Life of Sir Roger Mortimer ruler of England 1327-1330*, (Pimlico, 2004), pp.129–31.

4. John Stow, *The Survey of London*, (J.M. Dent & Sons), p.54 (now an ebook at www.gutenberg.org/files/42959/42959-h/42959-h.htm).

5. John Bale, 'Brief Chronicle concerning the Examination and Death of … Sir John Oldcastle …' in *Select Works of John Bale*, (CUP, 1849), pp.46–49.

6. *Gesta Henrici Quinti*, (trans. and ed. F. Taylor and J.S. Roskell), (Oxford, 1975), p.6.

7. John Stow, George Buck and Edmund Howes, *The annales, or generall chronicle of England*, (London, 1615), p.344. The account of the revolt in Stow's *Annales* is taken from a very detailed London chronicle of which the original appears to be lost. That the escape took place *noctanter* (at night) and *subdole* (deceitfully) is confirmed by the original of the writ to the sheriffs of London announcing Oldcastle's escape. Guildhall Library, London Letter Book I. f.129.

8. Robert Redmayne, *Vita Henrici Quinti*, (Longmans, 1858), pp.16–17.

9. Walsingham, p.405.

10. Some sources say that Fisher was captured in August 1415 at the time of the failure of Oldcastle's rising in Malvern, but as his trial would then have not taken place till over a year later, this is unlikely, and an alternative date of October 1416 is now usually agreed. See, for example, Maureen Jurkowski 'Henry V's Suppression of the Oldcastle Revolt' in *Henry V: New Interpretations* (ed. Gwilym Dodd), (York Medieval Press, 2018 [paperback]), p.120.

11. www.british-history.ac.uk/old-new-london/vol2/pp60-76#p27.

12. C.L. Kingsford, *Henry V, the typical medieval hero*, (G.P. Putnam's sons, 1901), p.104; *Gregory's Chronicle* or *The Historical Collections of a Citizen of London in the Fifteenth Century*, (Camden Society, 1876), p.108.

13. *A Chronicle of London from 1089 to 1483* (Longmans, 1827), p.97.
14. Kightly, p.481 referencing Calendar of Letter Books of the City of London, (ed. R.R. Sharpe), (London, 1899–1912), Book I, p.119.
15. Maureen Jurkowski 'Henry V's suppression of the Oldcastle revolt', Chapter 4 in *Henry V: New Interpretations*, (Boydell & Brewer, 2013), p.107.
16. *CPR, 1413–16*, p.103; *CCR, 1413–19*, p.41.
17. TNA, E 403/614.
18. BENC, p.167.
19. Margaret Wade Labarge, *Henry V, The Cautious Conqueror*, (Secker and Warburg, 1975), p.46.
20. Michael Turner, *Eltham Palace*, English Heritage Guide to the site.
21. Kightly, p.486. Parchmyner was accused of harbouring Oldcastle only until the 6th January, Kightly, p.481.
22. *CCR, 1413–19*, pp.114–15.
23. Walsingham, p.395.
24. According to the *Gesta Henrici Quinti*, (trans. and ed. F. Taylor and J.S. Roskell), (Oxford, 1975), pp.10–11, his arrival was greeted by the appearance of a meteor.
25. John Stow, George Buck and Edmund Howes, *The annales, or generall chronicle of England*, (London, 1615), p.344; Kightly, p.489.
26. BENC, pp.166–79.
27. R.W.M. Griffiths, 'Prince Henry, Wales, and the Royal Exchequer', *Bulletin of the Board of Celtic Studies*, 32, (1985) p.210.
28. *Proceedings and Ordinances of the Privy Council*, (ed. Sir Harris Nicholas), (Eyre and Spottiswoode, 1834), Vol. II, p.64; J.H. Wylie, *The reign of Henry V*, (CUP, 1914–29), Vol. I, p.271, n.i.
29. Kightly, p.282.
30. In the early part of 1413, Colefox and Oldcastle were involved in the sale of a clasp of gold set with jewels, that had belonged to Sir Lewis Clifford for the princely sum of 1,200 marks to Henry V. They had received a down-payment in the Spring, and on 20 July, a month before Oldcastle's citation for heresy, Henry had given them a promissory note that the balance would be paid by Michaelmas 1414. *CPR, 1413–16*, p.73.
31. Kightly, p.196 and see p.146.
32. Kightly, pp.500–01.
33. TNA, E 368/187, m.300.
34. www.historyofparliamentonline.org/volume/1386-1421/member/cheddar-richard-1379-1437; Rit. Parl. III, 525 (French) reproduced (in English) in *English Historical Documents*, Vol. IV, 1327–1485 (ed. David C. Douglas), (Eyre & Spottiswoode, 1969), pp.458–59.
35. *CPR, 1413–16*, p.175.
36. *CCR, 1413–19*, pp.109–10.
37. Kightly, pp.493–94.
38. Kightly, p.364.
39. Kightly, p.496.
40. *CPR, 1413–16*, pp.13, 176; *Gregory's Chronicle* or *The Historical Collections of a Citizen of London in the Fifteenth Century*, (Camden Society, 1876), p.108.
41. Kightly, p.508.
42. John Stow, George Buck and Edmund Howes, *The annales, or generall chronicle of England*, (London, 1615), p.344; C.L. Kingsford, *English Historical Literature in the Fifteenth Century*, (Clarendon Press, 1913), pp.284, 293, 324; Adam of Usk, *Chronicon* (ed. E.M. Thompson), p.121; *CCR, 1413–16*, p.54.
43. Kightly, pp.35–39.
44. www.historyofparliamentonline.org/volume/1386-1421/member/chaworth-sir-thomas-1459.
45. Kightly, pp.134–39; www.historyofparliamentonline.org/volume/1386-1421/constituencies/leicester. For Roger Goldsmith see www.historyofparliamentonline.org/volume/1386-1421/member/goldsmith-roger.

46. Kightly, pp.141–42.
47. Kightly, pp.265–48.
48. Kightly, p.291.
49. Kightly, pp.251, 285–87.
50. Kightly, pp.285–90.
51. Rymer's *Foedera* January 1414 for January 11 accessed at: www.british-history.ac.uk/rymer-foedera/vol9/pp80-112.
52. *CCR, 1413–19*, p.379.
53. *CPR, 1413–16*, p.162; Kightly, pp.493–94.
54. https://www.historyofparliamentonline.org/volume/1386-1421/member/cheyne-roger-1362-1414; Kightly, p.393.
55. Margaret Wade Labarge, *Henry V, The Cautious Conqueror*, (Secker and Warburg, 1975), p.48; https://www.historyofparliamentonline.org/volume/1386-1421/member/cheyne-roger-1362-1414.
56. *Political Poems and Songs Relating to English History*, (ed. Thomas Wright), (Rolls Series), Vol. II (1861), p.247.
57. Maureen Jurkowski 'Henry V's suppression of the Oldcastle revolt', Chapter 4 in *Henry V: New Interpretations*, (Boydell & Brewer, 2013), p.110.
58. Kightly, p.207, referencing TNA, SC6/1222/13.
59. Kightly, p.207, referencing BM. Add. Ms. 38525 f.34.
60. W.T. Waugh , 'Sir John Oldcastle', Part II, *EHR*, Vol. XX, p.651 and n.64.
61. Edward Hasted, *The History and Topographical Survey of the County of Kent*, (Canterbury, 1797), Vol. III, pp.677, 692.
62. www.historyofparliamentonline.org/volume/1386-1421/member/darell-john-1438; Kightly p.288; Maureen Jurkowski 'Henry V's suppression of the Oldcastle revolt', Chapter 4 in *Henry V: New Interpretations*, (Boydell & Brewer, 2013), p.115.
63. Maureen Jurkowski 'Henry V's suppression of the Oldcastle revolt', Chapter 4 in *Henry V: New Interpretations*, (Boydell & Brewer, 2013), pp.115–16.
64. Kightly, pp.145–46, 293.
65. Walsingham, pp.405–06. Maureen Jurkowski in 'Henry V's suppression of the Oldcastle revolt', chapter 4 in *Henry V: New Interpretations*, (Boydell & Brewer, 2013), p.120 suggests that Fisher wasn't arrested till October 1416.
66. Kightly, pp.275–77, 293–95; Thomson, p.12.
67. www.historyofparliamentonline.org/volume/1386-1421/member/ruyhale-richard-1408.
68. Thomson, p.11.
69. *Concilia Magnae Britttaniae et Hiberniae*, (ed. David Wilkins), (London, 1737), Vol. III, pp.371–75; Walsingham, p.406.
70. Walsingham, p.406.
71. www.bedandbreakfast availability.co.uk/malvern.php consulted 15 Feb. 2009.
72. www.british-history.ac.uk/vch/worcs/vol4/pp29-33.
73. *Gesta Henrici Quinti*, (trans. and ed. F. Taylor and J.S. Roskell), (Oxford, 1975), pp.18; Thomson, pp.8–9.
74. Thomson, p.14.
75. Kightly, p.293, referencing KB9/209/36.
76. Kightly, p.209 referencing Register of Henry Chichele, Archbishop of Canterbury (ed. E.F. Jacob), (Canterbury and York Society, 1937–47), Vol. IV, p.151.
77. John Howells, *The History of the Old Baptist Church at Olchon together with the Life and Martyrdom of Sir John Oldcastle, The Lord Cobham*, (South Wales Printing Works, 1996).
78. I am indebted to Miriam Griffiths, the librarian of the Longtown & District Historical Society and current owner (in 2020) of Olchon Court for this information.
79. Hyett-Warner, p.90.
80. Kightly, pp.29–30.

81. Kightly, pp.470, 531–32.
82. Kightly, pp.20, 526–27, Thomson, p.12.
83. Kightly, p.41.
84. Walsingham, p.418.
85. *ibid.*
86. Kightly, pp.532–34.
87. M.E. Aston 'Lollardy and Sedition, 1381–1431' in *Past and Present*, 17 (1960), p.21.
88. Kightly, pp.146–47, 401–03.
89. Kightly, pp.26–27.
90. Kightly, pp.146–47, 297.
91. J.H. Wylie, *The reign of Henry V*, (CUP, 1914–29), Vol. III, pp.86–87, referencing Thomas Elmham, *Liber Metricus*, p.148.
92. Kightly, pp.349–50.
93. *CCR, 1413–19*, p.459.
94. Rudolph Fiehler, *The Strange History of Sir John Oldcastle*, (American Press, 1965), p.112.
95. Kightly, pp.209–10.
96. www.historyofparliamentonline.org/volume/1386-1421/member/merbury-john-1438.
97. www.historyofparliamentonline.org/volume/1386-1421/member/brugge-john-1436.
98. *CCR, 1413–19*, p.379.
99. Christopher Allmand, *Henry V*, (University of California Press, 1992), p.313.
100. Douglas Biggs 'An Ill and Infirm King: Henry IV, Health, and the Gloucester Parliament of 1407' in *The Reign of Henry IV, Rebellion and Survival, 1403–1413*, (ed. Gwilym Dodd and Douglas Biggs), (York Medieval Press, 2008), p.207, n.25.
101. *CCR, 1413–19*, pp.434–35.
102. www.historyofparliamentonline.org/volume/1386-1421/member/harry-john-ap-1420.
103. Rudolph Fiehler, *The Strange History of Sir John Oldcastle*, (The American Press, 1965); https://en.wikipedia.org/wiki/Owain_Glyndwr.
104. *CCR, 1419–22*, p.196; Thomas Elmham, *Liber Metricus*, p.158; C.L. Kingsford, *English Historical Literature in the Fifteenth Century*, (Clarendon Press, 1913), p.308.
105. According to one version of the *Brut*. C.L. Kingsford, *English Historical Literature in the Fifteenth Century*, (Clarendon Press, 1913), p.308.
106. Henry Ellis, *Original Letters illustrative of English History*, second series, Vol. I, (London, 1827), Letter XXVIII, pages 86–89.
107. James Tait, *Dictionary of National Biography*, (1885–1900), Volume 42.
108. Walsingham, p.428.
109. *Rotuli Parliamentorum,*, (London, 1767–77), Vol. IV, p.107 (in French) reproduced (in English) in *English Historical Documents*, Vol. IV, 1327-1485 (ed. David C. Douglas), (Eyre & Spottiswoode, 1969), pp.863-4. For Fabyan's comment see: *The new chronicles of England and France*, in two parts: by Robert Fabyan, (ed. Henry Eliis), (London, 1811), p.583.
110. TNA, E. 364/52, m.1d.
111. Thomson, p.15.
112. Walsingham, p.428.
113. As recounted in C.L. Kingsford, *English Historical Literature in the Fifteenth Century*, (Clarendon Press, 1913), p.41.

Chapter 9   Traitor, Martyr, Hero and Falstaff

1. https://www.historyofparliamentonline.org/volume/1386-1421/member/waweton-thomas.
2. HARC, CF50/242.
3. A.T. Bannister (ed), *Register of Thomas Spofford* (Hereford, 1917), pp.152–55.
4. William Robert Tremaine, 'A Critical Edition: Poems by Thomas Hoccleve' in HM 744, thesis, University of British Columbia, April 1968.

5. F.J. Furnivall (ed), *Hoccleve's Works, I. The Minor Poems*, Early English Text Series, Extra Series LXI, (1892), p.xxiv.

6. Flavius Vegetius Renatus (known as Vegece), was the author of *De re militari*, which was translated into French in the fourteenth century as *De la chose de la chevalerie* by Jean de Vignay.

7. In 1414 Prophete petitioned the king to build a chapel of St John the Baptist in Hereford Cathedral, but this was never built, see Michael Tavinor, *Saints & Sinners*, (Logaston Press, 2012) p.99 and *CPR, 1413–16*, p.226. See also note 8.

8. The information about Felde, Prophete and Hoccleve in this paragraph, and the information in the one preceding and the four following, is derived from C.S. Stokes 'Sir John Oldcastle, the Office of the Privy Seal, and Thomas Hoccleve's "Remonstrance Against Oldcastle" of 1415' in *Anglia* (Journal of English Philosophy), Vol. 118, issue 4, (January, 2000), pp.556–70.

9. MS Cotton Vespasian B, xvi, fol. 2, v, from Thomas Wright (ed), *Political Poems and Songs relating to English History composed during the period from the Accession of EDW. III to that of Ric. III*, Vol. II (Longman, 1861), pp.243–47.

10. Kightly, pp.148–49, 261–63.

11. John A.F. Thomson, 'Oldcastle, John, Baron Cobham (d.1417)', *Oxford DNB*, OUP, Sept. 2004; online edn, May 2008 [http://www.oxforddnb.com/view/article/20674, accessed 27 June 2009].

12. Brian Walsh, *Shakespeare, The Queen's Men and Elizabethan Performance of History*, (CUP, 2009), p.64.

13. B.M. Ward, 'The Famous Victories of Henry the Fifth: Its Place in Elizabethan Dramatic Literature' in *Review of English Studies* IV (July, 1928), pp.287, 294; Scott McCrea, *The Case For Shakespeare: The End Of The Authorship Question*, (Greenwood, 2005), pp.157–58.

14. John Dawtrey, *The Falstaff saga; Being the life and opinions of Captain Nicholas Dawtrey sometime seneschal of Claneboye and warden of the palace of Carrickfergus, immortalized by Shakespeare as Sir John Falstaff*, (Routledge, 1927).

15. Susan Ann Royal, (2014) John Foxe's 'Acts and Monuments' and the Lollard Legacy in the Long English Reformation, Durham theses, Durham University. Available at Durham E-Theses Online: http://etheses. dur.ac.uk/10624/ p.118.

16. *ibid*, p.99.

17. *ibid*, pp.49–50 and Patterson, Annabel, 'Sir John Oldcastle as Symbol of Reformation Historiography' in *Religion, Literature, and Politics in Post-Reformation England, 1540–1688* (eds Donna B. Hamilton & Richard Stricr), (CUP, 1996), pp.6–16.

18. *Holinshed's Chronicles, Richard II 1398–1400 and Henry V*, (eds R.S. Wallace and Alma Hansen), (Clarendon Press, 1917), Henry V, p.4.

19. *ibid*, pp.9–10.

20. The copy of James's letter and much of the discussion about the course and timing of events that follows is owed to James M. Gibson, 'Shakespeare and the Cobham Controversy: the Oldcastle/ Falstaff and Brooke/Broome Revisions', *Medieval & Renaissance Drama in England*, vol. 25, 2012, pp.94–132. JSTOR, www.jstor.org/stable/24322475 and, taking a rather different view, Gary Taylor, 'William Shakespeare, Richard James and the House of Cobham' in *Review of English Studies*, xxxviii (1987), pp.334–54.

21. R.J. Fehrenbach, 'When Lord Cobham and Edward Tilney were at odds; Oldcastle, Falstaff and the Date of I Henry IV' in *Shakespeare Studies*, Vol. 18 (1986), p.94.

22. *ibid*, p.95.

23. For full details of the correspondence and the circumstances surrounding it a good source is R.J. Fehrenbach, 'When Lord Cobham and Edward Tilney were at odds; Oldcastle, Falstaff and the Date of I Henry IV' in *Shakespeare Studies*, Vol. 18 (1986), pp.67–101.

24. R.J. Fehrenbach, 'When Lord Cobham and Edward Tilney were at odds; Oldcastle, Falstaff and the Date of I Henry IV' in *Shakespeare Studies*, Vol. 18 (1986), p.93. For full details as to how ord Cobham became involved in the Ridolfi Plot, see D.B. McKeen, "A Memory of Honour', A Study of the House of Cobham in Kent in the reign of Elizabeth I', (Thesis, July 1964), pp.314-383. In brief, Lod Cobham's brother, Thomas Brooke, was a pirate and a schemer who constantly landed

himself in trouble. He was drawn into a plan to aid the Duke of Norfolk put Mary, Queen of Scots on the throne, and, with the help of Francis Bertie, one of Lord Cobham's servants, managed to have some treasonable texts and letters smuggled into England through the Cinque Ports, of which Lord Cobham was Warden. In trying to protect his brother, Cobham handed on some of the secret correspondence to one of the plotters, so landing himself in deep water, from which he was subsequently saved by his friend, Lord Burghley. Thomas Brooke was held in the Tower for a while, but was eventually released, dying a few years later in obscure circumstances.

25. John Fastolfe entry in the *Oxford Dictionary of National Biography*, written by G.L. Harriss.
26. https://www.british-history.ac.uk/no-series/survey-of-london-stow/1603/pp216-223. This text of Stow's *Survey of London* reprinted form the text of 1603, includes a summary paragraph about 'Candlewicke street warde' which includes this information, a paragraph which the edition edited by William J. Thoms and printed by Whittaker & Co. in 1842 doesn't include but mentions the fact in a footnote on p.82. In *Old London taverns : historical, descriptive and reminiscent, with some account of the coffee houses, clubs, etc.* published in 1899, Edward Callow says that the Eastcheap Boar's Head Tavern is mentioned in the reign of Richard II, but gives no reference, before going on to say that Stow alludes to the riot in which Prince Hal's brothers took part as occurring here, when Stow mentions no inn and indeed specifically says, as mentioned above, that there was no tavern in Eastcheap then.
27. https://www.culture24.org.uk/history-and-heritage/literary-history/art79367.
28. L.W. Vernon Harcourt, 'The Two Sir John Falstaffs' in *Transactions of the Royal Historical Society*, Vol.4 (1910), pp.47–62.
29. For more on Jaggard and the various claims made for plays as written by William Shakespeare, as well as a for a discussion regarding the play *Sir John Oldcastle*, see James J. Marino 'William Shakespeare's *Sir John Oldcastle*', in *Renaissance Drama*, New Series, Vol.30 (1999–2001), pp.93–114.
30. James J. Marino, 'William Shakespeare's Sir John Oldcastle' in *Renaissance Drama*, New Series, Vol.30 (1999–2001), pp.93–114. This article also covers much ground concerning the attribution of plays, the rewriting of plays, the issue of control of texts and ownership of those texts.
31. John Rittenhouse (ed.) *A Critical Edition of I Sir John Oldcastle*, The Renaissance Imagination, Vol. 9, (Garland Publishing, 1984), pp.1–9.
32. *ibid.*
33. www.bl.uk/treasures/shakespeare/henry4p1.html.
34. Stanley Wells, *Shakespeare, a Dramatic Life*, (Sinclair-Stevenson, 1994), p.140.
35. More information on all the authors of the play can be found in John Rittenhouse (ed.) *A Critical Edition of I Sir John Oldcastle*, The Renaissance Imagination, Vol. 9, (Garland Publishing, 1984), pp.46–50.
36. I am grateful to Jools Holland for pointing out this story to me.
37. Edward de Vere Newsletter No.17, accessed in pdf format through www.oxford-shakespeare.com › newsletter.
38. Foxe, *Acts and monuments*, (1583 Edition), Book 5, p.606.

Chapter 10   Afterword
1. The possibility of Oldcastle having three wives has been discussed in Chapter Four; see p.88.
2. www.historyofparliamentonline.org/volume/1386-1421/member/whitney-sir-robert-ii-1443.
3. Duncumb, *Collections towards the History and Antiquities of the County of Herefordshire*, Vol. 1, (Hereford, 1804), pp.90–91.
4. Ruth Elizabeth Richardson, *Mistress Blanche, Queen Elizabeth I's Confidante*, (Logaston Press 2007, reprinted with additions, 2018), p.89.
5. According to a handwritten note in John Duncumb's researches for his *Collections Towards The History and Antiquities of The County of Hereford* (published in 1804) and held in Hereford Archive and Records Centre, CF50/242.
6. The *Historical Church Guide to The Church of St Nicholas, Ash* by Sir Reginald John Tower, revised 2010, says that Maud Oldcastle was married to Richard Clitherow, but gives no evidence for this.

L.S. Woodger in historyofparliamentonline.org/volume/1386-1421/member/clitheroe-richard-i-1420, mentions *CPR, 1399–1401*, p.222, which mentions Richard Clitherow's wife's son or stepson, a Thomas Mountford. In *Calendar of Wills Proved and Enrolled in the Court of Husting, London: Part 2, 1358-1688*, p.557, the will of William Gregory, an Alderman, mentions the Knolles Chapel in the church of St Antonin in Watling Street, between The Vintry and Cheapside, that included a bequest for the souls of various people, including for 'Richard Clyderowe, esquire, and Alice, wife of the same'. Richard Clitherow's wife therefore seems to have been an Alice Mountford. Richard Clitherow was buried in the Charterhouse, part of what was then a Carthusian monastery near Smithfield.

7. J.R. Planché, *A Corner of Kent, or Some Account of the Parish of Ash-next-Sandwich, etc*, (London, 1864).
8. J.G. Waller, 'The Lords of Cobham, their monuments and the church' in *Archaeologia Cantiana*, Vol. II (1877), pp.99–101.
9. https://www.historyofparliamentonline.org/volume/1386-1421/member/brooke-thomas-1391-1439.
10. www.historyofparliamentonline.org/volume/1386-1421/member/whittington-guy-1440.
11. According to a handwritten note in John Duncumb's researches for his *Collections Towards The History and Antiquities of The County of Hereford* (published in 1804) and held in Hereford Archive and Records Centre, CF50/242. This reference too for the information regarding his two daughters.
12. www.british-history.ac.uk/vch/worcs/vol4/pp29-33.
13. *List of Early Chancery Proceedings preserved in the Public Record Office*, Vol. VII, (Kraus reprint Corporation, 1963), Bundles no. 864 and 865.
14. E.K. Chambers, *William Shakespeare: A Study of Facts and Problems*, (Oxford, 1930), Vol. II, pp.213, 217–18.
15. Thomas Fuller, *The Church History of Britain from the birth of Jesus Christ until the year M.DC.XLVIII* (London, 1665; new ed. London, 1837). The quote is taken from the 1837 volume (so with some modified spelling), Book IV, p.489.
16. *The Miscellaneous Works of Oliver Goldsmith*, (John Murray, 1837), Vol. I, pp.155, 188.
17. Rudolph Fiehler, "Sir John Oldcastle Reconsidered' in *Concordia Theological Monthly*, (August, 1957), p.579.
18. William Eusebius Andrews, *Review of Fox's Book of Martyrs*, Vol. II, (London, 1826), p.63.
19. Christopher Allmand, 'Writing History in the Eighteenth Century', Chapter 11 in *Henry V: New Interpretations* (ed. Gwilym Dodd), (York Medieval Press, 2018 [paperback]), notably p.282.
20. Maureen Jurkowski 'Henry V's Suppression of the Oldcastle Revolt', Chapter 4 in *Henry V: New Interpretations* (ed. Gwilym Dodd), (York Medieval Press, 2018 [paperback]), notably pp.110–11, 121–29.
21. See Richard A. Sylvia, 'Reading Tennyson's "Ballads and Other Poems" in Context' in *The Journal of the Midwest Modern Language Association*, Vol. 23, No. 1 (Spring, 1990), pp.27–44.
22. Stanley Wells, *Shakespeare, a Dramatic Life*, (Sinclair-Stevenson, 1994), p.140.
23. Walsingham refers to his time at Oxford in his chronicle, notably at the time that Pope Gregory XI sent a bull to the university in 1378 aimed at restraining the teachings of Wycliffe: 'It can easily be seen how far the modern day provosts or rectors of this university have departed from the good sense and wisdom of their predecessors, if I tell you that when they heard the reason for the arrival of the pope's envoy, they debated for a long time whether they should honour and accept the pope's bull or do him the dishonour of completely ignoring it. O university of Oxford, how far have you tumbled and fallen from the heights of wisdom and learning which were yours!' Walsingham, p.50.
24. See the introduction to Walsingham, pp.29–30.
25. Walsingham, pp.29–30.
26. For the details of Henry's involvement in the Council of Constance see Christopher Allmand, *Henry V*, (University of California Press, 1992), Chapter 11.
27. For more details on the case of John Croft at least, see Ruth Elizabeth Richardson, M*istress Blanche, Queen Elizabeth's I's Confidante*, (Logaston Press, 2007, revised edition 2018), pp.87–88.

Index

Page numbers in italics refer to illustrations or their captions

Scogan, Henry 95
Scott, Thomas 168
Scrope, Henry, Lord, of Masham 107, 112, 175
    Richard, archbishop of York 82
Scudamore, Sir John *68*, 69, 87
    Philip 85
Shakespeare, William 73, 89, 91, 95, 100, 194–96,
    197–214
    Henry IV Part I 5, 71, 76, 89, 194, 199,
        200–07, 209, 210, 224
        evidence for name of Oldcastle 199-200,
          202–04
        Boar's Head Tavern *206*, 207
        version with Oldcastle's name, 1986 231
    Henry IV Part II 18, 76, 98, 132, 194, 202–03,
        210, 211
    Henry V 113, 185, 194, 195, 198–99
    Henry VI Part I 205
    Merry Wives of Windsor 200, 205
    suggested authorship of *Famous Victories* 195
    use of Holinshed 198–99
Shamley, Kent 89
Sharp, Jack, rebellion, 1431 187
sheriffs, duties of 28, 30
Shelwick 9
Shrewsbury, Battle of 75
Sigismund, Holy Roman Emperor 178
Silverstone 178
Sir John Oldcastle (inn) 89, *90, 155*
Sir John Oldcastle's Field *90*
Sluys 62, 117
    Battle of 64
Smith, William 48
Smyth, John (a yeoman of Oldcastle) 79
soldiery 76–78
Somer, Sir Henry 188, 190
Somenour, John 82
Southampton Plot 142, 172–73, 211, 214
Speed, John
    views on Oldcastle 222
Spofford, Thomas, bishop of Hereford 187
Stafford, John, bishop of Bath and Wells 193
Stanhope, Sir Richard 122, 168
Stapleton, Thomas
    translation of Bede's *Ecclesiastical History* ...
      196
Stationers' Register, the 194, 200
Staunton-on-Wye 182
Strata Florida Abbey 70
Steven, Laurence 45
Stokesley, John, bishop of London 193

Stow, John
    on Cobham's Inn 89
    on Coldharbour 92
    on 'an affray in East-cheap' 94–95
    on conduct of the princes 95
    on Oldcastle's escape from Tower 159
    on Oldcastle's rising 162
    on Boar's Head Tavern 207
Strecche, John
    on Oldcastle on the run 175
    on Oldcastle's death 186
Sturry, Sir Richard 51, 52
Sudbury, Simon, archbishop of Canterbury 44, 47
Swarkston Bridge 177
Swynderby, William 35, 40, 48–49, 50, 58, 168
    trial by Bishop Trefnant 53–56
Symonds, Revd W.S.
    Malvern Chase 173, 175

Taillour, William 143
Talbot, Gilbert 85
    Henry 166, 178
    John 83
    Sir Thomas 166, 170, 173, 178
Tanner, Thomas, bishop
    Bibliotheca Britannico-Hibernica 60, 138
Tarleton, Richard 195, 196
taxation 103–04
    poll tax 46
      of 1379 13–14
Tennyson, Alfred, Lord 227
    'Sir John Oldcastle, Lord Cobham (in Wales)'
      227–31
Thomas, duke of Clarence (brother of Henry V)
      92, 94, 95, *95*
    army in France, 1412 123
Thorpe, John 149, 193
    William 36
Tilney, Sir Edmund 197, 200, 202–03
Tiptoft, John 106, 112
Tirwhit, Robert 98
Toly, Matthew 171
treasurers of war 81, 104
Trefnant, John, bishop of Hereford 15, 25, 48, 51
    trial of Walter Brut 56–57
    trial of William Swynderby 53–56
Treloscan, John 80
Trussell, Sir John 51
Turmyne, William 173
Turnastone 79
Turnour, Philip 172, 178

Also from LOGASTON PRESS (www.logastonpress.co.uk)

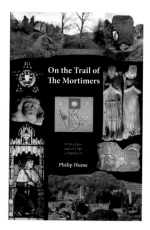

On the Trail of the Mortimers
Philip Hume
144 pages, 234 × 156 mm
75 colour photographs, as well as maps and family trees
ISBN: 978-1-910839-04-1
Paperback with flaps, £7.50

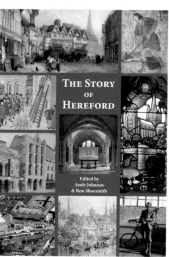

The Story of Hereford
Edited by Andy Johnson and Ron Shoesmith
336 pages, 242 × 171 mm
Over 160 colour and b&w illustrations
ISBN: 978-1-906663-98-8
Paperback, £15.00

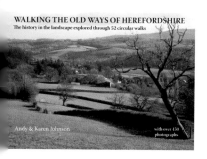

Walking the Old Ways of Herefordshire
The history in the landscape explored
through 52 circular walks
Andy & Karen Johnson
384 pages, 148 × 210 mm
Over 450 colour photographs, 53 maps
ISBN: 978-1-906663-86-5
Paperback with flaps, £12.95